Creating Futures: Leading Change Through Information Systems

NADA K. KAKABADSE and ANDREW K. KAKABADSE

Ashgate

Aldershot • Burlington USA • Singapore • Sydney

Published by
Ashgate Publishing Ltd
Gower House
Croft Road
Aldershot
Hampshire GU11 3HR
England

Ashgate Publishing Company
131 Main Street
Burlington
Vermont 05401
USA

Ashgate website: http://www.ashgate.com

British Library Cataloguing in Publication Data
Kakabadse, Nada
  Creating futures : leading change through information
  systems
  1.Social change 2. Information technology - Social aspects
  3.Computers and civilization 4.Organizational change
  I.Title II.Kakabadse, Andrew
  303.4'833

Library of Congress Control Number: 00-132828

ISBN 1 84014 879 9

Printed in Great Britain by
Antony Rowe Ltd, Chippenham, Wiltshire

Contents

List of Figures   *vii*

List of Tables   *ix*

List of Contributors   *xi*

Acknowledgements   *xiii*

Introduction   *xv*

1   Information Rich vs Information Poor: Issues for Public
     Policy   1
     Nada K. Kakabadse, Alexander Kouzmin and
     Andrew K. Kakabadse

2   Information Technology's Impact on Quality of Democracy:
     A Philosophical and Administrative Framework   31
     Andrew K. Kakabadse and Nada K. Kakabadse

3   Information Technology for Public Sector in Developing
     Countries: Designing Relevant Infra-Structural Capability
     or New Colonialism?   73
     Nada K. Kakabadse, Andrew K. Kakabadse and
     Alexander Kouzmin

4   Information Technology – Enabled Communication and
     Organisational Effectiveness   101
     Nada K. Kakabadse, Alexander Kouzmin and Andrew K.
     Kakabadse

v

5   Current Trends in Internet Use: E-Communication,
    E-Information and E-Commerce   127
    Nada K. Kakabadse, Alexander Kouzmin and
    Andrew K. Kakabadse

6   Knowledge Management: Understanding and Praxis   159
    Nada K. Kakabadse, Alexander Kouzmin and
    Andrew K. Kakabadse

7   Decentralised, Interactive and Available: Fundamental
    Changes for IS/IT Professionals   185
    Andrew K. Kakabadse and Nada K. Kakabadse

8   'Profession' and Professional Ethics: An IT Perspective   217
    Andrew K. Kakabadse and Nada K. Kakabadse

9   Leadership Determinants for Effective IS/IT Adoption   233
    Andrew K. Kakabadse and Nada K. Kakabadse

10 Technostress: Over-Identification with Information
    Technology and Its Impact on Employees and Managerial
    Effectiveness   259
    Nada K. Kakabadse, Alexander Kouzmin and
    Andrew K. Kakabadse

Bibliography   *297*
Index   *371*

List of Figures

7.1   Role Analysis   207
7.2   Role and Contribution of IS/IT Professionals   208
7.3   Work and Contribution of IS/IT Professionals   209

9.1   Leadership Philosophy Impact on Effective IS/IT Adoption   255

List of Tables

7.1   IS/IT Competencies: Results of Research   202

9.1   Three Cluster Analysis   243
9.2   Summary of IS/IT Factors   244
9.3   Cluster 1 (Team Players) – Factor Summary   245
9.4   Cluster 2 (Radicals) – Factor Summary   245
9.5   Cluster 3 (Bureaucrats) – Factor Summary   246
9.6   Team Players – Demographic Characteristics   247
9.7   Radicals – Demographic Characteristics   248
9.8   Bureaucrats – Demographic Characteristics   249
9.9   Leadership Influence on IS/IT-Training (IS/IT1)   251
9.10 Leadership Influence on IS/IT-Deployment (IS/IT2)   251
9.11 Leadership Influence on IS/IT-Skills (IS/IT3)   252
9.12 Leadership Influence on IS/IT-Impact (IS/IT4)   252

List of Contributors

Professor Alexander Kouzmin
Graduate School of Management, University of Western Sydney, Nepean,
Australia

Acknowledgements

For our parents, Elfrieda and George Kakabadse and Mila Lisa and Dmitar Korac, with heartfelt love and respect.

Very many thanks to Pauline Thomas and Alex Britnell for all your help, support and dedication to preparing this manuscript for publication.

Introduction

Creating Futures

Open virtually any text in the management, strategy and public administration field and the word 'change' is likely to be liberally distributed throughout each document. Change is no new phenomena, but is a normal, if not poorly integrated, experience of our daily lives. However, regular exposure to change does not necessarily assist in appreciating the nature of the prime drivers of change, their impact and limitations. How many could answer the following questions? In organisational terms, has the breakdown of the vertically integrated enterprise allowed the human resources department to become a prime strategic influence on the progress of the organisation through its potential to impact on the development of people? Is the information business and its accompanying technologies driving through change in the organisation, or, is it in reality, just another set of tools that conveniently facilitates change processes to occur in organisations? Have IS (information systems) professionals substantially impacted on the organisation, repositioning it to be more effective in its prospective markets or community, or acted more as technological junkies, being operationally clever, but strategically inept?

In addressing these questions, this ten chapter volume focuses on the influence of, and additionally explores the value adding contribution of, information systems and related technologies on the development of society and private and public sector enterprises. The chapters are 'stand alone units' representing the research work and thinking of the Cranfield School of Management husband and wife team, Nada and Andrew Kakabadse in conjunction with the Australian thinker and researcher, Alex Kouzmin, University Western Sydney-Nepean. The initial opening chapters of the book examine the impact of IS/IT (information systems/information technology) on society and organisations. As the book progresses, attention is then given to exploring the effect of IS/IT on individuals within the information arena and more broadly within varying walks of life.

Chapters Overview

Chapter One explores the impact of government IT policies on society at large. Introducing the metaphore 'harem', which originates from the Islamic haram, forbidden, as opposed to 'halal', permitted, conveying the idea of secret or separated from the rest of the world highlights that at the societal level, the impact of IS/IT applications are promoting, or inadvertently giving rise to, particular invisible barriers in society, especially so in terms of the poverty divides in the world, the inequitable technology transfers taking place between societies and the snooping and fast growing political surveillance applications of information technologies. The overall conclusion is that the balance between being an enabler of social development rather than a disabler of quality of life improvements, is that the disabling nature of information technology based applications is gaining precedence.

Continuing with the theme of information technology's societal impact, Chapter Two examines how E-democracy is likely to be affected by IS/IT. Exploration of the nature of democracy is undertaken, highlighting that the present day disillusionment with democracy is the result of developments in society rather than a problem with democracy per se. The conclusion reached is that technology is likely to have a mixed impact on communicating the sentiment of citizens to policy levels in government. Certainly, technology will enable citizens to have more direct access to their political representatives. However, technology is equally likely to provide even greater opportunities for powerful, minority lobby groups, to strongly press home their point(s). Such a development would mean that the mass of citizens would not be able to resist the overtures of the influential few, due to the lack of organisation of the many. The current disillusionment with politics and democracy, as much due to the influence of unrepresentative, strong lobby groups, is likely to increase, as these groups, through the use of up to date information systems, are likely to gain the upper hand in the battle of voicing those opinions that will eventually become societal practice.

In keeping with the theme of information systems and their impact on society, chapter three examines how information technology could negatively impact on developing countries. The need for a global response to those parts of the world who have a low information infra-structure and low levels of capital, is vital. The requirement is for policy designers to focus on those technologies that help bind nations or regions. The alternative is to enhance the existing societal gaps, thus extending the gap between the rich and poor and threatening a broad destabilisation.

Stepping down from the societal level of analysis to that of organisational processes and functionings, Chapter Four provides analysis of how IT enabled communication supports greater organisational effectiveness. The nature of communication is analysed, as are its impact and its benefits. The overall conclusion, obvious to some, is that groups and individuals now have greater choice in terms of selecting a variety of communication media, with one proviso, not only are the electronic channels here to stay but are likely to dominate the scene.

Whereas Chapter Four provides more of an introduction to the concepts of electronic and non-electronic communication, Chapter Five explores, in considerable depth, the nature of current trends: E-information, E-communication and E-commerce. Originally considered in the 1960s as an information system capable of surviving nuclear attack, the Net has grown into an extremely complex network connecting millions of sites, with a projected membership, in the USA alone, of 137.5 million, within the next two years. The services provided through the net cover almost every aspect of life, now turning cyber services into a bizarre bazaar. How the Net will be developed is the intriguing question, for as it currently stands, it is the ultimate unregulated democracy.

In keeping with concept of a fundamental paradigm shift in information sourcing and communication, the very concept of knowledge is scrutinised in the next chapter. Chapter Six provides an examination of the meaning of knowledge, ranging from the ancient Greek divisions of myths and logos, to the current day sub-divisions of rational, implicit and contextual knowledge. Distinction is drawn between knowledge and 'know-how', with know-how being firmly placed as the value added component to knowledge praxis and understanding.

Inevitably, such progress in information management and electronic modes of communication has substantially impacted on the role and contribution of the IS Professional. From a position of supporting developments in organisations to now being a key driver of organisation change, the IS/IT Professional has had to make and will continue to have to make, considerable shifts, both of behaviour and mindset, in order to become a leader in driving through change in organisations. In keeping with the driving through change theme, therefore, Chapter Seven concentrates on understanding the leadership imperatives for promoting strategic change through the application of IS systems and the challenges the IS Professional faces in helping realise changes. The greatest shift of all is turning from being systems oriented to being context responsive, through recognising and respecting the intricate and unique nature of particular circumstances in organisations and through that insight, appreciating how to apply innovation in a way that situationally works.

As rapid change is the catch phrase within the field of IS/IT, forcing considerable shifts in the views, values and adaptiveness of IS professionals, the question raised is, is the IS professional a member of a 'true' profession which now requires to have tabulated its own ethical parameters and codes or not? Attention, therefore, is given, in Chapter Eight to exploring this theme. The meaning and nature of profession is explored leading to the conclusion that the IS/IT arena, if to be recognised as professional, now requires an acceptable and codified set of ethics, which highlight its philosophical direction and equally provide guidelines for appropriate conduct.

Certain fundamental themes as, transformational change, leadership and ethics, run continuously through this book, with change processes and the leadership capabilities to drive through change being positioned as central. As leadership is such an important element of this book, a study of leadership effectiveness, in terms of the leadership required for effective IS/IT adoption in the Australian Public Service, is reported in Chapter Nine. One particular finding to emerge from the study is that the leadership skills necessary to drive through change are of secondary importance to the philosophy and values held by each leader. Critically, demographics are identified as primary sources of influence of the philosophies adopted by leaders. Those individuals who hold a positive, outward looking attitude, who have considerable tenure in the organisation and are older, are more likely to effectively introduce and bed down change into the organisation. Why?, because of their appreciation and responsiveness to context! Other demographics as gender, education, role etc. emerge as immaterial to effective leadership application.

As the book chapters progress from, initially, broader policy issues, to strategy and leadership issues to the impact of IS/IT developments on the individual, the final chapter, Chapter Ten, analyses the topic of technostress. Technostress is defined as the level of individual arousal through exposure to technology. Technostress may be experienced by individuals through them having to continuously adjust to new developments in technology or, alternatively, through them becoming more and more dependent on technology. Either ways, the chapter highlights the present day danger of technology promoting a state of perpetual urgency, resulting in people displaying 'Pavlovian dog like reactions' to technology stimuli. It is purported that the perpetual encroachment of technology into each individual's private and discretionary time, can lead to depression, burnout, lower motivation to work and general irritability. Ways of addressing such concerns are equally addressed in the chapter.

Finally, this text of original, selected readings, which range from broad policy to individual performance, are an attempt to encapsulate in one volume the enormity of impact of the developments in information technology on our lives with, in reality, a humility being presented, that we have a considerable way to go before the full impact of all of these developments are fully realised.

1 Information Rich vs Information Poor: Issues for Public Policy

NADA K. KAKABADSE, ALEXANDER KOUZMIN AND
ANDREW K. KAKABADSE

Abstract

This chapter[1] explores the effects of current IT policies and corporate and
government praxis in the arena of technological development and use. It
also explores global trends that lead toward futures that a majority of the
world population, arguably, would not choose and should actively seek to
avoid.

It emphasises growing discrepancies between information rich and
information poor, segregated by an invisible technologically-imposed
boundary and further controlled by surveillance technology creating newer
social cleavages and IT-harems. The chapter also explores current visions
for the future of employment in an information society and concludes with
'wicked' policy issues for urgent consideration.

Introduction

The once widely embraced notion of modern capitalism, in its strictest
form, has been replaced by pragmatic national quests for policies that
promote economic growth in an increasingly globalised economy. The
trend in a number of political systems has been to reduce *direct* state
intervention (cutting taxation, privatising functions previously performed)
in areas such as education and employment creation (Wilson, 1992);
although states have generally been unable to control, by political means, a
number of variables of macro-economic importance - a phenomenon
reflecting rising uncertainty about production and markets with respect to
the increase in international trade (Ohmae, 1995). The curbing of direct
state intervention appears to be a response to the New Right, Public Choice
Economics perspective which argues against state intervention and against
the growth of the size of the state. The economic climate of the late 1970s

1

and 1980s had already appeared to favour capital over labour, only to affirm it in late 1990s (Reich, 1991; Drucker, 1993; Soros, 1999).

The rapid economic transformation to 'market fundamentalism' has been coupled with the rise of (neo)conservative governments, employers and powerful business factions which threatened macro-economic balance (Soros, 1999). The emergence of 'market fundamentalism', the idea that markets need only be regulated by forces of profit and competition, has distorted the role of capital to the extent that it 'is today a greater threat to open society than any totalitarian ideology' (Soros, 1999). Both developed and emerging economies, alike, irrespective of their political alliance, are attempting to improve economies by adopting the 'market' as the arbiter of 'good' in a range of policy areas; most notably the work force.

The waning of direct state influence in the industrial sphere in recent years reinforces the elitist situation in which state agencies respond to capitalist demands over and above the claims of others between election times. Thus, employers (particularly large corporations and confederations) have had the resources to secure even greater access to the policy ear of the state. This is further reinforced by IT polices that provide further power to those who, already, have disproportionate influence within the large corporations and the state. Phenomena such as this, in turn, assists the generation of significant inequalities amongst citizens in their capacities and opportunities for participating as political equals in governing the state (Dahl 1985, pp.54-55) - as Rokkan (1966, p.105) has stated it more laconically: 'votes count, but resources decide.'

Globalisation and the Changing Role of the State

A growing number of national policies are being built upon the widely-held belief of economists that the state should divest itself of many traditional areas of activity in both social and market environments on the premise that the natural operation of markets will result in 'efficient' outcomes. The main argument against this assumption is that it requires a great deal of faith in the notion that individual agents participating in the market operate in a rational, fully informed and consistent manner (Dahl 1985; Ormerod, 1994). Many question the rationale behind this economic liberalisation, as in virtually every economy, where such policies have been implemented, it is commonly observed that this is only achieved at the expense of reduced levels of social welfare, rising rates of unemployment and, in some cases, instability in financial markets (Ormerod, 1994; Krugaman, 1999; Soros,

1999). This is not to say that free market policies are always wrong, but the 'real' world is far more complex than is allowed for in the model of 'Rational Man and Competitive Equilibrium' (Ormerod, 1994, p.70).

The underlying complexity of the 'real' world is a source of criticism of mainstream economics and also in development models of the economy. Economists have traditionally resorted to models with many simplifying assumptions, exemplified by the Phillips Curve (1958). The central conclusion from Phillips' (1958) work is that, from a policy maker's perspective, it is impossible to have both full employment and price stability; the two are simply incompatible goals. Although many policy makers and politicians have subscribed to this view, in terms of their economic prescriptions, there is increasing concern Phillips's hypothesis, supported by evidence from a number of countries where low levels of unemployment and inflation have been observed simultaneously for some years (Krugaman, 1999). It is often the case that in order for a particular model to even loosely depict the state of the economy, the assumptions which are made, along with the restrictive nature of linearity assumed in a non-linear world, cast much doubt about the efficacy of these models (Ormerod, 1994). Too often, the defense for this process has been grounded in the idea that any model is better than no model at all. This outlook may be acceptable in the confines of a laboratory, but given the influence that economists have had over policy development in recent times, and the impact that such policies have had on society, an autonomous approach such as this is inappropriate as the 'crisis in unemployment has finally come to attract the attention of the world's political leaders' (Ormerod, 1994, p.145).

Until the twentieth century, many states impinged upon individuals through regulatory and judicial activities; only in relatively recent times did they become heavily involved in the provision of services and in the operation of the economy. For example, in 1821, the number of bureaucrats in Great Britain was 27,000 whilst by, 1985, the number grew to 1,056,000 (central government servants only), only to reduce to 495,000 (476,000 permanent civil servants and 19,000 casual staff) by 1997 (Finer, 1932; Rose, 1985; Foreign and Commonwealth Office, 1997). The roles of modern state agencies have gradually converged to the extent that they are now located in an increasingly international and interdependent economic, political and social system.

Some see globalisation, or the global economy, as a 'corporate Olympics', a 'series of games played all over the world with international as well as domestic competition' and where 'global games are increasingly team sports requiring collaboration across national, cultural, social, ethnic and economic differences' (Kanter, 1985, p.18). Others observe that current global transformations re-arrange the politics and economics of the coming century so that 'there will be no national products or technologies, no national corporations, no national industries' (Reich, 1991, p.7; Ohmae, 1995; Reich, 1991, p.77) further argues that there will no longer be national economies. What will remain 'rooted within national borders are the people who comprise a nation'. Notwithstanding that nationality still has meaning for companies who are financed by local debt and serve local markets with locally-traded goods produced by local workers, the meaning of nationality is disappearing for the growing population of corporations serving global markets or facing global competition and 'global Webs' - whose products are international composites (Reich, 1991; Ohmae, 1995. p.10). Reich, (1991, p.113) points out that what is increasingly being traded between nations is 'less finished products and increasingly more specialised problem-solving (research, product design, fabrication), problem identification (marketing, advertising, customer consulting) and brokerage (financing, searching, contracting) services, as well as certain routine components and services, all of which are combined to create value'.

The emergence of the 'global option' would have been inconceivable without advancements in IT, particularly telecommunications (Castelles, 1989; Henderson, 1991), since the root of global re-structuring is a 'techno economic' process establishing a whole range of new organisational possibilities, facilitated by computer-related physical technology, and creating a new world order.

In as much as there has been some state withdrawal from services and benefits to citizens, the increased importance of other state activities and the continuing significance of more 'core' governance functions mean that individuals still remain affected in almost all aspects of their lives by the actions of the state, including a substantial portion of those who are employed by it, exemplified by increased *surveillance*. The expansion of surveillance in the modern political order, in combination with the policing of 'surveillance', radically transforms the relation between state authority and the governed population, compared with the traditional state. 'Administrative power now increasingly enters into the *minutiae* of daily life and the most intimate of personal actions and relationships' (Giddens, 1985, p.309). With ever increasing dependency on the electronic modes of storage, collection and dissemination of information, the possibilities of accumulating information relevant to the practice of government are almost endless.

'Control of information within modern, pacified states with very rapid systems of communication, transportation and sophisticated techniques of sequestration, can be directly integrated with the supervision of conduct in such a way as to produce a high concentration of state power' (Giddens, 1985, p.309). Proudhon's 1851 writings summarise this state as he writes that to be governed 'is to be watched, inspected, spied upon, directed, numbered, regulated, enrolled, indoctrinated, preached at, controlled, checked, estimated, valued, censured and commanded by creatures who have neither the right, the wisdom nor the virtue to do so' (Proudhon, 1923, p.293). As an anti-centraliser and advocate of worker's self-rule by *mutualite,* Proudhon (1923) saw government as an intrusion on citizens' life.

The IT-Harem Metaphor

The invisible IT-harem is a metaphor for an invisible barrier set up against disadvantaged individual's potential (physically challenged, 'have-nots', women, ethnic minorities, poor).   IT-harems are considered to be enclosures without walls, but ones that are implicitly constraining (Korac-Boisvert, 1994).   The Islamic word 'harem' comes from *haram,* 'forbidden', the opposite to *halal,* 'permitted'. Traditionally, in Islam, women were both the forbidden ones and those to whom almost everything was forbidden, separated from the world of man by a *huddud,* a secret barrier.

The *abaya* or *chuddar,* the outer garment worn by women in traditional Muslim societies, which covers women from head to toe, is perceived by some, and in particular those with fundamentalist values, as liberating - it provides personal freedom in allowing women to roam, away from the roving eyes of men, and social freedom, women being protected from view as an object of desire, thus, providing women with reassurance of their value and self-respect in society (Di Giovanni, 1998).   Others argue that *abaya* is a symbol of oppressiveness, as it imprisons women and impinges on their rights for self-expression and liberation (Di Giovanni, 1998).

In a similarly contested vein, some have argued that IT has a liberating power, particularly for those who are socially, economically, physically or geographically handicapped (Turkle, 1984). Others have urged that IT has a power to enslave, as it gives power to those who know how to exploit IT over those on whom information is recorded and manipulated (Webster, 1990). Thus, like fundamentalists who perceive the *abaya* as a return to traditional values, optimists perceive a society transformed radically for the better and IT as a tool for liberation and empowerment (Turkle, 1984). Pessimists see IT as a tool for increasingly inhumane and despotic capitalism (Webster, 1989, 1990) in the same vein as the secular modernist perceives any attempt to force women back into *abaya,* or even the home, as an imprisonment, exploitation and misery (Di Giovanni, 1998).

The reality of IT advancement has been, like all technical innovations, varied in its impact across different categories of social sectors but with a higher magnitude. Although it is plausible to believe that power can be distributed equally for everyone by giving equal access to the same technology, such as IT, new technologies do not necessarily empower the powerless. The technocratic dream of a technological 'fix' cannot be extended to all social ills (Korac-Kakabadse and Kouzmin, 1996; Kouzmin, Korac-Kakabadse and Korac-Kakabadse, 1999a). This is perhaps most evident in developing societies, over the last decade, where often highly divisive effects of attempts to introduce high technologies into developing societies' programmes are found.

There are numerous examples of redemptive introductions of technologies in developing societies in an attempt to alleviate deficiencies in quality of life without sufficient attention being given to formative context and appropriate social policies or their failure (Korac-Kakabadse and Kouzmin, 1996; Kouzmin, Korac-Kakabadse and Korac-Kakabadse, 1999a; 1999b). The crucial question is whether there is the will to bring about social justice through IT policies. Will IT promote a more caring, sharing world or will IT development and implementation be dominated by media and technology multi-nationals which promote more selfish values that give free reign to redistributing wealth in their own favour?

IT and 'Invisible' Barriers

The Internet, for example, is considered at the moment to be the most egalitarian mass media since the public meeting. With the volume of content growing at a rapid rate, users will, increasingly, turn to others, the 'infomediaries', to help them find the content of interest (Hagel and Singer, 1999). The others they will turn to are, in the most part, the media and technology multi-nationals which will have an interest in making some sort of information easier to find than others. However, with increasing access to pornography (Hollands, 1999, p.7), there is a tendency for introducing censorship or, at least, there will be a need for swamping: search engines are increasingly getting more effective at finding the main commercial sites (where questionable values are explicitly promoted) and, in doing so, are less often returning the sites of critics.

Some argue that the new information technologies will help the poor become literate, learn how to plant new crops or sell their services within an expanding information marketplace. However, such 'opportunities' are dependent on citizens being provided with the communication systems; hardware, software and training needed to join the 'IT-harems', otherwise known as the 'information club' (Dertouzos, 1998; Kouzmin, Korac-Kakabadse and Korac-Kakabadse, 1999a). In the absence of such help, they cannot even get started. Computing and technology have implications for praxis and, as such, are as political as any other sort of practices with social repercussions (Dertouzos, 1998). IT policy discourse that arises is political, to a greater or a lesser degree. Some try to demonstrate their a-political nature, by ignoring or concealing what is at stake, socially, in terms of technological change.

The information gap between rich and poor in the world is not difficult to assess. For example, the Bangladesh economy devotes one-tenth of one per cent to hardware and software products and related services. In the US, the corresponding figure is 100 times larger - ten per cent of the US economy goes to IT (Dertouzos, 1998). Since the average Bangladesh citizen is 30 times poorer than the average American, the disparity, per person, between US annual expenditure on IT is even more staggering - an average of US$3,000 for each American compared to US$1 for each Bangladeshi (Dertouzos, 1998). Similarly, with poor Americans, there is an equally obvious dissonance between IT expenditures in the inner city and the suburbs – 'people struggling for daily bites of food having nothing left over for 'bytes' of information' (Dertouzos, 1998). Whereas the rich, who can afford to buy the new technologies, use them to become increasingly productive and, therefore even richer, the poor stand still. Thus, left to its own devices, the information revolution will increase the gap between rich and poor nations and between rich and poor people within nations.

IT and Social Isolation

Even across America there is a troubling 'digital divide'; a study by the Progressive Policy Institute (PPI) ranks the 50 states on how well they are adapting to the new E-Economy. The study uses criteria such as the number of high-tech jobs, quality of educational technology, percentage of population on-line, commercial Internet domains and available venture capital. The reports identifies a clear geographical pattern; the West Coast and Eastern Seaboard, from New Hampshire to Virginia, are at the forefront of the 21st century economy, whilst the Deep South and the upper Midwest lag far behind (Dunham, 1999). For example, whilst 52 per cent of Alaskan populations are on-line, only 17 per cent of the population are on-line in Mississippi (Dunham, 1999). Similarly, whilst the state of Michigan is the highest investor in R & D, with 4.9 per cent of its total economy invested, Hawaii invests zero per cent, followed by Montana, South Dakota, North Dakota and Louisiana with 0.1 per cent (Dunham, 1999).

Furthermore, the SRI's psychographic analysis of the US's Web population identifies two broad categories of the Web 'audience'; the 'upstream' and 'downstream' segment (Freeman, 1995). The 'upstream', or 'actualisers', represents 50 per cent of the Web population but only ten per cent of the US population. This group consists of successful men and women with high self-esteem and active 'take-charge' lifestyles, of which 77 per cent is male and 97 per cent have some college education (Freeman, 1995). The 'downstream', or 'other half', already on-line represents the 'led/user' of the 90 per cent of US society. This group consists of younger people (70 per cent under 30) and on their way to being just as educated (89 per cent have at least some college education), of which, 64 per cent are male and 36 per cent female (Freeman, 1995).

Social isolation is defined as 'the state where one's achieved level of social contact is lower than one's desired level of contact' (Caldwell and Taha, 1993). Isolation is increasingly problematic for information societies as personal relations are seen by sociologists 'as the mortar of society'. It is through such relations that people are taught norms that make for smooth social interaction, are assisted in times of trouble, and become contributing members to a broader social life. When individuals are alone, they, by definition, do not benefit from a social life; when a society has made isolated members 'it is prone to crumble' (Derlega and Margulis, 1982, p.160; Fischer and Phillips, 1982, p.21; Peplau and Perlman, 1982, p.8).

Increasing social isolation is proving to be technology-based on two accounts; due to loss of 'off-line' social skills (Turkley, 1997) and, secondly, due to socio-economic depravation of 'virtual connectivity' or 'information reach'. These currently limit those who have physical access to required technology (Evans and Wurster, 1997; *The Weekend Australian*, 1999, pp.6-7). The policies that government, public and private sector adopts now will shape the socio-economic opportunities for the next ten or 20 years.

Problematic Technology Transfer

The notion of technological capability, which has become increasingly prevalent (Forester, 1985; 1989; Dodgson, 1989; Madu, 1990), is designed to capture, conceptually, precisely the idea of competence - of being able to understand, and hence control, the way in which a new technology is deployed for socio-economic ends. This has been emphasised largely because most technology transfer mechanisms fail to bridge the 'technology gap' between rich and poor countries (Perez and Soete, 1988), further promoted by the invisible barrier and IT-harems. The problem is further compounded by industrialised countries' intensified technology 'dumping' of superseded technologies incompatible with end-users' needs (Kouzmin, Korac-Kakabadse and Korac-Kakabadse, 1999a). This process of technology dumping is sometimes extrinsic and obvious, such as in the case of weapons technology, and at other times, intrinsic and subtle, as in the form of aid.

The past practice of developed societies' and multi-nationals' mode of investment in developing societies' assembly technology, not in *full* production capabilities, has produced the current skepticism that foreign investment in export-oriented intermediate processing will do very little to assist the development of the host society (IDRC, 1989; Henderson, 1991). Some argue that there is an increased effort by the IMF, WTO and World Bank to liken the rest of the world more and more like 'home' (Noi, 1999). Research and development continues to be performed in the exporter country, building host societies' dependencies for the supply of spare parts and expertise. Despite having almost 80 per cent of the world's population, developing economies are responsible for only four per cent of global research and development (UNDP, 1992: 40). 'Poor infrastructure may be the most visible distinguishing characteristic of developing countries' (Austin, 1990. p.53). In 1985, over one billion people in developing societies were living in poverty; one third of their total population (World Bank, 1990). Research and development in developing societies capacity is highly restricted, constrained by capital shortages, foreign exchange shortfalls, lack of infrastructure and other contextual factors. Considering the price of hardware, software and Internet access, those that are most in need of getting their social justice cause publicised via Internet are those least likely to be able to publicise it. Meanwhile, the economic effect of IT industries is (and will remain) to redistribute wealth, overall, to those already wealthy.

Thus, exported technology 'really exports a new form of dependency' (Morgan, 1986, p.311). This is further exacerbated by the multi-nationals' disguise of 'excess' profits and the avoidance of 'paying appropriate taxes in host nations through creative 'transfer pricing' (Morgan, 1986, p.311). Thus, undue confidence in the redemptive power of technology can often prevent policy makers from exploring other strategies needed to empower the 'powerless'.

From the perspective of developing countries, donors often satisfy their own needs at the expense of the recipient country's objectives (IDRC, 1989). Too much effort has been concentrated on structuring systems and centres rather than on evaluating the relevance of services to users; from policy-makers to peasants (IDRC, 1989). International Development Research Centre (IDRC) participants from developing countries concluded that, at present, in general, the statistical information available in Africa is inadequate, out of date and inaccurate. Those who use the information make plans and promises that can never be fulfilled (IDRC, 1989).

Furthermore, the lack of appropriate information accessing tools and technologies to assist the information seeker is compounded by language problems and computer-technology's abounded usage of jargon, proclivity for great promises and, often, the delivery of great disappointments (IDRC, 1989).

From the perspective of the developing countries' policy-design elite, gross disparities in economic performance, research and technology underlie a 'new imperialism' that threatens to keep less-developed nations in a position of 'perpetual thralldom' (IDRC, 1989; Henderson, 1991). Castelles, 1989, p.16) suggests that the real cleavage in societies may be 'between countries integrated in the international structure of production and those excluded from it'. Furthermore, in developing countries, information is expensive and not accessible to everyone, leading to information being withheld from development initiatives at grass-root levels (De Soto, 1989). This is further compounded by the fact that in some developing countries it is not only that the information is not free, but also that one must strive to get it.

Theorists of social power distinguish between power as 'power to' and 'power over' (Olsen, 1997). Notwithstanding that new technologies can give the 'power to' perform actions that one could not perform before, there is insufficient evidence to suggest that technologies, by themselves, can give individuals new 'power over' the conditions of social disadvantage - rather, they require significant support systems. However, the idea of new technologies empowering the 'powerless' and disadvantaged is a plausible one. Without social polices for social justice, these often prove to be another tool for focusing power in the hands of those who already have power - for example, multi-nationals who produce computer hardware and software and telecommunications companies who make use of information and communications technologies for securing profits.

General IT users are among those who will be more subject to the technology than controlling it. Those who are actually able to exploit IT to gain more power are tiny minorities of the population. Knowing how to exploit IT and having the resources to do so may well be two very different things. Although computer usage is growing, currently, less than five per cent of the world's population uses computers (*Hong Kong Business*, 1998). Whilst there is growing research in benefits of IT, very little is done in addressing the issue of Social Darwinism that is increasingly being created by IT policies and praxis. For example, in Canada, the major banks received a $350M R & D tax credit for installing ATMs in late 1990s. The fact that 60,000 tellers lost their jobs is considered irrelevant.

Similarly, in the UK, it is reported that since ATM introduction in 1967, the technology has cost over 150,000 jobs - or around one third of the bank work force (MINTEL, 1996). Current business practices are often short-term and destructive. Companies that realise that they can do business for a fraction of the cost in India or Eastern Europe, may win in the short term - until their competitors adopt the same practice and, then, create a job drain to overseas economies which, eventually, leads to a lack of domestic demand for the product.

Some have argued that IT has a liberating power, particularly for those who are physically or geographically handicapped. However, the downside is that one factor in the liberation of disabled people is having provision made for access to buildings and transport facilities: if it is seen as less important that disabled people have access to buildings and transport, or if access is dependent on the individual having equipment, less provision-for-all disabled will be made. Equally, if disabled people are making use of technology to telework and shop from home, they will be seen less and so the current trend of rising awareness of disabled people among the general population (in the UK, at least) will be reversed and they will become another 'invisible' segment or another 'harem' created by technology. Technology requires resources in order to deliver 'freedom' or access to the disadvantaged. In increasingly corporatised governments, in developed and developing societies, there is an unresolved debate as to who should bear such costs, the individual (directly or indirectly through tax distribution), the government or the private sector.

Indirectly, providing access to IT for all, requires policies that allow IT to be equipped with devices which make it possible for all to use them. For example, radios with closed captioning screens for the hearing impaired and TVs with oral closed captioning describing the images for the visually impaired, should be provided. Or do disadvantaged/impaired individuals also have the responsibility to equip themselves with technology (user-configurable browsers, text to speech software, Braille output encoders) in order to render Web pages and other public utilities interpretable to them?

Perhaps, one should adopt policies on Web page design so that disadvantaged/impaired individuals can use Web pages. For example, even if Web pages are designed in multiple formats, modes, languages and particular style (which involve elements of design, typography, content and language), this will not empower all disadvantaged but the associated costs would be borne by Web page providers. One single company, Axiom Corporation in Conway, Arkansas, has a database combining public and consumer information that covers 95 per cent of American households, whilst governments use data-processing technologies for many entirely legitimate reasons, such as tracking benefits claims, delivering better healthcare, fighting crime and pursuing terrorism; all of which inevitably means more government surveillance (*The Economist*, 1999).

The Development Problematic: IT and Poverty

Uptake of electronic banking, shopping and the development of other electronic services might further increase social division within, and between, societies and between 'haves' and 'have-nots' within society. Even today, people without telephones, credit cards and bank accounts are marginalised, whilst, in the future, the same will happen to anyone lacking access to the Internet (Bray, 1997). Whilst globalisation has been held as a facilitator of universal prosperity, an estimated 1300 million people live in absolute poverty (Muller, 1998). Furthermore, two billion inhabitants on this planet do not yet have electricity and about half of the current world population has never made a simple telephone call. By the year 2001, three-quarters of the households in the US, along with over a half a billion people, globally, are expected to subscribe to a wireless communication service. Of the 4.4 billion people in developing economies, almost three-fifths lack basic sanitation, one-third have no safe drinking water, one quarter have inadequate housing, while one-fifth are under-nourished and the same proportion have no modern health services (UN, 1998).

The World Bank calculates that 3.3 billion people in the 127 countries of the developing world suffer from water-related diseases; amongst them diarrhoea, schistosomiasis, dengue fever, infections by intestinal worms, malaria, river blindness and trachoma and that the deaths from water-related diseases are almost six million each year (Gupte, 1999). Even within wealthy economies, there is a large disparity between the consumption patterns and living standards of the richest and poorest. For example, at least 37 million are unemployed, 100 million are homeless and nearly 200 million have a life expectancy of less than 60 years (UN, 1998). Equally worth noting is the degree of future social division, illustrated by the findings of the United Nations Human Development Report for 1998. The report (UN, 1998) shows that while the consumption bill of the planet is US$24 trillion a year, the global distribution of the consumption bill is alarming. For example:

- 86 per cent of the world's goods and services are consumed by 20 per cent of people living in high-income economies whilst, by contrast, the poorest 20 per cent consume just 1.3 per cent (UN, 1998). Indeed, the richest fifth consumes 45 per cent of all meat and fish, 58 per cent of all energy used, 84 per cent of all papers and has 74 per cent of all telephone lines and owns 87 per cent of all vehicles;
- The three richest people in the world have assets that exceed the combined gross domestic product of the 48 least-developed economies;
- The US population consume £8 billion a year on cosmetics, which is US$2 billion more that the estimated annual total needed to provide basic education for everyone in the world;
- Americans and Europeans spend US$30 billion a year on pet food, which is US$4 billion more than the estimated annual additional total needed to provide basic health and nutrition of everyone in the world;
- Of the 4.4 billion people in developing countries, nearly three-fifths lack access for safe sewers, a third have no access to clean water, a

quarter do not have adequate housing and a fifth have no access to modern health services of any kind;

- The average African household today consumes 20 per cent less than it did 25 years ago;
- Two-third of India's 90 million lowest-income households live below the poverty line.

The belief that globalisation or information technology, somehow, will contribute to developing poorer economies by spreading available global capital more evenly than before, is difficult to sustain in developing economies.   Some have argued that rather than promoting integration, globalisation has shown itself to be a factor for exclusion, exemplified by the current debt of the global South, which stands in excess of US$2 trillion (Muller, 1998).   These, the poorest of the world's economies, repay US$250 to the rich North every minute of the day (Muller, 1998).   It is to no surprise that some 4000 people, most of whom belong to various environmentalist groups and the little-known movement, called J18, have opted out of the system altogether and organised the protest carnival against developing nations' debt which coincided with the Group of Eight Economic Summit in Cologne (Taylor, 1999).   Their philosophy is anti-capitalism which, they say, is destroying the environment and forcing millions into poverty (Taylor, 1999). As capital becomes more mobile than labour, there are concerns that companies will exploit that greater mobility by playing off competing jurisdictions against one another, leading to the situation where governments cannot promote fair taxes, uphold fair labour standards or protect the environment (Lary Sommers, quoted in Noi, 1999). Moreover, critics of the IMF-supported bailouts, of more than US$100 billion, argue that much of the landed money has simply gone to multinational banks and the various currency speculations of billionaires making bad decisions; exemplified by the Wall Street-based Long-Term Capital Management (LTCM) 'hedge' fund, near collapse, saved only by a hasty and massive rescue effort (Muller, 1998).   Western banks, exemplified by Morgan, Chase, Bankers Trust, Goldman Sachs, Deutsche Bank, Barclays and Society General were in a completely illicit relationship, lending money to LTCM, in which they invested and for which they traded (Muller, 1998).   Hedge funds are unregulated private partnerships, except that individuals must invest at least US$5 million to join, whilst an institution must invest US$25 million. For example, in South Korea, western over-investment was followed by the sudden withdrawal of funds and credit, inducing a financial crisis.

When the IMF came forward with bailout funds and its infamous 'restructuring' programmes, South Korea was forced to change social and labour polices which were not directly responsible for the financial crisis. Furthermore, the IMF 'rescue funds' did not go to South Korea at all, but were, rather, used to repay the external investors whose market manipulations had caused the collapse (Moore, 1998). Similar examples can be drawn from Southeast Asia, Africa and the former Soviet Union economies (Moore, 1998). In addition to the fact that globalisation undermines democracy, as governments relinquish power to transnational corporations (TNCs) and multilateral insinuations, under current arrangements, only a 20 per cent minority benefit from free-markets and free trade (Muller, 1998). TNCs have evolved into gigantic engines for generating capital growth and TNC-dominated bureaucracies, exemplified by the IMF, World Trade Organisation (WTO) and World Bank, are being given global decision-making power over a wide range of issues loosely called economic. These insinuations are rapidly taking over roles previously carried out by the national governments.

This new power is most prominent in the global and regional surveillance systems which are carried by various governments, often for the benefit of large corporations. Some have observed that these changes are underpinned by technical dynamism, coupled with scientism; 'materialism'; commercial exploitation; nationalism (the military-industrial complex); colonialism; short-term thinking; and defects in the western industrialism worldwide - particularly short-term thinking and the hegemony of instrumental rationality that has led to a culture that is, fundamentally, anti-life (Slaughter, 1999).

IT and Political Surveillance and Control

Surveillance technologies are one of the fastest growing areas of the technology of political control. Instead of investigative crime, a reactive activity, the fastest-growing trend is towards tracking certain strata, social classes and races of people (Korac-Boisvert and Kouzmin, 1994), living in red-lined areas *before* any crime is committed (De Courcey, 1998). For example, with the new surveillance system, Memex, it is possible to quickly build a comprehensive picture of virtually anyone by gaining electronic access to their records, cash transactions and cars held. Surveillance technology can be defined as devices or systems which can monitor, track and assess the movements of individuals, property and other assets (EUDGR, 1998). Much of surveillance technology is used to track the activities of dissidents, human-right activists, journalists, student leaders, minorities, trade union leaders and political opponents (De Courcey, 1998).

A report by the European Union's Directorate General for Research (EUDGR, 1998) shows that the technologies for intrusive monitoring of almost every action of almost every citizen already exists.   These technologies, if and when employed, will prove significant weapons in the fight against terrorism, but widespread use, even in democratic countries, could lead to the severe abuse of power.   These technologies can be classified in three broad categories, namely *surveillance, identification* and *networking* and are often used in conjunction with video cameras and face-recognition or biometrics and ID cards (EUDGR, 1998).

These technologies facilitate mass and routine surveillance of large segments of the population without the need for warrants and formal investigation.   For example, new surveillance technology can exert a powerful 'chill effect' on those who might wish to take a dissenting view. Few will risk exercising their right to democratic protest if the cost is riot policing with equipment which may lead to permanent injury or loss of life. In the UK, electronic tollbooths and traffic-monitoring systems can record the movement of individual vehicles, whilst closed-circuit TV cameras, initially developed in the UK, now scan increasingly large swathes of urban landscapes in many societies *(The Economist,* 1999).   Particularly successful are heli-tele versions which allows cameras to track human heat signatures in total darkness - an offspring of the night-vision technology developed as a result of the Vietnam War (EUDGR, 1998).   Similarly, the art of bugging systems does not even require physical entry into the home or office.   The multi-room monitoring system of Lorraine Electronics, called DIAL (Direct Intelligence Access Listening), allows an operator to monitor several rooms from anywhere in the world, without effecting an illegal entry.   Neural network bugs go one step further.   Built like a small cockroach, as soon as the light goes out they can crawl to the best location for surveillance.   In fact, Japanese research has taken this idea one step further, controlling or manipulating real cockroaches by implanting microprocessors and electrodes in their bodies.

A range of surveillance technologies is increasingly evolving. Included in the repertoire are night-vision goggles; parabolic microphones to detect conversations over a kilometre away; laser versions to pick up any conversation from a closed window in line of sight; stroboscopic cameras which can take hundreds of pictures in a matter of seconds and individually photograph all participants in a demonstration or march; and the automatic vehicle recognition systems which can identify a car number plate then track the car around a city using a computerised geographic-information system (EUDGR, 1998). One kind of system is trained to recognise number plates via neural technology and can see both day and night. Initially, it has been used for traffic monitoring, but its function has been adopted in recent years to cover security surveillance and has been incorporated in the 'ring of steel' around London. The system can record all the vehicles that entered or left the cordon on any particular day. Although these systems have an important role in tracking criminals, the danger is that their infrastructure is essentially a massive machinery of supervision that can be targeted fairly quickly should the political context change.

Such a powerful form of artificial intelligence needs continuously scrutinised policies and re-assessment. Such surveillance systems raise significant issues of accountability, particularly when transferred to authoritarian regimes. For example, the cameras in Tienamen Square were sold as advanced traffic control systems by Siemens Plessey (De Courcey, 1998).

Whilst mobile companies are busy installing equipment which allows them to track the location of anyone who has a phone switched on, this technique can be used by interested parties who can adapt laptop computers and simply tune in to all the mobile phones active in the area by cursing down to specific numbers. Such parties can search for numbers 'of interest' to see if these are active (Pike, 1998; *The Economist,* 1999). There are, increasingly, growing numbers of electronic devices and software packages that contain identification numbers that can interact with each other and, at the same time, collect information on users - exemplified by Microsoft personal computers - that transport unique identification numbers whenever a personal computer user logs on the Internet (*The Economist,* 1999).

However, the bugs and taps pale into insignificance compared to the national and international state-run interception networks (Pike, 1998). For example, what is not widely known is that built into the international digital telephone system protocol, CCITT, is the ability to take phones 'off the hook' and listen to conversations occurring near the phone, without the user being aware that it is happening (Poole, 1998). This effectively means that a national dial-up telephone-tapping capacity is built into these systems from the beginning. Similarly, the digital technology required to pinpoint mobile-phone users for incoming calls means that all mobile phones in a country, when activated, are mini-tracking devices, giving their owners' whereabouts at any time, and with this information being stored in the company's computers for up to two years (EUDGR, 1998).

Furthermore, within Europe, all E-mail, telephone and fax communications are routinely intercepted by the United States National Security Agency (NSA), transferring all target information from the European mainland, via the strategic hub of London, then, by satellite, to Fort Mead, in Maryland, via NASA's biggest base for electronic spying and crucial hub, at Menwith Hill, in the North York Moors of the UK (Poole, 1998; Port and Resch, 1999). The ECHELON globe-trading system, run by the NSA, is a combination of spy satellites and sensitive listening stations. It eavesdrops on just about everything - electronic communication across national boarders, phone calls, faxes, telex, E-mail, Internet, plus radio signals; including short-wave, airline and maritime frequencies (Port and Resch, 1999; *The Economist*, 1999). It stretches around the world to form a targeting system on all the key Intelsat satellites.

ECHELON springs from a secret pact between the US and UK and also signed, in 1948, by Australia, Canada and New Zealand, the countries running ECHELON's main listening posts (Poole, 1998; Port and Resch, 1999; *The Economist*, 1999). Unlike any of the electronic systems developed during the Cold War, ECHELON is designed for primary non-military targets: governments, organisations and businesses in virtually every country. ECHELON works by indiscriminately intercepting very large quantities of communication and then siphoning out what is valuable, using artificial intelligence aids, such as Memex, to find key words. While there is much information gathered about potential terrorists, there is alot of economic intelligence, notably intensive monitoring of all countries economic activities (Poole, 1998). Like other technological tools, ECHELON is subject to political abuse, as illustrated during the Reagan Administration, when intercepted phone calls by Michael Barnes, then a Democratic Congressman from Maryland, to Nicaraguan officials via transcripts, were leaked to the press (Port and Resch, 1999).

ECHELON also backfired in two, known, instances where Canadian intelligence officers, collaborating with the US, used ECHELON to pick up information on a pending US and China grain deal so that Canada could steal the business with lower prices (Port and Resch, 1999). Under the 1948 UK-US Agreement, the NSA is the lead organisation, with American's Anglo allies deemed 'second parties'. Although most NATO countries, and a few others such as Japan and Korea, have since joined the UK-US alliance, they are deemed 'third parities', meaning they only get funnelled intelligence by the NSA and are seldom allowed to see anything from other contributors (Port and Resch, 1999). Unfortunately, information encryption is no guarantee of privacy either. The NSA has little trouble unscrambling messages encoded with most commercial software as the NSA can break 'crypto' schemes with crypto-keys as long as 1,028 bits and, perhaps, more (Port and Resch, 1999).

The European Parliament is working on a junior version of ECHELON. A resolution outlining the technical standards for tapping new technology systems, such as the Internet, was approved on 7 May, 1999 (Port and Resch, 1999). The Enfopol is a purported FBI/European Union-led initiative to conduct surveillance on phone conversations and Internet access. Whilst business executives worry that the worldwide electronic marketplace will be ruined by a patchwork of inconsistent local regulations, exemplified by Kuwaiti decency standards, European privacy laws and Iowa sales taxes, and the possible threat by government regulation (France, 1999), the reality is the government and big business are implicitly controlling the Internet. The current practice of Internet's self-regulation and some policies made by the quasi-governmental World Intellectual Property Organisation (WIPO) do not provide sufficient checks and balances (France, 1999). Issues such as electronic contracts and cyber squatting, in addition to Internet taxation and privacy, seem to be too important not to be dealt with in a transparent way (France, 1999).

Some argue that the power of the Intranet, in its current state, lies in its resistance to governmental regulation and that its ability to speed information past censors and across borders makes it a force for freedom of expression (Gibson, 1999). The reality is that, in addition to these attributes, there is a down side to the Internet as it is, and can be, used as an electronic vehicle for propaganda, government control, spying, misinformation, vengeance and even terrorism (Gibson, 1999). With growing concern about the Internet's potential to invade people's privacy, politicians are considering new laws to prevent the revolutionary communication channel from being misused. However, proposed regulations will not prevent Internet misuse by governments themselves, as exemplified by their use of the ECHELON system.

Scenarios of IT-Driven Futures

Dominant trends, well-established within the global system, do not lend themselves to a world of peace, prosperity and plenty; rather they lead to a world devastated and dominated in nearly every respect (Slaughter, 1999). A World Health Organisation study predicts that of all diseases in the next decades, *depression* will rank second among leading illnesses *(The Economist,* 1998).   The prediction is based on current rates of disease projected on the demographic model of the world to come. In terms of the number of years of productive life lost to disability, it will be surpassed only by cardiovascular disease. It has been estimated that, in the US alone, the cost of brain disorders in terms of work-time lost, medication and insurance is over 700 billion US dollars a year *(The Economist,* 1998).

In celebration of the modern computer's 50th birthday (in 1948, at Manchester Institute of Technology, Professors Willimas and Kilburne developed 'Baby'), the British IT systems and service company, ICL Systems, has completed an in-depth forecast entitled *The Next Step* (Prodromou, 1998).   The study predicts how the next 50 years of technology will radically change lives. A snapshot from *The Next Step* study suggest that (ICL, 1998):

- Children will be given an electronic identity at birth, a unique global electronic address that will be used throughout their lives;
- The concept of the weekend will disappear, as people will mix work and discretionary time to fit their lifestyle;
- Virtual doubles will exist and carry out many mundane tasks;
- Patients will use the global network to access specialist medical advise, with interviews, tests and diagnosis carried out remotely;
- Individual organ cloning will be performed at birth;
- All domestic appliances will be voice-activated and will be programmable with different personality profiles;
- Screens the size of a credit card will be used as global video phones;
- There will be single global currency;
- New diseases and medical conditions such as 'information overload' and 'information shock' will emerge; and
- There will be a need for a statutory body to ensure security concerns are met in order to ease fears of 'big brother' controlling people's lives.

Notwithstanding that the process of globalisation is unlikely to be reversed, it can be planned for. As globalisation and IT impacts sovereign nations, there is a need to strengthen international institutions that can protect weaker societies. The global economic tendency to reduce job security, increase distress, corrode cultural diversity, limit access to knowledge and human rights when less than five per cent of the world's population uses computers *(Hong Kong Business,* 1998) is disturbing. Although driven by economics, the globalisation process is basically a new political structure (Johnston and Kouzmin, 1998). Globalisation co-exists with rising poverty, unemployment, exclusion and inequality. There is a need for a comprehensive definition of a global structure based on rules of the information society that affects all societies. As the economy evolves towards high value-added, information-based products and services, the accusation is that capital increasingly gravitates at the core, not at the periphery. Thus, national, local and regional economies are shifting from a position of dependent exploitation to structural irrelevance.

The US work force is moving steadily towards a 24-hour-a-day, seven-days-a-week economy in which only 55 per cent of US workers are employed full-time during the day (Presser, quoted in Kleiman, 1996). Some studies suggest that over the past 20 years, working hours have gone up, in the US, by the equivalent of one extra month a year (Handy, 1995). Extensive downsizing through informatisation and management restructuring throughout the global economy has led to longer hours for those who have jobs (Sharp, 1996). In the US, for example, employees believe that working harder and longer is necessary to keeping a job (Sharp, 1996). In self-imposed downsized or 'anorexic' organisations, top management assumes that remaining employees will devote 50, 60 or 70 hours a week to get the job done (Clark, 1997). IT has facilitated downsized business executives to follow itineraries that place them on a global, round-the-clock time schedule, subject to laptops, modems, faxes and E-mail at any time of the day (Tonn and Petrich, 1998).

In the past 20 years, in the US, the vacation time has decreased for the average worker by three-and-a-half days and commuting time has gone up by 23 hours per year (Tonn and Petrich, 1998). A Wall Street Journal poll found that 80 per cent of respondents describe their lives as busy to the point of discomfort as the info-age produces a society in a 'real time' mode composed of people who are 'economically pressed, politically depressed and socially stressed' (Beeman, 1996, p.3). The time pressure associated with prolonged working hours has a negative impact on the quality of life. Research findings suggest that children of successful executives are more likely to suffer a range of emotional and health problems than children of 'less successful' parents (Tonn and Petrich, 1998). Furthermore, parents are spending 40 per cent less time with their children than they did 30 years ago (Tonn and Petrich, 1998).

Although there always has been tension in industrial society between work, family and leisure, it is more so in an information-economy where work places major constraints on the amount and quality of people's discretionary time and attention (Lobel, 1992). This increasing conflict between work and *discretionary time* adversely effects the well-being of men and women in both domains, as living in electronic 'real time' causes 'time poverty' in both spheres. Increasingly, more people are working longer hours, seemingly by choice, but in actuality, with little recourse. Lives are harried and, necessarily, self focused.

The UK culture of long working hours may pose a threat to the stability of family life and reduce quality of life. A study of 6000 couples, aged 33, found that more than one in four fathers work more than 50 hours a week and that their absence had a detrimental effect on joint family activities (Ferri and Smith, 1996). Like their counterparts in the US, men who work longer hours admit to having poor relationships with their children, causing family distress and negatively impacting on relationships with a partner (Delong and Delong, 1992). Longer working hours among men also places a disproportionate burden on women who often combine the double shift of care and work with paid work (Lewis, 1997). There is a sense that families, increasingly, live in a situation of 'compressed time', as work provides both the public and private sphere, and is equally shared in the UK (Daly, 1996, p.117). Research shows that people who work long hours are often unable to communicate on an emotional level in a private sphere, which produces stress and strain in private relationships (Delong and Delong, 1992). Although the demographics of work have changed drastically in the last 30 years, work often remains a place built on 'face time' or long hours in the office for any recognition, reward and advancement (McKenna, E.P., 1997; McKenna, R., 1997). Thus, although some companies make provisions for flexible working hours and working from home, they often marginalise those who use these provisions, such as women and the disabled (McKenna, E.P. 1997; McKenna, R. 1997).

Unemployment and Economic Exclusion as 'Wicked' Public Policy Dilemmas *Par Excellence*

Rittal and Webber (1973, p.160) first coined the phrase 'wicked' problems not because these properties are themselves ethically deplorable but because they are akin to that of being 'malignant'; 'vicious'; 'tricky' or 'aggressive'. In addition to problems of poverty, environmental crisis, crime and discrimination, IT and its development is a new 'wicked' issue for public policy. Wicked problems are those for which there are no obvious, established or easy solutions and, often, do not sit conveniently within the responsibility of one organisation or agency.   They are intractable as they have 'no definite formulation and hence no agreed-upon criteria to tell when a solution has been found' (Harmon and Meyer, 1986, p.9).   This is often because of uncertainty about how to define the problem. Even if there are indications of the nature of the problem, there is uncertainty or disagreement about the source.   For example, the existence of crime is very real, but the cause of crime is much more difficult to unravel.   Even if the cause can be discerned, solutions may still be hard to find.   'These are the problems with no solution, only temporary and imperfect resolutions' (Harmon and Meyer, 1986, p.9).

The resolution of the IT wicked issue inevitably requires action but not by government alone.   The IT wicked issue, by its nature, is intertwined in established ways of life and patterns of thinking, thus requiring changes in ways of life, working and patterns of thought.   It may not be clear what the problem of IT in the future will be and it will certainly not be clear what the solution will be.

Recognition of inter-relationships between IT and other wicked issues is important as breadth of understanding and attention needs to be given not only to IT but, also, to sustainable development, community safety and a safe environment.   There is a need to be inclusive, not exclusive, in the search for connections and to resist the trappings of the organisational perspective (Clarke and Stewart, 1997; Korac-Kakabadse, Korac-Kakabadse and Kouzmin, 1998).   Although the existence of formal agencies to make public policy is necessary, most organisational designs are based on the need to focus, achieve problem simplification, order, efficiency and effectiveness.   These assumptions need to be challenged or at least expanded to include inter-disciplinary, inter-organisational and inter-issue dependencies and capabilities (Clarke and Stewart, 1997).

The Australian Government's re-invention of *unemployment policy*, for example, carries little more than its own ideological jargon despite the previous government's considerable investment of some AUD $700 million in upgrading IT.   The previous Labour government investment in IT had not provided evidence of increased job placement through the Commonwealth Employment Service (CES).   Subsequent Liberal government policy introduced quasi-competition under the banner of 'Job Network', a network of private, community and government organisations, working under the banner 'connecting the right person to the right job', and facilitating government payments to each non-government agency for each eligible individual *taken off* the unemployment queue.

Currently, the unemployed are no longer called 'job seekers' but 'flexible labour exchange services' (FLEX) and access to job assistance depends on the sub-category individuals fall into. The new language masks massive cuts to government spending, where a 'choice of agencies' for job placements being public or private translates to the proliferation of under-researched, private sector agencies (some 300 government licensed agencies), many of which are now downsizing or going out of business (Cohen, 1999). Competition to increase putative effectiveness of public agencies means gutting the long-established government employment service. Similarly, 'mutual obligation' in unemployment policy means that long-term unemployed must work for their benefits, but the government is not mutually obliged to provide any training which may increase job prospects (Cohen, 1999). Furthermore, job seekers are not unemployed - they are a FLEX in a 'job-ready' state, but, in reality, those 'FLEXs' in category 3 (long-term unemployed) have very slim chances of finding a job (Cohen, 1999).

Complexity of employment policy is far reaching, incorporating IT policy and encroaching on crime, societal well-being and the environment. Textual 'white noise' in public policy fulfils many of the functions of romance novels, as it describes market-driven relationships, how one is to come together with technology, declining services or ineffectual public policy (Cohen, 1999). Because unemployment is a wicked issue, it represents intractable problems, imperfectly understood. It is important that it is widely discussed in order to achieve better understanding and to draw upon the experience of those who face these problems at their point of greatest impact - the unemployed (Clarke and Stewart, 1997). The voice of those who are unemployed, who are discriminated against, live in crime-ridden areas, face poverty and are already located in 'IT-harems', have to be heard if the rarity of these issues is to be understood (Clarke and Stewart, 1997). There are, naturally, sharp conflicts and strong disagreements in, and between, components of an effective policy but these disagreements are more frequently about ideology, tactics, priorities and language, than about effective public policy to reduce unemployment in the face of the information revolution.

Conclusion: Transcending Over-Economised Employment Policies

Government policies of the political right have not been able to show, once the active role of government is withdrawn, how individual liberty, alone, can answer the insecurity and remorseless inequity of an open, information-driven economy. Equally, the Left has found it difficult to sustain the conventional functions and fixed structures of government as a workable response to new sources of social and economic exclusion. There is a need for a new way - a choice between market freedoms, with its army of the working poor, and unreconstructed public provision, with all the failings and burgeoning costs of the welfare state.

That economic globalisation should precipitate a multi-leveled crisis for public policy at national, regional and local levels is increasingly understood by political actors across the ideological divide. In Australia, political parties are striving for new 'paradigms' of governance suited to the demands of an information society and economic globalisation - new paradigms that acknowledge that *knowledge* has joined *capital* and *labour* as a core factor of production. At a time when economics has dominated, so overwhelmingly, public policy and public management discourse, the conspicuous inability of economics to theorise about the strategic emergence of knowledge as a central variable in increasing information-driven contexts is particularly startling. As Latham notes (1998, p.52), following Peter Drucker, 'so far, there are no signs of an Adam Smith or a David Ricardo of knowledge' (Drucker, 1993, p.167). Quite remarkably, new pools of knowledge are regarded as outside the parameters by which economic growth is modelled within conventional theories of economics. The fact that IT companies, which generate employment multipliers of 20 times that of heavy industry, can be ignored in economic policy, as is the ongoing role of government in fostering economic growth, is of policy concern to many. Public policy needs to focus on the deficiencies of conventional economics as much as on the deficiencies of that 'church' of economics called Public Choice Theory, which drives 'small-government' rhetoric and posturing, seeking to further diminish the strategic role of government, not only in economic growth, but in wider social-capital requirements of maintaining integration and equity and also facilitating economic inclusion in the face of Neo-Liberal attempts to impose wider tolerance levels for strategic economic exclusion (Johnston and Kouzmin, 1998; Andrews and Kouzmin, 1999).

In the transition of capital from predominantly national to multi-national features of ownership, control and mobility, Latham (1998) usefully reminds one that, in a post-industrial era, political issues are being driven by much more than the conventional dichotomy between capital and labour. 'The political spectrum no longer lies flat with an easy continuity from left to right. It has additional layers of partisanship grafted-on-through the upward movement of capital, the rise of information skills and the changing nature of social connectedness. The political divide is now best conceptualised as a four-plane matrix' (Latham, 1998, p.xxiv) split by:

- The struggle between capital and labour (the class question);
- The policy conflict between economic nationalism and economic internationalism (the nation/state question);
- The emergence of the information rich and information poor (the cognitive skills question); and
- The difficult realignment of social relations between individualism and community (the social/identity question).

    Latham (1998) argues that, in many countries, parts of this matrix have served as a catalyst, not only for re-casting the political system, but by raising fundamental challenges for ideology and public policy and creating a crisis for economics, in particular, with the advent of knowledge work and an information-based society.

    One of the more challenging epistemological issues of today is how to account for the successful economic attack on the public sector - culminating in 'small government' rhetoric (Kouzmin, Leivesley and Korac-Kakabadse, 1997) that has led to dismantling and hollowing-out policies that render competent public sectors de-skilled and outsourced, merely responding to the increasingly strident demands of global capital. Neo-Liberal-driven Economic Rationalism argues that the role of government resides in reducing the cost burden for business or, more strategically, in a rent-seeking way, that the role of government is to furnish business welfare subsidies and protective policies for industry rather than dysfunctionally facilitating the welfare provisions demanded by the increasingly socially-alienated and economically-excluded citizen.

    The most important conventional failing in macro-economic policy and public policy, in the face of globalisation pressures, is that of the failure of economics with regard to the central importance of developing human capital in a post-industrial age - the litany of omission in economics is contrasted with the enormity of the policy response required in creating new and spatially-distributed skill formations, necessitating a renewed government intervention at national and regional levels to mediate the impact of socially-irresponsible mobile capital.

    What is clear is that traditional government intervention into the economic arena - more subsidies, more regulation, more protection, in an attempt to exercise leverage over private capital, is failing in the sphere of

IT and globalisation. Such measures may have influenced nationally-defined capital and may have been defensible within the relatively-closed economics of the Keynesian state (Galbraith, 1995), but such interventions represent an inadequate response to the internationalisation of capital. Much economistic rhetoric is geared to 'an impression, in the public arena, that failures of national competitiveness are simply a product of the inadequate public subsidy of capital. The fiscal crisis of the state becomes more acute as the costs of production are socialised while the returns to capital remain privatised on a globalised scale' (Latham, 1998; p.61). This process not only erodes public legitimacy of the state and the public sector, but also frames public policy around a cycle of industry assistance which ignores the *failings* of business and industry in many strategic ways.

The public sector has important roles to play in easing the strain of economic adjustment. According to Latham (1998, p.69), this can be done through the creation of new forms of employment, relying on the enhancement of fixed economic assets of nations and regions, especially in the public investment in infrastructure and direct employment creation. Yet, 'the semi-permanent high rates of unemployment in most western nations are a result of market failure - a catastrophic mismatch between the mobility of capital on a global scale and the relative immobility of labour market skills and participants at regional and local levels' (Latham, 1998, p.100). These problems of market failure in skill formation and employment location lie outside the scope of orthodox economic theory. Thus, the unemployment crisis for many western economies reflects a crisis in economic theory. Hirschman (1970; 1991; 1995) long ago reminded the reader, inclined to inter-disciplinary sensitivities, of the dangerous misunderstanding of the limits of economics.

The crisis in economics centrally focuses around the need to reformulate epistemological and methodological policy approaches to employment issues. Supply-side economics - as Galbraith (1995) wryly observes, may be the revenge of micro-economics over Keynesian macro-economics - a humiliation suffered by micro-economics over the last 50 years as a result of systematic government interventions necessary to forestall the crisis of the depression.

Problems of economic exclusion in skill formation and the spatial distribution of employment have rarely entered into the political debate in most western liberal democracies. The preoccupation with current account deficits (putting aside, for the moment, whether public - or private-sector borrowing is the major contributory factor to such deficits), ignores the central importance of *human capital* deficits in enhancing national gain sharing in equitable and socially cohesive ways.

But, how is the 'dismal' science of economics to respond to such public policy challenges provided by its natural ally – 'footloose' capital? Factors of technology and management in economic analysis are, conventionally, disregarded as 'externalities' (Marglin, 1971) – an epistemological device known only to the discipline of economics as it assumes away the complexities of industrial, increasingly informational and corporatist, economies.

Economics is a discipline obsessed with, and exalting, a cult of efficiency which, nonetheless, ignores the legitimacy of ends over means; over focuses on costs of operations rather than looking for innovation; and, thirdly, links myths of markets to putative efficiencies by ignoring macro-measures of wastage of human and capital resources in business failures associated with distorted market mechanisms actually operating (Kouzmin and Korac-Kakabadse, 1997).

This is the same discipline that projects the rent-seeking behaviour of private-sector entrepreneurs and corporate board members and managers onto altruistic public sector officials; projections which, when combined with agency and control issues, equally drawn from business failure, give rise to the ideological edifice of the need to instrumentally subordinate and fiscally control public sector agencies while, at the same time, seeking to reduce or eliminate public sector mandates along the way. This is the same discipline that associates business confidence with rent-seeking behaviour and maintenance of privilege (industry welfare) - where any business failure is a problem of inadequate governance and economic mismanagement. This is the same discipline that preaches the dogma of 'revealed preferences' in order to methodologically overcome the embarrassment of 'empirical reality' occasionally not matching the ideological assumptions underlying methodological individualism (Kouzmin, Leivesley and Korac-Kakabadse, 1997, p.26). This is the same discipline that, in supply-side economics, believes that it has finally surmounted the 20th century 'problem' of the cost of labour while losing the plot regarding the strategic importance of investment in human capital, knowledge-based industries and research and technology development. This is the same discipline that underpins the neo-liberal political repositioning of global elites and buttresses the politically outrageous interventions of Bretton Woods instruments of globalisation (IMF/World Bank) (Caulfield, 1998), so dysfunctionally brought to partial account with recent and ideologically-misplaced interventions into the economic and political sovereignty of Asian economies.

The centrality of the government's role in developing human capital is of particular significance. Globalisation and IT developments are having a profound impact on the nature of work and social organisation. Apart from the long-term political issue of profound economic exclusion, the change in the employment base of an economy, from manufacturing output to services, has been associated with politically unacceptable manifestations of a 'pink-collar' work force - the emergence of a part-time, casual and highly-feminised work force (Kouzmin, Korac-Kakabadse and Korac-Kakabadse, 1999b). The significance of a knowledge-based society is not reflected in current, over-economised public policy - a priority, which, in Australia, for example, currently correlates negatively with the political conversion of mass tertiary education and training into a private commodity and 'benefit', thereby rendering education and training less accessible to those most likely to be economically excluded from the consequences of globalisation and the information revolution.

Notwithstanding economic rationalism (Kouzmin, Leivesley and Korac-Kakabadse, 1997) and an economics-dominated public policy, the information society witnesses a smaller, weaker, hollowed-out, outsourced, de-skilled public sector very much under 'capture' from rent-seeking business interests and unaccountable management consultants imposing 're-engineering' and 'downsizing' strategies through 'template' consulting (Micklethwait and Wooldridge, 1997) designed, arguably, to capture declining public-sector revenues as appropriate rents. Contrary to fiscal crisis arguments of the state, a dismantled state will need to be eventually 're-invented', as 'a smart state', concerned with a shrinking public domain and with the need for strategic development of *human capital* at a very time when its revenue-base to perform these functions and sustain related costs are at a minimum. This central contradiction of a future 'smart state' mitigating 'footloose' capital and the employment-displacing abuse of IT will hopefully not depend so slavishly on current limited epistemological capacities of economics in the face of globalisation-doom and public policy impotence projected by many (Boyer and Drache, 1996). The combination of an informational/knowledge illiterate economics, driving a Neo-Liberal and globalising policy agenda, with an aggressively innovating and digitising IT industry, should raise concern about social and economic exclusion increasingly predicated on IT-harems.

Note

1   This chapter was presented at the Public Administration and Development Jubilee
    Conference on 'The Last Fifty Years and the Next Fifty Years: A Century of Public
    Administration and Development'; St Anne's College, Oxford University, April 1999.

2 Information Technology's Impact on Quality of Democracy: A Philosophical and Administrative Framework

ANDREW K. KAKABADSE AND NADA K. KAKABADSE

Abstract

The perennial debate over the future of democracy reaches new heights with the proliferation and penetration of information technologies in all facets of human life. Humanity has arrived at a moment of immense democratic and entrepreneurial opportunities made possible by information technology. However, these opportunities at the same time pose potential threats if not timely debated and planned for. Democracy, that includes concepts of citizenship, human rights, free speech, voting, election, constitutions, economic and political freedom, self-determination, balance of power and position of public office, is conceptualised in this chapter as the vessel that holds hope for a better life.

The chapter[1] examines current problems of representative democracy and the impact of information technologies on current and future quality of democratic life. Four generic models of 'electronic democracy', made possible by interactive information technologies, are analysed in terms of their applicability and impact. These are 'Electronic Bureaucracy', 'Information Management', 'Populist' and 'Civil Society' models. Information technology's impact on the roles, responsibilities and accountability of citizens, elected representatives, media and corporations is examined. In order to take current and future hopes for a better life into the 21st century, the chapter proposes strategies for ways forward or the reinvention of the democratic vessel, including community values, accommodating debate, and providing access for citizen participation in policy analysis.

Introduction

The word democracy has western origins, with its roots in ancient Greece. Democracy is derived from the Greek word 'demokratia' that stems from two related words, 'demos', the people, and 'kratein', to rule. In its Athenian construction, democracy symbolises rule by, and of, the people.

In *The Republic*, Plato (1987, p.83) characterises democracy as a 'charming form of government, full of variety and disorder', which ultimately leads to tyranny. Plato (1987) feared that if people were allowed to make decisions collectively, they would simply endorse their own self-interests, which would result in policies that were nothing more than the lowest common denominator of individual greed and desire for personal security. While Plato (1987) opted for the rule of 'philosopher king', Aristotle (1987) deliberately described democracy as the rule of the poor in their own interests. Mill (1991, p.45) advocated a regulated 'rational democracy', one ruled by 'an enlightened minority accountable to the majority in the last resort'. In contrast, de Tocqueville (1994) saw a predicament, in the American context, in integrating democratic, political culture with a socially democratic society. He perceived that social democracy does not necessarily lead to political democracy in the sense of self-government. Thus he opted for the middle and argued that the democratic culture should be institutionalised to prevent governance by faceless bureaucracies. Marx (1964), on the other hand, thought democracy as the rule of the proletariat.

The major contemporary justification of democracy is that it serves interests by bringing them into debate and decision procedures; that democratic participation enhances autonomy; and in so doing democracy is the best form of government for political equity; and that it is the natural form for consent through deliberation. Democracy serves welfare, autonomy, equity and agreement and it tends to diffuse power, which as a consequence inhibits the corruption of a highly concentrated power elite. Therefore, it is usually less tyrannical than all the other systems of government tried, until now. The negative claim for democracy is a variant of Winston Churchill's quip, that democracy is the worst form of government, other than all the other forms we know, that is because democracy always leads to the imposition of the will of the majority on minorities (de Spinoza, 1951). Hence, democracy is valuable for what it prevents than for what it creates. Democracy is not, in itself, a political paradigm, but rather is a vehicle for implementing a political paradigm, based on conservative, liberal, authoritarian or libertarian philosophy.

This text examines the contemporary conditions of representative democracy, its aspirations and its shortcomings, which can largely be attributed to the structure of governance and the proposed direct liberal democracy made possible by the development of information technology. The impact of information technology on the quality of democratic governance and democratic form is then discussed. It is concluded that whichever democratic form, or combination thereof, is adopted, a crucial consideration is that the role of the elected representative is not undermined. Effective governance requires integration of responsibilities from accountabilities, through utilising means which give society at large greater access to the implementation of policy, but maintains their elected representatives' accountability for its outcomes.

Democracy and Individual Rights

Representative democracy practised this century emerged out of the political philosophy of liberalism (Jones, 1991). The concept presupposes a social order based on liberal democracy, where society is simply a collection of 'free' individuals. The individual is seen as absolute, irreducible, separate and ontologically a priority over society. Thus, the link between the person and his/her parents, children, extended family, ancestors, community, environment and nature are not made (Sardar, 1996). The notion of the community and social duties, which was so central to ancient and simple past forms of participatory governance, was abandoned in favour of independence. In this liberal framework, the individual is constantly faced with the paradox of the community and feeling perpetually threatened by their drive for independence. The individual's main concern is to help keep his/her identity intact, separate from all others, preserve boundaries at all costs, to enclose around oneself a protective wall. Thus, the individual has to make a moral choice between self and society, between the comfort of belonging and the freedom to choose and re-choose different pathways. Therefore, there can never be substantive agreement between the individual and the community as a whole. Morality becomes a matter of individual behaviour; the emphasis is not on what is of ultimate value and what ends should be sought, but of how others can be persuaded to accept the ends of certain individuals (Galbraith, 1992; Hughes, 1993; Stivers, 1994). The goals of liberal democracy therefore focus on providing the individual with all possible avenues to persuade others of what is desired, by the person even at the expense of the community. As such, the practice of liberal democracy creates a paradox for government, by pursuing a pathway towards communal social, cultural, economic or political goals which would ensure an equal distribution of wealth or to provide certain basics, such as equal education and healthcare opportunities for all, but then to leave each individual to fend for him(her)self (Parekh, 1993).

This paradox is even more explicit in constitutional democracy which entails, definitionally, a simultaneous commitment to the principles of democracy and constitutionalism, which are incompatible at the extreme and a presiding tension at best (Holmes, 1988). According to the democratic principle, the will of the majority should govern. Thus to the pure democrat, limits on majoritarian power are unjustifiable. Unlike the democrat, the constitutionalist is somewhat wary of majorities, in particular of the majorities' willingness and ability to protect individual autonomy (Croley, 1995, p.702), to the point where certain rights possessed by individuals and minorities can override majoritarian will. Thus, democracy affords all qualified members of the political community a voice in political decision-making.   In practice, however, societies commonly called democracies fall far short of this ideal due to inequalities in wealth, access to communication technology and other factors, which translate directly into inequality of political power (Dahl, 1989). Once citizens of the polity are political equals, that is, once they have an equal voice in the decision-making process, it follows that policy alternatives attracting the greatest number of voices will prevail. 'Democracies do live by the idea, central to the process of gaining the consent of the governed, that the majority has the ultimate power to displace the decision-makers and to reject any part of their policy' (Bickel, 1986, p.27). The identification of 'democracy' with political equality, popular sovereignty, and rule by majority is promulgated through the whole history of democratic theories (Dahl, 1989, p.34).

Constitutional theory, on the other hand, on which many democracies rest today is not a simple majority theory. The constitution is designed to protect individual citizens and groups against certain decisions that the majority of citizens make, even when that majority acts in what it takes to be the general or common interest (Dworkin, 1977, p.132). Constitutions may be written or unwritten, and the rights they contain may be enumerated or implied. The central purpose of a constitution is to delineate the border between majoritarian power and individual autonomy, or between legitimate and illegitimate exercise of majoritarian power (Croley, 1995). Among other things, the application of universal rights supports individual autonomy, by restricting the powers the majority may exercise, in terms of 'substantive rights' or the manner in which the majority may exercise its power, 'procedural rights'. Thus, majoritarian power loses legitimacy whenever it invades the protected spheres of individual autonomy or otherwise interferes with individual autonomy (Croley, 1995, p.705). Therefore 'constitutionalism, from a certain perspective, is essentially antidemocratic. The basic function of the constitution is to remove certain decisions from the democratic process, that is, to tie the community's hands' (Holmes, 1988, p.195). As such the freedom of 'the majority to govern and the freedom of the individual not to be governed, remain forever in tension' (Bork, 1990, p.139). For example, in the information age, the majorities' demand for certain information to be made readily available by government agencies may impinge on the privacy of the individual or minority groups.

Democracy and Context

In most indigenous cultures, such as Australian Aborigines and American Indians, for example, the individual is defined by the tribe or the clan; the individual cannot be distinguished from the tribe and seek his/her fulfilment as an integrated part of the whole tribe (Geertz, 1973). Similarly, the Chinese see the family as an organism linked to the past, the ancestors, but also with the present and the future, the descendants (Smith, 1994). The individual is seen not as a separate being, but in living union with his/her ancestors. Similarly, Muslims see the individual as an integrated part of the society, which in the local areas is displayed by attendance at the Friday mosque, and on an international level by collectively of all Muslims, the *ummah.* Overall, society is a priority to the individual and social obligations come before individual dictates (Davies, 1988).

   In many African cultures, prior to colonisation, power was collectively shared through a council of elders. The plurality inherent in the membership of the council checked any tendency towards tyranny. Thus, the traditional African system of governance involved both participation, responsibility and accountability. Sithole (1959) argues that it is 'bad history' that has led many western scholars to declare that Africans never had democratic principles until the coming of the white man. What Africans did not have is the modern national state. The notion of the state with its impersonal institutions and emphasis on geographical boundaries, was not only alien to Africa but when introduced led to a total dislocation and disruption of African society, destroying the indigenous social fabric of the village and community, chieftancies and kinship (Sardar, 1985). The fragile state structure, the crises of legitimacy and economic underdevelopment, has all reduced Africa to ruins (Sardar, 1985). The difference in the philosophy of democratic societies in the west and philosophy of the indigenous people, can help explain why western style, liberal representative democracy is not easily adaptable in the non-western societies (African, Muslim, Japanese). Even in western societies, with a tradition of liberal representative democracy, democratic principles are contextually redefined, according to the prevailing political philosophy and adopted mechanisms for upholding democratic principles (government structure), namely the democratic vessel. Hence, although the cargo, in this case democratic principle, is the same, the vessel that carries the cargo (prevailing political philosophy and government structure) is different according to the waters in which it has to sail (the societal context; culture, history, values, attitudes).

For example, the election of the people's representative in the UK is based on the principle of 'first past the post', whilst in the USA, it is based on proportional voting. Furthermore, elections are held every three years in Australia, every four in the USA, every five in the UK and every seven in France, to mention just a few. In Australia, voting is a compulsory activity, while in most other societies, it is a voluntary activity. Switzerland has adopted a form of more 'direct democracy' whilst the UK, the USA, Canada, Australia and others have adopted a representative democracy model. Furthermore, whilst the USA has adopted a congressional system of government, the UK, Canada and Australia have opted for a Westminster system of government or their variation.

Similarly, the structure of political parties and prevailing philosophies are as varied, although all evolve around democratic principles. Whilst Australia and the USA (the constitution and the Bill of Rights) have a written constitution, the UK with an unwritten constitution has a constitutional monarchy. Thus, the interpretation of democratic principles is dependent on the prevailing philosophy and context that defines their meaning. For example, the human rights principle, although universally acknowledged and recognised, is interpreted differently in accordance with local context. Therefore, human rights principles interpreted in certain contexts, in terms of political and civil rights, do not satisfy the quest of the poor for human dignity and social justice (Muzaffar, 1993). Life and liberty, food and freedom need to go hand in hand if society wants to develop a more holistic, integrated vision of human rights (Muzaffar,

1993). As a result, there exist all kinds of vessels that carry democratic cargo, depending on the nature of the waters (context); deep sea vessels, river boats, paddle boats, catamarans and even surfboards.

Models of Democracy

Although all societies have democratic potential, they also all have the design for promoting their democratic model or preventing its appearance. The democratic potential is the capacity of citizens to effectively and knowledgeably participate in socially constitutive processes, to exercise power. One can distinguish democratic potential per se by focusing on the state as the systemic level of interest. It is, however, an identifying feature of today's environment that state affairs are increasingly influenced by processes at the inter-system and individual levels, and part of the task of understanding the nature of democratic practice and citizenship is to unravel what that means (Mouffe, 1992).

Some theorists link specific information technologies with particular political processes and forms: orality to democracy and the city-state; print to bureaucracy and the nation-state; and the emergence of the net, or the global information infrastructure, with models of 'electronic democracy'. There exists a variety of democratic modes of governance, and it can be said that each society has its own unique model that reflects its 'formative context', such as institutional arrangements, cultural values, ethnic tastes, training, historical background and cognitive frames that shape the daily routines of citizens, ideology and objectives (Unger, 1987; Korac-Kakabadse at al, 1996) However, from the myriad of practices, three generic models of democracy are identified, Aristotelian style direct democracy, representative democracy, and electronically facilitated and mediated 'direct democracy'.

Direct Democracy (Aristotelian)

Aristotle argued in the fourth century BC that democracy could not work in a country larger than a small city-state such as Athens. One reason was that in a democracy all citizens should be able to assemble at one place to hear a speaker. Thus, the range of the human voice limited democracy's size. As late as the mid 18th century, political thinkers continued and argued against the possibility of large-scale democracy, in part because of communication limitations. After the birth of the United States, a huge democracy by historical standards, such arguments were discarded. The early 19th century invention of the penny press for printing newspapers, made the acquisition of political information by the masses both convenient and affordable. This, in turn, greatly facilitated the extension of suffrage during that period.

The advent of radio and television led to the growing influence of the media in political elections. The development of mass media, such as newspapers and television, extended the political message not to hundreds or thousands within the physical range of voice, but to the tens of millions that can watch television. With the advent of computerised information technology emerges, amongst other things, the possibility of the direct democracy. Today, the emergent interactive, direct and unmediated communication holds the possibility to revolutionise not only the entertainment industry, but also the nature of public and political discourse. Furthermore, the news media allows vast amounts of information to be processed almost instantaneously, whilst also accommodating a broader base of civic access and participation.

Mediated or Representative Democracy

In its simplest form, democracy entails having all citizens participate in voting on policy. However, in large states this is not sensible or even possible and participation takes place in sequential forms. First, representatives are chosen and then they decide on policy. Many critics of direct democracy have argued that the average person does not have the resources, the time, ability or inclination to become an expert on issues and political candidates. Individual motivation for action is incompatible with collective preferences, when the latter are well defined (Downs, 1957; Olson, 1996). Direct democracy, which inevitably leads to information overload can, at best, only be in part palliative to the political information problem (Downs, 1957).

It is widely believed that different structures for representation produce substantially different outcomes. Hence, there is no simple formula for representative democracy that relates popular preferences to political outcomes in larger political forums. Unfortunately, the technology and institutions of democracy are no longer keeping up with its growth. Many societies continue to have democratic ideals, but not an informed and engaged electorate able to act upon those ideals. The result is often government that neither knows, nor implements, the public's will. Examples can be drawn from the savings-and-loan scandals exemplified by Boesky, Milken, Maxwell, Lloyds, Elders IXL, *et alia* in the USA, the UK and Australia, and many other financial crises in the latter half of the 1980s, such as insider trading on Wall Street that cost shareholders, investors and tax payers billions of dollars, and rocked the market capitalist system to its foundations (Premeaux and Mondy, 1993; Korac-Kakabadse and Knyght, 1996).

Complete failure by certain corporations to enforce legal, moral or safety constraints, raises obvious moral problems as well as the undesired nature of governing bodies that have tolerated them (Bishop, 1991). If the governments of these societies had regulated banks in the public interest, tax payers would have saved hundreds of billions of dollars. For many individuals who lost confidence in the ability of both elected representatives and the media to act in their interest, direct democracy, such as the ballot referendum or the town meeting, offers an appealing alternative.

Electronic Democracy

Electronic democracy can be understood as the capacity of the new communications environment to enhance the degree and quality of public participation in government. For example, the Internet can enable certain citizens (namely those with access to it) to vote electronically in elections, referenda and plebiscites. The Internet can also facilitate opinion polling. As such, it has the potential to strengthen interaction between government and citizens and between political candidates and voters and, as such, further impact on the nature of democracy. The technological innovations that make these activities possible include increasingly sophisticated computer chips, lasers, fibre optics, low power television, digital recording, telefax, and public and commercial satellite access.

Although scholars and researchers have explored the civic potential of new electronic technology since 1960 and phrases such as 'teledemocracy', 'technopolitics', 'the new media', 'instant polling', 'satellite politics', 'video democracy', 'electronic democracy', 'cyberdemocracy', 'virtual polis' and 'couch-potato democracy' (as people can participate from home) have been in common usage for some time, the substantive debate is taking place in the 1990s. There exists a variety of proposed electronic democracy models. However, four generic models emerge through the literature: the 'Electronic Bureaucracy', 'Information Management', 'Populist' and 'Civil Society' models.

The 'Electronic Bureaucracy' model refers to the electronic delivery of government services. This model already enjoys increasing success at the federal and state levels in the USA and Australia where the 'government on-line' (electronic information available through the Internet) and 'one stop shop' (the office that handles business of multiple government agencies) are operational.   The 'one stop shop' concept is receiving consideration in the UK as stated in the Green Paper 'Government Direct' and other OECD countries (ICL, 1997; OECD, 1996).   The goal of this model is to allow for easier, quicker and cheaper transactions with the government on behalf of businesses and citizens and to reduce, over time, the size of the public sector.   However, some have argued that the enhancement of the service creates problems of inequality between those 'information rich' individuals and businesses that can gain access to the technology necessary to use the electronic service, and those 'information poor' who cannot.   Many equate service enhancement with differential pricing and regard both as unacceptable.   Changing people's attitude towards technology may be a worthy aim, but some would consider it more appropriate as an intervention to enhance education and training than to use such facilities as a cut-back pricing mechanism.

The 'Information Management' model refers to more effective communication bridges between individual citizens and candidates or decision-makers.   This model is also receiving some acclaim as a number of state and federal governments (the USA, Australia) are providing electronic public services and information, on-line, at the point of use. Using multimedia, such as touch screen kiosks, in public places (libraries, shopping malls) or personal computers from home, citizens can obtain government information and/or send messages to their representatives or government agencies.   In the USA, the Clinton administration is exploring this model.   Presidential orders, speeches and other communications are transmitted on-line directly to the people, 'bypassing' the news media. The easy access to bills being introduced to Congress as well as government publications may result in a more informed citizenry.   For example, the ability to circulate government 'white papers' designed to generate political action quickly, is a unique phenomenon of information technology.

The 'Populist' model, endorsed by Ross Perot, enabling citizens to register their views on current issues, is most often equated with direct democracy.   The model received proliferation since Ross Perot popularised the term 'electronic town hall' in his 1992 presidential campaign, whose centrepiece was the notion of electronic town halls (to recreate the spirited gatherings of New England townspeople in a national scale through the medium of interactive technology) (London, 1994).   With the first electronic town meeting taking place in New York State on 5 October

1992, and Santa Monica's interactive computer network PEN (Public Electronic Network) which facilitates 24 hour electronic town meetings (London, 1994), there emerges the age of unmediated communication, where newspaper editors, the mail carrier and television journalists are no longer essential intermediaries between citizens and the officials. In this manner, the electronic town meeting refers to civic discourse that is quick, direct, interactive and inclusive (London, 1994). Some suggest that town hall meetings may be used to educate people on the issues or to decide on policies. Considering that politics involves dialogue, not only the dissemination of facts and information, but also electronic forums can be used to serve both ends, but then the outcomes must rest on the deliberative process that thrashes about in order to define the right questions and the range of alternatives. Electronic referendum fosters the notion that an electronic transaction is an authentic democratic choice. In the USA there are numerous projects underway that suggest that electronic town meetings will soon be a regular part of political life. On 15 January 1993, for example, an electronic town hall in Dallas, through CNN, put to the citizens for instant telefeedback, issues of deficit reduction, campaign financing and lobbying regulations.

The 'Civil Society' model refers to the transformation of political culture and, as such, it can only be appreciated within the context of the broader transformation brought by communication technology. Its goal is to strengthen connections between citizens, thereby promoting a robust and autonomous site for public debate. Whilst in America debate has focused on whether there exists a need for an 'electronic bill of rights', citizens in Sweden and Germany are fretting about the impending age of no privacy, in a democracy that is becoming more and more an electronic tyranny. In addition to the USA, the interactive on-line systems for everyday use are already available in several societies, such as Canada's Teledon, France's Intelmatique and Minitel and Japan's Hi-Ovis being a few examples, although their utilisation is limited, as no one nation is wholly wired with fibre optic cable (the US will be within the next ten years) to accommodate equity of access.

Although all four models have their usefulness and application, it is considered that the 'Civil Society' model is the one that requires more intensive debate. The quality of public dialogue in the future will be influenced by changes in interpersonal relations, employment patterns and organisational structure. The growing cultural and commercial value of information will also be relevant, as will government response to such policy issues as technology, privacy and regulation. The effects of new technology on policy making hold ramifications for democracy. Whilst none of these issues are directly about democracy, each will have considerable impact on the shape that democracy actually takes, as opposed to its formal nature. Analysis of such areas will reveal more about the future of democracy than an examination of the technicalities of electronic voting or managing E-mail deluges. This approach is premised on a particular view of democracy, namely that it is more than a mechanism for determining government, rather than, as the term implies, genuine opportunity for popular participation; open and accountable government; and broad input into the policy debate.

Critiques of Current Models of Representative Democracy

Democratic societies have shown that it is possible to protect human rights, foster citizen participation in the political process (voting, lobby groups), provide economic freedom, and tolerate free speech and freedom of the press which, it can be argued, benefits present and future generations. However, on the eve of the third millennium and democracy's arrival on a global scale, the disillusionment with representative democracy has begun to be openly expressed (Gillwald et al. 1992). A deep cynicism towards representative democracy's model in many democratic societies is emerging (Gore, 1994). Many disenchanted voters are demanding a shift from 'representative democracy' to 'direct democracy' (Sardar, 1996). The cynicism is created, in part, by democratic processes that foster self-centred interest groups over wisdom, deviation over tolerance, short term gain over spirituality, fierce economic competition over collaboration and community change over stability (Gore, 1994). As such, the cynicism is not directed towards democracy or democratic principles, but towards the governance of democratic processes in a variety of contexts. Notwithstanding that a deep cynicism is directed towards political and governing processes (the democratic vessel) rather than towards democratic principles (the cargo), many citizens do not make this distinction and as a result many misinterpret as unsatisfactory liberal representative democracy, instead of democratic processes.

Today's liberally constituted representative democracy, defined and structured within the limits set by liberalism, appears to promote rampant individualism (personal and corporate), the breaking of moral taboos, frenzied consumerism and other absolutes of liberalism, that provides fertile ground for the make-up-as-you-go-along morality of liberalism

(Sardar, 1996). Indeed, liberal secularism in its present form and as practised in the west, appears to be unable to deal easily with any kind of collective identity, except those defined by geography (Sardar, 1996), as exemplified by the 'corporate cowboys' attitude of the 1980s, when the irresponsible behaviour of many individuals at the top of corporations led to the stockmarket crash late in that decade. With the globalisation of markets and capital, and the inability of liberal democracies to provide means by which to enhance community values, ethnic values are coming to the fore.

Similar tensions can be found when western societies insist on exporting liberal democracy to non-western societies, whereby they often deny their histories, destroy the coherence and integrity of their ways of life, and prepare them to mimic imported alien norms (Parekh, 1993; Korac-Kakabadse et al. 1996). African political thought evolved on an organic concept of social and political order hung on the natural formation of kinship (Mazuri, 1990), which has continued to dominate the political formations of contemporary African societies (Sogolo, 1991) but, as such, is at odds with western liberal representative democracy philosophy (Korac-Kakabadse et al. 1996), because their communal and sharing of values are ill-equipped to cope with the dictates of aggressive individualism. In sub-Saharan Africa, for example, intervention by Bretton Woods organisations such as the International Monetary Fund (IMF) and World Bank structural adjustment programmes, based on western values and philosophies, impose harsh reductions on government spending on basic needs on the one hand, and high interest rates on the other (Korac-Kakabadse et al. 1996; Sardar, 1996). The result has been a massive de-industrialisation and a steep rise in poverty, as social and economic infrastructures were gradually destroyed (Seabrook, 1993). World Bank's and IMF's prescriptive recipe for the restructuring of developing societies as a prerequisite for obtaining aid, has produced anti-sentiment towards the western model of liberal representative democracy (Korac-Kakabadse et al. 1996).

Even in western societies, the adopted liberal representative democracy models appear to have an in-built bias against citizens in unorganised and/or informal sectors, who are not highly focused, in contrast to those driven by single issues, such as gun law lobbyist or gay and lesbian rights campaigners. Groups that are more multi-interested, and/or, without resources as such cannot have an influence on political processes as can highly focused, organised groups with resources (Balagopal, 1989). Powerful interest groups, with the resources and a clear focus, often get elected and then divert resources to their own causes, inevitably hijacking political agendas. For example, an interest group consisting of gay mothers, may win seats in local elections under a variety of platforms, and when elected divert resources towards their own causes instead of being representatives of their broader community. Hijacking agendas and resources for singular causes deprive communities of having their needs addressed. Even foreign powers with resources can buy access and perhaps policy favours, which by nature hijack government agendas. For example, it is alleged that the Chinese government has bought influence at Capital Hill (Hosenball and Thomas, 1997). When Clinton accused Bush of 'coddling dictators' and threatened to cut off normal trade relations with Beijing to punish the Chinese for human rights abuses, the Chinese were eager to find a way to deal with the new administration. Through its state owned company, China Resources (Holding) Co., the Chinese government bought a 50 per cent stake in a Hong Kong bank owned by the Lippo Company, whose boss and family patriarch, Mochtar Riady, had access to Clinton, and through that avenue wrote Clinton a personal and confidential letter urging him to drop his threat to restrict trading ties with China. Riady's son, James, had contributed US $100,000 to Clinton's inaugural election campaign in 1993 while Lippo's vice chairman in the United States, Huang, in 1994, became principal deputy assistant secretary of commerce for international economic policy in Clinton's administration (Hosenball and Thomas, 1997).

Similarly, powerful lobby groups are able to mobilise resources and influence government agendas for their own causes, while groups without resources, or no single focus have no mechanism through which they can influence government policies and process. Even when measures are taken to shift power away from professional politicians to ordinary citizens by adoption of the ballot initiative, as was the case in Oregon, California and other western states, where any citizen may draft a petition and provided their petition attracts a set number of signatures it is then put before the voters in a referendum, these do not assist the ordinary citizen (*The Economist*, 1998). Although many attempt this process, only the special-interest groups and lobbyists, corporations and unions can take advantage of the process, as no single individual was ever able to collect the 72,000 signatures in Oregon and more needed in other states, in order to get the issue before the voters (*The Economist*, 1998). Further, although petitions can sometimes galvanise government, they also can choke it, particularly if poorly drafted and their meaning is ambiguous or in conflict with other laws or are unconstitutional, eventually ending up in courts only to be amended or struck down *(The Economist,* 1998). The lobbying impact imbalance is probably one of the most serious issues that can be found in the current liberal representative democracy models. Political interest lobbying and concern for the long term prosperity are often incongruent with each other. For example, lobbying by corporations like Boeing and American Express, who need access to global markets, play a key role in American foreign policy but their presence steers policy in particular directions (Hosenball and Thomas, 1997). Special-interest lobbying represents groups of people, who with significant financial resources press government to make specific decisions on specific matters favourable to them in the short term, to the exclusion of other people and other issues, and in so doing undermine long term prosperity (Tonn, 1996). Lobbying is a controversial, but seemingly accepted, form of competitive political interaction, because of its purity of power and winner takes all outcome. However, a number of writers recommended that caring-oriented governments should be more concerned with consensus, wisdom and community interests at large than about power or competition (Sternberg, 1990).

Some have argued that the current democratic processes disable people of wisdom from meaningful involvement in political processes (Tonn, 1996). The political process, especially at national level, values people who have stamina, determination, self-centredness, the capability to withstand abusive criticism, and the ability to manipulate the media (Tonn, 1996, p.415). There are no other job requirements beyond getting one more vote than one's opponent, being below or past a certain age, and not being convicted of a felony (Tonn, 1996, p.415). People of wisdom, on the other hand, are creative, intelligent, insightful, knowledgeable about life, sagacious, open to change, able to deal with uncertainty and conflict, compassionate, mentally flexible and visionary (Sternberg, 1990), hold a strong sense of value (Tonn, 1996, p.415) and hence are ill-equipped to cope with the current democratic processes.

Some argue that now more than ever there is a need for the emergence of moral leadership in liberal representative democracy (Jeannot, 1989, p.14). As such, moral leadership presupposes traits of character and qualities of mind as 'self-possessed individuals, possessed of humanity, principles, vision and the craft to make them real' (Jeannot, 1989, p.35). People of wisdom are not self-selected or self-centred (Sternberg, 1990), that is they do not normally declare to the world that they are the wisest, because that would violate their values (Tonn, 1996). Like Socrates, they do not proclaim their wisdom. Furthermore, wisdom is not easily conveyed through a 20 second TV commercial and bumper stickers. However, wisdom can be recognised through close association with a wise person in various difficult and trying contexts (Sternberg, 1990). Current political processes tend to drive people of wisdom away from the fore, as many political parties do not hold wisdom as a central characteristic necessary for political office, and are often incapable of identifying people of wisdom or nurturing their growth over the years (Tonn, 1996, p.415). These parties forget that the concern for further prosperity cannot be realised without vision and wisdom (Kakabadse, 1991). The literature search suggests that the vessels of democracy in which we currently sail, with their attendant civic frustrations, political abuses, ubiquitous Gallup polls, and media pontificators, require improvement which may occur with the onset and excitement of hi-tech politics, which holds the potential for vastly increasing direct citizenry participation, and even the possibility of speeding up many processes of government (London, 1994).

The Need to Refocus Debate

Some have argued that in the newly democratised states, such as those of the former eastern block, and in some not so new, such as Canada, Ireland and Spain, democratisation has opened powerful floodgates of ethnic aspirations with nascent democracies having to cope with scores of political parties organised along narrow ethnic lines (Sardar, 1996). Democracy and ethnic revival seem to go hand in hand, as electoral competition stimulates ethno-nationalism, when ethnic groups realise that ethnicity can become the source of their political power and additionally bring in a few other benefits (Inayatullah, 1992). Some argue that representative democracy alone has not been able to provide people with a sense of identity, hence the rise of ethnic nations (Sardar, 1996). The perceived failure of representative democracy to provide its citizens with a sense of belonging, has brought fundamental contradiction to the fore (Sardar, 1996). Thus, some perceive democracy to be a double-edged sword especially in the newly democratic states (Sardar, 1996).

However, these arguments seem to ignore the fact that only democracy can bring to the surface issues and tension in society for debate as opposed to social unrest, revolution and wars which leads to loss of life. Once democracy brings issues and tensions to the surface for examination, then political processes can take over towards their resolution. Thus, ethnicity tensions are brought to the surface through democratic means for debate, but then the manner in which these issues are resolved is dependent on the prevailing political processes, structures and political philosophies. In the non-democratic societies, ethnic issues are not allowed to emerge for debate as in, for example, the former Soviet Union republics, where ethnicity was not a publicly debated issue, but deeply buried in people's minds. However, people may expect certain solutions, as they make assumptions that representative democracy is equal to the ideal solution. They forget that representative democracy only provides the form that brings together issues, philosophies and people which can create solutions, but does not guarantee a solution. Furthermore, when the emergent solution is not in the line with the citizens' held philosophy, desired or perceived solution, their frustration may be vented on the representative democracy. Although the emergent solutions may be unpalatable to the general public, they are derived by democratic processes.

Further, many have equated democracy with economic prosperity, and when the economic growth starts to decline, the disillusionment with representative democracy equally shows (Sardar, 1996). For some, growing disenchantment is partly rooted in representative democracy's failure to meet economic expectations (Sardar, 1996). Others, as Fukuyama (1992), equate the triumph of the free market economy with that of representative democracy. However, these views have raised even more questions about the true nature and capability of representative democracy. Some pose the question as to why democratic Russia is facing economic ruin, whilst communist China has a flourishing economy? (Sardar, 1996) These questions hide, for example, that democratic Russia is still struggling to establish governing mechanisms and a political philosophy that reflects the new context of the democratic state and thus a new identity, in a circumstance of the newly democratic Russian state inheriting an almost bankrupted economy left over from the previous regime. Furthermore, whilst the Chinese economy seems to flourish on the surface, no-one knows exactly the nature of the tensions and contradictions that are deeply buried and not debated.

Others like Adonis and Mulgan (1994) suggest that a fundamental weakness of the modern western state is the divorce of politics from society, and of political responsibility from citizenship, producing low citizen involvement, limited choices, and poor delivery. That is the governing mechanisms for designing and delivering social policies are not aligned with community needs. Governments are often dominated by an elite who offer simplistic and often one dimension solutions to problems that concern the voters (Adonis and Mulgan, 1994). Citizen choices are based on the choices of catch-all policy programmes, which are often vague and which political parties often abandon once in power. Even in the case when policies are carried out, they are all too often seen as ineffective (Adonis and Mulgan, 1994). Thus the political system in many democratic states has shown little capability to make difficult decisions under uncertainty (global climatic change) and even less capability to promote learning over time. Weiss (1989) has argued that today's representative democratic processes (not principles) are not sound enough to sustain societies over the long term, and they are certainly not in a position to meet the challenges of even the most basic obligations to future generations.

Democratic Potential through New Technology

The growing literature on the democratic significance of new information technology has focused on its ability to enhance direct participation by citizens in the political process. Modern technology is commonly perceived as being of greater value in registering the political attitudes and inclinations of the public at large. New interactive media can now accommodate dialogue, which can flow in a circular fashion across interested stakeholders grouping. This kind of exchange has the potential to return the meaning of 'dialogue' to its Socratic usage. In this way, IT promises new ways to build consensus, common ground, and energise the citizenry. Regular dialogue and feedback keeps both citizens and officials in touch with the ebb and flow of public values and judgements. The value of citizen feedback, combined with the new media technologies, has several distinct advantages: it has the capacity to vastly enlarge the scope of political dialogue; it serves as an educational process that brings issues into public focus and gets them defined (London, 1994). Besides engaging citizens, it also promotes a deeper commitment to and understanding of public policy; and it allows public officials to consider a broader range of possible policy options on any given issue, based on the real life concerns and testimonies of everyday citizens (London, 1994).

For example, the Citycard project holds up the eventual prospect of the transformation of relations between the citizen and his or her local authority. Its main goal is to involve the citizen much more in the activities of the local authority, and not just through better dissemination of information. If a resident, for example, believes that a road traffic system is not working, Citycard will enable him or her to communicate their views and advice directly to the local authority officers concerned. Clearly, the officials would be obliged to respond by giving some explanation for the current policy, and an appraisal of the citizen's suggestion. Still in its pilot phase, the Citycard project is led by two software companies (MARI from the United Kingdom and OMEGA from Italy), in cooperation with Lagotex (Portugal) and the cities of Wansbeck and Bologna. While not exactly the democracy of the Athenian public meeting, this application of the information technologies promises to close the gap between governors and the governed, in the process making public officials more accountable to the people they serve (OECD, 1997). There is still more of a democratic promise to Citycard, because the venture will be designed to enable citizens to discuss issues amongst themselves and to pass on proposed solutions to local problems. Discussion groups will even have the facility to produce edited documents for passing to the authorities. However, here lies also the danger and a paradox, as those discussion groups can become lobby groups with a new tool.

New technology facilitating new forms of voting and thus direct participation, which is based on the theoretically elegant but heretofore impractical voting systems, may now come into widespread use (Snider, 1994). For example, instead of physically going to the polls, individuals could vote from their homes. With more convenient and less expensive voting systems in place, individuals could be expected to vote more frequently and on more issues. Ballot referendums and polls could proliferate. Institutional willingness for ballot referendums which is a sensitive issue in the UK, has not shown itself so in either the Californian or Swiss context, where regular referenda are held, which suggests that for certain countries technology may be a less important issue than political and institutional will (Perri, 1997).

While instant polling and referendums can simply make the public as non-reflective as legislatures sometimes are, there exists the potential for far more reflective democratic processes. Experiments over the last two decades with televoters have highlighted the potential in this area. In addition, a recent senatorial election in Oregon, USA allowed voting by mail. The voter turnout was 67 per cent, almost doubling the national average voter turnout over the last 20 years for senatorial elections in non-presidential elections (*Washington Post,* 1996). Combined with citizen movements towards growing healthy communities, sustainable development and enhanced community dialogue, electronic messaging in this arena could become transformative (*The Economist,* 1995).

Other benefits of the new information technology are improved access to the deliberation of public bodies. In the USA, cable channels already cover House and Senate Chambers and congressional hearings, as well as at state level (California House and Senate Chambers and legislative hearings) and at local level (city councils and school boards). In the future, coverage of such meetings at local, state and national level is likely to expand dramatically, thus making government deliberations much more accessible to the average person (Snider, 1994). New technology also facilitates via television, computer or some synthesis of both, electronic town meetings, where citizens are offered direct contact with public officials, unmediated by journalists. The idea is to force politicians and the media to talk to the public about important issues that might otherwise escape the political agenda. Combined with televoting, the electronic town meeting offers a potentially significant improvement on the ballot referendum which is poor at fostering deliberation and thus has led to uninformed voting. Government records could also be made more accessible, which would be an improvement on the cumbersome procedures necessary to gain access to information, under the Freedom of Information Act adopted in many western democracies (the USA, Canada, Australia, New Zealand). However, information pertinent to individuals, groups or security needs still have to be protected.

Electronic communication's role in political outcomes is growing, from instant opinion polls to chat lines. Technology is shaping the scope and nature of the political process. The likelihood is that some form of electronic democracy will, amongst other things, fuel effort to make technology universally accessible (*The Economist,* 1995). The argument has been put forward that the perceived or assigned shortcomings of liberal representatives democracy can be remedied with the new information technologies, which will also help to humanise liberal democracy (Sardar, 1996). Some claim (Szilagyi, 1994; Sardar, 1996) that technology will enable citizens to have direct access to their representatives, thus bypassing pressure groups, party politics, the media, special-interest groups and other undemocratic channels of opinion formation. Sardar (1996, p.846) suggests that the elected representatives will perform their function, only on people's daily sufferance, which will lead to the loss of the old grandeur of parliament and political parties. While Szilagyi (1994) argues that the information revolution will change the political system, it will also lead to the collapse of representative democracy as it is known today, replacing it with the 'democracy of the information age', a form of direct democracy. Politicians will be selected according to a free competition of ideas, with a power base that is decentralised, creating a culture where success and status in society will not depend on the exercise of political power. However, the impact of the use of information technologies on societal democratic potential depends on the ever growing sophistication of information and communication technologies; rules restricting the use of information and communication technologies; and the nature of the entity that makes the rules about the use of information and communication technologies (Braman, 1994). It is considered that nations will prosper or falter in the next century, depending on their investment in building an information infrastructure (Davis and Davidson, 1991).

Downside of Electronic Democracy

Considering that human knowledge presupposes information, the collective intellectual abilities of a nation, its human capital, will depend on access to information in electronic form (Crawford, 1991). The advancement of information technology (IT) such as telecommunication networks, satellites, fibre optics, databases, to mention just a few, and the special nature of computer literacy, process knowledge related to the effective use of information, have promoted in many scholars and citizens the vision of a technological future. At the same time, today's jumble of regulations is increasingly hard to maintain as voice, images, data, and text coalesce into one massive 'telematic' network, and as hybrid technologies like virtual reality (VR) blur the line, dividing speech from action (Fogelman, 1994, p.295).

Thus, the broad means of conducting elections represent one downside to electronic democracy, as democracy is about the articulation of common interests and shared concerns between citizens. However, digital democracy is mainly about the expression of the individual in front of one's own keyboard or other electronic gadgetry. Therefore, it will be harder to aggregate preferences in an acceptable way without institutionalised ways of persuading and ensuring collective action. Furthermore, excessive participation at the wrong time could lead to government paralysis. Electronic democracy can dangerously over-extend the sphere of democratic decision-making into what ought to be the sphere of individual or corporate decision-making, because the institutional constraints that have been developed in analogue democracy do not exist in the digital setting. For instance, a national electronic 'town meeting' on environmental protection versus economic development could result in interminable debate, little consensus and no decisions (Deleone, 1994, p.91). Witness the controversy in the Pacific Northwest and the debate as to where to bury radioactive waste materials. In times of political crisis, the inability to reach a decision could be dangerous. Under more normal conditions, open citizen participation in decision-making would almost surely present delays (Deleone, 1994, p.91). Some argue that the availability of the instant response provided by interactive technology will discourage deliberation and thoughtful exercise of democratic choice.

Although no form of vote tabulation is completely risk free from external interference, paper ballots have a three to five per cent error rate, the electronic vote casting practised in 70 per cent of the US has high potential for vote tampering (O'Meara, 1998). In the new computerised systems such as Direct Record Entry (DRE), used by 8.8 per cent of the precincts or nearly 13 million Americans, the most important step in the voting process, the physical ballot marked by the voter, is omitted leaving opportunity for fraud as computers can be programmed to perform erroneous counting at any time (O'Meara, 1998). Transferring trust to the wonders of electronic voting systems smacks of Stalinism, for it was Stalin who quipped that the people who cast the vote decide nothing but the people who count the vote decide everything (O'Meara, 1998).

Still others suggest that although much of the technology needed for the vision of 'electronic democracy' already exists in a number of societies, no-one can really tell whether these technologies will acutely enhance participative democracy participation or lead to further fragmentation and individualisation (Ogden, 1994). Information technology, as currently implemented and likely to remain so in the near future, should equitably facilitate citizenry access to direct democracy to only a small and atypical minority group (young, affluent, liberated, etc.) as they are the only ones who are on-line.

The very idea of the citizen sitting in front of his or her computer terminal interrogating political representatives, takes individualism into a new dimension (Ogden, 1994). Information age direct democracy poses new social segregation challenges between those who are information rich and poor, on an individual and societal basis (Kapor, 1992; Korac-Kakabadse et al. 1996). Poor individuals will not be able to influence political agendas. For example, by the year 2000 it is estimated that nearly one quarter of the new workers in the work force in the USA will be immigrants, many of whom will have a relatively low level of formal schooling and limited English skills (SLCI, IPP, 1995). Considering that projected growth of 2.7 billion people will be added to the world population between 1995 and 2025, of which 93 per cent will occur in Africa, Asia and Latin America, giving these regions 83 per cent of the world's population, the differentiation in information rich and poor societies may be significant (United Nations Population Fund, 1994). Moreover, by the year 2000 over half of the world's population will be under the age of 20, raising the generation and socio-cultural divide between the information rich and information poor citizens (Peterson, 1994). The fact that about half of the current world population has never made a simple telephone call, and that by the year 2001 three quarters of households in the US, along with over half a billion people globally, are expected to subscribe to a wireless communication service, highlights the degree of future social divide (Zysman, 1995).

Furthermore, the current IT problems that range from Internet pornography to on-line forgery, credit card theft, virus attacks, unauthorised access to a system to destroy data, hacking in to read E-mail and cracking passwords and taking over an account, may also erode electronic democracy. Not all technology related crimes fit the popular definition of 'computer crime', crimes committed involving computers and/or telecommunication systems. Some, notably the get-rich-quick schemes, are traditional fraud, given new impetus by technology such as Web pages and E-mail. Although the motivation for computer crimes is commercial gain, the motivation is not always what can one get out of it directly. Often it is what one can get out of it by seeing the competition go broke. Thus, using technology to modify voting patterns may be a new avenue of computer crime. In Australia, for example, the second (America being first) informatised society in terms of computers per capita, computer crime units are a relatively recent innovation in policing, emerging only since the 1990s (Creedy, 1997). However the number of complaints received by crime units for investigation have tripled in the last three years. The Institute of Criminology suggests that officially reported computer intrusions represent the tip of the iceberg (Creedy, 1997). In the increasingly interconnected economies exemplified by stock exchanges and frontierless capital markets, globalised production and marketing, IT crime combat and prevention requires global policies and co-operation. Moreover the emergence of regional trading blocks and economic dominance increases the potential for IT crime.

Furthermore, with a growing amount of commerce occurring over the Internet, electronic transactions are becoming the norm. Monitoring and tracking paper exchanges for tax and tariff purposes can become even more complicated by the ease of moving a virtual organisation's headquarters offshore, or with the creation and issuance of new electronic media of exchange (Merritt, 1995). The lack of adequate monitoring policies for electronic commerce and electronic-money (E-money) taxation, may lead to great difficulties for governments that regulate and tax their business citizens. Fuelled with the current pressure of a growing national debt and socially conservative policy making leading to an overall shrinking of federal government expenditure on social polices, additional hardship for the underprivileged is almost destined to be a future reality.

IT, Democracy and International Concern

Facing pressure to do more with less, government, and the public and private sectors have turned to IT as a tool for increasing both efficiency and quality of services. These improvements have been wide-ranging, including faster processing and less expensive storing of information, quicker responses to information requests, and better integrated information to serve customers. However, IT can be a double-edged sword. While IT has enormous potential to increase the efficiency of government operations and the effectiveness of communication, it can also have negative effects if it is not well managed. A poor choice of what to purchase, a badly conceived contract, or inadequately trained staff, for example, can all lead to problems such as a restricted ability to communicate, degraded performance, or excessive costs required to adjust to continuing technological change.

IT advances also raise broader issues related to how governments communicate with citizens. Potentially IT can enhance government accountability and citizen participation in democratic decision-making through clearer and more accessible communication, by fostering direct communication between citizens (e.g. the Internet) in an effort to build public debate which is dominated neither by political parties or the news media. However IT has also a potential downside as it can isolate individuals, providing better access to information only to the well-educated, technologically well-equipped, organised and those with resources (Perri, 1997). As such IT has potential not only to professionalise lobbying but also to facilitate lobbying on a large scale.

In the USA, the Minnesota E-Democracy project is a non-partisan and a citizen-based project, which has a mission to improve democratic participation in Minnesota through the use of information networks, and on-line civic participation centres (Clift, 1997). Similarly, Washington State Government Electronic Democracy provides to public agencies by the Department of Information, services for the benefit of the citizens of

Washington State and the Internet community. In Australia, the Victorian government initiated the Australian Electronic Democracy project, in an effort to enhance the quality of political debate by communication technologies.

The European Commission's (1994) 'Europe and the Global Information Society' report (often known as the Bangemann Report) represents the views of an eminent group of businessmen and community leaders that forms the basis of much of the European Commission's work programme and strategic planning for the Information Society (ICL, 1997). Influenced by the Bangemann Report, the G7 recently launched a series of pilot projects to address the social, political and technical issues raised by the advent of the information society, including a project called 'Government On-Line'. Government On-Line seeks to facilitate development of on-line information systems to help governments in four key areas: international government co-operation and exchange of information; more efficient collaboration among government departments; closer links between government and business; and greater interaction between government and the general public (OECD, 1997). The other project launched by the European Commission is the 'Information Society Project', which includes the creation of an 'Information Society Forum', which, in turn, attempts to bring together government and expert participants to address issues including access to public services through 'electronic democracy', more transparent and better quality public services, and the protection of the individual (OECD, 1997).

In response to the Bangemann Report and the Hedsor Memorandum, a call for Europe to embrace the full potential of the Global Information Society, a number of groups and symposia have emerged to debate the impact of the Information Society and the changing roles/responsibilities of public administration, business, academia and the citizen (ICL, 1996). The January 1997 'Information Society Symposium' (a 'think-tank'), for example, attempted to foster a discussion with a select group of people from government, business, arts, academia and politics in order to analyse and discuss the long term impact of IT, which may go beyond regulatory political constraints, and to generate outputs which will contribute to the policy debate (ICL, 1997). The symposium identified five areas which may provide potential leverage to move the UK towards the sort of society and governance system needed to thrive in the information society of 2010, namely, the quality of democracy and a number of social issues such as employment, education, the role of the media in serving the public interest and services for the citizens. Questions brought to the surface for a wide debate were (ICL, 1997):

- What can the UK do to improve the sharing of the vision of an information society, in which there are clear and demonstrable improvements to citizens lives?;
- What leadership style should the UK adopt in the information society?;
- What are the issues for the quality of democracy in the information society?; how can IT be used to improve the quality?;
- How can the UK participate to the greatest extent in the job creation potential of the information society?;
- What are the roles of central and local government, of governors, parents and teachers, in exploring improvement in education through the use of IT?; and
- How can the media contribute to the debate on the information society?

In addition to the information society initiative, 'Government Direct', a proposal for the electronic delivery of government services, (UK Office of Public Service, 1997), the UK government has also launched under the banner 'IT for All', an information and communication technologies awareness initiative (UK DTI, 1996).

Electronic democracy is an emerging global trend and at this moment in time is a part of 'operational democracy' (Rosell, 1992, 1995). It is not a replacement. However, it is changing the nature of democracy. It will only thrive and lead to improved democracies across the world if governments, individuals and organisations come together to build shared meanings and accessible on-line infrastructure to all citizens. To build an on-line infrastructure that is accessible to all citizens requires local and regional co-operation, visionary policies and long term individual and organisational commitment. Thus there is a hope because there is 'something' in the air, or as Pascal called it, a 'je ne sais quoi' that technology can facilitate improvement of democratic processes. The danger there is a political tendency to go with certain opinions, rather than asking questions from those who will be affected by these opinions when implemented.

Information Technology's Impact on Citizens' and Representatives' Roles

Perhaps the most serious problem of 'electronic democracy' arises from its ability to divorce responsibility from accountability, which is twofold. First, whilst individuals, at least those who can afford technology, will be responsible for influencing the political agenda, they will not be held accountable for their impact on policy implementation (Kapor, 1992). The very problem Plato (1987) feared and wanted to guard against, was that of people simply endorsing their self-interests, which would result in policies that were nothing more than the lowest common denominator of individual's greed and desire for personal gain or security. Second, elected representatives driven by an aggregation of electronically democratic demands, will be held accountable for policies for which they are not responsible and over which they have little influence. The bargaining power of elected representatives will be undermined and as such will not be able to see through agreements. Furthermore, fragmentation and a lack of coherent policy will lead to social vulnerability. For example, if, in a society with information based direct democracy (cyberdemocracy), every individual (or majority) were to vote to abolish nuclear weapons in that society and that policy was to be carried out, then in the case of threat or invasion by another society that has a nuclear weapons policy, the former society will be only temporarily democratically satisfied, as exposure to threat would probably mean ultimate loss of freedom.

Under the current representative liberal democracy, the elected representative is implicitly operating under a social contract obligation, as they are responsible for supporting particular principles and accountable for their actions. Any social institution, of which government and business are no exception, operates in society via a social contract, which needs to meet the twin test of legitimacy and relevance by demonstrating that, on the one hand, society requires its services and, on the other, that the groups benefiting from its rewards have society's actual or implied approval (Shocker and Sethi, 1974, p.67). In electing representatives, citizens place onus on the representative to provide an account of their actions (Gray et al. 1987, p.2). The failure by representatives to deliver the electorates' expected outcomes leads to dissatisfaction in policy and a change of representatives. Thus giving and demanding of reasons for conduct (Roberts and Scapens, 1985) defines the relationship between citizens and representatives, in contractual or principal and agent terms (Laughlin, 1996), where the agent acts on behalf of the principal under a contract existing between them, which has to be neither written nor need to be explicit (Gray, 1983; Tricker, 1983; Stewart, 1984). This assumes that the principal 'society' can be identified along with its concomitant aims, aspirations and interests (Power, 1991, p.34). In the implicit contract, the principal, the citizen, typically gives instructions to the agent, the political representative, on what actions are expected from him/her, given certain powers of remuneration from citizens' tax, power over resources, policy design and implementation. In so doing the principal, the citizen, holds the agent responsible and accountable for their actions (Gray et al. 1988, p.3). Using information technology to influence the representative's agenda on a daily basis, leaves the representative accountable for decisions for which he/she is not responsible in terms of generating, may not be in agreement with and may not have the opportunity to present an alternative case. Such circumstances within an organisational setting are akin to holding a manager accountable for the actions of their subordinates, whilst having no control over what they do (Kakabadse, 1991). Divorcing accountability from responsibility leads to the ultimate demise of the implicit contract between the representative and the citizen. The social technology of representative democracy binds agent and principal together, thereby generating a relationship of accountability, which is fundamental to the 'social contract' of political theory. Being a theoretical construct, social contract theory assumes that the 'individual chooses' to enter and subject themselves to social and political arrangements involving the delegation of authority' (Power, 1991, p.34). The social nature of the relationship suggests the superiority of an accountability framework over the decision usefulness of operational frameworks such as IT technologies (Ijiri, 1983; Roberts and Scapens, 1985; Williams, 1987).

Thus instead of creating a community based on consensus, unthinking information technology application could easily create states of alienated and atomised individuals, that communicate with each other through computer terminals, terrorising and being terrorised by all those who value conflict, or are determined to pursue their own agenda (Ogden, 1994; Sardar, 1994). For example, in the past two decades violent crime has increased 200 per cent in the US, and the situation is expected to worsen (Stone, 1995). Considering that scientists and leading-edge entrepreneurs are developing interactive technologies to immerse users in a totally convincing illusion, seeking to assemble a 'real' and sharable environment within a cybernetic 'teleplace', the synthetic equivalent of a fully 'inhabitable' alternate world, in which increasingly alienated individuals will have difficulties distinguishing between real affection and 'technoaffection', the long term results of such development could be societally dangerous. Some research laboratories and pleasure arcade virtual reality (VR) implementations, already enable the user/participant, masked or wrapped in sensory effectors, to walk through unconstructed buildings, feel the pull of molecular gravity, or engage in a high-tech shoot-out with a computer or a human operator. Although VR peripherals are limited, at this point, to primitive step platforms, data-gloves, and bulk head-mounted audio/video displays (HMDs), tactile effectors are already being tested. Systems with tactile effectors, which transcend current definitions of simulation, may become a convenient substitute for reality. For example, the tactile effectors, such as 'remote intimacy' dimensions, have the potential to alter forever the legal and social landscape (Fogelman, 1994, p.299). Furthermore the truly persuasive, fully-sensory depictions could give rise to a new epoch of high-technology crime and alienation. While current technology is now able only to violate system security by trashing files or spreading obscure viruses, network pirates could someday employ recorded or counterfeit 'bit streams' to commit heinous acts of breaking and entering: 'virtual sexual harassment', 'information kidnapping' or even 'remote statutory rape' and 'remote murder' (Fogelman, 1994, p.299; Stephenson, 1995). As information becomes increasingly critical to success in both business and personal lives, the threat of being cut off from information by cyberspace criminals, like being held hostage or being kidnapped, is a very real possibility. Terrorists could cut off communication to an individual, a group, a community, or to an entire government or create information agents designed to mug consumer information agents as they make electronic transactions (Cetron, 1994). Considering that the 'telemedicine' will include the automatic transfer of data from consumers to their medical records, and that home care will increase (Olson, 1996), sending counterfeit 'bit streams' to patients can induce murder. Anarchy, violence, drugs and other deadly enemies often thwart good intentions of IT policy. Too often the institution's culture is simply dislocated from the citizen's world (Comer, 1988). The potential for cyberspace harassment to cross into daily life is real as it has been demonstrated in the US, where the first cyberspace stalker has been charged with stalking and harassment on the Internet (a new crime), computer fraud and solicitation for rape (Driscoll, 1999).

Thus, the criticism focused on representative democracy and desire to change it to the 'direct democracy' needs to be re-evaluated and refocused on examining adopted mechanisms of government, the structure of political parties and adopted philosophies. It is projected that industrial workers will be no more than 13 per cent of the work force in every developed society in the world and that, in the US alone, knowledge workers will constitute up to 30 per cent of the work force; there is a need for the development of economic policies appropriate to a world economy in which knowledge is the key resource, as well as a political philosophy and institutions for effective governance in a knowledge-based society (Drucker, 1994).

Given the centrality of computers to information flow, computer literacy may become the *de facto* prerequisite for citizenship in the next century, if the direct democracy model is adopted. Traditional literacy can be defined not just as the ability to read, but the possession of certain background knowledge without which the act of reading becomes meaningless (Bransford and Johanson, 1972; Hirsch and Mulcahy, 1987). Computer literacy is as profound as the ability to read, as it requires a range of abstract understandings about how information is accessed, managed and manipulated, and understanding what transcends particular makes and models of computers and software. Computer literacy will provide extraordinary access to information, but only for those who understand the process of information seeking (Paisley, 1987, p.5). Thus, the distinction between those who have the facility and access to information technology and those who do not, will become as distinct functionally as the difference between those who can read and those who cannot. In the UK for example, research shows that 38 per cent of the UK population are both unconvinced and unconcerned with regard to the new technologies that lead to the growing Informant Society, whilst 16 per cent of the population feel alienated from it (UK, Department of Trade and Industry, 1996). Twenty one per cent of the population accept new technology and only 25 per cent of the population are enthusiastic about the new technology. Those who are, characteristically, are young upmarket men and women (UK, Department of Trade and Industry, 1996). The need to redesign democratic vessels is real, but it is the container that needs to be redesigned to a new aerodynamic shape that can cope with new winds and depths of water, rather than its cargo, the democratic principles. The emerging new information technology's ethical, legal and policy ramifications should be modelled and investigated before they personally, even physically, touch our lives.

Information Technology's Impact on Media and Corporations' Roles

While the role of government is, and remains, central to the democratic processes of governance, in the information society more and more players, voluntary organisations, interest groups, the private sector, think-tank groups and the media become involved in the process. Communication and information ethnology, globalisation of markets, technology in the workplace, the consumer focus (or the rise of the customer as the boss), increased work force diversity, the changing citizen profile, and the emergence of democracy as the major political framework worldwide, are all agents of governance in our changing society and organisations (McLagan and Christo, 1995; Korac-Kakabadse et al. 1996).

Alvin Toffler's (1980) description of the Third Wave shift in civilisation, the transition from industrial to information based economies, suggests that companies will increasingly help shape the Fourth Wave shift. This prediction is made from the ecological perspective, which sees organisations as being active in their environments, and where environment no longer represents external forces, but instead takes on a role of negotiated instruments (Gray et al. 1991), and as such needs to carry without a social responsibility. The truly responsible and visionary corporations will need to form visions that include a high level of commitment to values, such as corporate responsibility and citizenship (Collins and Porras, 1994).

Role of the Media

Some have argued that what people want is trustworthy information sources that will do the hard work of gathering and digesting political information for them, the very task that is currently performed by the media, albeit not always reliably. Today's passive role of the media is likely to be replaced by a new type of interactive multimedia, characterised by highly specialised media outlets often described as 'information agents' (Snider, 1994). The present day reporters who work for newspaper organisations could well become, in the future, independent information entrepreneurs, selling their information wares directly to the public over the telecommunications networks. Using information technology these information agents will gather and digest information and disseminate it to their clients just as high-priced consultants do today. Among the current media technologies are: computers (with conferencing capacities, electronic mail, and bulletin board systems); cable television (providing, in most cases, local community access, and in some cases, interactive services); satellites (which allow for direct broadcast simultaneously all over the globe); videotex (easy to use, low cost, computer-based information services); interactive television; and, perhaps most importantly (at least in the short term) fibre optic, computer integrated telephone networks.

Increasingly, the role of the media and the media's responsibility in helping to revitalise the public's trust in society is receiving attention. For example, some argue that journalists have a specific role to play in ensuring that the democratic community continues (Merritt, 1995). While the concept that journalists can do more than just simply transfer information from one point to another may be unsettling for those in the journalism field, many feel that journalists must heed the higher calling of civic journalism (Merritt, 1995). Some have argued that journalists need to be people first, reporters second (Fallows, 1996). Further accentuated by the movement of political discourse through new forms of media such as the Internet, the roles journalists choose to take in addressing the problems in society, as information agents, will go a long way towards the final outcomes of those discussions (Fallows, 1996). Notwithstanding that the existing mass media has attracted vast criticism, the potential for more competitive, diverse and customised media in the future carries with it new opportunities, hopes and ills. For example, traditional self-promotion through television advertisements and by political candidates may become obsolete. Similar repercussions may confront lobbyists and special interest groups, who derive their power from the ability to fund a candidate's media campaigns, but who may find themselves undermined when voters can buy critical information from independent information agents (Snider, 1994). The guiding logic of Ross Perot's 'United We Stand' alliance, enabled by 'electronic town links' for town meetings, was to facilitate discussion and wide ranging debates at the grassroots level and not at the lobbyists' level (London, 1994). However, a problem with the electronic town meeting is the supervision of the agenda or who determines what will be discussed (Van de Donk and Tops, 1995). Examples from the Netherlands show that even a moderator does not always succeed in managing the (democratic) quality of these debates (Van de Donk and Tops, 1995). Teleconferencing, for example, is relatively easy to manipulate by lobby and interest groups (Van de Donk and Tops, 1995).

On the plus side, it forces some groups to place their buried issues and hidden agendas on the political agenda (Barnouw, 1982; McLean, 1989). However, this alternative assumes universal access to the coming information highways, otherwise it furthers the gap between those who can purchase critical information from information agents and those who cannot afford to. Furthermore, new information technology will make possible new ways to publicly finance elections, where instead of money going to candidates, money could be given directly to the voters (Snider, 1994). Instead of tens of millions of dollars in communication vouchers being given to the USA presidential candidates to spend on 30-second television advertisements, money could be given directly to citizens to spend on information about presidential candidates. Voter-based vouchers are far more democratic than candidate-based vouchers, but such a switch has not been practically feasible to implement until present day developments in IT (Snider, 1994, p.18).

Role of Corporations

Considering that a contractual (explicit or implicit) relationship exists not only between a business and its shareholders, but also with employees, customers, creditors and other stakeholders, corporations need to be accountable to their constituents (Benston, 1982). Thus, it is possible for the notion of accountability to be extended beyond a narrow two-party contract, to social responsibility, accepting that other parties, such as employees, consumers and even society at large, need to be considered (Pallot 1991, p.203). Thus, contractual responsibility is likely to encompass others than merely owners and shareholders. Managing a business exclusively for the shareholders alienates the very people on whose motivation and dedication the modern business depends, the knowledge workers, as the knowledge worker will not be motivated to make shareholders rich (Drucker, 1993, p.80).

Already, the demand for organisations to be socially responsible is increasing. Organisations, through social pressure are being tested to accept full responsibility for their impact on communities and society, from effluents that are discharged into a local river, to the traffic jams that can be created through internal work schedules. Increasingly, as consumers are able to learn about an organisation's actions through multimedia communications, social responsibility becomes an even more important trait in gaining and keeping customers. Corporations, in order to keep credibility with their stakeholders, will need to seek to serve as global stewards with the desire to leave a valuable legacy for the future (Maynard and Mehrtens, 1993). With the ever-increasing demand for similar responsibility to be displayed by corporations, corporate governance and ethics will be increasingly more important. Corporations, like government, operate under a mandate from society (legitimisation) and face having that mandate withdrawn if they do not behave responsibly (Parsons, 1956; 1960; Dowling and Pfeffer, 1975; Wilkinson, 1983; Guthrie and Parker, 1989). Legitimisation is the process whereby an organisation justifies to a peer or superordinate system its right to exist, that is to continue to import, transform, and export energy, material or information (Parsons, 1960; Maurer, 1971, p.361). Corporations may need additional strategies to enhance and maintain the legitimacy of the organisation's domain, when attempting to manage their organisation-environment relations in a rapidly changing landscape (Miles, 1980, p.182). Social norms and values are not immutable. Changing social norms and values constitutes one motivation for organisational change and one source of pressure for organisational legitimisation (Dowling and Pfeffer, 1975, p.125). The corporation thus needs to disclose enough information about itself for society to judge whether or not it has been, or is being, a 'good citizen' (Perrow, 1970, p.101; Harvey et al. 1984, p.11). There is also the concomitant requirement to better communicate corporate actions and intentions to the organisation, stakeholders and society (Mathews, 1993, p.31). The disclosure of information is necessary to prevent organisations from what Gross (1978, p.370) calls, inherently criminal behaviour. The consideration that all organisations hold a strong emphasis for goal attainment as a measure of performance and effectiveness whilst operating in uncertainty suggests that, if necessary, goals will be attained through criminal or illegitimate behaviour (Gross, 1978; Clegg and Dunkerley, 1980). Although this argument represents an extreme position, examples such as the Lockheed bribes scandal in the USA and the Guinness debacle in the UK, suggests that there is more than an element of truth in that viewpoint. The poor performance of certain corporations; the hostile takeovers; the leveraged buyouts; the acquisitions; and the divertissements which created the 'bubble economy', that collapsed in a series of financial scandals (Drucker, 1993), are examples of irresponsible, if not, illegitimate behaviour. The perception is that irresponsible corporate behaviour exists, is widespread and is not just confined to company boards, but also to boards of non-profit organisations (Cadbury, 1995).

The Way Forward: Reinventing the Democratic Vessel

Notwithstanding the danger of replacing representative democracy with the new form of 'cyberdemocracy' or 'virtual polis', there is room for redesigning the vessel of representative democracy. The focus is not only on the choice between grassroots, participatory cyberdemocracy versus current participatory democracy, but also between top-down, repackaged and controlled 'virtual mercantilism' versus free trade (Rheingold, 1993). Thus, there is a need for a vessel design, which is more responsive to community needs and the needs of the disfranchised poor.

In many societies, voluntary voting produces elections and policies by referendums with only a fraction of the population exercising their choice. For example, in the USA, after a vigorous and very expensive campaign, 47 per cent of voters voting is considered to be a good show at the polls. In Pakistan, at the last election only 29 to 35 per cent (depending on the region) of Pakistanis voted. However, the elected president has wide powers entrusted to him or her, although (s)he represents a minority desire. He or she can change the constitution in his or her favour, which will affect all citizens, although the president got there by a minority vote. It can be argued that in electronic democracy (one where access to electronic communication is available to all), the voting percentage may not increase, unless the voluntary voting system is replaced with a compulsory one.

However, if society adopts compulsory voting, it will ensure that the elected representatives will carry out polices agreed by the majority and not only the espoused majority. Further, the compulsory voting model would bring together citizens to responsibly elect representatives and be held accountable for electing that representative. If society desires to enhance their democratic system, they have to be committed and work hard to achieve it, thus casting duty and obligation to the forefront.

Furthermore, in order to enable representation of the minority groups, proportional representation needs to be added to the model. The model of proportional representation in the USA has much to offer, as it would allow small communities to be represented on an equal footing with large ones. Thus when society adopts electronic democracy, with a communications infrastructure available to all citizens, voting patterns would truly represent the will of the majority.

However, much can also be learned from the Swedish concept of local democracy and its relation to central government and, above all, its significance for the individual citizen. The Swedish concept of subsidiarity, closely developed to the concept of a 'bottom-up' as opposed to the 'top-down' approach, provides a guiding principle for governance in Sweden after possible accession in the European Union (Michalski, 1994). Swedish local democracy might serve as a stimulating example of the division of power between local, regional, national and European levels.

The citizen's right to govern is currently realised by a structure of three levels: national through parliament, regional thorough the county *(landsting)* and local through the municipality *(kommun)*, having the possibility of extension to the fourth, namely that of the European Union (Michalski, 1994). At all three levels, the citizens hold the right to elect, through proportional representation, individuals who are deemed suitable to represent the people's voice and adopt, implement and follow up decisions on their behalf. The principle of local democracy is based on municipalities (which vary in geographical and demographic size from 10,000 to 50,000 inhabitants), whose self-government relies on four principles: the municipality's general competence (enshrined in law in 1992, ranging from education, social, energy and housing policy, childcare, waste collection, water, electricity and sewage, public health, environmental protection, local planning and local transport to culture, sport and leisure activities); the municipality's right to levy income tax (in addition to the county tax, a system of double local taxation which rises the total tax burden for individual citizens); the provision of a national system for the transfer of funds from rich to poor municipalities); the municipal planning monopoly; and the citizen's right to political accountability (assured by a comprehensive system of democratic forms for choosing their local representatives) (Michalski, 1994). In the decentralised form of the Swedish democratic system, municipalities are assuming an increasing important role concerning economic and welfare political objectives. Thus the role of local governance for the individual will become increasingly important concerning both the direction of its policies and the effective management of municipal services (Michalski, 1994).

In order to avoid information 'overload', facilitated by communication technologies (Korac-Boisvert and Kouzmin, 1995) and at the same time facilitating government responsiveness to citizens' needs and citizen participation in policy analysis and design, the model also needs to adopt decentralised governance, where local issues can be dealt with at the local level, societal issues at the state level, and the global issues at the regional and international level.

Thus, it is argued that to improve the quality of democratic governance, by making governance more efficient and accessible to citizens, the challenge is a policy issue and not an IT issue. The use and application of information technology is open to choice and as such falls in the policy domain (Korac-Kakabadse et al. 1996). For example, while no government has built the Internet, the US government had a policy that provided the founding to DARPA (the predecessor of ARPA - 1960s

Pentagon's Advanced Research Project Agency) to develop RAND Corporation's (the USA's premier Cold War think-tank) idea of a decentralised, 'blastproof', packet-switched network. Therefore, governments need to have developed a policy on governance enhancement that will utilise IT developments and not just leave it to the private sector, as the emerging electronic democracy is an important issue that needs to be debated.

Considering that the policy problems themselves never subscribe to a single disciplinary positioning or are value free, there is a need to adopt multifaceted policy analysis (Deleone, 1994) which can include an articulated value component previously untapped or unknown. Policy analyses need to encompass values related to society, interdependency, partnerships, motivation, connectivity and trust. These values are most appropriate for highly uncertain situations and can be expressed in actual policy only through a policy development process that specifically includes them. That is, there is a need to recognise the limitations of the economist method of economic and political action synthesis (Rose-Ackerman, 1978, p.216) and go beyond the multidisciplinary approach of policy analysis to a broader appreciation of what constitutes policy research and makes it effective regarding matters of context, process and client (Fischer and Forester, 1993).

For example, Rein's (1978; 1983) value-critical analysis identifies ways in which a stronger statement of the values underlying both policy means and ends can be made more explicit and, hence, can provide insights on assumptions inherent in policy design. Habermas (1990) proposes a model that he calls 'discourse ethics' as a way to address complex questions of social justice and fairness policy. He argues that pluralism and the complexity of modern life make it impossible to formulate universal, abstract or strictly objective solutions to problems. Instead, such solutions must be based on uncoerced and reasoned agreement. Others emphasise cultural variables (Douglas and Wildavsky, 1982; Wildavsky, 1987); focus on policy change and learning (Sabatier, 1991); and investigate fundamental human values (Wilson, 1993) that offer new perspectives in policy analysis, that allows for 'value-critical' principles (Stern, 1986). While new empirical methodologies, such as technical risk analysis, contingent valuation and super-optimum solutions might claim a certain elegance, they, at best, can be seen as useful but not sufficient for policy analysis, as they may violate the value-critical principle (Stern, 1986).

The philosophy underlying the value component in policy analysis and design is an applied synthesis of Jeffersonian democracy and Habermasian critical theory, namely and respectively, that all affected parties should have a political voice and that these voices should be heard without prejudice or advantage or 'ideal speech position' (Habermas, 1990). Considering that the essential need in a democratic society is 'the improvement of the methods and conditions of debate, discussions and persuasion' (Dewey, 1927; Torgerson, 1992, p.229), the proposition does not involve citizens on a nominal basis, as in precautionary legislative or administrative hearings, or by the medium of indiscriminate public surveys, but enables them through the means of discursive democracy (Dryzek, 1990) to participate in the design of programmes that tangibly affect their well-being (Deleone, 1994, p.88). Considering that policy design's greatest asset is an understanding of the impact of policy upon citizens' participation, the focus should be less on the ends and more on the means. The basis of participatory policy analyses is to better inform the policy process, and through direct citizen involvement concomitantly give the citizens opportunity for increased participation in, and allegiance to, the political system and its processes (Deleone, 1994, p.88). However, only well informed citizens can successfully participate in the democratic political process. Therefore, making policy information available to the citizens and educating citizens how to use communication technology to access the information, needs to be incorporated in the policy design and implementation processes.

Accomplishing this requires accessibility, equitability and adaptability of policy information. Accessibility means the process is one to all stakeholders, with multiple and reciprocal pathways for information flow, which may require actively soliciting input from significant stakeholders, not only from lobby groups and institutions, but through creating structures to foster communication. Equitability means taking explicit care to balance potential costs and benefits among all stakeholders, which presuppose openness to differing or conflicting perspectives and assumptions (LaPorte, 1975; Janis and Mann, 1977; Brewer, 1986). Adaptability means the willingness and the capacity to continually re-evaluate policies in the light of changing circumstances, new knowledge, and/or unexpected outcomes. For example, although many government bodies, regulatory agencies, industries, public interest groups and individuals are actively engaged in developing policy to address compact environmental issues, only some of them carry this process with open communication with the stakeholders. The utility of the selected approach(es) measured in terms of policy insights should be the continuing, albeit difficult, litmus test for development of more democratic procedures through focus on policy definition and design (Deleone, 1994).

For example, adopting the policy to introduce 'civic participation centres' or 'town meetings' without assessing how the model will work in practice, may not guarantee democratic enhancement. A speaker, for example, can in effect frame a question in such a way so as to limit, wrap, or actually guarantee the desired answer from citizens (London, 1994). Similarly, the availability of a communication infrastructure to all citizens, may not produce enhancing results if the important policy issues are dealt with at such a speed that it does not allow citizens to think them through and participate in the debate.

On the other hand, if citizen participation were sought for each and every policy and operational issues, in a truly democratic way, there would be very little use for politicians. Instead there would be only the need for administrators who would respond to the citizens' majority demands on a daily basis, which does not provide for direction and planning for the future. Powerful lobby groups could choose a future that will benefit only a select few. Therefore, the level of citizens' participation in policy design and implementation is of immense importance, if aspects of the elected representative's role are to be preserved, namely their responsibility and accountability elements. The danger of over-extending the shape of democratic policy design and implementation into the desired shape of the individual (elected representative) or corporate decision-making, is more prevalent with electronic democracy (Perri, 1997) which ultimately leads to a split between responsibility and accountability. Allowing citizen participation on daily and operational policy issues, modifies the elected representative's role to the extent that he or she is responding to the citizens' demands, without consideration of the issues from the platform agenda for which he or she feels responsible, but still being accountable for the implementation of citizens' demands and their own platform. On the other hand, citizens will be responsible for policy design but not accountable for its practice and pursuit. The dismemberment between responsibility and accountability may well limit the usage of electronic democracy to important issues that require referendum.

With an appropriate information infrastructure, one that provides universal citizen access, important issues such as whether one society should join the European Union or not, can be debated and voted in a manner that is more comfortable for citizens (using communication technology from home), and once the infrastructure is in place, in a significantly more economical and efficient manner, there is no need for the

manual handling of ballot papers.   Caution is needed as theoretically
elegant, but practically deceptive, voting systems could come into
widespread use, possibly leading to information overload which can, at
best, only be a minor palliative to political information problems (Snider,
1994).   What citizens want are trustworthy information sources that will
easily provide concise political information (Snider, 1994).   Thus, the main
advantages of information technology in attempting to improve the
democratic vessel are: to promote participatory policy analysis in order to
better inform the policy process, as constructive action is impossible
without an understanding of how our fellow citizens think and feel about
issues; and to educate citizens through their involvement so that they can
make informed choices.   The challenge is to find a way to pool the good
judgement and foresight of the public (Elgin quoted in London, 1994).
Furthermore, there are non-technology-based approaches for improving
democracy, for example, instilling a better sense of civic duty in schools, or
overhauling campaign-finance laws in order to minimise the influence of
special-interest groups (Snider, 1994).   Only with forward-looking and
informed public policies can new technology be used to bring the
democratic ideal much closer to reality.

Conclusion

While information has always played a key role in democracies, its current
role is both expanding and transforming.   Multiple models of information
transfer are used not just locally, but nationally and internationally.
Information transfer and the infrastructures that support it are understood to
have profound effects on economic prosperity (Martinez, 1994).   In the
increasingly interconnected and rapidly changing formative context of the
information society, traditional ways of organising and governing, which
are based on a more restricted flow of information and limited
interconnections, in public and corporate organisations or in democratic
national states, seem to be overwhelmed.   Thus, what is becoming
increasingly clear, in a world of rapid and continuing change, eroding
boundaries, multiplying interest groups, and fragmenting institutions and
belief systems, is the need to invest more time, energy and attention to
developing a shared understanding of where society should go, within a
more systematic process of agenda setting and further within an acceptable
and agreed value system.

Hinging on equitable access to information technology is whether that technology will make society more cohesive and collectively prosperous, or undermine the bases for democracy and further polarise the nation into a dispossessed and a wealthy elite, defined not just by investment portfolios, but also by monopoly of information (Martinez, 1994). Technology can enhance the learning of conceptual knowledge, but also the knowledge of process, in particular, enabling forms of information seeking required and engendered by information technology. However, technology can also influence the 'knowledge gap' to grow wider (Paisley, 1987). The future of the IT influence will require vigilance and a guarantee of access to ensure that the electronic revolution draws more to reconcile society than to render it. The quality of democracy is only enhanced by IT if the citizens are better informed, without suffering from information overload.

At a time when humanity has full possession of a mass of forces that could destroy the world, through nuclear, genetic and other altering chemicals, the realisation that what people do really does make a difference, requires dramatic changes or a shift in governance. The move to participation is probably the greatest shift of our times. It acknowledges that we live and work in a highly interdependent world, making complex decisions that have many effects that we cannot, by ourselves, anticipate and see. It also reflects that the real value of diversity, while it increases the chance of conflict, it also increases the possibility of more creative and sustainable solutions to problems we face, whether in society, work or private life. The price of change is one of testing, making mistakes and building skills and confidence in people who only know the old way. Nature itself relies heavily on the participation of all species in creating the balance of forces that sustain our lives on this planet. Governments and business are only now discovering the survival advantage of participation in their own spheres. Humanity has arrived at a moment of immense democratic and entrepreneurial opportunity made possible by information technology, and the opportunity should not be wasted, but used wisely. Besides good governance, democracy also requires mechanisms for conflict resolution, a political culture of tolerance and compromise and, above all, the wisdom in leadership to steer it through. Modern democracy and polity require a large and complex governance because the private sector alone simply cannot provide many vital services such as defence and environmental protection (Snider, 1994). New information technology, combined with leadership wisdom demonstrated by the forward-thinking public policies, can help bring the democratic vessel to sail safely through troubled waters.

A community orientation concisely demands some discipline and sacrifice on the part of individuals. No community can exist if every individual goes his or her own way and defines his or her own morality, irrelevant of their context and community. The concept of cyberspace or 'environment in flux' that coalesce around visions of virtual community-centred and network citizen-controlled 'Jeffersonian network' or an autonomous collective of virtual communities, is rather a concept of a transcendent or meta-community (Rheingold, 1993). Individuality without a community orientation leads to further alienation and fragmentation of society and upsets the ecological balance (Sardar, 1996). The shift to community values and needs is necessary to take place at the individual level and at the corporate level. As each individual and organisation needs to take responsibility and accountability to make the world a better place, thus there is a need for a new philosophy that will emphasise the virtue that ensures continuation of democratic principles and connects the individual with the community. How might and how should the democratic principles such as rights and freedom of new 'speech' (through the multidimensional worlds of sight, sound and touch, over invisible and ubiquitous 'terabyt' highways) be applied in the era of the information superhighway, needs to be further examined. Preservation of democratic principles, such as freedom, can be 'expensive, dangerous, unpredictable and sometimes ugly and offensive' (Berry, 1992, p.6).

Note

1   A shortened version of this Chapter is published as 'Information Technology's Impact on Quality of Democracy: Reinventing the "democratic vessel"', in Heeks, R. (ed.), *Reinventing Government in the Information Age: International practice in IT-enabled public sector reform*, Routledge, London, pp. 211-228.

3 Information Technology for Public Sector in Developing Countries: Designing Relevant Infra-Structural Capability or New Colonialism?

NADA K. KAKABADSE, ANDREW K. KAKABADSE AND
ALEXANDER KOUZMIN

Abstract

The proliferation of information technology (IT) offers challenges to developing countries which struggle with basic human needs. Yet the key to their survival may lie in information which is inaccessible to them. Facing these challenges, developing nations start from a position of frailty based on low levels of capital; a limited information infra-structure; dependencies on foreign aid and multinationals; and an ever-increasing population growth. It is essential that foreign technology inflow is adopted strategically within the pre-existing framework of national policies for technological development and with an emphasis on technology transfer. The broad policy direction needs to be towards the establishment of an information infra-structure and a contingent perspective for the meta-policy process of designing appropriate IT infra-structures.[1]

Introduction

In the last 30 years the world has been experiencing an information technology (IT) revolution propelled by extraordinary scientific progress and an array of rapidly advancing micro-electronics technology (James, 1985; Bahalla and James, 1991). While industrialised countries are moving towards an information-economy, many developing countries are still in the infancy of the industrialisation process with an enormous task at hand for informatisation (James, 1985; International Monetary Fund, 1986;

73

World Bank, 1989a; Madu, 1990; Bahalla and James, 1991; Scott, 1992). In the 1970s, approximately 40 per cent of economically-active North Americans were in information-related occupations (Schmoranz, 1980), while developing countries were predominantly rural societies receiving short-term interventist 'poverty programmes' (Hanna, 1990) from donor agencies such as the US Agency for International Development (USAID), La Cooperation and the Bretton Woods organisations: the International Monetary Fund and the World Bank (Hage and Finsterbusch, 1987; Rondinell, 1987).   The IT sector of developing countries is small, approximately under 25 per cent, as compared with 40 to 65 per cent in developed countries (United Nations Economic Commission for Latin America, 1987).   Since the 1980s, every structural adjustment loan from the World Bank has included a considerable component of information upgrading (Annis, 1987; Feinberg, 1987; Hanna, 1990).   A similar shift towards information activities has also taken place within other donor organisations, such as the International Development Research Centre's (IDRC) Information Science Division (ISD), which provided 141 grants for information activities in 34 African nations during 1989 (IDRC, 1990).

There are approximately one billion poor people in the world, approximately 25 per cent of the world's population (World Bank, 1989b; 1990).   These people have substantial needs, insufficient relative income and, in most cases, there is no income even for basic needs.   Generally, the causes of poverty in these societies are attributed to dated post-colonial economies, socio-political instability and growing populations (Hage and Finsterbusch, 1987; United Nations Economic Commission for Africa, 1989).   The sub-Saharan Africa or Sahel (Ghana, Liberia, Malawi, Niger, Nigeria, Somalia, Sierra Leone, Sudan and Zaire) is one of the least-developed regions of the world today (World Bank, 1989b; 1990). Seventy per cent of the countries officially classified as 'least developed' are found in the Sahel region.   The World Bank (1984) has expressed the view that no list of economic and financial statistics can convey the human misery spreading in the region.   Furthermore, many societies in the South-Asian region and Latin America, although not classified as least developed, nonetheless struggle with the populations' most basic needs (World Bank, 1989b; 1990).   Even under hopeful assumptions about economic recovery, 'the absolute number of poor in the world at the turn of the century will probably be higher than in 1985' (United Nations, 1992, p.30).

Although various regions face different threats to basic human needs they all have a common root to the problem - the economy.   Developing

Latin American countries (Argentina, Brazil and Uruguay) have staggering debt situations (Ferrer, 1985; World Bank, 1989c). Asian, or at least the South and South East Asian, developing countries' threat to basic human needs is highest among the landless rural-poor, further propelled by an identity crisis (Lipton, 1977; Gunasinghe, 1984) and the recent fiscal crises generated, in the main, by burgeoning corporate-sector debt (Cauldfield, 1998; Latham, 1998).

To devise ways out of an unenviable situation, developing countries require not only financial resources but also substantial co-ordinating efforts (De Soto, 1989; Scott, 1992). This need for co-ordinating effort is depicted even in the most basic tasks such as food distribution. Furthermore, a critical issue in co-ordinating tasks is the time factor (Clark, 1985; Kouzmin and Jarman, 1989; 1990) and relevant information, which is not always available. Without information exchange technology, policy-designers in developing countries are unable to obtain timely, quality information (World Bank, 1988; 1990) or maintain effective linkages with other regional and international research organisations.

There are ample examples highlighting the fact that initiated research projects suffer from a lack of awareness of development elsewhere, thus reproducing slow and frustrating processes of innovation as well as misplacing valuable resources (Hirschman, 1991). Research findings relevant to developing countries, such as agricultural research and, perhaps most importantly, tapping the knowledge of local, indigenous people that may provide a key to self-sustaining development, are not widely disseminated, causing basic development programmes to founder due to a lack of strategic communication; notably, 'inadequate and ineffective links with agricultural research' (Hage and Finsterbusch, 1987, p.108) and agricultural extension systems. For example, the accurate weather forecast of rain during the monsoon season in India holds the key to agricultural production in the country; while information on the prevention of the simplest of disease in Africa can save thousands of lives (World Bank, 1988).

The absence of an information infra-structure is not the only factor for the failure of technology transfer. The United Nations and Bretton Woods institutions, for example, have been criticised for their single-image formula model for restructuring (Hage and Finsterbusch, 1987; Williams, 1987). This model has been prescribed in the past, or imposed with donor programmes, and has failed to deliver the developmental dream (Borda, 1986; Esteva, 1987; Williams, 1987; Rahnema, 1990; Escobar, 1992). For example, during 1985-1986, some 24 African countries, among other developing countries, undertook structural adjustment programmes supported by the Bretton Woods organisations' assistance. Years later, under the handicap of severe financial stringency for repayments, the majority of these countries face a debt crisis (Williams, 1987; World Bank, 1989c). It might be argued that the dogmatic application of the western developed economic model, imposed by donor organisations and multi-national IT organisations, hinders the formation of new social systems needed to overcome the basic dilemma of developing countries (Ramos, 1981).

Limited Discourse, Paradigm Barriers

The proliferation of information technology, which most certainly reaches the affluent first, is also beginning to penetrate the isolation of poverty (Hills, 1990). Increasingly, literate, information-hungry people in developing countries are driving social change at grass-root levels (De Soto, 1989). The process is, however, slow as the provision of end-user technology, such as telephone communications, demands outlays of adequate expansion (Carmody, 1989) developing countries cannot afford; being barely able to keep pace with population growth (O'Connor, 1985; Agi, 1987) and industrialised countries' technology 'dumping' (Ziauddin and Davies, 1992).

Western social science and IT development 'are not prone to acknowledge the viability of non-western societies on their own value grounds' (Ramos, 1981, p.171). Thus, traditional intellectual paradigms, founded on the conventional political debate of North-South prospects in relation to market barriers, mechanisms and technology transfer, have not helped the developing countries' cause. The last 50 years of debate (Hage and Finsterbusch, 1987) has oscillated between two extreme positions - the advocacy of state control to mobilise resources and the advocacy of market mechanisms (Kaufmann, 1991). Elements of 'Formative Context' (Unger, 1987), such as institutional arrangements, cultural values, ethnic tastes and cognitive frames, that shape the daily routines of people were largely ignored (Borda, 1986; Hage and Finsterbusch, 1987). The donor organisation's inability (Ramos, 1981) to incorporate into development programmes formative context has produced anti-development sentiments in many developing countries (Borda, 1986; Esteva, 1987; Rahnema, 1988; 1990; Escobar, 1992).

Advocates of the state control position (Fisher, 1950; Habermas,

1971) have argued that market mechanisms, on the whole, do not promote sufficiently rapid and equitable rates of economic growth; they also tend to increase the problems of developing countries' dependency on industrialised countries (Ziauddin and Davies, 1992). Some argue that centralisation promotes innovation, the latter being vital to entrepreneurship (Martin, 1965; Perrow, 1972; Hage and Dewar, 1973). Conversely, proponents of the free market position hold that state control increases bureaucracy, stifles entrepreneurship and discourages the efficient allocation of resources (Ostrom, 1973; Chartland and Morentz, 1979; Morgan, 1986). Furthermore, a commonly held view is that 'increasing the factors of production increases economic production' and, ultimately, raises the standard of living provided that 'population growth is kept within a reasonable limit' (Hage and Finsterbusch, 1987, p.1).

Traditional developmental debate has inspired policy perspectives of a dualistic nature, where debate is enunciated between two extreme rhetorical positions (Ramos, 1981; Kaufmann, 1991); state control and the market mechanism, with an underlying theological theme of good and evil, or a philosophical one of reason and passion. Although proponents of each position may agree that an extreme view over-simplifies the nature of the issues involved, policy advice is, nevertheless, enunciated within the framework of cognitive dualism. Proponents of each position have a 'single-image formula' (Hage and Finsterbusch, 1987, p.2) for developing countries. Some have advocated bureaucracy, others decentralisation and, some others, flexibility. The 'rhetoric of intransigence' (Hirschman, 1991, p.168) has produced policies of cognitive dualism, exemplified in Bretton Woods organisations' policies for developing countries advocating restructuring as a condition for the stabilisation of finance for many African and other developing countries (Hage and Finsterbusch, 1987; Williams, 1987; Escobar, 1992). These polices find support in Chandler's (1962, p.16) assertion that 'growth without structural adjustment can lead only to economic inefficiency', but ignore differentiation and interactions of various spheres of society (Kaufmann, 1991). While specific programmes differ, the framework for common structural adjustment includes restraint on domestic credit and money supply; reduction in government deficits; thorough cuts in subsidies and wages; reduction in external borrowing; and the adjustment of interest and exchange rates (Williams, 1987).

Some developing countries such as Brazil (Hobday, 1985; Botelho, 1989) and India (Lavakare, 1985; Botelho, 1989) followed a trend towards decentralised economies, but found expression in policies that demanded national control over telematics technology. In this way they reduced dependencies on foreign multinationals by shielding domestic firms from international competition through market-reserve policies (import tariffs, limits on royalty payments and the length of licensing contracts). Similar polices were used by Japan for some 30 years to promote the electronics and semi-conductor industries (Botelho, 1989). Thus, it can be argued that the theme of an effective policy-design for developing countries cannot be explained within the framework of either centrally-planned or free-market economies but with a contingent approach to policy design based on a society's specific needs, capabilities and emerging structures (Ramos, 1981). The domain of information technology adoption should be aligned with other dynamic parameters in order to ensure structural, environmental and infra-structure fit in the short versus the long run.

Traditional intellectual and policy IT frameworks act as a 'cognitive strait-jacket' (Kouzmin, 1983; Morgan, 1986; Kouzmin and Jarman, 1989, 1990; Korac-Boisvert and Kouzmin, 1995a) which, at best, over-simplifies and, at worst, misleads policy-designers. The conventional paradigm provides no account of the structural dynamism of socio-economic and technological parameters (Morgan, 1986; Korac-Kakabadse and Kouzmin, 1996) and since policy-designers have no clear ideas about changes that occur, they have little cause, or opportunity, for policy intervention (Kouzmin and Jarman, 1989). There is a need for new intellectual paradigms and policy platforms of a dynamic and contingent nature which address emerging structures created by socio-economic and technological changes in highly volatile environments (Ramos, 1981). The trend of planning technology policy from the centrally-planned economy perspective or free-market perspective is a pre-emptive, deterministic policy-design process (Kaufmann, 1991). Policy-designers need to search for a synthesis (Scott, 1992) of macro-social perspectives of technology dynamics (Braverman, 1974; Kraft, 1979; Ramos, 1981; Wood, 1982; Noble, 1984) as well as the micro-social perspective (Rice, 1958; Giddens, 1984; Zuboff, 1988).

While there has been substantial research on the effect of technology change, there has been much less sustained work on the nature and dynamics of technological change (Tushman and Nelson, 1990). There is a need for studies of the dynamics of technology and structure which integrate the flow of influence by which the two dynamics mesh (Giddens, 1984; Barley, 1990). Furthermore, there is a need to utilise longitudinal studies to examine technological dynamics and effects before adaptation and after design, as well as related adaptation time lags. Diachronic analysis can plot the dynamics of technological change in relation to 'before and after' design. Synchronic studies, such as contingency analysis, can help chart the relationships of entwined and contingent variables (Moberg and Koch, 1975; Barley, 1990) during the adaptation process. The synthesis of diachronic and synchronic analysis (Barley, 1990), together with combined macro-social and micro-social perspectives (Anderson and Tushman, 1990; Scott, 1992), are needed for an effective understanding of the dynamics of technological change (Tushman and Nelson, 1990) and its effect in developed and developing societies (Korac-Boisvert and Kouzmin, 1994).

The Development Problematic

The information gap between rich and poor in the world is not difficult to assess. For example, the Bangladesh economy devotes one-tenth of one per cent to hardware and software products and related services. In the US, the corresponding figure is one hundred times larger - ten per cent of the US economy goes to IT (Dertouzos, 1998). Since the average Bangladesh citizen is 30 times poorer than the average American, the disparity, per person, between US annual expenditure on IT is even more staggering - an average of US$3,000 for each American compared to US$1 for each Bangladeshi (Dertouzos, 1998).

Similarly, with poor Americans, there is an equally obvious dissonance between IT expenditures in the inner city and the suburbs - people struggling for the daily bites of food having nothing left over for 'bytes' of information (Dertouzos, 1998).

The notion of technological capability, which has become increasingly prevalent (Forester, 1985; 1989; Dodgson, 1989; Madu, 1990), is designed to capture, conceptually, precisely the idea of competence - of being able to understand, and hence control, the way in which a new technology is deployed for socio-economic ends. This has been emphasised largely because most technology transfer mechanisms fail to bridge the 'technology gap' between rich and poor countries (Perez and Soete, 1988). The problem is further compounded by industrialised countries' intensified technology 'dumping' of superseded technologies incompatible with end-users needs. This process of technology dumping is sometimes extrinsic and obvious, such as in the case of weapons technology, and at other times, intrinsic and subtle, as in the form of aid.

The past practice of developed societies' and multinationals' mode of investment in developing societies' assembly technology, not in *full* production capabilities, has produced the current skepticism that foreign investment in export-orientated intermediate processing will do very little to assist the development of the host society (IDRC, 1989; Henderson, 1991). Research and development continues to be performed in the exporter country, building host societies' dependencies for the supply of spare parts, modernisation and expertise. Thus, exported technology 'really exports a new form of dependency' (Morgan, 1986, p. 311). This is further exacerbated by the multinationals' disguise of 'excess' profits and the avoidance of 'paying appropriate taxes in host nations through creative "transfer pricing"' (Morgan, 1986, p.311).

From the perspective of developing countries, donors often satisfy their own needs at the expense of the recipient country's objectives (IDRC, 1989). 'Too much effort has been concentrated on structuring systems and centres rather than on evaluating the relevance of services to the users; from policy-makers to peasants' (IDRC, 1989). The International Development Research Centre (IDRC) participants from developing countries concluded that 'at present, in general, the statistical information available in Africa is inadequate, out of date and inaccurate. Those who use the information make plans and promises that can never be fulfilled' (IDRC, 1989). Furthermore, the lack of appropriate information accessing tools and technologies to assist the information seeker is compounded by language problems and computer-technology's abounded usage of jargon, proclivity for great promises and, often, the delivery of great disappointments (IDRC, 1989).

It appears that small developing economies are at the mercy of industrialised countries and multinational information technology giants and have little chance, in the near future, of developing their own electronics or telematic technology (Hobday, 1985; Sussman, 1988). Furthermore, from the perspective of the developing countries' policy-design elite, gross disparities in economic performance, research and technology underlie a new imperialism that threatens to keep less developed nations in a position of perpetual thralldom (IDRC, 1989; Henderson, 1991). Castells (1988, p.16) suggests that the real cleavage in societies may be 'between countries integrated in the international structure of production and those excluded from it'. Moreover, the most dangerous perceived threat to developing countries is military; advanced weapons systems with micro-electronics components and computers which are all concentrated in North America, Western Europe and the former Soviet Union. The threat is not only posed by new military technology but also by 'the unmanaged nature of technological change' (Croft, 1989, p.466). The other drawback in developing countries is that information is expensive and not accessible to everyone, leading to information being withheld from development initiatives at grass-root levels (De Soto, 1989). This is further compounded by the fact that in some developing countries it is not only that information is not free, but also that one must strive to get it.

Along with technology assembly lines, developed societies have exported western specific values of rationality, calculation and efficiency and a techno structural ideology to developing countries which hitherto may have had an ideology of self-fulfilment, spontaneity and experimental richness. The Japanese case of industrialisation (Abegglen, 1958) seems to indicate that the organisational models of the west are not essential to successful industrialisation. Abegglen (1958) also found that Japanese organisations were consistent with, and a logical extension of, the relationships, values and ideology existing in Japan prior to industrialisation. Technology transfer has also produced a cultural transfer (Soesastro and Pangestu, 1990) and also highlights the unanticipated 'cultural contradiction of capitalism' (Bell, 1976; 1980). For example, Brazil produces soya beans and cheese for export, although local taste prevents their domestic consumption (Hage and Finsterbusch, 1987). As Crozier and Friedberg (1977, p.107) argue, 'information is a rare commodity and its communication and exchange are not a neutral and free process'.

Most studies on the impact of information technology or telematics on society have confined themselves to two main areas: employment (Boucher, 1981; Soete, 1985; Vickery, 1986; Pattel, 1988) and work skills (Machlup, 1962; Soete; 1985; Senker, 1992). This is because the social concern is principally directed at these two areas in view of the inherent threat to jobs and those work skills acquired through years of training and experience. More recently, studies extend to other areas, such as occupational structures of the labour force and organisational design (Rajan, 1985). They are, however, predominantly studies for developed societies or are largely prescriptive; overlaid with contentious values and insensitive to indigenous developing countries' needs (Borda, 1986; Esteva, 1987; Williams, 1987; Rahnema, 1990; Escobar, 1992). An example can be drawn from the World Bank's and IMF's prescriptive brief for specific restructuring of developing economies as a pre-requisite for receiving aid.

Lessons From Developed Economies

While developed economies struggle with their own structural conditions, political instability and balance of payments short-falls, answers to problems do not lie in information technology. Information technology requires enormous support, such as an educational infra-structure that encourages the use of information services and scientific and technical infra-structures that make use of the data processing and communication systems (Saracevic, Braga and Afolayan, 1985). Above all, information technology can be introduced only to well-defined functions or problems. If the problem is not understood or manual procedures are not in place, information technology cannot solve the problem (Perrow, 1967; 1968). Conspicuous examples can be drawn from many situations. An Algerian case involved the 1986 financial reforms, when the State-owned banks (the Banque Extêrieure d'Algêrie, Banque Nationale d'Algêrie and Crêdit Populaire d'Algêrie) had adopted a computerised banking system in 1989 without introducing, in the first place, an adequate accounting system (*The Economist,* 1989; *Le Monde,* 1990). The electronic system did not improve the inadequate banking system but made it even more visible as previous manual errors, visible to only limited viewing, were made very much more public through computerisation (*Middle East Executive Report,* 1990). Algeria was trying to render its currency convertible and the IMF requires, among other pre-requisites, that a country has an accounting system in place in order to assess the country's credit rating.

Even in economies with advanced information-technology infra-structures, based on a high-technology culture, development of large-scale information technology projects can be risky. The risk may lay in the capital costs and critical time over-runs involved. Morrow (1981) states that 'severe under-estimating of capital costs is the norm for all advanced technologies'. An examination of large computing projects within Australia reveals the same pattern. The Australian Public Service's projects such as MANDATA, Job-Seeker/Job-Bank and Stratplan, the Commonwealth Bank's Hogan project and Westpac Bank's SP90 project all failed to meet budget and time criteria (Aspect Computing Pty. Ltd. and Thompsett, 1988). MANDATA and the Hogan project were abandoned once it became clear that development requirements were facing severe compromise following budget and deadline blow-outs (Aspect Computing Pty. Ltd. and Thompsett, 1988). Stratplan and Job-Seeker/Job-Bank both faced massive cost and schedule over-runs but were developed as the requirements for the projects were achievable and the political pressure for implementation was high (Aspect Computing Pty. Ltd. and Thompsett, 1988).

Similarly, the British public sector experienced difficulties and frustrations with the re-development of the on-line unemployment benefits project, National Unemployment Benefits System 2 (NUBS2), which was to replace the operational NUBS1 developed in 1960 (Employment Service, 1992). Although the functionality of the system in its basic form was automated (NUBS1), and thus a substantial *a priori* development knowledge existed, NUBS2 faced a requirement and compatibility crisis (Kwan, 1992). Because of the long lead time required to develop NUBS2, some of its required specifications were already out of date. During the 'Business Pilots' implementation at the strategically targeted offices in February 1992 (Employment Service, 1992), NUBS2 fell short of meeting operational requirements. A nationwide implementation, planned for November 1992, required major enhancements planned for the subsequent release during 1992-1994 (Employment Service, 1992). Implementation of the Wide Area Network (WAN) required to support NUBS2 was also planned for 1993-1994 (Employment Service, 1992).

Similarly, after much deliberation, and an estimated cost of £400 million, in March 1993, the London Stock Exchange project TARUS (Transfer and Automated Registration of Uncertificated Stock) was abandoned. TARUS was considered too complex and problematic to continue (Water, 1993b). Conceived in 1990 as a total paperless trading system (share ownership would be stored electronically and investors would not receive share certificates), it was to link some 280 financial institutions, serving a range of stakeholders from registrars, brokers, market-makers, custodians to wage investors (Water, 1993a). The projected annual staff cost savings by Coopers Lybrand, Deloitte for the period of ten years was about £230 million, with the estimated build-up of approximately £50 million (at then current prices) over the period of four years to spring 1993 (Tilley, 1990).

The reasons for the abandonment of TARUS were threefold, related to technical, managerial and quality control issues (Water and Cane, 1993). First, software development was conducted on and ad hoc, incremental basis. The developer, ISE did not complete a full system design, even after industry-wide testing of the first phase. The selected software package needed 70 per cent re-writing and was carried by ISE in the United States, leading to fragmentation of the project. The software company was hired on a 'time and material' contract rather than on a 'fix-price' contract raising projected costs of £4 million to £14 million before completion of the task (Water and Cane, 1993). Secondly, TARUS was developed using government SSASM rule-book methodology that called for linear and 'logical' programming inadequate for complex large-scale projects; with inadequate project management. Thirdly, the absence of stringent quality control contributed to further delay and setbacks.

Further examples of failure are found in the Canadian Public Service, where Canadian On-Line Secure Information and Communication System (COSICS) phase I (1990) was developed to testing stage two years behind schedule, while phase II, dealing with classified communication, was suppressed as was a number of alternative solutions encompassing the COSICS system after the conclusion was reached that additional funding and a further six years for full implementation would be needed and that, even then, the objectives of every employee having a personal terminal would not ever be achieved (External Affairs and International Trade Canada, 1991). In September 1991, a new multi-tier IT alternative was selected, based on personal computers (PCs) and the Local Area Network (LAN) infra-structure, with an implementation schedule over a four year period (1991-1995) and the requirement that by 1995 100 per cent of employees would be connected to computing resources (External Affairs and International Trade Canada, 1991).

Developing countries with a limited information technology infra-structure should avoid over-ambitious and large IT projects if only for one reason; lack of financial resources (O'Connor, 1985; Agi, 1987) and the fact that costs can be enormous. For example, 'the COSICS value investment in hardware and software was CAD $38 million, a cost that was exceeded by the investment in training and staff experience (External Affairs and International Trade Canada, 1991). The Australian Taxation Office Re-development Project involved initial direct capital investment in hardware of A$700 million prior to application development (Carmody, 1989). The UK Employment Service's IT budget for 1992 operational costs (excluding capital costs and salaries) for NUBS2 and its related projects was approximately £21 million (Employment Service, 1992). If, however, the fiscal problem is compounded by the lack of an information infra-structure then the risk of failure may reach crisis proportions (Korac-Boisvert and Kouzmin, 1995b; Kouzmin and Korac-Boisvert, 1995).

In order for new technology to impact successfully on economic production it is necessary in some sense not only to transfer the technology itself but, in addition, to ensure its subsequent use as a dynamic resource for substantive change. Even developed societies have time-lags in technology transfer. Furthermore, technology transfer often fails as many economies institutionalise their past into physical components of society as well as into the existing information infra-structure (Hill, 1990; Escobar, 1992). For technology transfer to be effective, it should not consist of just the establishment of new production facilities with ancillary user manuals and manpower know-how. It also requires knowledge and expertise in the implementation of technical change. This, in turn, involves both the underlying knowledge of technology itself as well as the various techno managerial capabilities needed to evaluate and transform existing plans to meet new and innovative operating conditions in changing environments.

These capacities and pre-conditions, in general, do not emerge automatically and, thus, there is usually a need for a co-ordinating body or a degree of state intervention to ensure technological dynamism, especially where local levels of competition are weak. Government intervention can take a variety of forms (Kaufmann, 1991), usually requiring the creation of appropriate institutions and institutional linkages, technology policy design, capital outlay or some combination of all of them. Hage and Finsterbusch (1987, p.1), in their study of 12 donor programmes by international agencies, involving the Food and Agriculture Organisation (FAO), La Cooperation, US Agency for International Development (USAID), World Health Organisation (WHO) and the World Bank in developing countries, conclude that 'eventually it became widely recognised that factors of production require conducive institutional arrangements to have their full effects'. Their six success stories, Organisational Changes of the National Irrigation Administration in the Philippines; the Training and Visit System in India; the Health Management Appraisal Method in Jordan; Management-Improvement Teams in Agriculture in Guyana; Organisational Planning in Jamaica; and Integrated Planning and Implementation in Rural Development in Colombia, besides involving foreign management teams, all had in common government intervention, support and institutionalisation. Although their models of technology transfer were prescriptive, they highlight some contingencies of social engineering. The need for most developing countries is to break the vicious circle of technological dependency, bringing about greater indigenous technological integration into economic production. Furthermore, developing countries need to reduce export earnings-dependencies on former colonial masters (Britain, France, Belgium, Portugal) (Johnson, 1991).

Policy Challenges and Constraints

The increasing integration of micro-electronics components in factory automation, necessary for competitiveness and foreign exchange, highlights the need for information systems in a developing country's manufacturing industry and agricultural sectors. For the most part, a developing country's goal is to achieve some level of competitiveness in the international market in order to support national growth and meet the requirements of a balance of payments without undue dependence on aid and on multinational conglomerate giants.

With increasing competition, the opportunities for the production of technical components and infra-structure for a national information system are limited for most developing countries. Japan and then South Korea, Singapore, Hong Kong and Taiwan, opted for industrialisation through information technology; becoming competitive in the micro-chip industry with great success (Wang Ke, 1987; Soesastro and Pangestu, 1990; Henderson, 1991). These countries found middle-level standardised technologies (in relative terms, semi-conductor technologies), where the centralised co-ordination of investment and cheap labour allowed them to compete with the information technology giants of the United States and Europe. Their example has been followed by Malaysia, Indonesia, the Philippines and Thailand, with various degrees of success (United Nations Advisory Committee on Science and Technology for Development, 1989; Henderson, 1991). While Malaysia has managed to attract multinational IT organisations by supplying sufficiently trained labour in semi-conductor assembly production at a cost significantly below that of Singapore and Hong Kong, Indonesia, the Philippines and Thailand are trying to achieve a competitive edge (Henderson, 1991). Japan, South Korea, Taiwan and Hong Kong had first invested in an infra-structure through education so that the absorption and development of IT could evolve (Krause, Ai Tee Koh and Yuan Lee, 1987). For example, the use of numerically controlled machine tools (NCMT) is increasingly utilised in industrialised countries (UN, 1985), while its utilisation is very limited in developing countries and is largely confined to Korea, Brazil and India (UN, 1985) where an information infra-structure had been sufficiently established to absorb innovative 'know-how'.

With increased automation and capital investment, poor and small developing countries find it increasingly more difficult to subsidise their industries to the required level to achieve a competitive edge in high-technology industry. Market barriers and multinational monopoly in the

IT industry are an additional consideration for developing societies (Perez and Soete, 1988). Some nations find it more economical to continue their dependencies on industrialised countries for information technology needs and focus their resources in finding competitive niches in other markets, such as agriculture. They may also explore a self-reliance alternative. India, for example, in the mid-1970s, curtailed its dependency on the IBM multinational conglomerate due to a disagreement concerning equity operations and control over currency transactions (White and McDonnell, 1983; Lavakare, 1985). This encouraged the government-owned Electronic Cooperation of India Limited (ECIL) to fill demand and resulted in speedier technology transfer to India and the rapid dissemination of knowledge to Indian entrepreneurs (Girdner, 1987). Furthermore, India escaped the vicious circle of technology dumping, thus reducing the technological gap between India and the west. During the IBM era in India, the gap was 8.5 years but was reduced to 2.6 years in the early 1980s (Grieco, 1984; Girdner, 1987). Notwithstanding, multinationals such as the Japanese companies Sony, Panasonic and Toshiba used ingenious ways to penetrate the high-entry barrier of the blocked Indian market (Kotler, 1992).

Pakistan, Bangladesh and Sri-Lanka have also made attempts to follow India's example (Kahn, 1984; Korale, 1984; Sussman, 1988). Although they have made some progress towards telematic technology, their socio-economic instabilities and small populations have hindered progress. Lessons can be learned to some extent from other countries with similar socio-economic structures and lack of foreign exchange. Their dis-similarities, however, also need to be considered; factors such as size of the population; size of information sectors; level of information infra-structures; and socio-cultural needs and priorities. Developing countries' emerging need for information systems may then be addressed by a strategically applied contingency approach rather than prescriptive western methodologies.

For example, although Brazilian policy had been criticised as the policy which artificially shielded domestic markets, it has been largely successful (Botelho, 1989). The so-called 'Brazilian miracle' cannot be easily exported to other countries; it is orientated towards domestic markets and thus would face major difficulties in countries with small domestic markets such as Argentina (Botelho, 1989) with its own unique problems and a low level of information infra-structure, let alone political and economic cleavages. Similarly, Singapore with a population of two million and a cultural affinity with South Korea cannot follow Korean policies since it cannot take advantage of economies of scale (Soesastro, Pangestu and Mckendrick, 1990). Furthermore, Korea had established an IT infra-structure which allowed for the supply of higher value-added inputs, whilst Singapore's under-developed IT infra-structure supports only low to medium technologies (Krause, Ai Tee Koh and Yuan Lee, 1987). Only 12 per cent of Singapore's youth are enrolled in higher education and less than 75 per cent in secondary schooling, in contrast to the comparable figures in Korea of 26 per cent and 90 per cent respectively (Krause, Ai Tee Koh and Yuan Lee, 1987).

Thus, each individual country has to re-think reflectively information technology strategies; at what point in time should IT policy be adopted and how are adopted technologies going to affect the country at large (Marien, 1989). For example, South Korea, India, Taiwan and Brazil have information technology policies that reflect their own development strategies and economic alliances (United Nations Economic Commission for Latin America (UNECLA), 1987), while India, South Korea and Taiwan are concentrating on export and international competitiveness and Brazil's policy is domestic market-orientated (UNECLA, 1987).

Towards Policy Contingencies and Alternatives

Although the importance of information infra-structure for societal development cannot be over-emphasised, high-technology development should be carefully balanced against developing countries' basic needs (Dadzie, 1988). Reflective analysis of IT choices is necessary (Kouzmin and Jarman, 1989) as information systems and high-technology production in the short term very often do not address the pressing needs of the majority of the population; namely the rudimentary issue of employment (Castells, 1986; Dadzie, 1988). High-technology affects organisation and society itself, as it 'redefines the work content, changes managerial styles and culture, reshuffles power hierarchies and spawns a series of both man-designed and spontaneous adaptations' (Zelany, 1982, p.58). If only a small segment of a population enters an information age, the emerging structures will not set a scene for desirable or acceptable socio-economic outcomes for the remainder of the population in further accentuating the social difference gap between urban elites and the vast mass of urban and rural workers (Castells, 1986; Dadzie, 1988; Sheldon, 1987; 1990).

Even within the European Economic Community (EEC), which has strengthened its global economic position through technological advancement, there exists current disenchantment with technology since profits are unevenly distributed among the member countries (Roobeek, 1990). Roobeek (1990) also argues that technology policies contribute negligibly to the solution of structural problems. New problems are often created by technology policy. He ascribes the EEC's decline in unemployment in the mid-1980s to the decline in the birthrate and, thus, a shift in population demography rather than to the deployment of technology.

Policy-designers need to focus on technologies which help to bind nations or regions and not deepen existing societal gaps or lead to an "elitisation" (Saracevic, Braga and Afolayan, 1985) of information in privileged urban centres. Policies need provisions for the building of a database of existing local knowledge and practice, as well as the development or acquisition of tools for sharing information and accessing existing international databases (Mowlana, 1985). Developing countries need to set realistic goals for information technology and to set development priorities according to the realities of capital, equipment, human resources and existing information infra-structure. Over-ambitious goals are not only beyond the capacity of many developing countries (O'Connor, 1985; Agi, 1987) but also bound to disperse strengths and lead to negative results. Areas in which developing countries may attempt to develop information capacity encompass priority development in terms of information technology, economy and social benefits, information education and the improvement of basic communication networks such as telephones and microprocessors.

Developing countries also need to minimise on-going foreign support of existing technologies in wide use such as microcomputers, database management systems, local/wide area networks, computer-aided instruction, expert-system techniques and decision-support systems. The priority needs to be given - in the short and long term, to the building of local knowledge-base resources through education and training in order to establish an information technology infra-structure for existing and future development. Also, priority needs to be given to the improvement of existing capabilities of scientists and information technologists in order to facilitate effective transfer of technology at all levels. Notwithstanding, the rudimentary issue for developing countries is employment. Both in the short term, through foreign-backed production facilities and aid, and in the long term, through improvements in information infra-structure/education, policy-design for development should focus on strategies which will aid the achievement of technology transfer and skill acquisition which lead to indigenous growth of a knowledge industry.

In the case of an adopted foreign information technology for general use, technology must be well documented, with appropriate tools and methods, and be geared towards end-user relevant experience in information projects (IDRC, 1989). Thus, priority should be given to technology which encompasses methodologies and standards encouraging further development and knowledge transfer. An example is the well-planned IDRC's aided Economic Planning Information Project, in Algeria in 1987, which did not achieve its main objective of technology transfer, mainly due to the lack of political stability and under-developed information infra-structures. Developing countries need to acquire, adapt or develop and manage appropriate information-handling tools and technologies for general and well-defined usage for the country's formative context. For example, information systems for debt recording and management in portfolios such as trade; labour and employment; public finance; public health; education/literacy; and social justice which, in turn, should be accessible to the majority of the population. Moreover, adopted information systems should support development projects which can utilise local and regional knowledge and technologies. Various technology transfer mechanisms can be utilised, from the non-equity means of fixed price sales and licensing agreements to the equity means of joint ventures and wholly-owned subsidiaries (Santikarn, 1981): with the vertical flow from developed or other developing economies or horizontal flow within the country (Smith and Jordan, 1990).

All those aspects of planning need to be linked to the realisation of long-term goals. These include prediction of future needs; further education and training of appropriate professionals; acceleration of technology transfer; and the precipitation of information into all aspects of productive, social and cultural life by increasing the share of the information sector and enlarging circulation and information networks. The long-term development goal may encompass geomatics technology (semi-conductors, micro-electronics), computer-based processing of spatially-related data and digital form acquired from space-borne and airborne sensors and maps and physical socio-economic surveys, provided that an economy can support the financial outlays of such technologies. These projects can be regional or national in scope, such as the public health programme for famine prediction in the Sahel region or monsoon prediction in South-East Asia. Long-term goals may also encompass telematics technology or the twin fields of computing and telecommunications (space satellite communication, space-based surveillance, photovoltaics and laser applications) and the use of telematic techniques to support research and development activities. However, telematics technology demands large capital outlays and it may be more economical for developing economies to be involved on a regional basis with developing nations. In 1989, Gabon, through IDRC's aid programme, undertook its first telematic research project with some local success.

Regional co-operation may aid small developing countries to achieve geomatics and telematics technology goals in their own right. However, the wider utilisation of existing information technologies within the country of origin, by providing links between individuals, organisations (from the smallest private to the government sector), educators and scientists, provides short-term benefits of cost reduction as well as the long-term benefits of building an information infra-structure. Even developed economies, such as those in the European Economic Community (EEC), invest in regional research programmes (European Commission, 1987), as distinct from those organised by individual national governments, such as Bio-technology (BAP); Basic Research in Industrial Technology for Europe (BRITE); European Strategic Programme for Research and Development in Information Technology (ESPRIT); European Research in Advanced Material (EURAM); the Early Wide-Range Scientific and Technology Programme (EUREKA); Forecasting and Assessment of Science and Technology (FAST); Research and Development of Advanced Communications Technology for Europe (RACE); and Science and Technology for Regional Innovation and Development in Europe (STRADE). These research programmes demand heavy capital outlays and sophisticated information infra-structures (European Commission, 1987; Fels, 1988). Furthermore, there is an increasing trend, worldwide, towards 'techno globalism': resorting to joint ventures, strategic alliances and joint research and development programmes (Dodgson, 1991).

Developing regions can learn much from the European Community example as proposed in the Lagos Plan of Action in 1980 (Ravenhill, 1986), but much political goodwill among the members of the union is needed (Dodgson, 1991; Johnson, 1991). The Sahel region already has on-going unions, notably the "Communautê Êconomique de l'Afrique de l'ouest" (CEAO) and the "Union douaniêre et Êconomiqe de l'Afrique centrale" (UDEAC), but owing to socio-political dysfunctionalities, the desired high-degree of collaboration has not been achieved as yet (Ravenhill, 1986; Johnson, 1991).

Although micro-computer-based systems can provide services to a limited number of users or a region of users, inter-connecting systems (Internet) can achieve access to other regions (Crowther, 1987, pp.19-31). However, access to information and education is often language dependent and it needs to be assessed both in terms of the user's prior knowledge and cultural perspectives and in terms of access to the technology to access information and further education and development. There is also a need to be concerned about the impact upon local culture that may be made by imported materials (via Internet) and the developed world's cultural values that the materials embody.

In relation to database access, a large percentage of scientific research relevant to developing countries comes from other developing countries (Saracevic, Braga and Afolayan, 1985). Another advantage of regional systems is that they can be tailored individually to serve the specific interest and needs of its users. Different information resources, different accessing command menus and different language capabilities are all possible with the common technology for the fraction of the development costs of the technology for a single user. Considering that the costs of information technology is one of the elementary factors in developing countries, keeping costs low and providing adequate support are essential factors for making them a widely accessible tool of information rather than an elitist tool for a privileged few. Technology transfer to those who need it is a social responsibility and this social responsibility needs to provide the fundamental framework of information science (Belkin and Robertson, 1975).

A good example is the Brazilian Institute of Social and Economic Analysis (IBASE); a non-profit, non-government organisation that set up ALTERNEX, the high-end communication network using micro-computers for social and economic research and for data communication for end-users (Hobday, 1985). Established in 1989, with 24 hour operation, the network provides access to users from a small personal computer, costing as little as US$300, to large mainframe systems for a monthly fee of the equivalent of US$7.50, including one hour on-line connection (UNECLA, 1987). The concept is based on local messaging systems provided to prescribed users so that a user never needs to make an international connection even when accessing information from international databases (mostly based in United States and Europe). The system allows users, through a local call, to address their mail internationally. The local messaging system collects the international mail, bundles and compresses it and then sends it to the appropriate foreign messaging system for distribution using a special high-speed connection for the purpose, thus providing relatively low-priced services to subscribers which, for most users in developing countries, can be very expensive (up to 20 times higher than the communication costs in developed countries). Currently in Brazil, Internet covers about 600 academic institutions and 60,000 academic users and, also, a rising number of non academics as well as 19 Internet access providers, including IBM, Origin and Unisys (Townson, 1995). Research by the Internet Society estimated 11, 580 host installations in Brazil in July 1995 (Townson, 1995). Encouraged by the IBASE's success in Brazil, Nicaragua and other Latin American countries have adopted the same tools and methodologies to link educators, scientists, individuals and organisations throughout the world (UNECLA, 1987).

South Africa, a country of contradictions and where rich communities vie with those lacking even basic facilities, has a relatively low dependence on multinational corporations (MNCs) for technology transfer. Whereas in the past there was evidence of 'transplantation' of IT, expertise remained with visiting specialists. IT activities of local divisions of MNCs (especially in the oil industry) are today almost entirely in the hands of South Africans (Miller, 1996).

Policy Recommendations

Significant obstacles remain for users in remote locations where the public telephone system is not readily available or not well serviced. Although several alternative, creative technical solutions are available to overcome this limitation, these alternative solutions also call for large financial outlays beyond the capability of many developing countries. Developing countries with stable socio-economic systems can attract external finance for information technology projects through joint-venture arrangements and aid from multi-lateral agencies or 'knowledge-based institutions' such as the World Bank. However, the World Bank's role has changed considerably from capital-transfer in the past to idea-transfer with a large knowledge-base today (Annis, 1987). Moreover, the World Bank still predominantly supports structural adjustment projects with a heavy emphasis on information up-grading (Annis, 1987; Feinberg, 1987).

Emerging literature (Saracevic, Braga and Afolayan, 1985), as well as international organisations (UN, 1987; UNACSTD, 1989; IDRC, 1989), point to the underlying factors of the lack of information infra-structure in developing countries or the shortage of indigenous entrepreneurs at a grassroots level who can understand the dynamics of development and economic growth by analysing the problem and choosing the technology required.   Thus the need for significant growth in information infra-structure for effective transfer, absorption and adaptation of new technologies emerges.   Transfer of technology, in turn, requires the establishment of institutions for the training and development of the necessary entrepreneurial skills at a grassroots level as well as the training of scientists and managers.   To facilitate these training needs, there are requirements for the establishment of transport and communication links.

Markets of factors of production, distribution and consumption (Bollard and Harper, 1987) should be targeted at the national, sub-regional and regional levels, before an international competitive alternative is explored.   The important IT segment for developing societies in the immediate future comprises communication informatics, micro-electronic applications and information processing, while telematics and bio-technology segments can be introduced over a longer period of time. Short-term goals and needs require alignment with long-term goals. Long-term goals need to encompass the forecasting of future needs and the education and training of appropriate cadre at the professional and grassroots levels.

To move from old, traditional to new, innovative technology involves breaking down many barriers. To animate and make the process effective, a national system of innovation requires the interaction of many previously disparate organisations.   Many social and institutional changes may be needed to sustain the appropriate links between government, education, training, industry, science, technology and international organisations. Thus, collaboration and co-ordination of many multivalent economic, political and social units may be more appropriate than a traditionally directing role of hierarchy, as these units may prove to be more effective in the creation and utilisation of socially valuable information.

Prior to the introduction of new IT into the economy, a useful starting point for policy designers may be a strengths, weaknesses, opportunities and threats (SWOT) analysis so as to identify the maximum long-term impact as well as the contingencies and opportunities of new technology within specific formative context. Informatisation must not be pursued at the cost of sacrificing the necessary indigenous technologies.

It is also necessary to view IT policy as a dynamic process; one which is essentially integrated with economic and industrial policies and building on an existing infra-structure.   The emphasis must be on 'technology blending' (moulding of new, emerging technologies with traditional technologies and methods of production). The goals of IT development must be contingent, but congruent, with other socio-economic development goals.

- IT policy should promote investment and domestic or regional production and be able to support a substantial increase in the inflow of new technologies. Initiatives need to create the climate conducive for widespread exploitation of IT; create regional centres to train business people and the community at large; develop national awareness campaigns; and facilitate large scale deployment of IT in schools. A field of special interest for some developing societies may be the application of electronics in the machine-tool sector. The use of numerically-controlled machine tools (NCMT) and computer-based systems for co-ordination can facilitate not only manual activities but also activities associated with the planning and programming of production;

- IT policy should incorporate national telecommunication infra-structure - defining universal service; enabling the rapid expansion of telecommunication services; and forming an independent regulatory body that promotes a globally competitive telecom industry with international standards;

- IT policy should have provisions for the awareness of the nature and future of IT applications, research and economic benefits. One or more applied research institutions, jointly founded by government, industry and/or aid programmes, should be established to develop an IT infra-structure with the necessary critical mass for future innovation and development. Special attention should be given to technology transfer and applied research. Exogenous research should be linked to local technological applications through IT blending;

- IT policy should be based on an assessment of the national formative context and competitive capability of an economy, as well as the implications of new technologies for the principal production and service sectors of the economy. Policy development should be aided by expert advice from various disciplines, with the application of multiple theories and approaches;

- IT policy should make provisions for special research fields, identified as national priorities or sub-regional and regional needs, and international market opportunities for competitiveness. Awareness of the environment, both domestic and international, as well as the early forecast of future needs and trends, are necessary for strategic choices in policy;

- IT policy should provide synergy for the establishment of IT networks among government agencies, industry and research institutions on a national, regional and international basis. It should provide long-term 'leadership' for IT adaptation, technology transfer and technology blending;

- IT policy should make provision for the creation of a national IT committee. Such a committee would fund IT research at educational institutions, meeting national needs, and would encourage technology transfer at grassroots levels;

- IT policy should reflect national consumption, labour and saving patterns in order to create an environment favourable to economic growth;

- Technology transfer initiatives should include financial incentives to promote greater collaboration and the transfer of technology from local R & D groups to industry, incentives to encourage MNCs to establish local operations and training programmes and aggressive efforts to locate and attract donor aid sensitive to local context.

Although an information infra-structure is a necessary contingency for technology transfer, it is not a sufficient condition for a developing economy to migrate 'technologically up-stream' and become competitive in the international market. For example, the Philippines has a relatively advanced information infra-structure in urban society, yet it has been unable to capitalise on this resource to achieve a competitive edge in the semi-conductors segment of the international market. Its IT industry 'remains largely locked into a regime of absolute surplus value creation' (Henderson, 1991, p.164). High-technology industrialisation may not provide the panacea to the developmental problems of a majority of developing countries and, especially, poor, developing countries.

The experience of IT success of South Korea, through joint ventures, and Taiwan's, through licensing, may not be easy to emulate in other developing societies since the technology infra-structure in these two countries has been fairly uniquely developed. Korean technological progress is partly attributed to the government's policy control over credit allocation, foreign exchange and licensing decisions (Chia, 1985). Singapore, whose main concern was to increase the level of national income, attributes IT progress to policies that created an attractive business climate for foreign investment, thereby placing fewer restrictions on imports and allowing multinationals to operate without restrictions (Soesastro, Pangestu and Mckendrick, 1990). Notwithstanding, some countries, such as those of the sub-Saharan region, have lower opportunities to borrow on the international capital market than countries of the Asian region which have the highest probability of access (Fosu, 1991). Furthermore, western science (including IT), being of a reductionist nature (Ramos; 1981; Escobar, 1992), and having been linked to exploitative economic systems (Borda, 1986; Esteva, 1987; Rahnema, 1988; Henderson, 1991) and growing ecological crises (desertification, de-forestation and chemical poisoning), may be inappropriate to deal with problems of developing societies (Ramos, 1981).

IT development may not provide an answer for a competitive edge through the micro-electronic industry. The information technology infra-structure may provide alternative solutions for the competitive edge in other market niches such as natural resources and agriculture or simply provide an answer to famine and drought problems through anti-erosion techniques and technology blending. The development of an IT infra-structure is necessary to facilitate the flow of information as a two-way process: from the grassroots (farmers, urban poor), through the extension worker to the national, regional and global levels and back to the grassroots along the same channels.

Barbados, for example, uses new test-tube technology to revive cotton as a main export crop. Test-tube cotton plantations have some advantages over conventional cotton farming, including the ability of the 'test-tube cotton farmer' to manipulate the length and thickness of the commodity (*Business Week, 1985*). Laser-guided land-leveling activities in Egypt for agricultural leveling is another example of successful technology blending that improves accuracy and speed and increases crop yields (Jonish, 1988). However, technological advances, despite their pervasive impact on individuals and organisations, have not, in recent years, given rise to major increases in industrial output in developed countries; ones which have high research and development programmes, as illustrated by OECD (1987, p.254) data. Technological advances have contributed to a significant shift in the international pattern of specialisation and competitiveness (OECD, 1987, p.214), not only in Japan but in other developed societies which are highly exposed to foreign competition in manufacturing (Australia, Canada).

In some cases new technology may be adopted without significant acquisition of new technological capabilities in the host country. An earlier, efficient adoption of a new technology may be possible if the associated ability to select, install, establish, operate and maintain the technology can be obtained from foreign sources (Smith and Jordan, 1990). New technologies may be purchased from overseas suppliers or transferred though some form of equity involvement by foreign firms. While recognising that technological capability is a relative concept difficult to quantify, Thee's (1990, p. 231) study of 12 Indonesian firms in four industries suggests that the degree of technological effort in achieving local technological mastery is greater in the case of national companies which purchase technology through licensing arrangement than is the case with joint ventures between TNCs and national private or state-owned companies, particularly when management control lies with the TNC by virtue of its majority share-holding. Furthermore, it appears that local companies put greater emphasis on developing their own product based on off-the-shelf technologies rather than relying on production under licensing agreements. Companies from the outset were required to exert greater local technological effort (Thee, 1990; p.232). New technology acquired under licensing or off-the-shelf may provide greater stimulus to local technological effort, but not necessarily to indigenous human resource development. Smith and Jordan (1990, p.9) suggest that the design, production and servicing of capital goods embodying the technology may be very intensive in the use of human capital but the operation of the equipment may require only a low level of skill. This raises a fundamental question about the type of work organisation that develops in relation to adopting new technology (Suzuki, 1988).

When assessments of the relationship between new technology and human resource development is expanded to include the question of competitive performance, the choice between work organisations based on de-skilling employees and work organisations based on self-managing and multi-skilled work groups may be less open than strategic choice theorists suggest. Lazonick (1992) examines an historic evolution in which the 'proprietary capitalism' of British enterprise lost its ascendancy to American 'managerial capitalism' which, in turn, surrendered its dominance to the 'collective capitalism' of Japan. Given the recent occurrence of this latter shift, salient characteristics of Japanese work organisations would appear to have greater relevance for countries and organisations adapting new technology than would the older image of managerial capitalism.

In the west, knowledge about self-managing work groups, developed from studies and experiments in the British coal mines in the 1940s, to the Norwegian Industrial Democracy Project in the 1960s and, subsequently, spread to Sweden and other European countries (Emery and Thorsrud, 1976). To some extent these studies also occurred in the USA (Katzenbach and Smith, 1993). However, in many other countries, managerial capitalism was the dominant organisational form; 'scientific management' was entrenched as the basic pattern of work organisation and genuine workplace change had been piecemeal and slow. The network characteristics of Japanese enterprise and the role of government are central to understanding the rise of 'collective capitalism' but so, it appears, are the self-managing work teams of dominant networked firms.

Although it has attracted considerable attention, Japanese 'collective capitalism' has not served as a universal model for enterprise development in other countries, let alone its near neighbours in the Asia-pacific region. As noted, introduction of new technology has been accompanied by job enlargement in Singaporean and Sri Lankean banks, while Korean banks have further sub-divided tasks and recruited un-skilled female labour. The impact of adopted technology is strongly mediated by management strategies regarding employment practices and those embedded in product markets, labour markets and socio-cultural forces characterising industry and the nation (Wilkinson, 1988). In the case of developing countries, the possibility that technology transfers itself influences organisational choices does not appear to have been seriously investigated.

Although there exists a myriad of options and alternatives for IT development policies, supported by numerous cases of success and failure in developed and developing societies guiding informatics policy choice, no individual model can provide a panacea for future development. Learning by experience, guided by the formative context of society and existing IT infra-structural capability, produces the richest flavour in strategic development. The alternative which a developing society chooses voluntarily, reflecting its formative context, immediate and long-term needs and capabilities, and not being an *imposed* strategy imbued with western scientific values, may prove the more effective, alternative strategy for the development of an Information Technology Meta Policy (ITMP).

Note

1   This chapter was presented at the 5th International Speyer Workshop on 'Assessing and Evaluating Public Management Reforms', Speyer, Germany, October 1996.

4 Information Technology – Enabled Communication and Organisational Effectiveness

NADA K. KAKABADSE, ALEXANDER KOUZMIN AND
ANDREW K. KAKABADSE

Abstract

The chapter[1] explores the current understanding of IT-enabled communication in organisations and IT-media choice. It examines the central concerns and ideas in the field addressed by theories drawing from rational and interpretativist perspectives. Thus, theoretical fragmentation is recognised and the controversial views of the effects of communication are presented. Characteristics of IT-mediated communication are identified, positive and negative impacts on organisational effectiveness examined, as is the IT-mediated communication effect on group behaviour. It is concluded that the effective choice of communication media depends on organisational understanding of the message the organisation is trying to communicate to internal as well as external stakeholders and what specific behaviour an organisation is trying to promote.

Introduction

While communication processes and practices are inherent to the effective functioning of organisations, communication tends to be something that humans take for granted and, perhaps, for that very reason communication processes are difficult to improve. Some have argued that the communication process should meet accuracy; honesty; openness; timeliness; credibility; consistency; responsiveness to stakeholders needs; and productivity criteria (Harshman and Phillip, 1994; p.115), whilst others have argued that the greater the need to communicate, the more difficult it becomes (Falcione, Daley and McCroskey, 1977). Although there is no universally accepted definition of the communication phenomenon, Shannon and Weaver's (1949) classical mathematical theory of communication provides a useful starting point. They define communication as the process of transfer of a selected bit of information (a message) from an information source to a destination (Shannon and Weaver, 1949; p.7). The information is encoded, possibly using an error-correcting code, transmitted through a channel and the message is then decoded. The average effectiveness of this process is measured in the Shannon capacity of the channel, which is becoming increasingly relevant with high-speed telephone and computer networks.

Shannon and Weaver's (1949) definition was later re-defined by Redfield (1958), who postulated that the communication process involves the transmission from an information source to a receiver and destination, in the face of 'noise', which can distort the message. These definitions underpin traditional communication models, exemplified by the first communication process model developed in 1957 by two professors of journalism, Bruce Westely and Malcom MacLean, Jr., who viewed communication as a two-dimensional exchange of information; information transfer (Argenti, 1996). This information processing view of communication has been expanded so that in addition to the data transfer, communication involves the transfer of meaning (Mantovani, 1996); that is, both sender and receiver dispatch a myriad of messages through a multiplicity of channels, each of which contributes to perceived message meaning mediated by the formative context. This view is adopted by political and social theory explaining social action in terms of communication of meaning. The existence of social life depends on the creation of shared meaning and understanding which, in turn, depend on the communication of such meaning amongst actors. In this process, language plays a central role.

Because communication is concerned with the interactions of people, individually and in the groups, the communication subject is interwoven with semantics, sociology, anthropology, psychology and organisational complexity. This diversity of subject domain, theories and perspectives has also produced diversity of findings that are often difficult to compare. The classical (Taylor, 1911; Gulick, 1937; Fayol, 1949); neo-classical (Barnard, 1938; Follett, 1940; Simon, 1947; Waldo, 1948; Selznik, 1957); human behaviour (Mayo, 1933; McGregor, 1960; Likert, 1961; Argyris, 1964); open systems, including resource dependency (Katz and Khan, 1996; Thompson, 1957); political-administrative (Selznick, 1957; Kaufman and

Couzens; 1973, Gardner, 1990); technological (Woodward, 1965; Perrow, 1970; Pugh et al. 1963); management excellence, reinvention and quality (Peters and Waterman, 1982; Osborne and Gaebler, 1992; Cohen and Brand, 1993); phenomenological (Heidegger, 1962; Mereau-Ponty, 1962; Husserl, 1964); critical (Marcuse, 1967; Habermas, 1972; Horkheimer, 1974); leadership (Burns, 1978; Tucker, 1981; Bennis and Nanus, 1985; Kakabadse and Kakabadse, 1998) and post-modern (Barthes, 1967; Foucault, 1980) perspectives have all concerned themselves with issues of communication and have made different contributions to the domain of communication. Garnett (1997) provides a useful framework for assessing the contribution of various perspectives based on how they address nine, basic communication variables:

- Degree of formality - formal, sub-formal and informal;
- Focus - internal or external;
- Level of analysis - interpersonal, group, organisational, inter-organisational;
- Direction of flow - downward, upward, lateral;
- Communication role - sending or receiving;
- Purpose - task, motivation, other;
- Epistemological orientation - rational/positivist or interpretative/ subjective;
- Attention to communication - minor, indirect, major, direct; and
- Key contributions to knowledge - from classical schools of thought and importance of formal reporting, to post-modernist schools of thought and subjective interpretation and communication technology.

Communication facilitated by complex information technologies (IT) and information systems (IS) is increasingly complex and difficult because of the intricacy of the socio-technical system as well as the nature of the communicated subject matter itself. Although the need for effective communication has been recognised for some time and has increasingly received attention in a variety of disciplines, with the proliferation of IT and its unprecedented support capabilities, IT-enabled communication increasingly captures the focus of practitioners and academics alike (Mantovani, 1996). IT-mediated communication uses computer text and/or multi media processing and communication tools to provide high-speed information exchange (Sproull and Kiesler, 1992). IT-enabled communication broadly includes electronic mail (E-mail); voice mail (V-mail); computer bulletin boards (CBB); computer conferencing; GroupWare; group-decision support systems as well as other new forms of structured communication support via computers (Steinfield, 1992: p.349).

IT-enabled communication has attracted studies both from the positivist perspective, known as the natural-science mode of social-science research, with the focus on the object or technology, and from the interpretativist perspective where the focus is on the social actor (Nass and Mason, 1990). Where the positivist, technology-focused perspective is interested in identifying and understanding the effects of new communication technologies on organisations, groups and individuals, the social actor, interpretativist approach seeks to understand IT-mediated communication use from the perspective of individuals and their choice behaviour in IT-mediated environments. In terms of units of analysis, the majority of research, to date, is at the level of the group and the individual, whilst the *organisational* level has received the least attention. The positivist perspective holds that individuals will always make rational choices on the basis of task and message content characteristics. From a positivist perspective, communication in IT-mediated environments is conceptualised as a physical process of transporting meaning from one person to another and, thus, labelled as a 'conduit' metaphor (Contractor and Eisenberg, 1990). Furthermore, it holds that any difference in the meaning received cannot be an improvement but can only be a loss due to noise, interference and other deterioration in the 'signal' during the course of its transmission. Where conduits take an asynchronous form, such as E-mail, deterioration of the signal would be said to occur from:

- The lack of immediate feedback;
- The filtering out of social cues;
- The confinement to a single channel;
- The lack of personalisation; and
- The reduction in language variety.

As a 'conduit', the face-to-face medium is considered superior to documents for transporting meaning from the sender to the receiver without any loss in 'signals' such as loss of facial expression and other social cues. The positivist perspective concerned with IT-mediated communication is represented by two schools of thought: the social presence approach (Rice, 1984a;1984b; Sproull and Kiesler, 1986; Hiltz and Turoff, 1993) and the media richness approach (Daft and Lengel, 1984; 1986; Trevino, Lengel and Daft, 1987; Trevino, Daft and Lengel, 1990).

The positivist or rational perspective has most strongly been criticised by proponents of the socio-cultural interpretative tradition of a hermeneutic explanation for media choice. The interpretative tradition argues that rational theories of media choice are providing a narrow and deterministic perspective on IT-mediated environments, one which restricts the understanding of the role of new media in the social and organisational setting in which they are used. They argue that social actors create and attach their own meanings to the world around them and to the behaviour that they manifest in that world and, thus, themselves transform whatever 'lean' words and cues are received in an understanding of what the sender meant and enacting the original meaning to the message (Schutz, 1973; Lea, 1991; p.347; Markus, 1994). The Socio-Cultural or Interpretativist paradigm addressing IT-mediated communication consists of four major streams of thought: Structuration (Giddens, 1984; Weick, 1987; Poole and DeSanctis, 1990; 1992; Orlikowski, 1992; Yates and Orlikowski, 1992; Fulk, Schmitz and Rye, 1995); Symbolic Interaction (McLuhan, 1964; Trevino, Daft and Lengel, 1990; Chesebro and Bertelsen, 1996; Mantovani, 1996); Critical Social Theory (Ngwenyama, 1991; Treux, 1993; Hirschheim and Klein, 1994; Ngwenyama and Lee, 1997; Ngwenyama and Lyytinen, 1997); and Social Influence (Fulk, Schmitz and Steinfield, 1990; Markus, 1990; Schmitz and Fulk, 1991).

Whilst the proponents of Rational and Socio-Cultural paradigms present competing views of media choice, integrative approaches propose that only the integration of paradigms will improve the current, insufficient understanding of media choice (Sitkin, Sutcliffe and Barrios-Choplin, 1992; Bozeman, 1993; Webster and Trevino, 1995). Integrative approaches found that the explanatory power of the two competing approaches depended largely on the type of medium as well as on its 'newness' within an organisation. In conventional communication environments, individuals' choice behaviour is underpinned by rational influences (Fulk and Boyd, 1991). Conventional media for communication are in use over long periods of time, thus, members of the organisation widely agree on their use. In contrast, choice in IT-mediated environments is largely influenced by socio-cultural factors (Fulk and Boyd, 1991). Research, focused on the particulars of IT-mediated contexts, suggests that choice from traditional media tends to be informed by rational criteria whilst choice from IT-mediated environments tends to be based on socio-cultural factors (Fulk and Boyd, 1991; Sitkin, Sutcliffe and Barrios-

Choplin, 1992; Webster and Trevino, 1995). However, a dynamic view of media choice needs to be adopted in order to acknowledge the importance of rational and social influences on choice over time (Webster and Trevino, 1995). The use of communication media by the user community, over time, tends to converge so that choice increasingly matches the objective characteristics of the medium and the communication task (Yates and Orlikowski, 1992; Markus, 1994).

Characteristics of IT-Mediated Communication

The particular characteristics of IT-based communication media that have been the focus of attention are centred around the categories of synchronicity, transmission speed, textual and graphical nature of the medium, multiplicity of connections, storage and manipulation facilities (Garton and Wellman, 1995). Communication technologies have specific characteristics that condition their impact and use (Culnan and Markus, 1987; Finholt and Sproull, 1990). Electronic communication is an asynchronous, computer-mediated messaging system that uses computer text processing and communication tools to provide high-speed information exchange (Sproull and Kiesler, 1992). The uniqueness of IT-mediated communication is based on the assumption that technology is the mediating function in the communication process. Thus, although the interpersonal communication process, in its purest form, seems simple, it is not a sterile process and is mediated by the communication medium. Furthermore, effective communication requires sender and receiver to have a shared sense of the meaning of the symbols and metaphors with which they encode their message into one or more channels. They must speak the same language, know the same jargon, make sense of the same gestures and be able to filter 'noise' and 'distortion'. Thus, in order to fully understand IT-mediated communication, the message-generating implications of communication media needs to be recognised (Chesebro and Bertelsen, 1996). To understand communication media there is a need for sharing the meaning of its basic elements.

- Encoding - to encode a message is to put what one desires another to understand into some channel that carries the message (Robbins, 1994);

- Decoding - entails using personal knowledge, perceptions, values and cultural understanding by the receiver to make sense of received messages;
- Channelling - transports information between the parties involved in the communication act. The channel may be:
  - synchronous - where communications occur in time and require the presence of the communicating partners in order for communication to occur. This can be interpersonal (tele- and video-conferencing) or intersectional (face-to-face communication); or
  - asynchronous - where communication occurs independently of the temporal presence of the parties engaging in the communication process. This is impersonal, such as written form (print, E-mail) or audio-visual form (voice mail, video mail) (Sproull and Kiesler, 1992);
- Linkage - a medium which establishes levels of interactivity between the participants in the communication activity. Depending on the medium's capacity for speed of feedback or the bandwidth, communication channels employed, degree of personalisation of message, the range of meaning it conveys and interactivity, the media can vary from 'rich', at the one end, where context-dependent meanings can be communicated, to 'lean' on the other, where only context-independent data/information is communicated (Daft and Lengel, 1986; Daft, Lengel and Trevino, 1987; Trevino, Daft and Lengel, 1990). Media richness is defined by three aspects of the information itself: the bandwidth, or the amount of information that can be moved from sender to receiver in a given time, the degree to which information can be customised and the level of interactivity;
- Richness - media is capable of communicating high levels of message complexity, equivocality, ambiguity and enables interactive communication modes. Face-to-face is considered as being the 'richest' communication because it provides varied opportunities for immediate feedback and multiple cues in a natural language tailored to circumstance (Daft and Lengel, 1986);
- Leanness - media is capable of communicating low levels of complexity, equivocality and ambiguity. Written text, such as fliers, bulletins and reports are considered to be the lowest in richness and, thus, 'lean' (Daft and Lengel, 1986);

- Reach - the order of magnitude of people exchanging information. There are four major orders of magnitude in IT-mediated communication:
  - intranets - connecting individuals within organisation;
  - extranets - connecting companies to one another;
  - internet - connecting everyone (Web); and
  - satellite - connecting everyone (interactive television).
- Mode - the level of the communication interaction, which can be:
  - impersonal - written form, such as letters, reports or E-mail;
  - interpersonal via telephone; and
  - interaction such as face-to-face communication;
- Level of interactivity - communication media establishes varying levels of interactivity between the participants in the communication act. These can be:
  - non-interactive, one-way communication processes;
  - two-way interaction process; and
  - multi-way interaction processes;
- Noise - the environment in which interaction communication occurs and includes all possibilities for creating misunderstanding, interference, confusion and miscommunication during a communication episode;
- Distortion - interpretation of the sender's meaning by the receiver, producing an entirely different message than the sender intended (Steers and Black, 1994);
- Non-verbal cues - subtle, non-verbalised cues or memories and stereotypes play an important role in the interaction mode of communication, such as face-to-face communication. Research shows that only eight to 20 per cent of interpersonal commutation is verbal (Ruch, 1989). The popular wisdom suggests that 'action speaks louder than words'. Non-verbal communication has received support by contemporary research that postulates that people are more likely to believe what they 'see' and experience than what they read or hear (Bruce, 1990; Steers and Black, 1994). Because of the power to influence the outcome of communication episodes, non-verbal channels have been studied independently and have developed into a discrete sub-field of study:
  - Proxemics - the use of physical space in communication. This science studies the effects of closeness, distance, furniture

arrangements and environmental attributes in communication (Campbell, 1979; Morrow and McElroy, 1981);

- Kinetics or body language - is the science of understanding facial expressions, posturing, head and hand movements, touching and any other body movements as part of the communication episode (Birdwhistell, 1952; Henley, 1977; Goldhaber, 1993);
- Para-language - includes the use of silence in vocal communication as well as tone, rhythm, speed, volume, rate, pitch, accent, language, coughing and sighing (Moerman, 1988; De Vito, 1989; Ruch, 1989; Hall, 1991). These vocal intentions and variations supplement actual words spoken by making up about 38 per cent of non-verbal communication (Ruch, 1989);
- Physical characteristics - such as body size and shape, skin colour, hair colour, age and other physical features, all send a message about the person, supplementing verbal messages in face-to-face communication (Lyons, 1987; Hubber, 1989; Scott and Morgan, 1993);
- Artefacts - items that are closely allied with body language and physical characteristics. These are items with which the body is adorned as a means of conveying status, credibility, values, job responsibilities and so forth. They include clothing and accessories, as well as makeup, perfume and deodorant (Mollay, 1987; 1988, Ebin, 1979).

The use of high-speed information highways, capable of carrying increasingly more data and information, moves organisations towards increased reliance on IT/IS but, at the same time, often reduces information to data as it strips it of its original context and lends itself to further misinformation and error propagation. The media-task matching perspective suggests four determinants of rational media choice. They include the requirement for uncertainty reduction, message equivocality resolution, the task routines and the analysability of the task.

- Uncertainty reduction - in order to accomplish tasks, organisational actors need to acquire information through communication. The necessity to reduce environmental uncertainty in the absence of information determines individuals' media choice (Rice, Grant, Schmitz and Torobin, 1990; Rice and Shook, 1990);
- Equivocality resolution - the concept of the equivocality of the message relates to the message content which is open to multiple

interpretations by any given message receiver. This view holds that message equivocality is the core determinant of the communication media choice (Daft and Lengel, 1986; Daft, Lengel and Trevino, 1987; Valacich, Paranka, George and Nunamaker 1993);

- Task routines - the task routine view explains communication media choice in terms of matching the medium and the level of task routines (Rice, Grant, Schmitz and Torobin, 1990);

- Task analysability - the extent to which the completion of a task is based on known procedures is termed task analysability (Rice, Grant, Schmitz and Torobin, 1990). This view holds that task analysability determines medium choice. Higher levels of task analysability require less rich medium to effectively communicate the task.

Effective communication requires media capable of transporting data and meanings as the medium is more than the carrier of the messages. Some have argued that 'the medium itself becomes a message' (McLuhan, 1964; Trevino, Daft and Lengel, 1990: p.84; Garton and Wellman, 1995). Since meaning is socially negotiated and culturally determined, it is context dependent and requires a rich media. Rich messages require rich media; that is, a media capable of communicating complexity, equivocality and ambiguity. A rich media enables interactive communication modes for the participants to negotiate, discuss and clarify the meaning of the communicated message, such as face-to-face interactions, where communicating partners are enabled to negotiate, clarify and explain subjective understanding. Text-based communication media, such as written documents and E-mail, are low in social presence. Media based on audio and/or visual facilities, such as video and teleconferencing systems or voice mail, are rated comparably high in social presence. Text-based communication media are perceived as less appropriate for social, intuitive or emotional communication tasks, such as negotiating, and more adequate for less socio-emotional tasks, such as information exchange, resolving unequivocal issues and processing standard, objective data detached from alternative interpretations (Rice, 1984a; 1984b; Sproull and Kiesler, 1986; Hiltz and Turoff, 1993).

Determinants of Media Choice

From the rational, media choice perspective, the most prominent model of communication at the level of the individual is considered to depend on the match between the richness of the medium and the equivocality of the message (Daft and Lengel, 1984; 1986; Daft, Lengel and Trevino, 1987). Rich media are considered to be most effective in reducing high levels of ambiguity. Yet, since rich media are more costly to use than lean media, they are seen as inefficient for tasks low in ambiguity. Oral communication is perceived to be most effective in situations where equivocality is high, whilst written communication is most effective for situations low in equivocality (Daft and Lengel, 1984; 1986). Thus, for example, managerial tasks characterised by high levels of complexity (Mintzberg, 1973; Rice and Aydin, 1991), are perceived as requiring richer communication media in order to be effective.

Using 100 managers and 355 hypothetical communication incidents, categorised into 18 workplace situations, Trevino, Lengel and Daft (1987) found that face-to-face communication was more likely to be chosen (46 per cent) for communicating tasks involving ambiguity rather than telephone, written and electronic mail (25 per cent). Electronic mail was more likely to be chosen (62 per cent) for tasks involving situation constraints than the other media (telephone 51 per cent, written 43 per cent, and face-to-face 17 per cent). Trevino, Daft and Lengel (1990) later revised their proposition from the symbolic-interactionist perspective, suggesting that media choice is determined by an interplay of three factors: the complexity of the message (information richness model), contextual demands (time pressure, geographic distance) and the symbolic meaning of the medium (Trevino, Daft and Lengel, 1990).

El-Shinnawy and Markus's (1997: p.456) study of V- and E-mail choice in a large organisation found that V-mail was not perceived an adequate medium for resolving equivocality, but that V-mail was preferred for 'short, spontaneous, one-way drops of information, in contrast to the lengthy, ongoing, prolonged and ambiguous communication typical of equivocal situations'. In contrast, E-mail was used to deal with equivocality on grounds of its capacity in processing ongoing communication, of documentation, multiple addressability and absence of verbal cues which individuals find distorting. The results showed that individuals prefer E-mail over V-mail in situations of uncertainty; specifically for exchanging large amounts of accurate, technical, objective and quantifiable information. They found that 'individuals' media choices were a function of the medium's communication mode and documentation capabilities, as well as the user's role as message sender or recipient' (El-Shinnawy and Markus, 1997; p.458). E-mail was used less for its richness features as a communication medium, but for reasons that relate to a user's communication roles and richness features.

The ability to resolve equivocality may not only depend on the media richness features but also on other characteristics and functionality that typify IT-mediated communication - such as communication mode; saving; filing; retrieving; documenting and manipulating capabilities (El-Shinnawy and Markus, 1997). Individual's choices may be informed by their roles in the communication process as well as any other personal, task, social or organisational factors. In addition, El-Shinnawy and Markus's (1997) findings indicate that users may select new media for reasons other than those associated with the intent of resolving message equivocality. Furthermore, individuals differentiate media not only in terms of verbal versus written communication modes, but also spontaneous versus planned communication, inconsequential versus important, emotionally-poor versus emotionally-rich and requiring technology versus non - requiring technology (Lea, 1991).

A 'wide range of empirical evidence suggests that factors besides task analysability, and the resulting ambiguity, influence the choice of a medium in any given situation' (Steinfield, 1992: p.352). Environmental complexity and organisational structure (Burns and Stalker, 1961; Lawrence and Lorsch, 1967); group and inter-unit interdependence; need for uncertainty reduction; individual media preference; and ambiguity in communication situations are all influencing factors in media choice (Steinfield, 1992). Critical mass theory (Markus, 1990) and the social influence model (Fulk, Schmitz and Steinfield, 1990; Schmitz and Fulk, 1991) demonstrate that the social context is a source for explaining adoption, usage and impact of IT-mediated communication. This includes time and distance constraints, social and organisational norms, symbolic meaning of the communication medium and the user's media experiences (Trevino, Daft and Lengel, 1990; Steinfield, 1992).

The process of developing norms and patterns of usage of a new communications medium results from the interaction of individual assessments of the new technology and critical mass effects over time, especially operating at the local, work-unit level rather than at the global, total-network - usage level (Rice, Kraut, Cool and Fish, 1994). Steinfield's (1992) and other (Hiltz and Turoff, 1993) work shows that IT-enabled communications are also employed for non-routine types of communication tasks. Organisations vary in their attitudes to communication technologies and their patterns of use (Steinfield, 1992). Purposes of use vary from work-related, to social, non-work-related communications, to broadcast by groups and to political debate and conflict resolution (Finholt and Sproull, 1990). Exclusive focus on rational explanations of IT-mediated communication use is insufficient - social and contextual influences are far more influential in media selection processes (Steinfield, 1992).

Resistance to New Technology

Resistance to new technologies has been explained by individual-level perspective theories, such as rational choice theory, and by collective-level perspective theories exemplified by social construction theory (Markus, 1994). Actor's conservatism, fear of change, lack of involvement and motivation and incompatible cognitive styles have been major issues identified by individual-level theories trying to explain resistance to innovation (Markus, 1994). According to richness theory, the choice between communication media depends on the individual perception of how 'rich' or 'lean' the information-carrying capacity of each alternative medium is for the communication task at hand (Daft and Lengel, 1986; Daft, Lengel and Trevino, 1987). Information-carrying capacity is considered rich if feedback is immediate, cues are multiple and the language is natural and tailored to the circumstances. Since rich information needs media which can help improve human understanding and overcome differences, the theory assumes that individuals tend to match rich media with tasks that are underlying with ambiguity, equivocality and uncertainty.

Fear of undesirable effects on organisational structure, power distribution or possible cultural conflict between the system and the organisation in which an IT medium is to be implemented are some of the resistance factors to innovation issues that have been identified by collective-level theories such as Structuralism (Markus and Robey, 1983), environment-oriented (Markus and Robey, 1983), culture-oriented (Pliskin et al. 1993) and politics-oriented frameworks (Kreamer and Pinsonneault, 1993). Collective-level perspectives argue that diffusion of any technology is perceived as appropriate by the community of potential stakeholders.

Interruptions, though easier to accomplish in IT-mediated environments, are less disruptive than in face-to-face interaction because actors usually do not belong to the defined community or location. They are, really, over 'there' to be interrupted. Even if interrupted for a brief moment, they are usually not seen (Rafaeli and Sudweeks, 1994; 1997). This elimination of aspects such as gender, status, ethnicity, language skills and physical attractiveness, creates more neutral, more 'noise-free', communication. However, this can also introduce a lack of clarity, ambiguity and confusion. Thus, communication in IT-mediated environments, or 'virtual communities', may suffer from a lack of 'social cues' and may be low on 'social presence' (Walther, 1992) but can still be highly interactive and, therefore, amenable to many social uses, including political manipulation.

Network and Virtual Organisational Designs

New designs and structures, which have been depicted as the breakdown of hierarchy, are enabled through the emergence of IT-mediated communication (Marlow and Wilson, 1997). IT is considered to be a determinant of organisational change in driving the organisation to adjust its activities, processes and structures to the operational and structural framework that the technology fabricates (Lea, 1991). The IT-effect studies argue that the interactive, multi-level capabilities of communication technologies compel change in conventional organisational activities and designs and, as such, drive the emergence of new organisational forms, exemplified by the network or the virtual organisation. For example, the electronic group at work is a new social and organisational phenomenon that requires significant scrutiny in order to expand current understanding of organisational behaviour and design (Finholt and Sproull, 1990). In contrast to conventional groups, electronic groups are supported by IT-enabled communication media such as electronic mail and GroupWare systems (Lotus Notes; Microsoft Exchange). Research on IT-supported groups stresses the benefit of flexible work structures that the communication technology enables. In creating more flexible structures, experience and expertise of human resources can be assembled wherever it is needed (Finholt and Sproull, 1990). The GroupWare technology allows individuals to form groups for emerging purposes that cut across geographic and departmental boundaries. GroupWare substantially facilitates information exchange and decision-making in groups independent of physical location.

The value of new organisational forms, such as virtual organisations, has been specifically identified in relation to organisations' interactions with external constituencies. Bradley and Nolan (1998) argue that the new organisations capture value in shifting from the traditional 'make and sell' to the new, IT-mediated communication-enabled paradigm of 'sense and respond'. The new, interactive communication networks enable organisations to sense in real time their customers' needs and so to respond swiftly and effectively. The speed with which advances are currently being made in the business applications of information and communication technologies triggers unprecedented change in organisations, industries and society such that those who study them are only beginning to understand (Bradley and Nolan, 1998).

IT-Mediated Communication and Electronic and Virtual Groups

Whilst GroupWare technologies might produce efficiency gains, they alternatively might create new or different forms of groups and, as such, induce desirable and undesirable organisational consequences. Organisational-level consequences of electronic groups were explored by Finholt and Sproull (1990) who studied the differences between conventional and electronic groups.

Research on social groups in conventional communication environments extrapolated three sets of characteristics relevant to communication in groups - attributes of group behaviour; processes of group behaviour; and organisational consequences of group behaviour.

Attributes of Group Behaviour

Attributes of group behaviour are typified by four distinct characteristics.

- Physical setting - IT environments change the traditional attributes of group behaviour because they create communication environments where group members do not share the physical setting;
- Member characteristics - since mailing via distribution lists is independent of the sender's knowledge of the individuals on the list, and with the knowledge that receivers will actually read the mail, there are few clues to the identity and social presence of the parties

participating in the communication situation. As a consequence, individuals are less aware of the attributes of others who participate in the communication. Other than in conventional communication situations, electronic group members share less of a social context;

- Membership criteria - membership in the distribution list may either be required or discretionary. This parallels the concepts of formal and informal groups in conventional communication situations. Required groups mirror formal organisation - discretionary groups invite informal, voluntary group association. Similar to formal and informal groups, behaviour in required and discretionary electronic groups varies;

- Task type - group behaviour is also affected by the type of task the group is performing (McGrath and Hollingshead, 1994). Groups either engage in work-related or non-work-related tasks. Work-related task groups have been differentiated in terms of generic task types. These involve co-ordination, control, negotiation and collaboration. Collaborative work is seen to be most appropriately supported by richer, interactive media such as group-decision support systems and video-conferencing. Since co-ordination and control tasks tend to be routine and structured, they are best supported through 'leaner' media such as electronic mail and voice mail (Finholt and Sproull, 1990).

Processes of Group Behaviour

Social groups exert three communication-related processes: interaction, influence attempts and identity maintenance.

- Interaction - electronic communication environments modify group processes. In electronic groups, interaction is asynchronous because electronic mail is asynchronous;

- Influence attempts - social context cues emanate from physical settings and member attributes. They regulate influence attempts. In electronic groups, where physical settings are not shared and members are invisible, influence attempts can only emanate from the text of the message;

- Identity maintenance - group identity is pursued through differentiation. In conventional communication environments, groups differentiate themselves against others through a variety of verbal, social and contextual cues. Electronic groups can draw on text only for differentiation and identify determination and maintenance. If differentiation occurs at all in electronic groups, it should happen through the text of the message being communicated (Finholt and Sproull, 1990).

Organisational Consequences of Group Behaviour

The effects of conventional and electronic groups' attributes and processes on organisations are distinguished on three dimensions.

- Participation - in contrast to face-to-face groups, membership and socialisation in electronic groups is facilitated since it requires entry into the membership list and knowledge of the messaging style and occasions considered appropriate only by the existing members (Chidambaram and Jones, 1993). Because participants are invisible, conventional social regulators of participation, such as gender and hierarchical status, less constrain electronic groups than conventional groups (Siegel, Dubrovsky, Kiesler and McGuire, 1986; Hiltz and Turoff, 1993);
- Performance - conventional groups have been observed to generate increasingly inefficient performance due to process loss which results from groups transcending a certain size (Chidambaram and Jones, 1993). Process loss occurs if one individual monopolises the group or if too many group members engage in lengthy social interaction. Since electronic group members do not interact physically, process loss is reduced. Further, members reticent or of lower status contribute more equally in the electronic setting. Therefore, organisational performance is expected to benefit from electronic groups (Finholt and Sproull, 1990);
- Learning - electronic groups also provide sources for enhanced information and knowledge sharing due to the relative ease of access to the groups and their individual members. If group members ask and provide information, individual experience and expertise is turned into shared knowledge. Electronic groups have a high diffusion capability and rate due to the technological support of the communication process (Finholt and Sproull, 1990).

However, management policies strongly influence the nature of electronic group activities and the ratio of positive and negative consequences for the organisation (Finholt and Sproull, 1990). The application and the usage of the new communication media is dependent on the policy discretion and self-policing and, as such, may account for negative effects such as information overload or abuse. Research findings suggest that managers use electronic mail for a significantly limited range of communication tasks in contrast to use at the non-managerial level (Finholt and Sproull, 1990). Design guidelines need to consider both the technical and the social aspects of communication technology. For example, technical policies may include the installation of filters and group directories, whilst social-level norms and codes for use need to be endorsed to encourage responsible and effective technology use. These organisational design issues need to be addressed by the policy-designers and not left to system designers alone.

Pros and Cons of IT-Mediated Communication

Electronically-mediated communication has entered the world of organisational communication in the form of voice mail (V-mail), electronic mail (E-mail) and, of late, in the form of video-conferencing (V-conferencing). E-mail has been defined as an interactive communication medium that facilitates communication between individuals and groups (El-Shinnawy and Markus, 1997). E-mail, for instance, is asynchronous, fast, text-based, one-to-one, one-to-many or many-to many, whilst V-mail asynchronous, fast, voice-based and one-to-one (Adams, Todd and Nelson, 1993).

A study of 68 users of both E-mail and V-mail, representing 12 organisations, found that whilst electronic mail was perceived to exert fundamental changes to conventional communications in terms of scope and patterns, the impact of voice mail was considered insignificant (Adams, Todd and Nelson, 1993). The study found that E-mail was perceived by users to be a far more useful and versatile communication medium than V-mail. Although rated richer in communication features and capabilities than E-mail, V-mail did not expand the scope of communication or alter the pattern of communication. Thus, where E-mail was clearly seen as an alternative communication channel to traditional ways of communicating, V-mail, in contrast, was viewed as a supplementary answering device able to deliver lower level, internal efficiency increases (Adams, Todd and Nelson, 1993). Notwithstanding that E- and V-mail share common functions and capabilities, they are not homogenous and inter-changeable technologies (Adams, Todd and Nelson, 1993).

Due to rapid technological advances and rapid change, knowledge about the effect and implications of IT-mediated communication has not caught up with the availability of media choices. For example, both V-mail and E-mail carry a verbal message and hints from para-language. However, no cues from physical space, body language, artefacts or physical characteristics are provided. Although V-mail permits one to identify gender, and perhaps ethnicity and emotional state of the callers, and to recognise a familiar voice, the ability to question, clarify and respond is delayed, even if immediate action is taken (Bruce, 1997). Para-language cues in a 'lean' IT-mediated communication, such as in the case of E-mail, are sparse, although creative senders can enrich their message by use of different font styles and use of graphics. Even with creative use of fonts and font size, receivers of E-mail may be deprived of as much as 80 per cent of the communication cues to which they are accustomed. This can have positive and negative impacts depending on the context (Bruce, 1997).

The unusual capacity of face-to-face dialogue to capture the entire spectrum of human interaction (multiple cues), its opportunity to interrupt and repair relationships, as well as to elicit immediate *feedback* and *learning*, are lost in IT-mediated communication (Goffman, 1963; Trevino, Lengel and Daft, 1987), leaving especially crisis-mediating situations increasingly vulnerable (Korac-Boisvert and Kouzmin, 1995a; 1995b). In situations and relationships that call for high levels of trust, IT is conceptualised as a support mechanism and not a substitute for face-to-face dialogue (Nohria and Eccles, 1992; Korac-Boisvert and Kouzmin, 1994). Robustness and trust, critical to quality of dialogue (Kakabadse, 1991; Kakabadse and Kakabadse, 1998), are severely weakened in IT-mediated communication. Lying, fraud, sabotage and other anti-social actions are harder to detect in IT-mediated exchanges (Korac-Boisvert and Kouzmin, 1994). Without the full benefit of face-to-face communication, it is almost impossible to recognise whether actors are being profoundly sincere or totally deceptive (Stone, 1991). For example, increased white-collar crime and other 'soft core' (Kouzmin and Korac-Boisvert, 1995a) and creeping crises (Jarman and Kouzmin, 1994) illustrate cases in point.

Although the 'cooling' effect of the 'lean' IT-communication medium can enhance conflict management and strengthen support by keeping the expression of emotionality at a more moderate level (Rice, 1984a: 1984b; Poole, Holmes and DeSanctis, 1991), it can be unsuitable for consensus building on highly equivocal tasks (Daft, Lengel and Trevino, 1987), such as competing for scarce resources within organisations with lean-buffers (Kouzmin, Korac-Kakabadse and Jarman, 1996) inter-agency driven crisis mitigation efforts (Comfort, 1993; 1994). Although dialogue is more 'egalitarian', it is also more 'disorganised' (Williams, 1977), as its 'openness' makes it difficult to resolve issues and establish who has authority to make critical decisions. Furthermore, the spatio-temporal distance that IT interaction provides can lead to an open display of anger and escalating conflict, or 'flaming', behaviour (Kiesler, 1986; Solomon, 1990). Thus, IT-mediated dialogue can help in enabling information flows useful for mobilising action (Comfort, 1993), but face-to-face dialogue is vital to actually taking action (Nohria and Eccles, 1992: p.297; Korac-Boisvert and Kouzmin, 1994) and reducing potential organisational vulnerability. As the amount of IT-mediated communication increases, there is a need for a corresponding increase in the amount of face-to-face dialogue in order to maintain and build robust social infrastructure of relationships between actors (Nohria and Eccles, 1992; p.297; Korac-Boisvert and Kouzmin, 1994). One mechanism for improving quality of interaction and dialogue is feedback (Kakabadse, 1991).

On the positive side, the IT-mediated communication can expedite task-oriented communication between colleagues; provide timely communicative interchanges; remove geographic constraints; and can increase or decrease contacts with superiors; subordinates and peers as the decision-making process requires (Adams, Todd and Nelson, 1993). Furthermore, the rich multi media electronic communication supports printed and visual forms offering new imaginative ways for addressing organisational and management issues using film, drama, poetry, fiction and other creative forms of communication, some of which have been in practice for sometime but under-utilised in contemporary organisations. Sproull and Kiesler's (1986) study found that electronic mail was preferred for communicating negative news, avoiding open dialogue and conflict resolution. Electronic mail increases the reach of communication in terms of the breadth and capacity of the communication network. In contrast to conventional communication networks, a dramatic increase occurs in the number of participants in the messaging system, the number of inter-connections between them and the volume of message traffic flowing through the network.

E-mail also alters patterns of communication in increasing the vertical and horizontal communication flow through the organisation. For example, asynchronous media such as E-mail and V-mail are able to remove time zones and geographical barriers and to distribute messages to a large number of individuals simultaneously and rapidly. This has been seen as a core advantage of an asynchronous technology. Simultaneous distribution of information is perceived to enhance co-ordination of project groups, scheduling of meetings and general information exchange. In terms of scope, electronic mail increases the total number of participants in the messaging system, the number of inter-connections between them and the number of messages sent and received. In increasing the total number of communication participants, IT facilitates the establishment of new contacts within the organisation. In view of communication patterns, E-mail was found to be preferred over V-mail for communicating with peers, superiors and subordinates (Adams, Todd and Nelson, 1993). In respect of the communication task, E-mail improves co-ordination tasks within the organisation. It also enhances and improves control tasks such as monitoring activities and reporting results. At the organisational level, E-mail is seen as a device for improving effectiveness in expanding the range of information and expertise and facilitating its exchange across the organisation and amongst decision makers (Adams, Todd and Nelson, 1993).

On the negative side, lean IT-media, such as electronic messages, can be impersonal and sterile and, inappropriately applied to replace more meaningful face-to-face contacts, can inhibit synergistic interaction. Whilst V-mail and E-mail are far less rich than face-to-face, voice-to-voice interactions or V-conferencing, electronic channels are rapidly increasing in use and abuse. Notwithstanding that new communication technologies have the potential of altering and improving communication processes, the 'improvement will only occur if the system is properly matched to organisational structural factors and task contingencies' (Adams, Todd and Nelson, 1993: p.13). Others have argued that 'much of the trade and practitioner literature tends to tout advantages' but that real 'benefits are contingent on implementation factors such as training and the overall utility of the system' (Adams, Todd and Nelson, 1993: p.13). How new communication technologies affect individual and organisation performance and how people treat one another in the long term, needs deeper understanding and further research.

Conclusion

In Plato's (1997) *The Phaedara,* the usefulness of a new technology, the written word, was explained to the Pharaoh, by its creator, Theuth, the Egyptian god of invention, in the following manner:

> '...this invention, O King, will make the Egyptians wiser and will improve their memories; for it is an elixir of wisdom and memory that I have discovered'. However, Thomas, the Pharaoh, replied: 'Most ingenious Theuth, one man has the ability to beget arts, but to judge of their usefulness or harmfulness to their users belongs to another; and now you who are the father of letters may have been led by your affection to ascribe to them a power the opposite of that which they really possess. For this invention will produce forgetfulness in the minds of those who learn to use it, because they will not practice their memory'.

In a similar vein to Pharaoh and Theuth, Sproull and Kiesler (1991: p.3) postulate that the new forum for communication created by information technologies also creates a new social situation that is impoverished in social cues and shared experience as electronically-mediated 'messages are likely to show less social awareness'. They argue that 'the advantage is that social posturing and sycophancy decline. The disadvantage is that so, too, does politeness and concern for others.' Thus, communication in IT-mediated environments, or 'virtual communities', increasingly suffers, from lack of 'social cues', because it is low on 'social presence'. However, at the same time, it can still be highly interactive and, therefore, amenable to many social uses.

Increasing population diversity, technological innovation, resource conflict and credibility gaps make communication more complex, difficult and essential; triggering more attenuation by scholars and practitioners alike. The emphasis on communication technology, the 'high-tech' side, and on interpretation, the 'high-touch' side, needs to shift to more salient elements of communication in particular contexts in order to harness benefits of 'high-tech' and 'high-touch' interaction. Research shows that in contemporary organisations, the impact of communication is crucial in determining what lies within the scope of organisational communication, rather than the type of channel used to convey a message. This very issue of the impact of the message and used channel to deliver and receive messages requires further understanding and research in organisational settings. Thus, before organisations embrace new channels of communications they need, among other things, to answer two crucial questions:

- What message is one trying to communicate (internally and externally)? and
- What behaviour is the organisation trying to promote?

In order to effectively choose and manage communications, there is a need for understanding how people in organisations generate communicative interactions, as much as how they are impacted by them. Scholars and practitioners must explore how organisational actors perceive IT-mediated communication and what they want from it, rather than what technology can do for them. Due to its unique capacity in establishing and maintaining multi-dimensional and *resilient* relationships (Schlenker, 1980; McKenney, Zack and Doherty, 1992), face-to-face dialogue is often the choice for difficult and ambiguous dialogue (McKenney, Zack and Doherty, 1992) and for specific personal relations in networking (Granovetter, 1985; Korac-Boisvert and Kouzmin, 1994) for crisis situations (Korac-Boisvert and Kouzmin, 1995a; 1995b).

In the organisational setting, communication is the mutual exchange of meanings between active participants. Complex organisations consists of many social and cultural groupings and communication between them is likely to involve not only shared meanings but also contradictory and contested ones, thus requiring value and conflict resolution (Selznick, 1957) as well as quality dialogue (Kakabadse, 1991). Further, participants in communication may be equally active in (re)producing meanings, but they frequently do so from positions of unequal power (Korac-Kakabadse and Kouzmin, 1997). Quality dialogue is a resonance between the beliefs and cultural experiences of the participants, expressed through a shared familiarity with the *codes* in use (Kouzmin, Leivesley and Carr, 1997). Irrespective of how actors develop, feedback is required to help individuals be more responsive to addressing *contingencies* within organisational *contexts* (Kakabadse and Myers, 1995a; 1995b), enabling them to negotiate and share understanding of contexts and, thus, through learning, transcend proclivities for 'cognitive failures' (Kouzmin and Jarman, 1989; Kouzmin and Korac-Boisvert, 1995).

Un-informed organisations, overly sensitive to 'other-oriented' managerialist actions (Kouzmin, Dixon and Wilson, 1995), are vulnerable to threats from the outside and missed opportunities within (Barnard, 1938; Selznick, 1957; Peres, 1968; Wick and Leon, 1995; Kouzmin, Korac-Kakabadse and Jarman, 1996). In learning organisations, information flows with speed and honesty between all organisational actors. Openness is a lynch-pin of an organisation's ability to scan and position itself in the market and political space. By equalising the power between leader and followers, leaders are often able to gather information about what really is going on instead of what they hope might be going on in organisations. Learning organisations structure themselves and utilise IT in a way that speeds the flow of internal information. They create cultural norms that place a high value on honesty, even in the face of difficulties. Instead of covering up problems, learning organisations make problems visible in order to encourage participation in finding solutions quickly (Wick and Leon, 1995).

Vulnerability management, on the other hand, requires long-range planning capabilities, strategic policy making capabilities, high quality generative learning and new ways of policy reasoning sensitive to 'formative contexts' (Dror, 1987; Unger, 1987; Korac-Boisvert and Kouzmin, 1995c; Garnett and Kouzmin, 1999). These requirements are continually limited 'by micro-issues dependent, on the main, on economic rationalism - lacking historical and comparative depth; ignoring psychological and communicative factors; and suffering from additional features such as limited and simplistic notions of rationality which make policy and planning in governance and crisis communication contexts narrow' (Dror, 1987: p.92).

Thus, although individuals and groups increasingly have a choice to select from a variety of available alternatives of media for communicating, their choice may not always be rationally based but socio-culturally based and sensitive to variety of communication incidents that emerge (Kouzmin and Korac-Kakabadse, 1999). Communication technologies influence, and are being influenced by, people's behaviour and their attitudes. Individuals and their formative context shape the use of communication technologies and, thus, their organisational effects. Although organisational actors are influenced by communication technology and their circumstances, they are not contingent on the technological frames and have a *choice* in the manner in which to use such frames.

Note

1   This chapter was presented at the 9th Annual BIT Conference on 'Business Information Technology Management – Generative Futures', Department of Business Information Technology, The Manchester Metropolitan University, Aytoun Campus, November 1999.

5 Current Trends in Internet Use: E-Communication, E-Information and E-Commerce

NADA K. KAKABADSE, ALEXANDER KOUZMIN AND
ANDREW K. KAKABADSE

Abstract

Rapid developments in the application and use of the Internet create new opportunities as well as the reformulation of 'older problems'. This chapter reviews current trends in Internet use, realising that this is a 'snap-shot' subject to rapid obsolescence.

The chapter[1] clarifies the origins of the Internet and the World Wide Web, critically canvasses what is on the Internet and focuses upon the broadening opportunities for E-commerce - incorporating E-channels and E-marketing. More importantly, the chapter highlights emerging problems of Internet abuse, intrusions into privacy and the need for global management of the Internet at a time of increasing exposure and vulnerability of many stakeholders finding themselves dependent on, or addicted to, the Internet.

Introduction

In the late 1920s, John Maynard Keynes, the British economist, wrote that the globalisation or integration of the world economy to ordinary British people seemed 'normal, certain and permanent' (Keynes, 1981). Although globalisation today differs significantly from that of the gold-standard period (1870-1913), as the speed and complexity of 'virtual' transactions are incomparably greater, the situation at the end of the 20th century seems to be similar to that of the late 1920s. However, it remains to be seen whether the surge of the contemporary version of the earlier *laissez-faire* ideology, market fundamentalism, will prove to be as unsustainable within increased globalisation; the basic dilemma being that expanding and freewheeling global markets, and the rapid demise of sovereign national states, are both facilitated by the proliferation of information technology (IT), which spans time and space - exemplified by the Internet.

Like its progenitor, paper, invented by Ts'ai Lun, in China, in AD 105, the Internet also breaks the barriers of time and distance and permits unprecedented growth of opportunities. Although, the Internet is not a society, nor a communication method, nor a market, for many of its users it provides all these and more. The Net or the Internet, BITNET, FIDOnet, UUCPnet, and other physical networks, are an infrastructure that facilitates the creation of all these concepts for those who access it.

It is well known that the Net was originally conceived, in the 1960s, as a military project supervised by the Department of Defense's Advanced Research Project Agency (ARPA), created during the Cold War as an information system capable of surviving a Soviet nuclear attack (Miller, S.1996).

The Net grew in the 1960s when ARPA began research on the development and testing of computer communications networks that would conserve funds by avoiding duplication of computer resources. Those same features of decentralisation and flexibility that would make it militarily invulnerable contributed to giving rise to the Internet of today: an international, chaotic, dense bazaar inhabited by all kinds of people. The project attempted to connect incompatible mainframe computers and was named the ARPA Computer Network (ARPANET) - it had two major objectives (*The Economist*, 1995):

- To develop techniques and obtain experience in inter-connecting computers in such a way that a very broad class of interactions were possible; and
- To improve, and increase, computer research productivity through resource sharing.

The ARPANET was a success story and its lasting contribution was to demonstrate how a backbone infrastructure could serve as a connection between gateways (part of a computer programmed to receive messages from one network and transfer these onto another network). Furthermore, E-mail was seen as a source of major productivity increase. By 1983, the ARPANET officially shifted from using NCP (Network Control Programme) to TCP/IP (Transmission Control Protocol/Internet Protocol). A key point to TCP/IP's success was its simplicity. The ease and simplicity of operating over various platforms accounted for its continued existence as a *de facto* standard for the Internet up to the present time.

The ARPANET was supplemented by CSnet and, eventually, replaced by the US government funding of its successor, NSFnet. Both CSnet and NSFnet were created by the US Government in response to research scientists' and professors' petition to the National Science Foundation (NSF) for similar connectivity. The NSFnet was also created to provide access to the five supercomputers in the computing centres around the country. The NSFnet became the US backbone for the global network known as the Internet and provided an alternative route for the distribution of Usenet (*The Economist*, 1995).

The original prototype networks, ARPAnet in the USA, the network of the National Physical Laboratory in the United Kingdom, CYCLADES in France and other networks around the world, paved the necessary physical infrastructure for a fertile social network to develop. The Internet, BITNET, FIDOnet, other physical networks, the Usenet, VMSnet and other logical networks, have rapidly grown and a critical mass of people and interests have been reached (*The Economist*, 1995).

The initial intention was to produce an easy method of communicating with other users at the same site - to share local bulletin boards and global communication. Usenet grew as a grassroots connection of people. The gateway of ARPANET mailing lists into Usenet attracted a wave of users. These users became attracted to Usenet when two ARPANET mailing lists, SF-LOVERS and HUMAN-NETS, began to appear on Usenet. These lists provided interesting material and discussion, paralleling France's Telecom success with Minitel, which became popular only when Minitel users, serendipitously, discovered that they could have live and *anonymous* conversations with other users.

Similar to the ARPANET, NSFnet was a constant connection run over leased lines. One of the ways Netnews is distributed is by using the NNTP protocol over Internet connections, allowing for both the Netnews and E-mail to be distributed quickly over a large area. Internet connections also assist in carrying Usenet and E-mail internationally. The Internet class networks and connections include established government, university and business-sponsored connections. However, individuals are connected at home via phone lines and various versions of UUCP. For example, even as late as 1992, when 60 per cent of Usenet traffic was carried over the Internet via the instantaneous Network Transport Protocol (NNTP), 40 per cent of Usenet was still carried through the slower UUCP connections. There are still many examples of various types of connections using UUCP - by users at the 'fringe', for example. However, there is also a growing number of commercial services which, for a fee, provide connections for electronic mail and Usenet access, as well as access to the Internet provided an individual has a computer modem (that device that sits between the computer and telephone line, translating data into the digital form, to send and receive digital form to text so that it can be displayed on the monitor in a readable form) and the telephone connection.

An account with an Internet Service Provider (ISP), such as American On-line (AOL) and CompuServe, gives an individual access to the Internet and sets an individual E-mail address. Like other infrastructures, Internet operations and maintenance require resources which are not free. The Internet is operated, maintained and owned by MCI/Worldcom, SPRINT, UNET and many other multi-billion dollar companies. These companies maintain the backbone network of copper, fibre and satellite links on which all users 'piggyback'. Governments around the world, typically, own their own backbones, into which they 'tie' other backbones. This 'tie into process' is possible because protocols (TCP, IP, UDP, HTTP) were agreed which enabled individuals, companies or countries to join the Internet. This protocol is similar to the other two international protocols, POTS (plain old telephone service) which allows individuals to plug an analogue telephone into any country's analogue phone system and the worldwide standards for traffic signals (red/yellow/green).

Today, the Internet is an extremely complex network with thousands of geographically - dispersed networks including more than 100,000 individual computer networks owned by governments, corporations, universities and non-profit groups. The Internet is, effectively, a free form of global communication resource (Sharp, 1998). When an organisation connects its own private network, or Intranet, to the Internet, it must also manage, in addition to its own internal resources and people, other resources and people external to the organisation, greatly complicating network management.

However, there is a new Internet body, the Internet Co-operation For Assigned Names and Numbers (ICANN), which will gradually take over responsibility for co-ordinating technical tasks such as domain/name system management, IP address space allocation, protocol parameter assignment co-ordination and root/server system management. In the past, the US Government, with groups such as the Internet Assigned Numbers Authority (IANA) and Network Solutions, the company that has a monopoly on the registration of '.com', '.org', and '.net' generic top-level domains, was responsible for these tasks. The ICANN will take over these activities (Long, 1999).

There is no agreed-upon definition of the Internet, as it consists of a set of common protocols, a physical collection of routers and circuits, distributed resources and, even, a culture of connectivity and communications - a massive global network of inter-connected, packet-switched computer networks. The Internet requires synthesis of three perspectives: a network of networks, based on the TCP/IP protocols; a community of people who use and develop those networks; and a collection of resources that can be reached from those networks (Krol and Hoffman, 1993).

Some applications on the Internet (personal homepages) represent 'narrow-casting' in the extreme, with content created by consumers and for consumers. As a marketing and advertising medium, the Web has the potential to change, radically, the way firms do business with their customers - by blending together publishing and real-time communication, broad-cast and narrow-cast.

Internet Use

The size of the Internet user population is currently smaller than its extensive publicity might lead people to believe - however, it is growing. European Internet consultancy, Nua, has estimated that there are 153.25 million Internet users, of which 1.14 million are in Africa, 26.55 million in Asia/Pacific, 33.39 million Europe, 0.078 million in the Middle East, 87 million in USA and Canada and 4.5 million in the South America (*Asiaweek*, 1999b). Whilst there were 56 million Internet users in the USA, alone, in 1998, it is projected that by 2002 that this number will grow to 137.5 million users (IDC, 1998).

This eclectic collection of individuals adds to the interests and specialities of the whole Net community. Like its predecessor, the telephone, the Internet has a range of uses (and abuses), of which three aspects are most prominent:

- Communications (E-mail, chat rooms);
- Information provision; and
- Electronic commerce (for example, marketing, shopping and/or banking).

Similarly, when the telephone was first invented, it was used for relaying live concerts - then, large companies adopted it. Slowly, the general public came to use it, first from post offices and drugstores, then from their own homes. Now billions of pounds change hands via telephone sales and even more through TV sales. However, the rate of growth in Internet use outstrips all previous similar consumer and business media technologies such as radio, TV and cable (Bray, 1997). But, as Internet use grows, so does the amount of fraud due to the cheap and efficient reach to large numbers of people.

What is on the Net?: Information or What?

Prototype community network systems are forming around the world - exemplified by Cleveland Free-Net, Wellington Citynet, Santa Monica Public Electronic Network (PEN), Berkeley Community Memory Project, Hawaii FYI and National Capital Free-Net. Access to these community systems is as easy as visiting the community library and membership is open to all who live in the community. In addition to the living body of resources this diversity of 'Netizens' represents, there is also a growing body of digitised data that forms another body of resources. These span from digitising 'great' literature of the past, exemplified by the otherwise obscure Gutenberg Project, and Project Bartleby, gathering non-mainstream material such as various religions, unusual hobbies, gay lifestyles and fringe activities. As an operational model of distributed computing, the 'Net' supports:

- Discussion groups (USEnet news, moderated and unmoderated mailing lists);
- Multi-player games and communications systems (MUDs, irc, chat, MUSEs);
- File transfer (ftp) and remote login (telnet);
- Electronic mail ('E-mail'); and
- Global information access and retrieval systems (archie, veronica, gopher and the World Wide Web).

One can find on the Net Usenet; Free-Net; E-mail; library catalogues; ftp (file transfer protocol) sites; remote computing logging facilities; free software; electronic newsletters; electronic journals; multi-user Domain/Dungeon (mud)/mush/moo; Internet Relay Chat (IRC); the multimedia World Wide Web (WWW) with global information access and retrieval systems; variety of data banks; multi-player games and communication systems; and discussion groups and much more.

The Internet's strength is the network's ability to tame massive amounts of data and make it easily searchable (Sandberg, 1998). Different servers, such as WWW, WAIS and gophers attempt to order and make utilising the vast variety and widespread information easier by the provision of Net 'browser' or 'search engines' - the computer programme that allows an individual to send, and view, information such as Microsoft's Internet Explorer or Netscape's Navigator.

For a geographically-sparse group, the Internet allows users to share news and communicate with each other, giving a sense that there is a community with things happening, whilst an associated 'ftp site' allows art and text to be distributed. In the area of information provision, Nets have helped, enormously, in the dissemination of information from individuals, knowledgeable in certain areas, and specialised repositories, difficult to obtain otherwise. However, the millions of page information on the Net can make locating useful information, and enjoyable stops at Web sites, hard work.

The Internet and Web Sites: Anarchy or a New Information Freedom?

The World Wide Web has grown dramatically since its inception by Tim Berners-Lee, as well as the use to which the Web has been put. Once simply a means of accessing information stored across various platforms, the Web is now a widely-used medium for communication (Jackson, 1997). The hypertext system and the link are the essence of the World Wide Web. The link is a mechanism through which information can be passed across, otherwise incompatible, systems, platforms and networks. Berners-Lee (1990) conceptualised and led the development of the World Wide Web at the CERN - the European Laboratory for Particle Physics in 1990. Berners-Lee (1990) envisaged that the new system must allow any sort of information to be entered. Another person must be able to find the information, sometimes without knowing what he/she is looking for (Berners-Lee, 1990).

Acknowledging the philosophical vision of hypertext, Berners-Lee's (1990) proposal focused on the development of a system sensitive to the CERN context, which would be capable of the following:

• Accommodating a network of heterogeneous systems;

- Operating without any central control or co-ordination;
- Providing access to existing databases;
- Allowing 'private' links, to and from, 'public' information;
- Having a minimum of 'bells and 'whistles';
- Supporting data analysis; and
- Supporting links to 'live,' non-static data.

Thus, the software for *storing* information was separated from the software for *displaying* information, constructing the concept of the 'browser' and the notion of client-defined, rather than server-defined, information displays. Web users could construct their own documents, on their own systems, to link to various material accessible to the 'Web,' but they could not modify documents 'owned' by other users or other systems (Jackson, 1997). The original vision of the hypertext ideal of completely inter-locking text was abandoned, as was the notion of the undetermined path. The hypertext vision, independent of any specific technological implementation, is of information perceived by the user to be joined into a single document with each user being able to wander according to his/her own interests and motivations. Instead, well-planned links allow the user to reach specific information efficiently. Notwithstanding that the Web is also incomplete, it is hard to imagine that all possible links could be put in by authors, compared to the small number of links sufficient for getting from one site to another in the smallest number of stops (Berners-Lee and Cailliau, 1990).

Currently, there is no central repository of material accessible by Web browsers, which means that authors have no way of knowing of other documents to which they might link. There is no signed agreement that owners must make their information accessible, to all, for all time (Jackson, 1997). Documents on the Web are owned. Whoever owns such documents may elect to remove them from the Web, at any time, change their location or their name-creating 'dead links' in other documents that point to specified material. It is possible to have a completely self-contained and closed set of documents never accessible because no other documents link to them (Jackson, 1997). Divisions on the Web are identified by the phrase 'Web site,' denoting territory or property. Currently, the techniques practised by Web site owners is that they continually change their information so that people will want to re-visit. They also form alliances with other site owners and agree to link to one another in 'Web rings.' This empire-building technique undoubtedly will continue to grow (Jackson, 1997).

To the user, the 'World Wide Web' facilitates the movement of the user from one document, commonly called 'pages' or 'URLs', to another. Technically, however, the Web facilitates movement of documents from a server to a client computer, preserving issues of ownership, boundaries and territory (Jackson, 1997). To the increasing numbers of Web 'squatters' who want to entice users to return to, and stay within, their 'site' (the collection of documents over which an owner has complete control), the Web is a collection of destinations. Since these sites are increasingly in competition with each other for user attention, in the emerging commercial world of the Internet, one Web site might have to pay another in order for the second to establish a link to the first (Jackson, 1997).

The leading internet service provider (ISP), American On-line (AOL), with a market value more than General Motors, has more than 15 million subscribers and expects to command millions more with its acquisition of Netscape's popular Netcenter 'portal' - a 'launch pad' for exploring the Internet (*The Economist*, 1999a). The other elite Internet pioneers, Amazon (worth more than all America's bookstores, including Barnes and Noble and Borders, put together) and Yahoo (the aristocrat of the Internet, with a market capitalisation of over US$30 billion, and most visited site with 167 million page views a day), have also acquired blue-chip status with Internet enthusiast, creating pre-eminent Internet brands and defining the markets they inhabit.

The competition amongst ISPs is intense, ranging from existing and upcoming portals, which include Yahoo; AOL.com; AltaVista; Excite; Infoseek; Lycos; MSN.com; Netcenter and Snap. Portal sites provide search services and additional features that often include news; stocks; games, chat, free E-mail, free Web space, appointment diaries, directories, shopping and personalised start-up pages; whilst non-portal sites are destinations in themselves. Furthermore, portal sites are continuously adding new features such as private clubs, city guides and personalised features for users which are then matched by competitors - with Excite and Yahoo leading the pack (Branscum, 1998). For example, Yahoo's progress from search engine to content aggregator has been phenomenal. Whatever Yahoo provides, has been either copied or previously offered by rivals such as Excite, Lycos, Netcenter and MSN (*The Economist*, 1998). Excite's private club, www.excite.com/communities, provides a shared-group calendar, contact list, a discussion area for posting and responding to messages, a photo area and a live chat room. Similar facilities are provided by Yahoo's My Club Area (www.clubs.yahoo.com) (Branscum, 1998). However, none of the well-known portals have tried to make themselves distinctive by appealing to a particular group in the way that most other media do, preferring to be all things to all people (*The Economist*, 1998). Yahoo provides interest directories such as Yhooligans (www.yahooligans.com) for children and Seniors Guide (www.seniors.yahoo.com) which caters to the over-50 group. Although My Yahoo (www.my.yahoo.com) allows users to personalise the site in many ways, it takes time to customise a portal to ones own taste, making switching tiresome (*The Economist*, 1998).

However, there are also 'vertical portals' or 'central hubs', better known as 'hubs'. Whilst portals link to the whole Internet, hubs link only to sites in a chosen area - such as history, medicine, football or some other major area of interest. While there are half of dozen or so portals, there are hundreds of hubs. There are also 'destination sites' or 'content sites' which hold real information and of which portals and hubs make real use. Although it appears that portals are consolidating, the Internet is not shrinking (American On-line has taken-over CompuServe, Netscape, Mirabilits ICQ and MovieFone) as it is the destination sites that actually make the whole information provision aspect of Internet worthwhile.

E-Commerce: E-Channels and E-Marketing

The terms 'electronic commerce' and 'E-commerce' are simply references to business transacted by electronic means. Via electronic media, suppliers can advertise goods and services, customers can make purchase enquiries and arrange sales and payments. In the case of goods such as software and publishing, electronic delivery of goods and after-sale service are possible. The strategic importance and viability of electronic channels to market has been a continuing subject of debate for over two decades (Reynolds and Davis, 1988; Hoffman and Novak, 1995; Evans and Wurster, 1997; Peterson, 1997; Cavanaugh, 1998). Whilst adoption of on-line and Internet use is considered the most extensive challenge facing marketers today, effective usage is likely to lend itself to fundamental change in the nature of consumer behaviour. Research suggests that technology has overtaken the marketing industry's ability to exploit it (Reed, 1997). Organisations are now lagging behind in the generation of ideas and ways of doing business utilising the capabilities offered by IT. Moreover, many enterprises believe that innovative and successful application of electronic marketing and commerce will expand markets, motivate customers to pay higher prices and/or reduce costs of supply and overheads through greater competition.

The range of channels for electronic commerce and marketing are broad - each impacts, in a varied way, on consumer behaviour. Available channels are radio; television (both one-way and two-way transmission); computers and computer-based technologies (including databases); telephone and telephone-based technologies; facsimile machines; videography; CD-ROM technologies; interactive kiosks; electronic ticket machines; pagers; optical scanners; and smart cards.

It is now broadly accepted that the Web needs to engage users through effective information provision and that consumers need to be attracted to Web sites by innovative means. Commercial Union, for example, used its sponsorship of the popular television programme, 'London's Burning', to attract potential consumers to its financial service sites. Moreover, it is also important to integrate new electronic channels within an overall marketing strategy. A primary decision for a retailer is to determine whether its marketing assets are directly transferable to an electronic channel (Reynolds, 1994). Web sites, for example, publicised as an automated response to telephone calls, highlighted that advertisements can be used as effective information or sales channels (*Journal of Advertising Research*, 1997). In one of the early UK shopping sites, Barclay Square, the Innovations (catalogue shopping) Web site was reported to receive up to 5,000 visits a day, while the Argos site, also in Barclay Square, received 'little interest' (Miller, R., 1996). On examination, it was revealed that this was a direct consequence of Innovations including the Web address on all promotional material, which Argos failed to do (Miller, R., 1996).

The International Benchmarking Study carried out, in 1996, by the Department of Trade and Industry, found that 19 per cent of all UK businesses had established Web sites, but that only 12 per cent of them were using Web sites for on-line sales. The majority were treating their sites as experimental and not as key marketing channels (UK Department of Trade and Industry, 1997). The fundamental question marketers need to address is whether any Internet presence is to be purely informational, transactional in nature (value-added retail products and services designed for electronic environment, facilitate easier shopping of essential goods and services and improve the quality of shopping of non-essential goods and services) (Reynolds, 1994) or derivative. Marketing journals report that, at present, much of the money spent on advertising for on-line services is generated from research and development budgets, not marketing (*Journal of Advertising Research*, 1997). A lack of marketing focus could mean that high-potential innovations fail to be exploited or that diffusion is slowed by a failure to address the immaturity of markets. Indeed, some notable multimedia innovations are believed to have succeeded precisely because they were driven by marketing, not IT, departments. It is also important to integrate new electronic channels within an overall marketing strategy that takes consideration of each economy's political, economic, social and technological context. In the UK, for example:

- Political: UK government services make extensive use of 'back office' information systems, but few offer direct interactive use for consumers, thus creating an opportunity to outsource services to the private sector;
- Economic: In the UK, like the US, an over supply of goods and services has led to a breakdown of divisions between previously separate industries, thus opening new opportunities for business using electronic channels and leading to reduced costs of market entry and enhancing the influence of customers'
- Socio-cultural: Consideration should be given to those products and services which can successfully be sold electronically, such as commodity items and banking services, bearing in mind that other items remain more effectively sold by traditional channels.
- Technological: For effective E-commerce, consideration needs to be given to the comprehensive use of the following sophisticated technologies:
  - Web-Enabled Lead Collection, whereby a Web home page facility collects customer information (with the customers's permission and privacy provisions) and provides up-to-date service facilities to potential customers;
  - User-Friendly Marketing Information Browsers (Web browsers) integrated with sales and marketing information systems;
  - Internet Data Synchronisation Database and Replication Technologies that allow field staff to easily and rapidly synchronise laptop databases with corporate databases through dial-up modem connections;
  - Internet-Working Computing or Corporate Client/Server Applications that operate in real-time on the Internet;
  - Internet-Working, or Virtual Computing, which allows for detailed information on requests for product and services previously mass marketed (for example, providing individual measurements and design for tailor-made Levi jeans).

Ignoring these considerations is likely to be detrimental as change in technologies and services is occurring rapidly. The forthcoming introduction of digital interactive television and of the 'cashless (electronic) purse' using 'smart cards', both of which have been trialed in recent years and have began to be rolled out in late 1998, are likely to have considerable impact. The changes are expected to drive on-line banking, E-shopping and new ways of accessing the Internet and may further alter broadcasting from a mass to one-to-one communications medium (Reed, 1997). Thus, whilst retailers have an opportunity to take the initiative in designing the future, their initiative is contingent on the retailers' supply-chain economy within electronic channels and by the ability to re-position their asset base (Reynolds, 1994).

E-Commerce and Issues For On-Going Consideration

The most rapid developments are occurring on that portion of the Internet known as the World Wide Web (WWW). The WWW is a distributed hypermedia environment within the Internet which allows multimedia information to be located on a network of servers, around the world, which are inter-connected, allowing one to travel through the information by clicking on hyperlinks. Any hyperlink (text, icon or image in a document) can point to any document anywhere on the Internet. The user-friendly, consumer-oriented homepages of the WWW utilise the system of hyperlinks to simplify the task of navigating among the offerings on the Internet.

The present popularity of the WWW as a commercial medium (in contrast to other networks on the Internet) is due to its ability to facilitate global sharing of information and resources and its potential to provide an efficient channel for advertising, marketing and, even, direct distribution of certain goods and information services.

The concept of integrated marketing holds appeal and promise for business efforts on the World Wide Web, because the Web offers enormous potential for developing customer relationships and customising the offering to individual customers. There are a number of functional categories of Commercial Web Pages. Each function can be considered as an element in an integrated marketing programme in the context of digital commerce. However, these are rapidly changing and some Web pages and links may have changed or disappeared altogether. Some of the current functions are presented below (Gaffin, 1994; Cleland, 1995; Donaton, 1995).

- On-line Storefront - Web sites offer direct sales through an electronic channel via an electronic catalogue or other, more innovative, formats;
- Internet Presence (Flat Ad, Image and Information) - Internet presence sites provide a virtual 'presence' for a firm and its offerings;
- Content (Fee-Based, Sponsored, Searchable Database) - Fee-Based content sites where the provider supplies and/or pays for content which the consumer pays to access. Sponsored content sites sell advertising space to reduce or eliminate the necessity of charging fees to visitors. In Searchable Database, merchants or advertisers pay a provider for information placement in an organised listing;
- Mall - The site typically constitutes a collection of on-line storefronts, each of which may contain many different categories of goods for sale and where the provider charges rent in exchange for virtual real-estate and may offer a variety of services to the storefront;
- Incentive Site - This represents a unique form of advertising that attracts a potential customer to a site. The objective is to *pull* the user to the commercial site behind it, thus helping marketers generate traffic to their Web sites;
- Search Agent - The purpose is to identify other Web sites, through keyword searches of a database, that extend throughout the Web. Software agents are used to generate and/or assist the search through the database.

Commercial Web site design usually include On-line Storefront sites, Internet Presence sites and Content sites and are rapidly changing.

At its broadest level, E-commerce can mean any use of electronic technology in any aspect of commercial activity. The National Information Infrastructure (NII) Task Force on electronic commerce more narrowly uses the term to mean the use of a national information infrastructure to perform any of the following functions (NTIA Office of the Assistant Secretary, 1995):

- Bring products to market (research and development via telecommunications);
- Match buyers with sellers (electronic malls, electronic funds transfer);
- Communicate with government in pursuit of commerce (electronic tax filings); and

- Deliver electronic goods (information).

With the speed of developments in E-commerce, constant attention will need to be given to segmentation and the ever-changing demographics of consumer groups (Schneider, 1997). Currently, Internet users tend to be comparatively wealthy people with families. If services are targeted exclusively to these segments of society, the attractions of purchasing IT and on-line facilities will remain strongest for these groups - to the exclusion of older and less wealthy segments. There is increasing evidence that the use of Internet and electronic services are already biased towards the younger-age group. However, neglecting older customers may even risk alienating a further, potentially, highly-profitable group (*Bankers Magazine*, 1997). A further risk is that the electronic delivery of government services will be slowed, as many potential users of those services could be IT 'have-nots'.

An alternative, more optimistic view is that the rapid uptake in recent years of the World Wide Web, in particular of E-mail, indicates that barriers to change may not be as rigid as some expected. Although men initially took to the technology, women, as key household purchasers and managers of domestic finances, are likely to be increasingly targeted. Whether older consumers will be similarly included remains to be seen. Overall, consumers of differing demographic profiles are increasingly becoming Internet users in the US and this is likely to occur in the UK, as well. A summary of the evolving forces of supply and demand driving such changes in consumer behaviour, is highlighted below.

The key aspects of technology change shaping consumer behaviour are:

- Production technology altering production processes and offering greater customisation and variety;
- Distribution technology and developments in logistics, electronic data inter-change, point-of-sale applications and automation; and
- Technology for personal use, where one can expect to experience the fastest gains in price-related performance.

The key changes in lifestyle and demographics are likely to be:

- Negative growth birth rates and rising median age in developed societies (older consumers tend to respond more favourably to relationship marketing approaches than do younger consumers);

- More women in the work force, leading to changes in families and households;
- Lifestyle, income and ethnic diversity;
- Increase in regional differences, both within and between societies;
- Increased stress as the nature of work changes;
- Greater concerns for privacy;
- Emphasis on safety and security; and
- Entrepreneurialism, giving rise to niche markets.

Whilst electronic channels for marketing in the US are, increasingly, gaining momentum, European-wide trends toward market fragmentation suggest that channels to markets which permit the more careful targeting of identifiable market segments, such as electronic channels, will represent a considerably more efficient business development strategy for retailers. Europe faces considerable debate over the technical obstacles to widespread domestic Internet usage, particularly over bandwidth or speed of connectivity. In the UK, for example, there has been considerable experimentation with retail Web sites. A number of retailers are responding to fragmented markets through technology with strategies to generate more information about their customers' behaviour, database marketing and loyalty schemes (OXIRM and KPMG, 1996).

In addition, home shopping channels in European homes, particularly Germany, Italy and France, have come much later then in the US. However, the growth of ISP in Europe, including American providers such as APL, CompuServe, and national ones such as those provided by telecom companies - BT in the UK and Telecom in France, provide a variety of choices for marketers. Electronic channels provide unrivalled opportunities for shifting from a mode of one-to-many marketing strategy and communication to a mode of one-to-one, with an immediate feedback opportunity in a strategy for closer monitoring of consumer behaviour (Reynolds and Davis, 1988). However, current practice by retailers across Europe is a complex, dynamic and somewhat serendipitous activity, as the user often discovers services by chance (OXIRM and KPMG, 1996).

Although commercial use of the Internet is rapidly expanding, doing business on the Internet raises a number of legal and cultural issues which must be considered by business (Bennet, 1998; Farrell, 1998).

- Retailing on the Web is currently tough, as the sheer pace of on-line change and E-market immaturity makes trading fragile. However, in considering opportunities for electronic commerce, retailers need to determine whether marketing assets are directly transferable to an electronic channel. If so, then retailers need to determine whether Internet activity needs to be purely informational or transactional in nature;

- Advertisement and competition laws vary across the continent and countries. In France, for example, any Web site that is specifically aimed at the French consumers, by law, must be in French. In Germany, two-for-the-price-of-one offers and gifts with purchase offers are illegal. In Sweden, toy advertisement may not be aimed at children. Language and culture increase the costs of engaging in cross-border commerce. The need to present national-language Web pages can be a barrier to entry into the ranks of successful E-commerce venture;

- Legal uncertainties in cross-border trade are considerable. Who is liable if a product is faulty? What are the consumers' rights if they do not like what they have bought and want to return the product? Which country's value-added tax (VAT) or consumers tax rate applies? Not only do VAT rates differ in various European countries but, also, that rate, applied to certain types of goods, may differ. For example, the UK has a fully competitive book market whereas in Germany book prices are fixed;

- Payment systems: In the UK, for example, paying by credit card or debit card is common and widespread. In Germany, cash-on-delivery is a popular payment method. Thus, German catalogue retailers will not sell to customers who do not have a delivery address in Germany or an account with a German bank. Euro-cheques are common on the European continent but almost non-existent in the UK. Furthermore, any cross-border payment transaction that is not carried out using either a credit card or a Euro-cheque involves lengthy and costly procedures, so much so that for most low-value consumer goods, the cost of paying may exceed the value of the item;

- Delivery of consumer goods: Free movement of goods and services is enshrined in the European Union law. However, freely and easily obtaining goods are often difficult. For example, it is still more costly to ship an item 30 miles across a frontier than to ship the same item 300 miles within the same country. In addition, there are issues with insuring shipment and liability of damage. While consumers can select anytime from a Web site and pay for it 'securely', it takes three weeks to get the goods cleared through customs, complete with the payment of import duties, discouraging repeat purchase. Similarly, small merchants in most countries do not have one-stop agencies that can help with customer formalities and other import-export regulations, leading to a reduction of profit margins after shipment of goods to purchase;

- Companies often pay too little attention to the differences in Internet uptake in the various European countries and elsewhere. The differences in telecommunications environments are a major determining factor in the development of on-line markets;

- The need for writing: One can carry out business and make legally-binding agreements via the Internet. However, where a document is required to be in writing or where a signature is required by legislation (for example wills and land transactions), electronic data and digital signatures may not suffice. In some cases, transactions via the Internet may, therefore, not be legally enforceable;

- Offers to the world: Although the Internet offers borderless business, it also encounters several problems. Sales of certain goods and services may be prohibited in parts of the world. Also, the size of the potential market may cause demand to exceed supply. Thus, designing a Web site that offers to provide goods or services whenever consumers respond, should be avoided;

- Acceptance of offer: Uncertainty currently exists as to where electronic acceptance of an offer occurs - when the E-mail of acceptance is posted or received? What constitutes 'postage' or 'acceptance' of E-mail also goes unresolved. This is important in that it determines when a contract has been formed between the parties and because the law of the country in which an offer is accepted usually governs the contract;

- Consumer Protection: Internet transactions potentially expose business to consumer protection legislation in all legal jurisdictions of the world, irrespective of a country's laws governing the contract. Litigation on this issue in the US has, to date, divided courts;

- Fear of the Internet's double threat, privacy and security, by business and consumers, has stunned E-commerce (Sandberg, 1998). Business has traditionally been conservative about the Net, fearing hackers and the loss of trade secrets. Consumers, fearing the same thing, are also wary of exposing sensitive private data, ranging from name and address to financial information. The Electronic Privacy Information Centre acknowledges reports of hackers spraying digital graffiti onto Web sites and software giants, such as Microsoft and Netscape, having to plug security flows being a common occurrence (Sandberg, 1998).

For example, in a single week in September 1998, the Web site of a leading political party in Sweden was hacked, software used by on-line auction houses in the US exposed thousands of credit-card numbers to theft and a group calling itself, 'Hacking for Girlies', papered digitised porn on *The New York Times'* site.

Because of the speed with which the Web has swept through organisations, many Web sites have been developed 'on the fly', thus without the effectiveness that a more methodical approach would have brought. Although this *ad-hoc* and decentralised approach created opportunities for innovation, it also generated particular problems. Opportunities created by the free form and decentralised development of corporate Web sites produced a wealth of creative solutions to Web problems and large and diverse Internet facilities. However, drawbacks are the proliferation of duplicative and unmaintained information. The challenge for information providers is to integrate information in a way that helps users be more effective in finding what they need. This may involve adopting standards for metatags, developing an internal content classification system, deploying layered search architectures and adapting other knowledge infrastructure components.

Balancing creativity and innovation with the need for levels of standardisation and control requires time spent building support and developing corporate plans, guidelines and strategies. Business units can be responsible for developing the content of the information, but the corporate IT unit needs to be responsible for security policies, encryption, infrastructure and network performance issues. With increasing information flow, there is a need for corporate information librarians to be involved in selecting and implementing the company-wide crawler and search engine, indexing and cataloguing major content sites and over-seeing the process for authenticating Web sites. The value of library expertise in information retrieval, in cataloguing and indexing is increasingly more important in the Web context. Increasingly, librarians are seen as a strategic asset. As a result, librarians are likely to be asked to participate in cross-functional teams where their expertise would not have previously been sought.

E-Commerce on the Net

The Net has become a bizarre bazaar - for some, a global yard sale, for others, a mega-mall - accessible for the cost of a dial-up account and some Web software. People now, have the ability to pawn or purchase goods worldwide. For others this is an inaccessible dream or a frightening alternative for shopping. Retailing on the Web is tough, as firms are fragile due to their relative immaturity and the sheer pace of on-line change; exemplified by broadband cable systems and the move towards free Internet access, again, illustrated by the Freeserver and ISP, by Dixon, a British electronic retailer, and Energies, a telecom company. Furthermore, with falling prices of fibre-optics, the network bandwidth (capacity) is becoming incredibly cheap and, in a few years, the Internet will be piped through the offices and homes like other utilities such as the electricity and water supply (*Journal of Advertising Research*, 1997; Reed, 1997), signalling further jockeying amongst portal ISPs for market share.

However, Net advertising spending by industry continues to grow according to the Inter Media Advertising Solution Report which suggests that the top 25 industries, of 400 surveyed, increased their on-line advertising spending 86.7 per cent over the first three quarters in 1998, compared with the same period of previous year (Flynn, 1999). Although on-line advertisements accounted for 1.5 per cent of overall advertisement budget, close analysis shows that the highest spending, 17.3 per cent, was within computer and software industries. Internationally, Microsoft was the top individual spender on Internet advertising, during 1998, followed by IBM and Excite (Flynn, 1999). The fastest growing industries were pharmaceuticals, government organisations, direct response companies, retail and financial services (Flynn, 1999). Advertisement sales based on key words account for about a quarter of the advertising revenue generated by portal and search sites, such as Excite (Flynn, 1999). However, selling advertising access to so-called key words, so that their banner ads appear near certain search results, based on key words such as a competitor's brand name, is widespread in the Internet business, often ending in lawsuits in the US and challenging some fundamental assumptions of Internet advertising. A search on 'Amazon' on the Lycos search engine, for example, may display an ad for the Amazon.com bookseller's chief rival, Barnes and Noble. To find out how widely their names are being used in keyword purchases, companies can use a free service, Bannerstake (www.namestake.com), to display ads associated with their names (Flynn, 1999).

Despite potential threats, a growing number of transactions are performed on the Internet. Companies trading computers and accessories are doing well (for example, www.cdw.com, www.necx.com, www.isn.com). Similarly, whilst most traditional mass media have regulated pornography to their peripheries, the Internet has given 'smut-viewing a new lease on lust' (Sandberg, 1998). Commerce which plays to the Internet's strength as a communications medium also does well, such as on-line auctions (for example, www.onsale.com, www.ebay.com). Users, who bid for goods posted on-line, can view other buyers' comments and banter as they bid, as well as indulge in on-line brokering (for example, www.discoverbrokerage.com, www.schwab.com, www.etrade.com). Goods already familiar to consumers tend to do well on-line. For example, Amazon.com has rocketed from obscurity to the fourth largest bookseller in America in three years. A similar case is with CD stores. Buying a car (for example, www.autobytel.com, www.carpoint.com), shopping for financial services and booking traveller reservations (www.travelocity.com, www.priceline.com) are among the more mature segments of electronic commerce (Sandberg, 1998). The more commodified the product, the simpler it is to sell on the Internet.

Luxury goods, apart from hard-to-find collectibles, however, do not take well to the sight-unseen nature of on-line buying (Sandberg, 1998). To date, E-commerce has been built on the assumption that customers desire something in particular, such as a book on marketing, where the E-shopper can browse the Net for a particular book title or general marketing book. The very act of 'clicking on' a site before it can be seen, involves a degree of intention that is alien to many traditional shoppers (Auchincloss, 1998). Although many shoppers may have a shopping list, once in a store, inspiration often takes over and serendipity and unexpected discovery often provide the greatest satisfaction. Further utilisation of other senses, such as feel and smell, play important roles, in addition to the social experience of being in the shopping mall. Stroking a cashmere cardigan or smelling a bar of soap adds to shopping charm (Auchincloss, 1998). E-commerce assumes that shopping is a rational exercise, rather than a realm where false hopes, changed minds and sudden enthusiasm reign supreme (Blythe, 1997; Auchincloss, 1998).

Although on-line shopping has captured the imagination of the public, Internet transactions do not currently represent significant proportions of electronic transactions (Miller, 1997). The most prevalent forms of E-commerce used to date are business-to-business electronic commerce (B2B). In Australia, for example, in 1997, business-to-consumers Internet transactions accounted for only AUD$55 million of the AUD$16 trillion of electronic transactions completed in Australia. B2B E-commerce in Europe follows a similar trend. It is expected to grow from US $126 million, in 1997, to more than US $5 billion, in 2002, whilst B2B E-commerce will expand from US $1 billion, in 1997, to more than US $30 billion, in 2001. Although B2B E-commerce is still predominately done via 'closed systems', requiring proprietary software and private networks, such as Electronic Data Interchange (EDI), Automated Teller Machines and EFTPOS, there is an growing uptake of B2B via the Internet. This is especially amongst small and medium-sized companies which cannot afford the high costs of private networks considering that Internet solutions can be the simplest and least expensive to implement. However, currently, these solutions suit users whose needs are flexible in response to the Internet's variable speed. File size and network traffic affect the route and speed of devices, making delivery times somewhat unpredictable. The bandwidth also is dependent, or unpredictable, because the data route cannot be prescribed or predicted. Speed or rate of throughput is determined by the slowest of the networks and unpredictably routes 'packets' through different alternative paths to the final destination at the receiving site.

The Internet depends on the telephone companies' wires and fibres for transporting digital traffic (and, in some cases, satellite links). Compression software and increased bandwidth have potential to make Web-to-Web options an effective solution for data and time intensive customer applications in the near future. The Internet provides an 'open system' of E-commerce, involving the use of open networks, accessible by anyone, to complete transactions. Forester Research, a technology consultancy, expects worldwide, B2B, Internet transactions to double, in 1999, to US$109 billion, six times the forecast for on-line business to consumer sales (Erikson, 1999). They predict, that, by 2003, Internet retail sales in the US will be in the vicinity of US$108 billion as 40 million American households make purchases on-line. However, considering that the total value of American retail sales in 1998 was around US$1.7 trillion, with estimated on-line retail sales US$7.8 billion, it means that, by 2003, on-line retail sales will represent five per cent of trade (*The Economist*, 1999a). A September 1998 report by the Organisation for Economic Co-operation (OECD) stated that during 1997 only US$26 billion changed hands on-line, being 0.5 per cent of retail sales in the OECD's seven largest economies (Sandberg, 1998). Most of this came from B2B revenue. The percentage of E-commerce in Europe and other continents is even more anaemic (Sandberg, 1998).

Internet Abuse

Internet has magical and frightening opportunities as it frees the imagination from the everyday world. On-line context can remove people from a proper understanding of reality and of the proper tests for trust (Lacayo, 1993), as it is difficult to verify people's identity and connect on-line with real life. It is persuasive, far-reaching and clandestine (Lacayo, 1993). The Internet community, or the virtual community that is supported by global connectivity (global computer network), consists of Net users who exist as citizens of the world and are called, by some, 'netizens' (Net citizens). Although the Internet is a cheap and efficient way to reach a large number of people, quickly, there are those who take advantage of these efficiencies to carry out security fraud (Neuman, 1995). As the Internet grows, so the amount of fraud grows. The US Federal Trade Commission (FTC), for example, receives as many as 1,500 complaints a day in relation to the Internet fraud and that number is reported as being on the increase (James, 1998). It is also important for the Web site's front to mesh effectively with its back-office business systems. The new connectivity creates new value chains and new sources of competitive advantage, as well as new *vulnerabilities*. The emerging global connectivity presents not only a threat to established ways of working, but also presents new opportunities and new risks (James, 1998).

Using the Internet as a getaway to on-line trading databases, hackers can transfer money into their trading accounts, a crime previously limited primarily to banks. There are other, more subtle dangers; hackers do use the intimate details of various customers' financial positions to direct their own investments (James, 1998). Furthermore, because it is easy to set up and publicise a stock offering on the Internet, criminals can mount a stock scam at a fraction of the cost it would take to do so via traditional methods. The new medium allows them to commit crimes cheaply, immediately, efficiently and worldwide, right from their living rooms (James, 1998).

Currently, it is easy to impersonate others on-line, making the Internet a hothouse atmosphere for fraud (Hamilton, 1999). The best example is the method of connecting to file repositories, via FTP (file transfer protocol), by logging in as an 'anonymous' user. Most, if not all, World Wide Web Sites, Wide Area Information Systems (WAIS) and gopher sites are open to all users of the Net. Some think that there is a need for a system of certified electronic 'signatures', administered by a trusted third party, that are *almost* impossible to be faked. This strategy is adopted by Scandinavian and Hong Kong Post, operating as digital certification authorities. Cybershopping is still in its infancy; even in the US, shady practice is common. Examples of misleading advertising, inaccurate billing and orders never arriving are overwhelming (Withmore, 1999). The Internet is a new technology and rather than taking advantage of the Net's inter-activity to enhance customer service, many retailers have used the Net to lower costs and the number of staff. Often, incompetence poses a greater risk than fraud, with overpaying and double-charging being typical mistakes (Withmore, 1999).

The creation of the 'Dominion of Melchizedek' may serve as a harbinger of more to come in a field where today's law-enforcement officials are yet to develop expertise. Melchizedek, variously situated in Antarctic, the Pacific and, even, the Carpatian Mountains of Central Europe, exists only in cyberspace, (www.melchizedek.com), (Lintner, 1998). It made a brief foray into physical reality with arrests of its creators in November 1998. The Dominion of Melchizedekon, on the Web site, was offering a wide range of services, including passports, banking facilities, university degrees, lawyer's certificates and a virtual stock exchange (Lintner, 1998). In January 1998, the 'dominion' even managed to have the immigration authorities in both Singapore and Malaysia respond favourably to a letter asking whether a 'Melchizedek passport holder' needed a visa to visit those two countries. In the same month, the Asia-Pacific Parliamentarian's Union, in Taipei, issued a statement recommending observer status for Melchizedek, unaware that it is not an actual country, merely a virtual one (Lintner, 1998). The Australian Federal Police's Transaction Report and Analysis Centre stated in its most recent report that fighting 'cybercrime' will be the most important challenge of the 21st century (Lintner, 1998).

Privacy concerns are increasing as an elaborate electronic record is kept on E-shoppers with their likes and dislikes (Levy, 1998). The customer information helps Web retailers to mimic the intimacy some consumers have with local stores, as it lets them target their customers with sharply-targeted E-mail instead of onerous 'spam' or unsolicited cyberjunk mail (Levy, 1998). Consumers are actually asked if they would like these intimate relationships to take place. Some of the information is needed to allow devices to interact and get guarantee security, trisections, copyright protection or similar conveniences. Some digital identifiers can be used by marketers who want to build customer profiles by a totalitarian regime interested in persecuting those trafficking in 'wrong' ideas (Schenker, 1999). For example, news of strife in Indonesia's East Timor, through an independent 'virtual East Timor', has been assaulted by, allegedly, Indonesian government-backed hackers (*Asiaweek*, 1999c), despite the fact that Dublin Internet Service Provider (ISP), named Connect-Ireland, established the site with the backing of East Timorese 1996 Nobel peace prize winners, Bishop Carlos Belo and Jose Ramos Horta. A sophisticated hacker attack, coming from computer servers in Canada, Australia, the US and Japan forced Connect-Ireland to shut down it service (*Asiaweek*, 1999c).

'Cookies' are digital identification tags that track consumers as they page through Web sites and enable site operators to compile a portrait of a user's interest and, even, financial status (Schenker, 1999). Although dirty E-mails can be deleted, filtered or ignored, the big worry for Net users is the potential for cyberspace harassment to cross into real life (Manktelow, 1999). In the US, the first cyberstalker has been charged with stalking and harassment on the Internet, computer fraud and solicitation for rape (Driscoll, 1999). In the UK, Novell, one of the world's leading providers of network software, began researching computer 'spam', unsolicited electronic junk mail, in an effort to estimate the cost to business in terms of time and money wasted (Driscoll, 1999). Spam now makes up about ten per cent of all E-mail around the world (Hagell and Singer, 1999). As a spin-off from their research, they uncovered an alarming number of women, 41 per cent of regular Net users, who said that they had been sent pornographic material or had been harassed or stalked on the Net (Driscoll, 1999).

In summary, Internet abuse can be categorised in four major areas - international and domestic fraud, as in the case of the 'Dominion of Melchizedek' scam is one, slovenly reporting, which happens because the standards of accuracy on the Internet are low and speed of dissemination is high, is another. For example, in the case of Pierre Salinger, former television newsman, where, on the basis of a Web page of dubious origin, it was propagated that he claimed, at a news conference, that TWA 800, a passenger plane that crashed into the Atlantic killing all aboard in 1996, had been downed by a missile (*The Economist*, 1999b). Slovenly reporting also includes malicious gossip or fictions that one would have circulated in a small group. This now spreads across the world, instantly forwarded by E-mails and newsgroups. Then, thirdly, there is the 'Chinese whisper', which makes the Internet a perfect vehicle for urban legends.

Usually, somebody puts something on the Internet and someone else turns it into something else altogether, often into something intriguing. Lastly, there is invasion of privacy, exemplified by 'spam', unauthorised information collection such as 'cookies' and Internet harassment, even stalking.

Protecting rights and privacy is becoming more difficult. In the US, marketers expose an average consumer to roughly a million marketing messages a year, across all communication media, or about 2,750 a day (Hagell and Singer, 1999). There are new technologies which will permit consumers to challenge marketers for control of personal information, such as 'anonymisaton' software which allows people to shield their identities as they surf the Web, 'Cookie' suppressers that stop information collection by Web sites and E-mail filters that attempt to protect individuals from 'spam' (Hagell and Singer, 1999).

Managing the World Wide Web

The adoption, by consumers, of the World Wide Web element of the Internet is being presented as a revolutionary innovation, taking off only within the last few years. The Web's structure is largely governed and determined by the World Wide Web Consortium, known to insiders as W3C. The Consortium is headed by Web inventor, Tim Berners-Lee, now at the MIT Laboratory for Computer Science (LCS), and currently consists of 275 member organisations, including companies, non-profit organisations, industry groups and government agencies from all over the world (Garfinkel, 1998). The W3C is the closest thing to the governing body of the famously decentralised Web. According to critics, W3C merely rubber-stamps what its leader, Berners-Lee, desires to be done, inducing a steady decline of member attendance at semi-annual meetings to 110 out of 140 members, in 1996, to only 70 out of 240 members in 1998 (Garfinkel, 1998). Berners-Lee has a large influence on the operation of the W3C; its influence earned by his role in the Consortium of the Web itself. Essentially, what Berners-Lee invented was a scheme for linking a document from many kinds of sources to any computer and then to the Internet. Dubbed the Universal Resource Location, or URL, this innovation gave everything on the Internet its own unique address. Once one types an URL into a special programme called Web browser, the programme puts out to the Internet, fetches the information and displays on the user's computer screen (Garfinkel, 1998).

One of the biggest impediments to E-business is the fact that computers and Webs are not very effective in recognising context; thus, many Web searches result in unwanted information. The reason is that the Web's main language, HTML (hypertext markup language), is essentially superficial. It tells a Web browser how to lay out the contents of a Web page, but it remains ignorant of the content. The World Wide Web Consortium (W3C) developed an extension to HTML, called XML (eXtensible Makeup Language), which, in addition to describing content, also provides a way of indexing data (*The Economist,* 1999a). It is a system of tagging data with relevant information, allowing applications running on the computers to respond in an appropriate way. For example, XML makes it clear that 'The Times' is a newspaper and in a particular time zone. By using meta-tagging data that describes data, XML can also speed searches in the way a librarian's card index can. However, in order for XML to work effectively, there is also a need for some agreement on definitions. This can be achieved within particular professions, such as medicine, although there is a need for a shared language of business, on the Internet, across industry. Microsoft is using its market clout to enforce global standards via its product, 'BizTalk', which will be incorporated into Office, BackOffice and Windows (*The Economist,* 1999a).

The biggest issue on the Internet is privacy; a concern that has a significant commercial impact motivating the World Wide Web Consortium member's debate. According to some surveys, as many as 80 per cent of Internet users refuse to make purchases on-line because their privacy may be violated via the information they surrender in making transactions (Garfinkel, 1998). Whilst clicking onto one Web site may provide complete anonymity, on the other hand, a different site might secretly record a user's name, E-mail address and all information to which one has access (Garfinkel, 1998; Schenker, 1999). A new Platform, For Privacy Preference Project, overseen by the World Wide Web Consortium and backed by companies such as IBM, aims to allow users to be informed of Web site privacy practices and control what information users give out (Schenker, 1999).

Drafting legislation is fraught with problems, as political and business interests vie in having their view taken on board by legislators. The original aim of legislation, often, is lost and the end result fails to satisfy anyone. Some believe that if E-commerce is to be adopted successfully by UK companies, the regulatory regime should be acceptable and user-friendly to those businesses most affected by E-commerce whilst still giving adequate protection to the public interest. At the core of the debate is a proposal to ensure that the security services have access to the encrypted material being sent over the Net. European governments and the US have radically different approaches to data privacy. The European Commission issued a Directive, in October 1998, giving national data regulators wide powers to control what types of data could be processed abroad and to hold export of personal data to countries, such as the US, deemed to have inadequate protection (Schenker, 1999). The US government overly relies on industry self-regulation (Garfinkel, 1998; Schenker, 1999).

Putative Benefits of the Internet

The most often quoted benefits from the electronic delivery of information are timeliness and connectivity. The fact that the fundamental factor of globalisation rests, first and foremost, on reducing the costs of information and its transmission can never be over-stressed. Thus, the prediction that by the year 2001, three-quarters of households in the US, along with over a half a billion people globally, are expected to subscribe to a wireless communication service, highlights the degree of future communication patterns. Equally, it is worth noting the degree of future social division, exemplified by the fact that two billion inhabitants on this planet do not yet have electricity and that about half of the current world population has never made a simple telephone call.

Internet commerce is believed to shift the balance of commercial power to buyers as, on the Net, competition is just a click away, giving instant choice. Furthermore, people can easily find a wealth of information and can compare prices. Similarly, the Net allows consumers and corporate buyers to pool their purchasing power and get volume discounts. The Net also eliminates geographical protection through offering a global reach.

It is often argued that the information and the mechanisms for delivering information provide the basis for competitive advantage. Communication technologies (ICT) hold broad meanings and refer to computers, communication software and devices; satellites and cable networks; video cassette recorders and glassfibre cables; direct mail; electronic mail; video-, computer- and tele- conferencing; teletext; on-line database; interactive television and the Web - all of which have become realities of contemporary communication media.

In the traditional communication media, such as mail, informational components of value were deeply embedded in the physical value chain and these were often obstructive to the visibility of their separate existence. For example, when information was carried by traditional modes of communication, such as an individual or by direct mail, information was delivered to its intended destination following the linear flow of the physical value chain. However, in the electronically connected or wired environment, information can travel in many directions, simultaneously offering the possibility of being un-bounded from its physical carrier.

Notwithstanding that information technology provides gains in time advantage, in shipping information to destinations and that some have argued that allowing everyone to communicate with everybody is, essentially, a zero cost, there are associated costs with digital connectivity. For those organisations which work with multiple sites, speed, efficiency, reliability and flexibility provided by digital connectivity more often than not justifies the associated costs, provided suitable connectivity channels are chosen.

In addition, for example, the Net provided an easy way of evading government censors to facilitate news around the world - such as recent events in China. In a similar way, students in France used the French Minitel system to organise a successful fight against plans by the French government to restrict admission to government - subsidised universities. Those who use the Net control the information flow on the Net. There is a much more active form of participation than what is provided by other forms of mass media. Television, radio and magazines are all driven by those who own and determine who writes for them. The Net gives people a media they can control. This control of information is a great power not available before to the everyday person. For those who have no skills, or time, to exercise information control, there is a personal information intermediary, 'infomediaries', who aggregate information with that of the consumer and use this combined market power to negotiate with vendors on the consumer's behalf (Hagell and Singer, 1999) These infomediaries become the custodians, the agents and the brokers of information about consumers; marketing this information to business and giving them access to it while protecting the consumers' privacy (Hagell and Singer, 1999). In the US, the Fourth and Fifth amendments to the US Constitution defend the right to privacy or the right to be left alone. In 1928, Mr Justice Brandies, in *Olmstead versus United States*, declared that 'the right to be left alone is the most comprehensive of rights and the right most valuable by a free people' (Hagell and Singer, 1999; p.7).

Of course, if one does not have access to an Internet connection, or cannot afford the connection fees, it does not make any difference that information is on-line. What the Internet does do is bring down the cost of accessing information to a point that makes it realistic for many more people to use the Internet then ever before.

Conclusion

Each organisation's need for connectiveness will depend, in part, on environmental forces it faces and its own internal dynamics. The move to global or Web-to-Web connectivity will occur at different speeds and with varying intensity.

On the one hand, fears exist that electronic banking, shopping and the development of other electronic services might increase social division within, and between, social groups. Today, people without telephones, credit cards and bank accounts are becoming marginalised by society, whilst, in the future, the same is likely to happen to those who lack access to the Internet.

On the other hand, E-commerce will enhance competition, as 'standard assets' such as retailing, warehousing, factory and office space, lacking flexibility and functionality to meet new needs, will be driven out of the market. Enterprises will be required to:

- Develop a better understanding of technology and how it can be utilised to the company's benefits;
- In the face of rationing, learn how to attract and enhance customer loyalty;
- Behave ethically to build customer trust and loyalty;
- Learn how to work in an integrated fashion, in cross-functional teams, incorporating internet-librarians, and be oriented to meet customer needs; and
- Increase interactive, one-to-one marketing and trading.

Over the long term, enterprises that remain unprepared for E-commerce and consequent changes will experience crisis. Alternatively, enterprises that understand the implications of E-commerce will be able to adjust better and thrive. Carnegie Mellon University, for example, is offering a Masters degree in Electronic Commerce; a field that judging by the lack of profits from almost all Internet companies, no one has actually yet mastered. The curriculum is designed to train a new generation of managers, planners, analysts and programmers (*Asiaweek*, 1999a). Because the Internet is a neutral, free, open and unregulated communication channel, it implies that all users are connected but that no one is in charge in cyberspace (Friedman, 1999). The Internet is democracy, but without a constitution (Friedman, 1999). The Internet makes all 'netizans' broadcasters and, because of this, it is important to cultivate citizens that uphold critical values and ethical behaviour (Moor, 1985; Friedman, 1999).

The power of the Internet in its current state lies in its resistance to governmental regulation (Gibson, 1999). Its ability to speed information past censors and across borders makes it a force for free expression, as well as a 'spewing front' for propaganda, misinformation, vengeance and even terrorism (Gibson, 1999). Concern with the Internet's potential to invade people's privacy and cause untold additional havoc has politicians around the globe considering new laws to prevent the revolutionary communication channel from being misused. Business executives worry that the worldwide electronic marketplace will be ruined by a patchwork of inconsistent local regulations, exemplified by Kuwaiti decency standards, European privacy laws and, even, Iowa sales taxes (France, 1999; Port and Resch, 1999). Current self-regulation and policies made by the quasi-governmental World Intellectual Property Organisation (WIPO) do not have sufficient checks and balances (France, 1999). Issues such as electronic contracts and cybersquatting, in addition to Internet taxation and privacy, seem to be too important not to be dealt with in a transparent or regulated way (France, 1999).

Note

1   This chapter was presented at the 5th Annual Conference of the UKAIS on 'The Social and Cultural Effects of Technology-Based Information Systems', Cardiff, April 2000.

6 Knowledge Management: Understanding and Praxis

NADA K. KAKABADSE, ALEXANDER KOUZMIN AND
ANDREW K. KAKABADSE

Abstract

Within competitive advantage considerations, knowledge has emerged as one of the more strategic assets for organisations. This is notwithstanding a wider and specifically economistic discounting of knowledge as a factor of production. Intellectual capabilities and knowledge/information transformations now have a central place within globalising information economies.

Constructing, transforming and commodifying knowledge and information require new organisational understandings and newer cognitive capabilities of strategic management praxis. Part of this cognitive awareness is a deliberate organisational designing for the role of symbolic analysts. As well, there is an emerging need for the Chief Knowledge Officer function going well beyond the Chief Information Officer requirements as the need is less for information technology-driven restructuring of routine processes, and more for innovation creation capacities associated with critically non-routine functions within organisations.

The chapter[1] considers neglected institutional and organisational dimensions to knowledge creation and knowledge conversion - it reviews the renewed importance of internal recruitment and socialisation within institutions and details knowledge codification and application functions within knowledge-creating organisations. Knowledge management, as praxis, inevitably raises concerns about cognitive failure in leadership theory and praxis.

Introduction

In the last decade, knowledge has emerged as one of the most important and valuable organisational assets. The term 'knowledge worker', coined by Peter Drucker (1959), gained acceptance and became associated with the users of information systems and information technology (IS/IT) (Drucker, 1993). The ability to use intellectual capability and create new solutions for human needs now takes central place in the global info-economy. Human knowledge and capabilities have always been at the core of value-creation, but this truism has become more visible in the info-age where the 'intellective' component of work is increasingly important (Zuboff, 1988). For years, organisations paid lip service to the management of knowledge, being concerned with more tangible and physical assets. The knowledge component of the value-chain had been obscured by the tendency to think of work as fundamentally a physical activity (Zuboff, 1988). However, the potential advantages that intellectual capital brings in the form of greater earnings through licensing technology has revised this trend. The pursuit of knowledge for competitive advantage has become increasingly central to organisational strategies. Yet, few organisations have realised benefits from knowledge management initiatives (Murray and Myers, 1997). The reason for this is two-fold; there are various conceptualisations of knowledge and, thus, confusion as to what constitutes knowledge management and there is no coherent framework for implementing the management of knowledge in an organisation.

In order to effectively manage knowledge one has to understand the meaning and significance of knowledge, understand one's own ability and limitations of knowledge and its potential meaning for organisational endeavours. Knowledge about knowledge, or meta-cognition, requires individuals to recall, analyse and use knowledge (Habermas, 1972). The challenge for management is to use the vast knowledge potential of organisations to create value.

Understanding the Meaning of Knowledge

Plato (1953) first defined knowledge as 'justified true belief'. Plato's (1953) concept was debated from Aristotle (1928), a student of Plato, throughout continental rationalism (Descartes, 1911), British empiricism (Locke, 1987), German philosophers (Kant, 1965; Marx, 1976; Hegel,

1977) to 20th century philosophers (Dewey, 1929; Husserl, 1931; Sartre, 1956; Wittgenstein, 1958; Heidegger, 1962; Merlau-Ponty, 1962; James, 1966). Although imperfect in terms of logic, this definition has been predominant in western philosophy (Nonaka and Takeuchi, 1995).

Attempts to understand knowledge phenomenon in organisations can be traced throughout management history. Taylor (1911), in his 'scientific management', attempted to formalise worker's experience and tacit skills into objective and scientific knowledge without insight that the worker's judgement was a source of new knowledge. However, it was Barnard (1938) who shed light on the importance of 'behavioural knowledge' in the management processes. Drucker (1993), coining the term 'knowledge worker', later argued that in the 'knowledge society' the basic economic resource is no longer capital, natural resources or labour, but is and will be knowledge. Drucker (1993) further suggested that one of most important challenges for organisations is to build systematic practices for managing self-transformation. Knowledge received explicit acknowledgement in economic affairs by the neo-classical economist Marshall (1965, p.115) who argued that capital consists, in a greater part, of knowledge and organisation and that knowledge is the most powerful engine of production. Theories of learning (Bateson, 1973; Argyris and Schon, 1978; Senge, 1990), amongst others, also tried to understand knowledge and processes of learning in organisations.

Notwithstanding, the meaning and value of knowledge can be understood only in the 'knowledge context' within which that knowledge is known (Meacham, 1983). The knowledge context is determined jointly by one's perception of the extent of all knowledge that can be known and by one's perception of the proportion of what one does know to all that can be known. Thus, two persons can hold the same objective amount of knowledge, yet one might feel that she/he knows a substantial proportion of all that can be known, whilst the other might feel that she/he knows relatively little (Meacham, 1983).

In the vein of Greek philosophers' dualistic definition of knowledge as a *mythos* and *logos*, Schank and Abelson (1977) propose two classes of knowledge, 'general' and 'specific'. General knowledge includes information about, and interpretation of, human intention, disposition and relationships organised in term of 'goals' (satisfaction, enjoyment, achievement, preservation, crisis, instrumental) and 'themes' (role themes, interpersonal themes and life themes) (Schank and Abelson (1977, p.4). Thought and thinker, knower and known, is one single, indivisible unit

(Olson, 1977; Labouvie-Vief, 1989). Thus, knowledge is intensely personal. As such, *mythos* refers to that part of 'knowledge' that is arguable and can be demonstrated and identified with precision and agreement (Olson, 1977; Labouvie-Vief, 1989).

Specific knowledge is seen as a 'script'; a representation of the expected sequential flow of events in a particular situation (cooking, applying for a job). Cognitive psychologists define specific knowledge as expert knowledge under the assumption that the analysis of protocols (written or verbal) allows access to the content and structure of knowledge in a domain (Ericsson and Simon, 1984; Anderson, 1987). Thus, specific knowledge can be equated with *logos* that defines 'knowledge' that is derived from more conceptual aspects of knowledge or of the state of the world. *Logos* derives from gathering, reading and coming to connote counting, reckoning, explanation, rules or principles and, finally, reason. *Logos* implies that knowledge can be rendered purely mechanical, computable and deductively certain. Although *mythos* and *logos* represent two realms that constitute knowledge, they are also complementary and interactive poles of knowledge.

Schank and Abelson (1977) postulate that experts in a particular domain can be differentiated from novices in the domain - both at quantitative and qualitative (flexible use and organisation) levels; where quantitative aspects of particular meta-knowledge and strategies (use of intuition) appear to best distinguish top experts in domains in which many people are able to specialise or acquire knowledge through formal education. Expert knowledge is considered to be based on 'factual knowledge' and 'procedural knowledge'.

Factual knowledge implies having long-term memory, an extensive database about life - an analogue to a multiple cross-referenced encyclopaedia (Brown, 1982; Kahneman et al. 1984). Procedural knowledge, on the other hand, is represented as a repertoire of mental procedures or heuristics used to select, order and manipulate information in the database or encyclopaedia and is used for purposes of decision-making and action planning (Brown, 1982; Kahneman et al. 1984). Factual knowledge can be equated to Ancient Greeks' 'epist'm' (scientific knowledge) - theoretical or the western reductionist and cerebral mode of enquiry of knowing that is based on cognition. Procedural knowledge can be equated to technical (craft-knowledge) - the eastern mode of enquiry or knowing that combines the use of all senses: hands, eyes, feelings as well as cognition. The secret of technology is in being intensely personal and that it can be learned only in a network of relationships: the parent-child, master-apprentice, *gury-shisha*. This tacit-knowledge plays an important role in leadership effectiveness and effective design and implementation of IS/IT systems. This knowledge is based on the cultural norms and beliefs that are contextually imbedded.

Polanyi (1958; 1966) and, later, others (Bateson, 1973; Gelwick, 1977; Teece, 1981; Nonaka, 1990; Naisbitt, 1994; Von Hippel, 1994; Nonaka and Takeuchi, 1995) made distinctions between tacit and explicit knowledge. Polanyi (1966) defines tacit knowledge as personal, context-specific and, thus, not easily visible and expressible - nor easy to formalise and communicate to others. Individuals may know more than they are able to articulate (Polanyi, 1966). Tacit knowledge is based on the subjective insights, intuitions and hunches and is deeply rooted in an individual's actions and experience and ideals, values and emotions (Polanyi, 1966). People acquire tacit knowledge by actively creating and organising their own experience by what Polanyi (1966) calls 'indwelling' and Kakabadse (1991) calls 'reflection' and, as such, knowledge-creating activity is underpinned by the 'commitment' (Polanyi, 1958) and 'willingness' to reflect (Kakabadse, 1991). In order to be shared, tacit knowledge needs to be converted into words, numbers or pictures that can be understood by others (Polanyi, 1966).

Nonaka and Takeuchi (1995, p.8) expand Polanyi's (1966) tacit knowledge in a practical direction, segmenting it into two dimensions, technical and cognitive. Technical dimensions encompass craft and skills captured in concrete 'know-how' - exemplified by the master craftsman who is often unable to articulate what he/she knows. 'Know-how' cannot always be codified since it often has important tacit dimensions (Polanyi, 1966). The cognitive dimension of tacit knowledge encompasses 'mental models' (Johnson-Laird, 1983) such as schemata, paradigms, perspectives, beliefs, images of reality and vision of the future, which shape the individual's perception of the world. Tacit knowledge is created in a specific practical context and real time, 'here and now', and, thus, has an 'analog' quality (Bateson, 1973). Tacit knowledge is equivalent to cognitive psychology's definition of 'procedural' knowledge in the ACT model (Anderson, 1983; Single and Anderson, 1989).

Explicit knowledge or 'codified' knowledge, refers to knowledge that is transmittable in some systemic language - such as words, numbers, diagrams or models (Polanyi, 1966). As such, it is easily transmitted orally and in written or electronic form. It can also easily be manipulated and stored in various databases and repositories. Explicit knowledge is imbedded in the past events or objects and is oriented towards a context-free theory (Polanyi, 1966). It is sequentially created and captured by 'there and then' and, thus, possesses a 'digital' activity (Bateson, 1973). People acquire explicit knowledge by actively searching for it through education, repositories and work context. Explicit knowledge is equivalent to cognitive psychology's definition of 'declarative' knowledge in the ACT model (Anderson, 1983; Single and Anderson, 1989).

Habermas' (1972) framework recognises three complementary 'types' of knowledge - constitutive interests concerned with social consensus and understanding, emancipatory interests concerned with self-critical reflection and autonomy. Holliday and Chandler (1986) also define three categories of knowledge: a general competence (a dimension that overlaps with local intelligence or technical ability); an experience-based pragmatic knowledge; and reflective or evaluative meta-analytical skills and abilities. The western philosophical tradition has fundamentally shaped the disciplines of social science, which has shaped current thinking about knowledge and innovation (Nonaka and Takeuchi, 1995).

Information as Knowledge

The concepts of knowledge and information tend to be used inter-changeably through the literature and praxis. For example, the management of information captured on corporate databases is often considered as an example of corporate knowledge and knowledge management. Information and data management are important pillars of knowledge management. However, knowledge management encompasses broader issues and, in particular, creation of processes and behaviours that allow people to transform information into the organisation and create and share knowledge. Thus, knowledge management needs to encompass people, process, technology and culture.

In the era of widespread economic and ethnological change, understanding the changing nature of work is important to understanding organising and re-organising (Barley, 1996). The adoption of new IT also conveys a powerful cultural load, having the capacity to involve all organisational actors in its use - being inserted into organisational life in both material and discursive ways (Webster and Robins, 1986; Hill, 1988; Muetzelfeldt, 1988; Korac-Boisvert, 1992). Materially, IT provides the potential for a wide range of data collection, storage and processing. IT provides information on demand, builds banks of shared knowledge and enables real-time, structured learning events to transcend boundaries of time and space, becoming a tool for building solutions (McAteer, 1994, p.68).

The theoretical link between information gathering and decision is framed in western societies within an Apollonian context where the value of intelligent and rational choice is paramount (Nijsmans, 1992). The belief that more information leads to better decision-making implies that having information in an organisation is a good in itself (Nijsmans, 1992). Meyer and Rowan (1977, p.340) argue that the symbolic meaning of information represents mythical and ceremonial symbolism, often independent from its immediate efficiency criteria or internal logic. Thus, the link between decision and information appears to be weak or 'loosely-coupled' (March, 1962, Allison, 1971; Brunsson, 1985; Weick, 1995).

The process of information gathering in organisations can be seen as 'representation of basic social value, the ability to account intelligibly for rational decision-making process' (Nijsmans, 1992, p.139). However, an individual's ability to attend selectively to information, disregarding unimportant stimuli in favour of those which pre-existing stores of knowledge indicate are relevant, is as important (Rumelhart and Nomran, 1990). However, this ability that advances individual capacity to remember, reason, solve problems and act is loaded with a potential Achilles Heel - allowing pre-determined experiences to exclude contradictory, novel and unfamiliar pieces of information entering one's analysis of the world (Weick, 1995), lowering one's capacity to classify information in knowledge structures and, even, adequately updating knowledge content. Walsh's (1995) comprehensive literature review, for example, demonstrates the lack of constancy in the understanding of knowledge structures, with some 70 alternatives for the meaning of knowledge structure.

Knowledge Definitions

Beckman (1998) has compiled a number of useful definitions of knowledge and organisational knowledge:

- Knowledge is organised information applicable to problem solving (Woolf, 1990);
- Knowledge is information that has been organised and analysed to make it understandable and applicable to problem solving or decision-making (Turban, 1992);
- Knowledge encompasses the implicit and explicit restrictions placed upon objects (entities), operation and relationships along with general and specific heuristics and inference procedures involved in the situation being modelled (Sowa, 1984);
- Knowledge consist of truths and beliefs, perspectives and concepts, judgements and expectations, methodologies and 'know-how' (Wiig, 1993);
- Knowledge is the whole set of insights, experiences and procedures which are considered correct and true and which, therefore, guide the thoughts, behaviours and communication of people (Van der Spek and Spijkervet, 1997);
- Knowledge is reasoning about information to actively guide task execution, problem-solving and decision making in order to perform, learn and teach (Beckman, 1997);
- Organisational knowledge is processed information embedded in routines and processes which enable action. It is also knowledge captured by the organisation's systems, processes, products, rules and culture (Myers, 1996).
- Organisational knowledge is the collective sum of human-centred assets, intellectual property assets, infrastructure assets and market assets (Brooking, 1996).

The Role of Symbolic Analysts in Making Sense of Information and Knowledge

During the 1980s, the cost of IT's material components (hardware) continued to decline (Kauffman and Weill, 1990), resulting in IT permeating every facet of organisation and, concurrently, becoming available for individual use. In the 1990s and beyond, IT further intensified its dominant role by the ever-increasing societal dependence on IT systems that have segmented the labour market into three generic groups: 'routine production servers'; 'in-person servers' and 'symbolic analysts' (Reich, 1993). The proliferation of IT has further re-defined traditional routine production work into sequences of repetitive tasks, to the extent that even the supervisors of such tasks are easily replaced. There is currently no shortage of such labour and it can usually be found more cheaply in a new market (Reich, 1993). Routine production margins are controlled, profits are usually predictable and workers have a high degree of exposure to global competitive forces.

Information, in many ways, defines pair-wise relations, such as the buyer-seller relationship, where, traditionally, much of the trader's margin depended on the asymmetry of information (Evans and Wurster, 1997). For example, in trade, the *caveat emptor* applies and the buyer of goods or services must look out for his/her own interests. Thus, a merchant is permitted to negotiate the best deal he/she can get and need not consider what is in the best interest of the customer. Thus, increasingly, customers, will value mediums which provide both rich and reachable access as he/she will need information that is complete, truthful, clear and contextual (establish context of information origin) (Ngwenyama and Lee, 1997). This validation of information pertaining to the completeness, truthfulness, clarity and contextuality, and the sheer breadth of choices of media and databases available to customers, will require services of an intermediator - 'symbolic analysts' (Reich, 1993).

Symbolic analysts access, analyse and synthesise information that adds to the value chain or produces 'symbolic goods' (with the focus on intellectual fields) (Bourdieu, 1971; 1979) and conditions the supply and demand for symbolic goods (the process of competition and monopolisation). For example, some organisations have an incentive to create or simply make available databases on interest rates, risk ratings and service quality histories. New opportunities emerge for third parties that neither produce a product nor deliver a primary service - intermediators (Evans and Wurster, 1997).

Navigators or agent brands have been around for long time. For example, restaurant guides influence readers towards a particular establishment. The Platform For Internet Content Selection (PICS) is a programming standard that allows net browsers to interpret third-party rating labels on Web sites. PICS enables users to rate anything and it makes those ratings ubiquitous, searchable, portable and costless (Evans and Wurster, 1997). The dramatic proliferation of networked matrices increase the need for such navigators and other facilitating agents; those that guarantee a product's performance or assumed risk (Evans and Wurster, 1997). The first need to consider is the means for transmitting and circulating the feedback effect amongst actors; focusing on symbolic enclaves (academics, other professionals in symbolic production) and their relationship with the increasing number of actors employed in the role of cultural intermediaries. These intermediaries administer the new global media-distribution chains (via satellite), rapidly circulating information between formerly sealed-off areas of culture (Bourdieu, 1971; Touraine, 1985) through conduits of intensified competition (Crane, 1987).

There is also a need to give consideration to competition, changing balances of power and interdependencies between the specialists of 'symbolic' production and intermediaries and their interplay with other actors (Elias, 1987) - especially the conditions of growth in the former's power potential as producers in the information-age, along with a further segregation between high-skill and very low-skill demands. The process of intensified competition on an inter-societal level is shifting the balance of power from isolated areas. With the emergence of 'globalisation' issues (Robertson, 1990), the struggle between the established and the outsider/newcomer is intensified (Elias and Scotson, 1965; Bourdieu, 1979). Outsider groups are often faced with a monopoly situation in which knowledge, in the form of a stable symbolic hierarchy, is transmitted to initiates through a patronage and sponsorship system operated by a stable establishment; outsider groups often may have to adopt usurpatory tactics (Marphy, 1989).

Because of the speed with which the new technologies such as GroupWare and Web swept through organisations, many Web sites, for example, were developed 'on the fly' and, thus, without the effectiveness that a more methodical approach would have brought. Similarly, GroupWare technologies (Lotus notes) databases are cluttered with data of dubious quality. Although this *ad-hoc* and decentralised approach created opportunities for innovation, it also generated particular problems. Opportunities created by the free form and decentralised development of corporate Web sites, for example, produced a wealth of creative solutions to Web problems and large and diverse Internet facilities. However, drawbacks are the proliferation of duplicative and unmaintained information. The challenge for information providers is to integrate information in a way that helps users be more effective in finding what they need. This may involve adopting standards for metatags, developing an internal content classification system, deploying layered search architectures and adapting other knowledge infra-structure components.

Balancing creativity and innovation with the need for levels of standardisation and control, requires time spent building support and developing corporate plans, guidelines and strategies. Business units can be responsible for developing the content of the information but corporate IT units need to be responsible for security policies, encryption, infrastructure and network performance issues. With increasing information flow, there is a need for corporate information librarians to be involved in selecting and implementing company-wide crawler and search engines, indexing, cataloguing major content sites and areas of knowledge and overseeing the process for authenticating Web sites and GroupWare databases. The value of library expertise in information retrieval and in cataloguing and indexing is increasingly more important in the IT context (Web, Internet, GroupWare). Increasingly, librarians are seen as a strategic asset. As a result, librarians are likely to be asked to participate in cross-functional teams where their expertise would not have previously been sought.

Institutional Knowledge Conversion

Knowledge Creation: An Internalisation Process

Many contemporary organisations have established higher levels of information sharing which constitutes the bedrock of a knowledge culture. The emphasis on knowledge-creation and aides both allows and forces an interpretation of the nature of value-creation. The emphasis of knowledge-leadership overthrows many conventional notions of value. New knowledge emerges as the result of the interplay between individual effort and social interaction. The exact conception of an idea that leads to an innovation, almost by definition, is not confined to place and time but, rather, can occur at any time (Usher, 1954). The creation of organisational knowledge, or intellectual capital, is driven by the interplay of human capital (employee knowledge and skills) needed to meet product or customers' needs, structural capital (organisational capability to respond to market demands) and customer capital (the strength of a customer base). The availability for 'tinkering' or 'slack' time for learning, thinking and reflecting may be one of the best vehicles for knowledge creation.

Knowledge Sharing: A Socialisation Process

Sharing implicit knowledge between actors is considered to be a socialisation process - externalisation or knowledge transfer as the individual or group of individuals share knowledge or 'know how' with each other or within the group. The act of knowledge sharing requires *gesinnung* or disposition-of-will; that is, the 'underlying common ground' of all the acts-of-will of a person capable of free choice (Kant, 1960). Organisational climate needs to be one of learning in order to motivate individuals and groups to share knowledge (Senge, 1990; Davenport and Prusak, 1997). For example, motivationally misleading situations can lead individuals to act in a way that is contrary to his/her intended plans and can stem from existential conflict of the will, such as between and among motives and values (Kant, 1960). Choice to share knowledge requires willingness to act or an act-of-will (Kakabadse, 1991). Creation and testing of knowledge is a social activity and, as such, requires environments that provide extensive opportunities for communication and experimentation (Senge, 1990; Davenport and Prusak, 1997).

Knowledge Application: A Codification Process

Many scholars link, theoretically and/or empirically, organisational performance to co-alignment between the organisational context and information technology and argue that technology utilisation is influenced by organisational context (Nolan, 1979; Venkatraman and Camillus, 1984; Tushman and Anderson, 1986; Anderson and Tushman, 1990; Venkatraman, 1990; Davenport, 1993; Currie, 1995). Both vertical technology transfers (the transformation of ideas into products) and horizontal technology transfers (the application of an idea into different domains) are long, expensive and difficult processes and require technological, physical and intellectual infrastructures (Korac-Kakabadse and Kouzmin, 1999).

One out of seven analysed organisations that had knowledge management initiatives in place had been more successful in knowledge sharing than other organisations - the differing factors being culture supportive of knowledge sharing and context and knowledge-structure management. In other organisations, where the culture of sharing was evolving, there were no structured processes in updating knowledge context and structuring the knowledge base, resulting in a knowledge repository of little use in finding more information. Considering that knowledge needs to be codified, classified and retrieved in a similar manner to information in the library, Information Librarians or Knowledge Structure Managers and Knowledge Content Managers may be required in addition to knowledge management in creating knowledge-sharing organisations.

Knowledge Management and Acquisition

Knowledge provides the basis on which both improvements and innovation take place in organisations. An organisational environment that is rich in opportunities for creation of relationships results in the re-evaluation of existing knowledge and the creation of new knowledge (Scharge, 1997). Managing corporate knowledge requires the development of comprehensive frameworks for managing every phase of the knowledge process and a way of measuring these intellectual assets. A first step is to visualise intellectual capital at the interchange from human capital, organisational capital and customer capital. The zeal to acquire knowledge has brought about the creation of new roles in organisations - Knowledge Managers and Knowledge Engineers, whose work is to ensure effective management of knowledge workers.

With the rapid pace of change and the complexity of problems facing many organisations, there is a need for people who can see new perspectives and can go beyond the current boundaries - whether of knowledge, available technology, social norms or, even, beliefs. The growing uncertainties and shortening time scales in the global information economy are challenging organisations - economically, organisationally, socially, managerially and technologically.

Accounting for intellectual capital requires managers to learn how to operate and evaluate a business when knowledge is its chief resource and result. In the emerging information economy, 'soft' assets (knowledge, 'know-how', programming) can be a better credit risk than 'hard' assets (office space, equipment) as the value of tangible assets can depreciate and, even, vanish overnight. For example, IT equipment depreciates at approximately 33 per cent annually. Knowledge is the genome of a corporation. Organisational learning depends on the business ability to generate new ideas and its adeptness at generalising ideas through horizontal and vertical knowledge transfer (Korac-Kakabadse and Korac-Kakabadse, 1999). 'Generic concepts' provide a collection of software applications, manuals and other structured 'know-how' which can easily be *are they talking about diff types here?*

??

customised to take account of local laws and regulations and support many lines of financial products.

Knowledge can be generated within organisation through R & D or it can be accessed from outside the organisation. If an organisation gets most of its knowledge from external sources, it is expected, over time, that this knowledge should be transferred internally by way of training or informally through on-the-job development/specialisation and it should, subsequently, be embedded in the organisation. However if, with time, an organisation still depends on external sources for this same knowledge then it has a knowledge management problem. Organisations with a high turnover of knowledgeable employees are very likely to have problems with managing knowledge. There are various strategies for generating knowledge: home-grown talent; recruiting; and consultancy/alliances.

Home-grown talent requires investment in the current work. As employees must find new ways to think about and do work, many organisations invest heavily in helping them learn new skills. Some learning can occur in formal training programmes and centres - much more occurs in structured on-the-job experience and development. Investing in employees' learning, in whom inquiry is coupled with action, results in new ideas replacing old and does lead to behaviour changes. Home-grown talent strategy is not just training but training that is tied to business results. It is development where action learning occurs and where systemic learning from job experience occurs.

By recruiting, organisations can recreate/buy highly-qualified talent. The process involves staffing and selection from the entry level to the executive levels. A recruiting strategy works when talent is available and accessible, but the risk can also be great. The organisation may not find external talent that is better or more qualified than internal talent. Furthermore, if the organisational culture is not conducive to knowledge transfer, newly recruited talent may not be effectively utilised or may leave.

Effectively using consultants or outsourcing partners may share knowledge, create new knowledge and design work in ways that both parties can benefit. Knowledge must transfer into the organisation by adapting consultant or partner tools so that employees can replicate and re-deploy them. The danger is becoming too dependent on an external consultant and not adopting the new knowledge (Korac-Kakabadse, Korac-Kakabadse and Kouzmin, 1998).

Organisations can invest in developing alliances and partnerships with outside partners who bring in ideas, frameworks and tools to make the organisation stronger. Partnership is developmental and takes a long time to establish. It can be argued that management's linguistic message and the image that it conjures are both problematic. Perhaps the adoption of the term 'proctorment' (proctoring, proctorship) or some other non-gender terminology that represents management activities may overcome some of the contextual problems. 'Proctor' has historically been applied to junior and senior appointed persons charged with a variety of functions. It can be argued that 'proctorment' may adequately replace management terminology without the burden of stereotyping (Korac-Kakabadse and Kouzmin, 1997).

Knowledge Management Praxis

Notwithstanding that the term 'knowledge management' implies formalised knowledge transfer, its essential function is developing specific strategies to encourage knowledge exchange (Davenport and Prusak, 1998, p.89). A Cranfield survey (TCISKS, 1998) carried out in 100 large and medium-sized European companies in the UK, Germany, France, Ireland, Benelux and Scandinavia, shows that business leaders define knowledge management as the 'collection of processes that govern the creation, dissemination and utilisation of knowledge to fulfil organisational objectives' (Murray and Myers, 1997; p.29). This means that organisations need to capture knowledge they have, share it and use it to some commercial benefit. The socialisation or transfer of knowledge is particularly critical for an organisation whose role primarily is the creation of knowledge or transfer of the knowledge - such as R & D organisations. Employee's attitudes to sharing knowledge are central to creating, socialising/sharing it and using knowledge for competitive advantage. Knowledge socialisation is part of organisational life and takes place whether or not organisations manage the process at all - people do talk formally and informally (Davenport and Prusak, 1998). However, at the same time, people do also provide major constraints to knowledge socialisation for the fear of losing expertise, influence or control.

The Cranfield survey shows that 89 per cent of respondents perceive knowledge as the key to business power and, as such, often are unwilling to share it (Murray and Myers, 1997). Sharing knowledge within focal groups is a primary and most common form of knowledge socialisation. However, sharing knowledge between key groups and making some of it available within organisations and, perhaps, outside, among partners, suppliers and customers, requires major re-thinking and new vision strategies. Sharing within organisation is often difficult if there is no sharing culture and the result is 'islands of knowledge', fragmented and separated into functional 'silos'. A sharing culture requires, also, effective structures which are flexible and responsive to change.

Although there are no proven solutions for knowledge management (KM), 87 per cent of European respondents believed that formal systems would help knowledge management, especially managing knowledge about customers, markets, products, services and corporate performance (Murray and Myers, 1997). Many organisations are looking for the solution in the arena of IT, as IT can assist integration, span cross-functional boundaries and facilitate existing and emergent networks at the organisational and global scale. On-line information systems (IS), document management, GroupWare (Lotus Notes), Intranets, Extranets and Internet are key technologies being used in knowledge management. Notwithstanding that IS/IT is a useful tool for capturing, tracking and sharing information, it is also necessary to have culture-of-sharing 'best practice' and 'know how'. Knowledge socialisation is not a single function or process but one that pervades the whole organisation. Knowledge is created and shared at all levels and in all processes and functions and, as such, requires a learning culture that rewards knowledge creation and sharing. The Cranfield survey suggests that 85 per cent of respondents believe that their organisation encourages their staff to share and bring forward new ideas, whilst 29 per cent explicitly reward (only six per cent on a regular basis) (Murray and Myers, 1997).

The advent of information technology such as Intranets, Extranets, Internet and intelligent agents has contributed significantly to the increased interest in knowledge management. As organisations are beginning to connect themselves in a way that they had not done in the past, groups, departments and teams now have the ability to share information in a way that they did not have in the past.

Information is shifting the vector of economic forces that define competitive advantage (Evans, 1999). Increasingly, in the search for competitive advantage, scholars are identifying a shift away from managing the information and technology itself towards managing the use of it: the human interface (Choo, 1998, 1999; Murray, 1999; Orlikowski, 1999). Davenport and Marchand (1999) similarly identify that facilitating access to a firm's repository of knowledge through improved information management is an important part of KM. They also highlight that companies have paid far less attention to how effectively employees apply and use their knowledge and the increasing recognition that KM is as much about managing people than it is about managing information and IT.

The Cranfield study (TCISKS, 1998) shows that because the topic of knowledge management is relatively new there are still a few outstanding examples to show where business is demonstrably delivering significant benefits from KM activities. Whilst many organisations are still deciding on the best forms of metrics and measurements, some have already implemented KM, but often in the secondary feeder process such as account management or internal networking. KM also requires investment and infra-structure. Organisations with inconsistent infra-structures and those who have been relaxed about data and information management and those who never discuss the role of information management in the performance of their business are unlikely to leapfrog into KM (Murray, 1999). The Cranfield study shows that organisations which have achieved success in KM had visionary leadership necessary for KM. The most progressive Chief Knowledge Officers (CKOs) all had wide experience in business and were respected within their organisation for their leadership qualities.

The future research agenda needs to address the general lack of understanding which connects the role of the employee and use of information/knowledge, its critical links to the optimisation of the available technology within the firm and the consequent achievement of competitive advantage. Such a research agenda would need to ask:

- What effect can data/information customisation have on the effective use and management of information and knowledge within an organisation?
- What activities, using both human and technical interventions, will enable individuals to be able to receive customised information of the quality and quantity they require to be able to perform at their optimum level?
- What are the critical issues directly affected by the use of information technology and knowledge management within the organisation?
- What are the issues relating to the relationships between the functions responsible for information and knowledge management? (HR, IT, Knowledge Management, Marketing, Internal Communications).

- What impact do these activities have on the competitive advantage of an organisation?
- What are requisite organisational structures and roles identified to manage these relationships and those with the employees within the organisation?

Barriers That Knowledge Management Needs to Manage

The Cranfield survey has identified four major categories of knowledge barriers across Europe, namely, people; management; structure; and knowledge (TCISKS, 1998):

People:
- Inertia to change;
- Too busy, no time to learn;
- No discipline to act;
- Motivation;
- Constant staff turnover;
- Transferring knowledge to new people;
- Teaching older employees new ideas.

Management:
- The fear of giving up power;
- The difficulties of passing on power;
- Challenging traditional company style;
- Imposed constraints;
- Lack of understanding about formal approaches.

Structure:
- Inflexible company structures;
- Fragmented organisations;
- Functional 'silos';
- Failure to invest in systems.

Knowledge:
- Extracting knowledge;
- Categorising knowledge;

- Rewarding knowledge;
- Understanding knowledge management;
- Sharing between key knowledge groups;
- Making knowledge widely available.

The process approach to KM is one of the principal emerging patterns in KM across Europe (TCISKS, 1998). It involves identifying knowledge-dependent processes and enhancing them through KM. It has the merit of tying readily into business benefits and also allows the possibly of more formal mechanisms, metrics and measurements (TCISKS, 1998).

Knowledge management, as a combination of disciplines and technologies, aims to manage knowledge. The disciplines have evolved from several areas, including business process re-engineering and human resource management. The ethnologies sprung from two main sources - the universal communications medium of the Internet and established software technologies such as information retrieval, document management and workflow processing.

The first attempts at KM started at about 3,000 BC. Knowledge was inscribed with a stylus in wet clay and then baked. However, the heating process and the lack of portability limited the author's ability to share knowledge. The papyrus was the new innovation technology in 2800 BC. Papyrus made capturing knowledge easier and allowed for the building of great libraries, such as those at Sumer, Akkad, Ebla and Alexandia. Parchment become available in 200 BC and paper in 100 AD. Being vulnerable media, due to fire and moisture, there was a need for making copies, often by the monks - the first knowledge professionals. In 400 BC, Greek philosophers Plato, Socrates and Aristotle (1928, 1984) laid down the foundations of understanding the nature of knowledge and its application (Skyrme, 1996).

Socrates invited debate, through dialogue, to challenge traditional thinking whilst Aristotle (1928, 1984) encouraged story telling. These methods are being re-discovered in contemporary management (Skyrme, 1996). The significant advancement in technology, the innovation of the printing press in the 15th century, made storage and distribution of knowledge cheap and widely accessible. With the advent of information technology (IT), computerised databases were the first tools for storing knowledge in the form of data and networks provided a means of sharing it. The first really useful IT knowledge management tool was GroupWare, exemplified by Lotus Notes, which allowed multiple users to share information and help in the creation of 'corporate memory'. The invention of corporate Intranets have provided a means of building GroupWare from a collection of less expensive software using Internet standards.

Fundamentally, the basic requirement for KM has not changed dramatically - what has changed is the wasted volumes of data, the speed and ease of content changes and the transformation of the workplace. Even the cultural barriers to learning and sharing have been fundamentally the same for some time.

Although KM means different things to different people, in contemporary organisations it implies a mix of people, process and ethnology to share information and to gain competitive advantage. Human resources (HR) experts see KM as part of re-casting the corporation as the 'learning organisation'. The consultant sees it as exploitation of 'intellectual capital' or the foundation for 'knowledge-centric' organisations. Currently, US companies are *technically* focused around KM and European companies think it is about people (Dempsey, 1999). The explicit knowledge held in intellectual property portfolios, databases and, increasingly, corporate Intranets need to be supplemented by tacit knowledge in the heads of staff. This, in turn, requires structure and culture that facilitate knowledge sharing between employees. Although the supporting technology ranges from telephone- and video-conferencing to GroupWare and Internets, these technologies are usually 20 per cent of KM components - the other 80 per cent are people.

Organisations need to design cultures where people have a desire to share knowledge. Whilst at its most basic form KM can be as simple as writing down contact telephone numbers in Filofax format, in its most advanced form, KM attempts to encode the unencodable. The driving assumption of many organisations is that, once formulated, the knowledge may be tapped by employees to do their jobs more effectively and, ultimately, improve organisational performance. Cranfield research shows that to capture relevant knowledge it is important to start with business objectives and then see how knowledge can fit in and how it can help meet those objectives. Only in highly effective research organisations is there an attempt to capture something as intangible as personal judgment. It is important to focus on knowledge that is critical - knowledge relevant to business and not lose energy on managing *all* knowledge.

The term's 'knowledge' and 'information' are often used interchangeably in the literature and praxis but a distinction is helpful. The chain is data - information - knowledge - action - wisdom. Knowledge is information put in the productive use, it implies action and through action and reflection one gains wisdom.

Ways of Working: Knowledge Leadership

To obtain information that one needs and to assess the value of information, one has, or needs to acquire, both explicit (or theoretical) knowledge and implicit (or practical) knowledge). Knowing how to use information in any given context requires wisdom. In order to effectively manage knowledge one has to understand the organisation. Managers need to understand employees, customers, suppliers and other stakeholders and be able to act on that knowledge in appropriate ways (Kakabadse, 1991). It requires, above all, effectively managing people and creating organisations that allow individuals to develop knowledge and engage with others to exploit the potential of that knowledge. Managers need to know how to manage specialist knowledge, a deep 'know-how' within one discipline and integrate it with more superficial knowledge about how it interacts with others (Leonard, 1998). They also have to know how to understand and manage, effectively, a diversity of cognitive styles as well as manning 'religious wars' about tools and methodologies an organisation adopts (Leonard, 1998). They also need to manage 'star performers' with their 'signature skills'. Leonard (1998; p.20) argues that companies' strategic advantage is based on four dimensions of core capabilities which may be readily absorbed by outsiders but that the synergy from unique competition is neither readily transferred nor imitated. Leonard (1998) defines these four interdependent core capabilities in pairs. Two may be thought of as dynamic knowledge reservoirs or competencies - namely employee knowledge and skill and the physical technical systems; and two that encompass knowledge control or knowledge-channeling mechanisms, managerial systems and values and norms (Leonard, 1998; p.19). Managing these synergies requires discretionary leadership (Korac-Kakabadse and Korac-Kakabadse, 1999).

The contrasting nature of discretionary leadership (Ghiselli, 1971, 1973; Kotter, 1982; McClelland and Boyatzis, 1982) is highlighted in the observation as to how dialogue emerges according to the predisposition of the actors involved. Information is the key resource contributing towards management's ability to add value (Strassman, 1995). Dialogue is viewed more as a quality process and facilitator of issue resolution. What happens to the senior executive grouping and the organisation if two or more top managers with substantially different held views as to the current configuration and future organisational identity and structure are in conflict? What if the experience of working within the senior management group is one of unworkable discomfort, whereby a restricted dialogue, debilitating tension at a personal level and minimal disclosure at the group level, become the norm? How do such experiences and processes impact on leadership practice and the future development of the organisation?

In attempting to address these questions, one aspect is clear - that fundamental to leadership and to learning within organisations is the concept of dialogue, involving a process of inner-reflection brought about through the sharing of experiences, especially over contrasting or conflicting agendas. Only individuals who reflect on their experiences can develop a competence or an ability to deal with new situations dissimilar to those they have already experienced. Through these rhythmic exchanges between participation and observation/distance, between action and reflection, knowledge grows (Korac-Kakabadse and Kouzmin, 1996). Thus, dialogue can be seen as the concept that expresses the dynamics of tacit knowledge. Fundamental to leadership and organisational learning is the quality, depth and breadth of dialogue. The quality of the dialogue encompasses the extent to which issues or relationships, considered as sensitive within the group, inhibit the discussion of key organisational concerns and, thereby, affect the future of the organisation and, in turn, how such experiences affect the extent to which the group members hold a shared view of the future direction of the organisation (Myers, Kakabadse and Gordon, 1995). Depth refers to the level of sensitivity displayed concerning the difficult issues discussed, despite differences of view that may exist amongst individual members, possibly affecting relationships, which may, in turn, negatively influence openness of conversation concerning the organisation (Myers, Kakabadse and Gordon, 1995). The breadth of dialogue refers to the variety of issues (internal and external) discussed.

Similarly, in organisational settings, actors' access to information and ideas can often depend on their position within organisational and networking opportunities. Thus, quality dialogue is a resonance between the beliefs and cultural experiences of the participants, expressed through a shared familiarity with the codes in use. While actors should take advantage of emerging electronic and telemetric technologies, they should use them in addition to face-to-face dialogue. Technology is only a support mechanism and not a substitute for personal contact (Korac-Boisvert and Kouzmin, 1995). Empirical studies show that some of the best communicators spend about 40 per cent of their time in face-to-face encounters, only because they do not have more time to give (Rice and Aydin, 1991). Irrespective of how actors develop, feedback is required to help individuals be more responsive to addressing contingencies within organisational contexts (Kakabadse and Myers, 1995a; 1995b), enabling them to negotiate and share understanding of contexts and, thus, through learning, transcend proclivities for 'cognitive failures' (Kouzmin and Korac-Boisvert, 1995).

Fundamental to relationship building, knowledge sharing and organisational learning is dialogue, involving a process of inner-reflection through the sharing of experience, enabling one to gain an understanding of one's practice. Face-to-face dialogue plays an essential role in establishing and maintaining the kind of multi-dimensional and robust relationships necessary for effective interaction and co-ordinated action in situations of uncertainty, ambiguity and risk (Trevino, Lengel and Daft, 1987; Nohria and Eccles, 1992). Even if disagreement or fissure occurs during dialogue, within the context of face-to-face communication, it is easier to repair situations and re-secure relationships because of its capacity for rapid feedback and multiple cues. Additional cues of caring, building teamwork, showing trust, acknowledgement of expert power and informality all add to the importance of dialogue.

Innovating, as well as maturing, organisations need to ensure high-quality dialogue amongst senior executives and with other organisational actors (Kakabadse, 1991). International studies of management competencies indicates that when quality of dialogue is high and the relationship amongst senior management is positive, the issues and concerns facing organisations tend to be more openly addressed (Kakabadse, 1991; 1993; Kakabadse and Myers, 1995a; 1995b; Korac-Kakabadse and Korac-Kakabadse, 1996). In organisations where relationships are tense and the quality of dialogue restricted, certain issues and problems tend not to be raised, because to do so would generate unacceptable levels of discomfort amongst certain, or all, of the members of the senior executive (Kakabadse, 1991; 1993). Such inhibition stimulates latent or creeping crisis opportunities (Kouzmin and Korac-Boisvert, 1995). In this context, dialogue encompasses knowledge transfer through the content of conversations concerning the present and the future of the organisation, the quality of relationships amongst actors, external developments which may affect the organisation and the views and responses of actors and groups within the organisation (Kakabadse, 1991).

Organisations need to ensure the existence of a high-quality dialogue amongst and between both senior management and other organisational actors (Kakabadse, 1991).   An audit of how issues are addressed, or unaddressed, by senior management is crucial to leadership, organisational learning and vulnerability management.   Senior managers are leaders and, within that framework, are also 'social wealth creators' (Kakabadse, 1991) who set agendas and identify appropriate strategies and, at times, put operational methods forward.   They need to discuss issues thoroughly, explore alternatives and seek opinions through stimulating debate about the organisation's present state and future prospects (Kakabadse and Myers, 1995a).   Although research evidence suggests that high quality dialogue is not easy to attain, its importance cannot be over-estimated (Westley and Mintzberg, 1989).   Furthermore, the quality of the dialogue is contingent on the quality of the relationship amongst group members.   Whilst strong and robust relationships promote a positive team spirit, where even the most delicate of concerns are aired, with poor relationships, undue attention is given to personalities and the issues that are deemed to be too sensitive to discuss tend to remain unaddressed, often with such dysfunctionality becoming a way of life (Kakabadse and Myers, 1995a; 1995b) and an avenue for crises.

A complex organisation consists of many social and cultural groupings and communication between and across these groups is likely to involve not only shared meanings but also contradictory and contested ones, requiring quality of dialogue as the means for improvement (Kakabadse, 1991; 1993).   Furthermore, participants in communication may be equally active in (re)producing meanings, but they frequently do so from positions of unequal power (Korac-Kakabadse and Kouzmin, 1997).   For example, in most contemporary western societies, a person's access to information and ideas can often depend on their class, gender, age and ethnicity, as can their access to means of communicating information to others (Korac-Kakabadse and Kouzmin, 1997).   Similarly, in organisational settings, actors' access to information and ideas can often depend on their position within the organisation and their orientation as networking opportunists.   In these circumstances, communicated messages are effective at the explicit level and at the broader cultural level of connotation, as shared connotations arise from shared experiences (Korac-Kakabadse and Korac-Kakabadse, 1999).

Note

1   This chapter was presented at the BIT World Conference, 'Business Information Technology Management: The Global Imperative', Cape Town, South Africa, June/July 1999.

7 Decentralised, Interactive and Available: Fundamental Changes for IS/IT Professionals

ANDREW K. KAKABADSE AND NADA K. KAKABADSE

Abstract

Historically, computers were the province of a few technicians who supported accounting and finance, but were otherwise isolated from the organisation. Now that IS/IT has changed the way that business is conducted in the world and accelerated the trend towards globalisation, highlighting a need for a better understanding of cultural issues, contemporary information systems (IS) developments are increasingly challenged as they are required to provide innovative solutions in response to complex problems. This challenge has also led to a vastly expanded role for the traditional IS/IT departments and IS/IT specialists. The new IS/IT development model goes beyond the technical specialist and makes use of cross-functional teams, which comprise both users such as accountants and sales people, IS/IT specialists such as systems analysts and programmers, as well as managers.

The responsibility of the IS/IT system professional is no longer focused on designing information systems, but instead on carefully directing the users to design their own systems. Changing the role of IS/IT from support to a driver of organisational strategies brings with it a need for a different set of skills and competencies in the IS/IT profession. To meet the information processing needs of the new global organisation, IS/IT managers and their IS/IT staff need to develop new skills, so that they may be more focused on the business rather than technical processes.

This chapter[1] provides a literature analysis of the changing skills of IS/IT professionals and identifies the new skills and competencies required for successful IS/IT development and utilisation. The chapter also presents capability-related models that suggest there is a need for improvement in the area of IS/IT leadership for effective IS/IT development and utilisation.

Introduction

Although it could be argued that the IS/IT industry is still in its infancy, IS/IT professionals are experiencing a third paradigm shift and at the same time are trying to change a stereotypic image acquired in the first paradigm and further propagated by the second paradigm. During the first paradigm, when large mainframes were introduced in organisations in the 1950s and 1960s, technological innovation was of an incremental nature (Applegate and Zawacki, 1997). IS/IT specialists adapted to changes in the hardware, software and programming languages and stayed ahead of the rate of change. The concept of 'fortress computing' (computer specialists living in their 'ivory tower') dates back to this period, when 'computer applications' were known as 'computer systems', whilst the combined disciplines of system development, operations and data entry (later supplemented by maintenance) became known as data processing (DP). During this period, the important skill to know and competently apply was programming.

Within the fortress, the separate disciplines of computing were segregated by organisational walls, each backed by elaborated grading systems and professional protocols. IS/IT professionals, in control of technology, were able to dictate to business units the technology they supposedly needed and when it would be available to them (Applegate and Zawacki, 1997). IS/IT professionals gladly accepted the role of solo expert providers of IS/IT and also the ones to whom businesses came for advice. The protected environment of the computer and the special status of its specialists, the 'high priests of IT', set DP departments aside from the rest of the organisation. Computers became the haven of bit-programmers and the maths wizards who did not make the time to talk to other people in the organisation to help them identify their needs (Daniel, 1996). Because of the frustration of not meeting business needs and the obvious isolation of IT departments, business units developed a negative view of IT departments and consequently viewed IT professionals as not understanding the business and not meeting their needs in a timely and cost-effective manner (Applegate and Zawacki, 1997). By the early 1970's, a smaller and less expensive form of technology emerged, the mini-computer and so thereby heralded the second paradigm shift.

The second paradigm shift, epitomised by more rapid technology changes, occurred during the 1970's and 1980s, when the term 'information technology' (IT) was introduced (Applegate and Zawacki, 1997). As technological and socio-economic change became more rapid, IT professionals managed to stay ahead of the hardware and software changes by working harder, working smarter (just-in-time inventory processes), and introducing more technology (mid-range computers, local area networks, wide area networks, client/server computing) (Applegate and Zawacki, 1997, p17). During the second paradigm shift, software became more user friendly and customers became more computer literate and hence more vocal about the quality of IS/IT service they experienced (Applegate and Zawacki, 1997). Systems analysis and design, supplemented by testing, became a specialist skill. Greater specialisation spawned the formation of professional associations (Association of Computing Machinery, ACM; British Computer Society, BCS; Data Processing Management Association, DPMA), whilst the use of IS/IT became associated with knowledge and information. The term 'knowledge worker' (Drucker, 1959) gained acceptance and became associated with the users of IS/IT. Thus, information emerged as the critical aspect of IT applications. Computer systems became information systems (IS) which provided information to management, thus promoting management information systems (MIS). Concepts of intelligent knowledge-based systems (IKBS) and decision support systems (DSS) emerged as information became a key ingredient for the running of businesses, so too emerged Executive Information Systems (EIS). Although the interaction between IS/IT professionals and user groups became increasingly closer, the traditional 'brick walls' were only replaced by the 'glass walls', whereby IS/IT specialists became more visible, but not integrated members of the business and of the Executive of the organisation. Information power stayed in the hands of IS/IT specialists (Daniel, 1996). Technology remained as the province of specialists, who supported accounting, finance and administration, but were largely isolated from the business units; thus further promoting the stereotypic image of IS/IT professionals as the sandal wearing, high-necked sweater and scruffy beard, absent minded scientists, introverts, poor communicators with poor knowledge of business (Patterson, 1992).

Despite the presence of such stereotypes, IS/IT as a competitive weapon and its capability to transform organisations attracted considerable academic interest in the 1980s, notably by the Harvard Business School (Ives and Learmonth, 1984) and MIT's Sloan School of Management (Scott-Morton, 1991), and in the late 1980s, by business and government, punctuating the third paradigm shift manner (Applegate and Zawacki, 1997). The 1990s have witnessed random and continuous change, epitomised by downsizing, rightsizing, re-engineering, and valuing less, individual effort (Applegate and Zawacki, 1997). With such turbulence, the philosophy of continuous improvement of business processes is rapidly being adopted as a fundamental strategy for coping with the random change of character of today's business environment and new technology. Technology has become open-ended and tailored, as in the case of the new IS/IT known as groupware (DeJean and DeJean, 1991; Applegate and Zawacki, 1997). Groupware technologies provide electronic networks that support communication, co-ordination and collaboration through facilities such as information exchange, shared repositories, discussion forums and messaging (Lotus Notes, Internet) (DeJean and DeJean, 1991). The traditional methods for adopting new IS/IT systems, exemplified by structuralist decision-making where the procedure for making 'rational' decisions is described as a sequential pattern of activities, whose different stages, variously defined are arranged in a 'waterfall' fashion, cannot keep pace with the required time frame of continuous improvement nor with open-ended technology which does not have a predefined sequence of operations and transactions, but tends to be general purpose tools that are used in different ways across various organisational activities and contexts (Korac-Kakabadse and Kouzmin, 1996; Orlikowski and Hofman, 1997). Whilst in the past IS/IT departments have perceived themselves as autonomous units that provided specific expertise to user departments, with today's emerging need for effective integration across the functions, IS/IT professionals are no longer autonomous, but have the potential to be equal members of a team of professionals, each with a specific contribution to make. The new open-ended technology has put more powerful tools at the user's disposal (from voicemail and laptops to multimedia for presentation and the Internet for real-time discussions), hence shifting the power of decision-making regarding IS/IT systems from providers to users (Daniel, 1996).

Propelled by a combination of new operating structures, increased demands from users and senior management's emphasis on the strategic and competitive value of information, the IS/IT professional faces an environment in which the traditional roles and skills for the design and implementation of systems no longer apply (Klenke, 1993). Adding to the challenges facing organisations are the accelerating pace of new technology development, the skills sets required to gain the benefits for such technology whilst simultaneously coping with the legacy of IT systems, old myths and stereotypes. This challenge is particularly relevant to IS/IT professionals who, by the very nature of their job, participate in the development of systems (software, work processes, communication) that transcend organisational and cultural barriers (Korac-Kakabadse and Kouzmin, 1996). However, IS/IT professionals are still perceived by many business units as 'techies' too far removed from business reality (Patterson, 1992; Sadler, 1994) and as such 'different' from 'normal' business people (Taylor-Cummins and Feeny, 1997) - a stereotypic image of the first and second paradigms, that built an invisible barrier or a 'glass ceiling', and is a major impediment to the mobility of talented IS/IT professionals into senior management. This concept of a 'glass ceiling' or 'barrier at the top' assumes that IS/IT professionals' under-representation at senior management levels is not a matter of choice or failure on the part of IS/IT professionals, but is a consequence of structural and sociological barriers erected through forms of direct and indirect interaction between IS/IT people and other organisational stakeholders.

Hence, this chapter examines the changing role of IS/IT professionals and the need for new skills and capabilities required in the third paradigm shift. The chapter also explores the current debate on the 'glass ceiling' (Fedanzo, 1995) in the IS/IT profession and appropriate ways forward through this impediment. A dynamic model for analysing the IS/IT role and required skills in the organisation is put forward, as well as the strategies for acquiring a new skill base, so needed for effective performance in the third paradigm.

The Nature of the Third IS/IT Paradigm Shift

As stated, current trends in IS/IT have not only changed the way business is conducted in the world and accelerated the trend towards globalisation, but have also vastly expanded the role of IS/IT department. The widespread restructuring of IS/IT services and functions has important implications in terms of the skills required for the IS/IT professional (Farwell et al. 1992). Driven by a combination of enhanced technologies, new operating structures, increased demand from users and senior management's emphasis on the strategic and competitive value of information, the IS/IT professional entering the field in this decade faces an environment in which accepted rules and roles no longer apply (Klenke, 1993). These concerns are intensified in a world where the pervasiveness and critical importance of IS/IT global development is now fully recognised (Palvia and Palvia, 1992). At the same time, IS/IT systems are made more complex by the cross-cultural nature of global business and the diversity of perspectives and personalities amongst the newly emerging IS/IT professionals involved. There is evidence to suggest that different *perceptions* apply within the IS/IT practitioner profession which may affect the ability of academic institutions to respond to the workplace requirements (Leitheiser, 1992). This has been described as the 'IS/IT paradigm shift' and implies that the IS/IT professional of the future may need to be more focused on business rather than technical processes.

A number of recent studies have suggested that an IS/IT paradigm shift has created different job descriptions for IS/IT professionals which requires them to acquire new knowledge and skills. The ideal IS/IT professionals of the 21st century will need to be multi-faceted, multi-skilled individuals. They will find it important to possess a combination of interpersonal, technical and business skills that will allow them to analyse problems, integrate applications, and implement new business processes built around information technology (Farwell et al. 1992; Leitheiser, 1992). A wide acceptance of this concept has renewed interest in research in the areas of IS/IT skills requirements, IS/IT staff motivation and IS/IT staff management. Several empirical studies suggest that in addition to specialised technical skills (analyst, programmer), IS/IT professionals need to recognise the importance of and develop other skills, such as diplomacy, political, interpersonal and business skills, and reconsider their traditional avenues of career development (Green, 1989; Nelson, 1991; Leitheiser, 1992; Chau and Tye Ng, 1993; Earl and Feeny, 1994).

Rockart et al (1996) identified eight imperatives that have an impact on the role of IS/IT professionals. Furthermore, 'Business' changes such as Re-engineering Operational Processes (traditional forms of BPR); Re-engineering Support Processes ('the back office' including the outsourcing of whole functions or sets of business activities); re-thinking Managerial Information Flows (to enable new organisational forms and new ways of managing to provide control with flexibility and empowerment); and Redesigning Network processes (inter-organisational and particularly opening up direct consumer IS/IT based services), are also considered as having a fundamental impact on the role of IS/IT professionals. Rockart et al (1996) also argue that Distributed Computing Environments; new software development tools and methods; the 'exploding' range of technologies used in organisations; the 'new' IS/IT industry, involving different types of suppliers and changes in the relative power of suppliers; the availability of outside suppliers and the services they can provide to take over many traditional IS/IT department activities and roles, are driving fundamental changes in the role and contribution of IS/IT services.

Role Ambiguity

New technology is viewed as enabling businesses to take advantage of contributions that, by nature, transgress several functional lines (Markus and Benjamin, 1997). However, although new IS/IT enables change, most staff and managers tend to remain within their prescribed roles. Line managers, IS/IT professionals and other organisational members although each may have been assigned a role, for example, process owner, design team member, transition management team member, coach or implementation team member, little mobility across roles is evident (Hammer and Champy, 1993). For example, line managers are expected to champion change whilst IS/IT professionals are excepted to provide support to the business units. When people fail to perform in their assigned role, the results are often project failure, in respect to traditionally defined success criteria (Korac-Boisvert and Kouzmin, 1994; Markus and Benjamin, 1997). In addition to the fact that people may not perform effectively in their assigned role, roles are also mediated by the new technologies (groupware IS/IT) as well by a rapidly changing context (Markus and Benjamin, 1997). The irony is that in contemporary environments, the failure to achieve planned outcomes are higher when all team members feel confident that they have performed tasks within their assigned role (Markus and Benjamin, 1997). However, evidence indicates that the success rate of organisational change programmes (restructuring, rightsizing, adoption of new IS/IT, re-engineering) is higher when all team members understand and practise multiple team roles (Markus and Benjamin, 1997; Korac-Kakabadse and Kouzmin, 1996). As change becomes more demanding and rapid, people are more likely to be required to be adaptable across roles. Effective performance in contemporary organisations requires not only different beliefs concerning work and standards of performance, but also a level of teamwork where members play different roles simultaneously. Demands made in today's organisations hastened by the application of new technology, exemplified by GroupWare systems, delete current role boundaries and introduce new role ambiguities. As role boundaries become more fuzzy or roles become more discretionary in terms of freedom of manoeuvre, or both, the more the personality, attitudes and views of the role occupant determine role-related behaviour. In essence, each role occupant increasingly moulds their own role boundaries (Korac-Kakabadse and Korac-Kakabadse, 1998) to their favour and satisfaction driven by each person's perception concerning the challenges they face and the nature of the persons with whom they interact

(Kakabadse, 1991; Korac-Kakabadse and Korac-Kakabadse, 1998). Hence, according to how a person perceives his/her role, how their role needs to be differentiated from other roles, and how, in turn, they should integrate their role with other roles, will determine how effectively discretionary choice is utilised (Kakabadse, 1991). Thus organisational technologies can be viewed as opportunities for action, as well as avenues for uncertainty avoidance or as stress factors, ultimately influenced by individual perception. Hence, it is no surprise to report that Groupware (Lotus Notes, E-mail, the Internet - 'virtual office' technology), top management demands, downsizing and restructuring have all been identified as stress factors leading to burnout amongst IS/IT professionals (McGee, 1996).

Burnout

The most commonly accepted definition of 'burnout' is that of a reaction to role related stress and 'is a syndrome of emotional exhaustion and cynicism' (Maslach and Jackson, 1981, p.101; Meyer and Allen, 1984; King and Sethi, 1997). The emotional exhaustion is characterised by a lack of energy and a feeling that one's emotional resources are used up. Employees have reported that they feel 'they are no longer able to give of themselves at a psychological level required for effective performance' (Maslach and Jackson, 1981, p.108). McGee (1996, p.37) argues that stress and burnout are more severe for IS/IT professionals than other employees, because IS/IT employees are expected to ensure that 'technology and systems work 24 hours a day'. Similarly Ludlum (1989) cites long and odd hours, unrealistic deadlines and the learning to adapt and become proficient with the proliferation of the varying technologies, as the main reason for burnout and job dissatisfaction among IS/IT professionals. King (1995) concludes that stress amongst IS/IT personnel is caused by companies increasingly deploying incrementally new and complex technologies. For example, help-desk workers are prone to burnout after 18 months (Meyer and Allen, 1984; King and Sethi, 1997).

Sonnentag (1994) surveyed 180 software professionals from 29 software development teams and found that work stressors were positively related to burnout. They found that a lack of control at work, work complexity and openness to criticism within the team were significantly and negatively related to a lack of identification with the workplace. The King and Sethi (1997) study suggests that IS/IT employees involved in user support and other activities that involve direct contact with users will demonstrate a higher level of burnout than in IS/IT development groups.

The stressors that lead to burnout are defined as those characteristics of the job and the immediate job environment that make considerable demands on the abilities or resource of employees (Abramis, 1994). Stressors typically involve a lack of predictability, and lack of control over and understanding of, environmental conditions (Cohen, 1980; Sutton and Khan, 1983). Research has identified two stressors in particular, as being particularly pungent, namely role ambiguity and role conflict (Kakabadse, 1991). Role ambiguity is associated with the need for certainty and predictability with regard to one's goals and the means of accomplishing them. Role ambiguity may occur if an individual lacks adequate information to accomplish the required activities (Jackson and Schulrer, 1985), and may also occur in the absence of proper procedures for performing tasks and uncertainty about evaluation criteria (Miles and Perreault, 1976). Role conflict occurs as a result of unclear, incongruous or unrealistic expectations covering performance and accomplishment communicated to an individual (Khan, 1978; Kakabadse, 1991). According to Rizzo et al (1970), role conflict may occur between an individual's internal standards and required job behaviour, the time allowed to complete particular tasks and activities, the inadequacy of the resources available to an individual, residing over a series of roles which are ill-fitting, all of which force the individual into contradictory behaviour and conflicting expectations and organisational demands. Brookings (1985) reported a significant relationship between perceived role conflict and role ambiguity and burnout.

Strong empirical evidence indicates that employee burnout leads to lower commitment, turnover, absenteeism and low morale (Maslach, 1976; 1978a; 1978b; 1979). A number of studies also show that emotional exhaustion (a syndrome of burnout) is highly correlated with lower level employees' commitment (Jackson et al. 1987; Leiter, 1991; Reilly and Orsak, 1991). Further, Mathieu and Zajac (1990) argue that highly committed employees identify with the organisation, hold a higher emotional attachment with their place of work and that increases their vulnerability to psychological threat. Less committed employees are more detached from their organisation, which allows them to avoid the negative consequences of stressful situations because of a lack of personal interest. However, IS/IT personnel fall into the highly committed category, emphasising their potential for burnout (Lazarus and Folkman, 1984).

'Glass Ceilings' and IS/IT Professionals' Credibility

Although IS/IT today vitally supports all of the company's business functions, and some argue that IS/IT is a business and not a support function (Whitman and Gibson, 1996), IS/IT professionals and IS/IT managers remain enmeshed in a system that they experience as biased against them (Fedanzo, 1995). Experienced professionals in accounting, human resources, or sales, are commonly thought of as capable of offering sound advice outside the bounds of their profession, by their senior management (Fedanzo, 1995). However, similarly experienced IS/IT professionals are almost universally presumed to be unprepared to do so, whether or not they have appropriate qualifications, such as MBA's (Fedanzo, 1995). In reality, most IS/IT veterans are just as knowledgeable about general business as their colleagues in other professions, as they have direct access to organisational information and are able to model and design processes necessary to support information flows (Fedanzo, 1995; Whitman and Gibson, 1996). It is, therefore, a natural extension of the IS/IT function to aid business (re)engineering strategies and implementation (Whitman and Gibson, 1996). Furthermore, the IS/IT profession is uniquely situated to apply enterprise modelling technology to overall business development, allowing systems designers to model current and proposed information systems as a precursor to development (Whitman and Gibson, 1996). Some argue that excluding IS/IT managers from critical decisions costs billions of dollars annually in duplicated effort, inefficiencies and lost opportunities (Fedanzo, 1995). Considering that the estimate for the worldwide IS/IT bill, hardware, software, support and training, is more than $1 trillion annually (Ahuja, 1997), and that actual and potential losses can be enormous, why, as academics and researchers have asked, are IS/IT managers not included in the making of important decisions? (Fedanzo, 1995; Damon, 1997). For example, company accountants advise on important investments, but although organisations invest large sums of money in the field of IS/IT, they seemingly are not driven to or do not take advice from IS/IT professionals (Currie, 1995). One powerful reason why is that a field as young as IS/IT leaves its users frustrated and angry, because the area is not well understood (Korac-Kakabadse and Kouzmin, 1996). Executives still lack knowledge and experience of new keystone technology (electronic commerce, the Internet) (Kanter, 1986; Thornton, 1997). When ignorance, fear, and anger are present, human nature responds with neglect and organisational abuse (Fedanzo, 1995; Bashein and Markus, 1997). In order to respond to the challenge, IS/IT professionals need to place themselves in a position where they can be considered as peers with their senior management colleagues, having developed, wherever necessary, their skills in business (Fedanzo, 1995; Korac-Kakabadse and Korac-Kakabadse, 1998).

However, the IS/IT function does not occupy esteem within organisations (Damon, 1997). Research indicates that the IS/IT director is viewed as an almost second class citizen to other directors (Catham and Ticombe quoted in Damon, 1997). This perceived lack of respect for IS/IT managers and their functions, means that IS/IT departments are often unrepresented at board level (Damon, 1997). A survey in the early 1980s by Benjamin et al (1985) found that only 20 per cent of IS/IT executives report directly to the CEO, whilst 80 per cent report to three or more levels down in the organisation. A survey in the late 1980s by Raghunathan and Raghunathan (1989) found that 22 per cent of IS/IT executives reported directly to the CEO, 56 per cent reported one level below and 12 per cent reported two levels down. A more recent study by Applegate and Elam (1992) found that 27 per cent of newly appointed senior IS/IT executives report directly to the CEO, whilst 44 per cent report to the finance director. In companies where IS/IT managers have a place on the board, IS/IT is more likely to be utilised strategically (Damon, 1997). Further, in organisations where IS/IT is viewed as an asset, and where IS/IT plays a role in transforming the business (Earl and Feeny, 1994), IS/IT professionals are perceived by other employees as change agents and thus (un)consciously avoided, which in turn prevents their full integration with the rest of the organisation.

The above-described developments have led some IS/IT professionals to feel that business people do not understand what the IS/IT specialists can do to help the organisation because, if understanding were greater, they would value their IS/IT colleagues and would not use them as scapegoats when policy and operations go wrong (Damon, 1997; Bashein and Markus, 1997). Unfortunately, many IS/IT specialists believe that other people's ignorance leads to negative stereotypes of IS/IT professionals (Sadler, 1994; Bashein and Markus, 1997). In turn, IS/IT specialists hold that many managers are technologically inept or averse (McLeod and Jones, 1986), and feel incapable of understanding, let alone managing, IS/IT (Patterson, 1992; Lacity et al. 1995). Although there may be some truth to this view, despite the fact that business people may hold an incorrect or incomplete view about technology, it is the IS/IT professionals who need to take the first step towards improving present circumstances (Ward and Peppard, 1996; Bashein and Markus, 1997; Markus and Benjamin, 1997). For example, a survey conducted in the Novel enterprise found that only 48 per cent of board directors viewed IS/IT managers as advisors or strategists, whilst 85 per cent of IS/IT managers perceived that a prime element of their roles is to convince senior management of the importance and benefits of new technology (Kavanagh, 1997). Grindley's (1991, p.116) study shows that over one quarter of the surveyed IS/IT directors believe that despite training and awareness programmes, the current generation of managers will never fully accept the role of information technology in their workplace. A UK survey highlights that only ten per cent of companies effectively managed the delivery of benefits from IS/IT projects (Ward et al. 1995). The image that professionals in the IS/IT function are often more attracted to work with the technology than to contribute to the success of the business, still persist in the 1990s (Ward and Peppard, 1996), as well as the belief that IS/IT professionals are too far removed from business reality (Patterson, 1992; Sadler, 1994) and as such are 'different' (Taylor-Cummins and Feeny, 1997).

Business people are encouraged to be strategic, broad minded, communicative, and persuasive. However, a relative weakness of many UK companies is the imbalance between the strong emphasis placed on recruiting and developing managerial 'high fliers' to the relative neglect of specialist, scientific, professional and technical talent (Sadler, 1994). Business people are sponsored to attend management development programmes, whilst the IS/IT specialists are encouraged to upgrade their skills relevant to new technology (Sadler, 1994). Engineers, scientists, software writers, designers and other IS/IT specialists have to fight their way into top jobs, often unaided by the extensive management development and career planning processes, enjoyed by their generalist colleagues (Sadler, 1994). The result of such practices is a divided culture, in which top-level decisions are in the hands of line managers who do not fully appreciate the technology they are managing, whilst purely technical decisions are delegated to specialists who do not fully understand business strategy (Sadler, 1994). These values, together with stereotypes and socialised roles and expectations, build barriers of 'glass ceilings', which are major impediments to the upward mobility of talented IS/IT professionals. The conclusion of many studies is that IS/IT professionals and business units each treat the other with suspicion or indifference, as much due to a lack of mutual understanding (Ward and Peppard, 1996). Thus, although organisational structures are changing, with the focus on teamwork and client services, negative perceptions of IS/IT professionals still persist. The use of cross-functional teams and new development methodologies (RAD, JAD) for the adoption of contemporary IS/IT systems and decentralisation strategies have, in many organisations, removed the 'glass walls' between IS/IT professionals and business units, enabling IS/IT professionals to better integrate with business units. However, this integration has not yet gained sufficient momentum, nor has it provided IS/IT professionals with the credibility that they understand the business as well as their colleagues in other business units, to enable them to shatter the stereotypical images which act as a barrier to policy integration (Patterson, 1992; Ward and Peppard, 1996). For example, a Price Waterhouse survey shows that 79 per cent of the managers surveyed see IS/IT as a support function and not an equal business partner (Price Waterhouse, 1993). Despite fundamental organisational changes, one reason why stereotypic images still exist is that IS/IT professionals are also found to be highly disciplined, have strong task orientation and prefer neat, tidy, lasting solutions to problems (Rochester and Douglas, 1990; Ward and Peppard, 1996). They fail to see the political nature of organisations, assuming that the problems at hand require technical solutions. As such they tend to have a low tolerance for ambiguity and often shy away from dealing with emotions (Ward and Peppard, 1996).

This finding is not surprising considering that many organisations use structured instruments such as the Work Profiling System (WPS) for the selection of IS/IT professionals which, unfortunately, can downplay certain qualities such as intuition. For example, since the late 1970's Saville and Holdsworth (SHL), at the forefront of occupational test development on behalf of British industry, found IS/IT staff exhibit a capacity to work through problems in a systematic and analytical manner (Keely, 1992). A range of jobs, from hardware engineers to computer operators, require skills in problem solving and the ability to work with symbolic or coded systems (Keely, 1992). Another important characteristic for IS/IT staff, is the capacity to be detail conscious, highly meticulous in their work and to follow complex instructions (Keely, 1992). Interestingly, the verbal skills required of IS/IT professionals are described as the ability to interpret and impart technical material to both a technically-sophisticated as well as non-technical audience, in the form of reading out the contents of documentation, and the ability to understand specification requirements (Keely, 1992). Additionally, IS/IT professionals are identified as needing to be proficient at the writing and interpretation of internal memos (Keely, 1992). Other skills of importance include the ability to understand numerical relationships and the ability to visualise spatial relationships (CAD, CAM, Graphic). SHL state that other characteristics are desirable, such as IS/IT staff should be receptive and innovative, as much of their work requires the ability to generate new and original ideas and an interest in planning skills, especially for software engineers and system analysts. To assess people's capability in these skills, SHL have designed a battery of seven tests for the selection of IS/IT professionals, through predicting job-related performance (Keely, 1992). Similarly, in the US selection batteries developed in the 1950s and 1960s (IBM and CPAB) have been frequently used, although they are now viewed as increasingly less relevant (Keely, 1992). The exclusion of certain qualities from the selection process may explain why the UK survey, conducted by the Butler Cox consultants, shows that 60 per cent of IS/IT managers exhibit poor management skills (Cox quoted in Patterson, 1992, p.8).

However, the possession of skills and talent do not by themselves guarantee a high level of achievement and effectiveness. People increasingly work in a more interactive way, where individual and team performance depends on the quality of interaction between them (Kakabadse, 1991). Thus, the skills and talents needed to perform effectively in the organisation consist of specialist skills and also a set of qualities of character and temperament, which will enable the IS/IT specialist to harness and focus talent to effectively respond to the demands of particular challenges. These characteristics need to include social and emotional intelligence constructed as drive, persistence, determination, emotional resilience, stamina, self-belief, self-awareness, social poise (Sadler, 1994; Goleman, 1995).

Recognition of Required Business Skills

Two major paradigms are predominantly used to explain superior organisational performance, the competitive forces view, particularly associated with the work of Porter (1980) and the resources based view (Prahalad and Hamel, 1990).

The competitive forces view holds that the success of an organisation's competitive strategy depends on the quality of choices that positions the organisation within its environment, particularly its industry, so that it can defend itself against competitive forces, such as the power of suppliers and customers, threat of new entrants or of substitute products, and rivalry amongst existing firms (Porter, 1980).

The resources based view (Prahalad and Hamel, 1990) holds that organisations should see themselves as a portfolio of core competencies capable of producing products through a combination of fuelling new business, and investing in new and existing product lines. As such, the resources based view holds that organisations need to develop two major capabilities: technological competencies which provide the key to the organisation's market position (for example, operational, financial, technical); and competencies which allow for speedy adaptation to marketplace needs (for example, management competencies), which are vital to organisational performance in order to promote an integrated organisation (Prahalad and Hamel, 1990). Prahalad and Hamel (1990, p.82) argue that 'core competencies are the accumulation of collective learning in the organisation'. As such, 'the senior management should spend a significant amount of its time developing a corporate-wide strategic architecture that establishes objectives for competence building' (Prahalad and Hamel, 1990, p.89). From this perspective, Senge (1993, p.14) argues that a learning organisation is one that is 'continually expanding its capacity to create its future'.

However, to be useful, competencies must relate to a particular organisation's strategic performance. Therefore, learning which is valuable to organisations is embodied in competencies to do things better (incremental improvement) or do different things (radical innovation). Thus, when an individual, group or organisation discovers new ways of achieving desired outcomes, a skill, competence or capacity to continuously use that learning to achieve its purposes (outcomes) is developed. These purposes relate to the organisation's current performance and its ability to learn to adapt and change for future performance. These purposes are achieved by recognition of what is needed now and implemented according to the existing will to act. The will to act, however, is often delayed until a competency or skill can be explicitly developed. As the relationship between the recognition to develop and the will to act is dynamic, new competencies emerge through trial and error, at times as an experimental problem-solving device, or viewed as an art.

Until the need for certain competencies is recognised, organisations will seldom invest in their development. Organisational competencies evolve from tacit knowledge, which is embodied in practical 'knowing how to' rather than the abstract 'knowing about' (Spender, 1993, p.246), through the accumulated experience of a few in the organisation, which may be extended to a group and the overall organisation, often in a piecemeal manner. These initial competencies are viewed as value-added competencies, which are contextual, tacitly used and are continuously evolving. Once value-added competencies are recognised in the organisation, they usually become a commodity competency. As such, commodity competencies can be explicitly codified and taught across the board. Commodity competencies are less context sensitive, as they draw from explicitly codified information, emerging as an explicit set of skills that others in the organisation can readily access.

The process from tacit to explicit may take a long time. For example, it took the modern British Parliament centuries, since its initial formation during the reign of Edward I (1297-1307), to develop explicit procedures and competencies for parliamentarians, in the form of two English government institutions, *Magnum Concilium* and *Curia Regis,* or at least since Sir Thomas Smith (1562-66) wrote an early formal statement of procedures for Parliamentarians in the House of Commons, *De Republica Anglorum* (published 1583). The procedures and practices were, and are today, intended to maintain decorum, to ascertain the will of the majority, to preserve the rights of the minority, and to facilitate the orderly transaction of the business of the Assembly. Only in 1995 on MP Teresa Gorman's and other MP's persistence for the recognition of this skill, did the British parliament introduce induction courses on parliamentary procedures for new MPs. Similarly, it took a Belgian government nearly 70 years after Henry Ford introduced the assembly-line mode of automobile production, The Model T, to recognise that there is a need for automobile driving skills, thus introducing driving tests (Team Consulting, 1995).

Current Trends Concerning IS/IT Professionals' Skills

Although a variety of issues and themes are addressed in the literature, the emerging consensus is that, in order to meet the corporate needs of the future, organisations require professionals with a combination of IS/IT knowledge, management skills, leadership experience and high motivation. Furthermore, because organisational realities are rapidly changing, organisations also require substantial cultural modifications, and as a result are likely to be faced with enormous challenges in retaining, redeveloping, replacing and recruiting IS/IT staff. Two crucial tasks may prove to be difficult and complex to accomplish, namely staffing key IS/IT positions with suitable candidates who are able to respond to the demands of ever evolving enterprises, and determining how to motivate with incentives and rewards those IS/IT professionals.

The analysis of empirical studies supports the notion of a paradigm shift, within which IS/IT professionals are required to develop interpersonal and business skills. Analysis of the perceived importance of system analysts' job skills, role and non-salary incentives in the USA, suggests that systems analysts recognise the importance of various skills, such as diplomacy and sales, for the adoption of effective IS/IT systems and for their own career development, whilst users expect systems analysts to exhibit technical skills, such as programming (Green, 1989). As a continuation of their 1980 research, Cheney et al. (1990) conducted another study through structured interviews with senior IS/IT managers in the USA, responsible for planning, training and hiring IS/IT professionals. The IS/IT managers were asked to rate the importance of 20 specific skill areas for each of three major IS/IT work job categories: project management, systems analysis/design and programming. The study conceded that senior IS/IT managers believe that human factor skills have and will continue to increase in importance for all IS/IT workers, particularly for project managers (Cheney et al. 1990).

A study of the perceived usefulness and proficiency of 30 IS/IT skills grouped under organisational and technical constructs, shows that the perceived usefulness of organisational skills were rated higher than those of technical skills (general IS/IT knowledge, technical skills and of IS/IT products) (Nelson, 1991).

A two year research project concerning the changing needs of IS/IT professionals, by the Boston Chapter of the Society for Information Management, found a shift in emphasis away from the traditional IS/IT activities and skills (Farwell et al. 1992). Further, a survey of 98 IS/IT practitioners, including IS/IT managers, user managers and IS/IT consultants, suggests that the ideal IS/IT professional of the 1990s should possess a combination of interpersonal, technical and business skills (Farwell et al. 1992).

Table 7.1 IS/IT Competencies: Results of Research

Author	Methodology	Database	Skills/Rank Order
Green (1989)	Questionnaire	872 system analysts and system users (US)	Analysts see important behavioural skills: • diplomacy • politics • sales Users see important technical skills: • programming • skills specialist
Cheney et al (1990)	Structured interviews	Senior IS managers responsible for planning, training and hiring IS professionals (US)	20 skills areas for project managers system analysts/ designers and programmers • Managerial/human skills increasingly more important for all three categories
Nelson (1991)	Questionnaire	275 IS professionals and end-users from eight US user organisations	Organisational skills: • organisational knowledge • organisational skills • organisational unit management Higher order technical skills: • general IS knowledge • technical skills • IS product
Farwell et al (1992)	Two year research project	98 IS practitioners: IS managers, user managers and IS consultants (US)	Combination of: • interpersonal • technical • business Future skills: • re-orientation of technology • solutions to business problems • integration and competitive advantage
Author	Methodology	Database	Skills/Rank Order
Leitheiser (1992)	Questionnaire	IS managers' perception of IS	54 IS skills in seven categories ranked as follows:

		developers skills	• interpersonal skills • business skills • analysis and design • programming • applications skill • knowledge of environment/platform • computer language
Feeny et al (1992)	Interviews	28 CEOs, CIOs (US)	Of the nine qualities for CIOs • six relate to soft skills and business • three to operational management (less important) Contributing beyond the IT functional role is rated highly
Trauth et al (1993)	Questionnaire	IS managers, end-user managers, consultants and IS professors (US)	Of the 18 IS abilities (human, business and technical), top ten consist of: • six human abilities • three business • one technical
McCarteny (1996)	Questionnaire	300 IS managers and IS professionals (UK)	• business experience • technical knowledge
Korac-Kakabadse and Korac-Kakabadse (1998)	Questionnaire and structured interviews	750 senior executives and middle managers (AUS)	• leadership capabilities • innovative IS/IT skills

Source: Korac-Kakabadse and Korac-Kakabadse, 1998

Further, a study of the most important skills for systems developers from the IS/IT manager's perception (Leitheiser, 1992), shows that interpersonal and business skills were ranked more important than knowledge of IS/IT environment/platform, and computer language.

Research into the key skills and knowledge required of future IS/IT professionals from the perception of four groups - IS/IT managers, end-user managers, IS/IT consultants and IS/IT professors - shows that the desired top six abilities lie in the human and business categories, whilst only one technical skill was ranked in the top ten (Trauth et al. 1993). Replication of Trauth et al.'s (1993) study in Hong Kong, by Chau and Tye Ng (1993), confirmed the same findings from a survey of valid responses from 116 IS/IT managers.

An additional survey of 300 IS/IT executives and IS/IT professionals shows that 40 per cent of IS/IT managers believe that business training, in the form of an MBA or hands-on managing experience, will continue to be a prerequisite for IS/IT career advancement (McCarteny, 1996). Some 50 per cent of respondents stated that their companies provided either business training for IS/IT specialists or technical training for business people (McCarteny, 1996).

A study based on the 750 senior executives and middle managers in the Australian Public Service (APS) at central government level, shows that successful adoption of new IS/IT in the organisation is strongly influenced by the leadership capabilities of IS/IT management and top general managers (civil servants) (Korac-Kakabadse and Korac-Kakabadse, 1998). The results of the same study also show that the level of IS/IT skills and appropriate training is strongly influenced by the leadership philosophy of the top management and the IS/IT organisational context (Korac-Kakabadse and Korac-Kakabadse, 1998).

Feeny et al.'s (1992) research of ten CEOs and 18 Chief Information Officers (CIOs) in 14 organisations, shows that CEOs consider soft skills and business orientation as vital for successful performance as a CIO. They rate highest positive relationships with other members of the executive team and being a good ambassador for the business. Operational management weaknesses can be tolerated, provided competent subordinates are in place (Feeny et al. 1992). An additional study highlights that all CEOs emphasise the importance of the CIO's contribution way and beyond the commonly accepted remit of their IT functional role (Feeny et al. 1992). The study reinforces Bock et al's (1986) argument of the need for positive business orientation qualities (Feeny et al. 1992).

Hence, empirical research (Table 7.1) suggests that a new-breed of IS/IT professionals will need to combine updated technical skills with:

- Business knowledge and aptitude;
- Solid interpersonal skills; and
- Customer and service-driven attitudes.

Thus, it will not only be skills in technology alone that will help make IS/IT professionals successful, but their attitude towards broader business skills and to the manner of their interaction with customers (Weldon, 1996).

The Cranfield School of Management IT Directors' Forum, consisting of 25 IS/IT Directors, analysed the question, 'why do IS/IT departments have a poor reputation and why do IS/IT specialists lack credibility amongst business managers?'. The reasons identified include organisational myths and legends, business managers' previous experience of IS/IT departments (usually negative), IS/IT professionals' lack of business knowledge, rate of IS/IT change, IS/IT hype directed at business managers, IS/IT jargon used by IS/IT professionals, inappropriate performance measures which do not fully appreciate IS/IT professionals' added value (IT Directors' Forum, 1997). The source of listed problems is considered to stem from a subjective evaluation of IS/IT systems, the arrogance of business managers and of IS/IT professionals and their territorial positioning (IT Directors' Forum, 1997).

Effectiveness of IS/IT Practice: The Work Performance/Contribution Model

Although there exists a variety of strategy formulating decision-making theories and models, most can be traced back to one of two distinctive paradigms: a rational-economic paradigm and a cognitive-managerial paradigm (Farjoun and Lai, 1997).

According to the rational-economic paradigm underlying most strategy formulation models (Christensen and Montgomery, 1981; Cool and Dierickx, 1993; Farjoun and Lai, 1997), there is little need to distinguish between the real world and the decision-maker's perception, as both are considered to substantially overlap, a perspective close to Porter's (1980) competitive forces view. The choices made can be predicted by the rational decision-maker entirely from knowledge of the real world and without a knowledge of the decision-maker's perceptions or modes of calculation (Simon, 1986, p.210). Thus, a first major assumption of this paradigm is that 'real' object similarity and 'perceived' object similarity (defining key stakeholders or client group) are one and the same, and therefore can be assessed using 'objective' or external data (Cool and Dierickx, 1993; Farjoun and Lai, 1997). A second assumption of this paradigm is that when assessing similarities between organisations, resources and markets,

ion-makers process data accurately and in a shared manner (Cool and
..ckx, 1993; Farjoun and Lai, 1997).

The cognitive-managerial paradigm presents an alternative view to the
rational-economic paradigm towards strategy formulation and decision-
making (Porac and Thomas, 1990; Ginsberg, 1990; Reger and Huff, 1993).
The paradigm breaks with the first assumption of the rational-economic
paradigm by acknowledging that decision-makers' perceptions are most
important and have a distinct impact on the quality of decisions made
(Farjoun and Lai, 1997). Perceptions are important because each
individual's actions are based on their perceptions and not on an assumed
'objective' reality (Farjoun and Lai, 1997). Further, because reality is
socially constructed, adopting such a perspective raises the likelihood that
perceptions are reality and do not merely reflect it (Smircich and Stubbart,
1985). Additionally, although externally determined inputs may be closer
to the 'right' decision (factors that need to be considered from a theoretical
point of view), nevertheless insiders may have tacit knowledge that is not
accessible to external observers and hence are less likely to 'know' what
will and will not work (Nayyar, 1992). Consequently, in the cognitive-
managerial paradigm, analytical concepts such as key stakeholders and
relatedness are viewed as cognitive constructs that both reflect and create
the material constructs determined in the rational-economic paradigm
(Walton, 1986; Porac et al. 1989). In this way, the cognitive managerial
paradigm is conceptually paralleled by the Prahalad and Hamel (1990)
resources based view of the firm.

As the literature strongly emphasises that IS/IT professionals need to
develop interpersonal communication, negotiation, business and marketing,
and leadership skills, as well as being more visible in the organisation, the
conceptual model closest to such considerations is the cognitive managerial
paradigm. On this basis, the development requirements of IS/IT
professionals reflect being context sensitive, a crucial consideration of the
cognitive managerial paradigm. One approach to deciding what the IS/IT
professional needs to develop is to first understand what the job requires
within a given context and the qualities needed to fulfil these requirements.
The resulting gap then becomes the focus of attention. Both the
requirements of the job and the qualities needed to perform in the role will
need to be customised at the individual level. Nevertheless, the individual
and the organisation will still need to maintain a general sense of generic
effective performance, in order to model how the skills and capabilities
required can be developed specifically and across the board, in order that
the organisation receives consistent contribution from individuals.

As stated, adopting a cognitive paradigm as the construct to explore the performance effectiveness of IS/IT professionals emphasises the importance of needing to be context responsive. The cognitive paradigm assumes that people view similar and dissimilar circumstances in similar and dissimilar ways. On this basis, an understanding of people in their context is necessary in order to gauge what elements of performance are considered as positive and contributory, as opposed to dysfunctional and inhibiting. The key factor to examine is role. Does the individual's role permit them to pursue and action their views, namely they can scope the boundaries of their role, or are the boundaries and parameters so clearly established that the role holder is only required to apply their skills to achieve the targets and objectives they have been set? The reason that such a distinction needs to be made is that those with a broader role remit are in the position to substantially influence their situations, thus making the influence process and its outcomes a unique contextual experience. A role with clearly assigned parameters is one that is prescribed, in that the individual occupying that role is assigned resources and given the specific brief to pursue a particular course of action (target) (Figure 7.1). The limited freedom of the role holder requires the person to apply existing resources, irrespective of whether they are considered adequate or inadequate to do the job, in a manner suitable to achieve the goals of the job, team, department or organisation (Kakabadse, 1991).

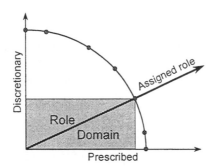

Figure 7.1   Role Analysis
Source: Korac-Kakabadse and Korac-Kakabadse, 1999

Roles of broader responsibility are termed discretionary, in that the role holder is required to establish the parameters of the role and the direction to pursue (Figure 7.2). The role incumbent has to provide clarity and shape to that role, by taking into account the internal organisational context in conjunction with the external, business and market context and simultaneously attempt to integrate, at times, contrastingly different forces and stakeholders (Kakabadse, 1991).

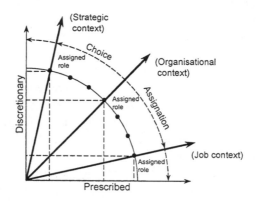

Figure 7.2   Role and Contribution of IS/IT Professionals
Source: Korac-Kakabadse and Korac-Kakabadse, 1999

In order to effectively discharge prescriptive roles, the role incumbent needs to apply specific skills in order to accomplish prescribed tasks (Figure 7.2). In order to display accomplishment in discretionary roles, the role holder needs to show that they can apply task-related skills in a manner that is suitable to the demands of specific situations when different stakeholders may be pursuing their own agendas.   The concept of appropriateness is crucial, as in broader context circumstances, people pursue their own goals, sometimes for good business reasons but also because of their own insecurities and personal desires (Figure 7.2).

Figure 7.3 Work and Contribution of IS/IT Professionals
Source: *Korac-Kakabadse and Korac-Kakabadse, 1999*

Figure 7.3 highlights the spread of skills and capabilities required when applying a managerial cognitive paradigm framework to IS/IT practice in organisations.   In order to effectively address job context demands (Figure 7.3), IS/IT practitioners are likely to occupy a limited amount of discretionary scope, namely East North East roles (see Figure 7.2).

Although working within a largely prescribed manner, namely according to how their project or role has been scoped, the IS/IT professional is afforded a certain degree of discretionary freedom concerning how to respond to users' needs and how to handle their queries and requests, in order to assure their continued interest in the present activities.

Organisational context refers to the peculiarities of how IS/IT work is conducted within each organisation.   The varying needs of users are reflective of internal organisational circumstances, as well as the manner in which IS/IT is applied and perceived by internal users.

Addressing concerns of a broader organisational nature will require of the role holder greater discretionary capacity and more effective use of choice. How to respond effectively to the varying needs of departments and different units in the organisation will require an appreciation of the varying IS/IT challenges facing each sub-unit, in attempting to improve its performance whilst integrating these into an organisational whole. Working within the arena of organisational context, IS/IT specialists would need to consider how to market their services internally in order to meet new and existing needs. In this respect, how to scope a project in dynamic circumstances needs particular attention. Requiring line management to specifically identify their needs, and in return provide a service by IS/IT specialists to specifically meet these needs, is unlikely to be satisfactory for users. In ever changing circumstances users may not be totally aware of all the relevant issues to introduce into the debate on providing needs-based IS/IT systems. As users may not be clear as to their requirements, IS/IT professionals are likely to apply consulting skills in order to assist users to think through the issues they face and, from those insights, then scope the project. In so doing, the IS/IT specialist will be required to have developed insights and be familiar with operational business management skills, concerning how budgets are devised and how the use of numbers can influence the behaviour and attitudes of line management. In addition to appreciating how to internally market IS/IT services, the IS/IT specialist will equally need insights as to the marketing issues facing the organisation, in order to understand how changes occurring externally are impacting on line management thinking internally. Such skills and insights are needed in addition to the more traditional project management skills required for the effective management of IS/IT projects.

In addressing issues of an organisational context (Figure 7.3), IS/IT professionals will need to occupy roles which allow for an almost equal spread of prescriptive assignation and discretionary choice (Figure 7.2). The prescriptive element of their role refers to the objectives that need to be achieved and the time frames that need to be met. The discretionary element of role highlights the need to be responsive to the issues facing users, with the requirement that each user should be uniquely addressed, according to the circumstances they face. The IS/IT specialist's role will need to adopt a North East perspective (Figure 7.2), allowing the role incumbent to pursue a fine line between achieving the targets set by senior management within the time limits set, whilst simultaneously addressing multiple and, at times, ill fitting needs, which will eventually require integration at the organisational level and which may also require a re-assessment of the objectives set. Addressing organisational context issues demands providing a cohesive IS/IT service, through finding flexible and durable pathways through multiple agendas and internal needs, by as much adopting a consultancy mantle.

Whereas organisational context issues require integrating varying internal to the organisation needs, operating within a strategic context, for the IS/IT professional, requires integrating external market, consumer, and community demands with internal capabilities to service and effectively respond to client desires. A far broader perspective needs to be adopted by the IS/IT specialist in order to effectively function in a strategic context, than in a job or organisational context. The issues to be faced by the IS/IT professional would concern the future shape, nature and identity of the organisation within its market(s), and the investment required by the organisation in order to achieve its strategic plans. In order to harness attention and resources to achieving the organisation's long term desires, effective leadership of both internal and external key stakeholders is required. Influential internal stakeholders would be the directors of the enterprise at both the corporate centre and in the business divisions and/or subsidiaries. Equally, the opinions and objectives of influential trade unionists and leaders of internal networks would also need to be taken into account. Important external stakeholders would include key shareholders, the press, local or national politicians, the chairmen and CEOs of supplier organisations, the top managers of competitor organisations, as well as the leaders of related organisations, such as professional associations. The IS/IT professional operating in the strategic context is likely to hold the role of director of the IS/IT function or, at least, a senior manager of general management status who holds responsibility for IS/IT in the organisation. Similar to the directors of the other specialist functions, such as human resources and finance, continuously engaging within a strategic context is likely to highlight the attitudes and philosophy of the role incumbent - is the individual one who thinks and feels as a director first and foremost, or are the person's loyalties to their specialist function, precluding thinking and feeling as a 'broad brush' director of the organisation? The strain and demands of the senior manager's role are likely to surface the personal philosophy and attitudes the individual holds. It is those philosophies and attitudes that will dictate the manner in which they mould and shape their role. Hence, operating effectively within a strategic context requires that the IS/IT professional displays a capability to shape and influence the varying demands and agendas of both key internal and external stakeholders, but in a manner in keeping with the fundamental views and sentiments they themselves hold. Stamping one's views and personality on a situation of contrasting demands and ambiguities requires leadership, namely the ability to drive through a cohesive and coherent policy and strategy, in a world of varying and contrasting demands. Those who operate within strategic contexts occupy roles of broad discretion, namely North North East roles (Figure 7.2), which require the role incumbent to shape their role as they discern appropriate, in terms of both the business logic and the values they themselves are pursuing. Hence, in effectively discharging North North East roles, the interpretation the IS/IT professional makes of the impact of stakeholders, the IS/IT professional's view of what is appropriate for their function and for the organisation and the nature, shape and flavour they would wish to see of their enterprise, now and in the future, will display their effective or ineffective exercise of discretionary choice.

Work Performance/Contribution Model Overview

Although the literature suggests that IS/IT professionals need to develop skills in interpersonal communication, negotiation strategy, marketing and leadership, as well as how to be more visible in the organisation, the question is how? The work performance/contribution model (Figure 7.3) addresses the question of 'how' by providing a way forward by indicating that different levels of skill, accomplishment and personal capability are required in order to effectively contribute in three clearly different contexts of job, organisation and strategy. Operating within job and organisation contexts will require the application of distinct skills, professional IS/IT skills, influencing skills, business skills and the skills to reorganise, and help to define most users' operational needs. The difference in skills application from job to organisation context is incremental, in that the IS/IT professional is still operating within prescriptive boundaries.

However, a far more fundamental shift is required in order to effectively function within a strategic context, in that the IS/IT professional is required to harness and apply leadership capabilities. The ability to work with ambiguity in the pulling together of constrasting stakeholder demands, whilst simultaneously promoting a desired mission and values for the future, on behalf of the organisation, requires different attributes to the more operational application of managerial and professional IS/IT skills. In effect, the person must be able to think, feel and act as a corporate director of the enterprise and from the insights they gain from holding such responsibilities, feel confident to position the IS/IT function so as to service the organisation to achieve its mission and strategic aims.

In making the distinction between job and organisational context on the one hand, and strategic context on the other, emphasises the difference between managerial skills and leadership skills. Managerial skills, by their very nature, are more explicit and more easily lend themselves to codification. Leadership skills are higher order value skills, which are difficult to codify, are learnt through experience and require the application of particular personal qualities such as maturity, robustness, wisdom, street skills, unorthodox decision-making and personal discipline (Kakabadse, 1991). Managerial skills can be taught within a classroom setting, whereas leadership capabilities are effectively developed through on the job experience, mentoring, counselling and feedback on open personal performance (Kakabadse, 1991).

The work/performance contribution model brings together the varying operational and managerial skills required of IS/IT practitioners, emphasising that their application must vary according to the needs of the context of the organisation and the person's role in the organisation, and also the broader market, external perspective, which necessitates taking into account leadership capabilities which, if effectively applied, can dramatically alter the direction being pursued by the organisation and, by implication, the nature of the markets in which the organisation finds itself now and in the future. This dynamic model brings together context, skills and capabilities and highlights the inter-relationship between these different strands of performance application for IS/IT professionals. The model equally draws a sharp difference between skills and capabilities. Where skills are operational, individuals need to ask the question, 'do I have the knowledge to undertake particular roles, tasks and activities?'. In the capabilities arena, the individual needs to ask the question, 'do I have the personal qualities and capability to discern trends, recognise opportunities and the personal qualities to pursue strategic challenges?'.

Requirements for the Future

It is probably still a truism to state that IS/IT professionals need to overcome considerable barriers in order to gain credibility and trust from the business units. The physical distance of IS/IT departments from the business units, differences in dress and language (technical jargon), different beliefs and attitudes about technology, a history of poor user experiences with technology and IS/IT specialists, are only examples of these barriers.   Catham's (quoted in Damon, 1997) point that IS/IT professionals tend to talk in jargon and not in a standard business language, which makes them unconvincing when presenting an argument, adds weight to this perspective (Catham quoted in Damon, 1997). If, as a result, IS/IT professionals are distrusted, they will not be credible to users, no matter how insightful their technical performance (Bashein and Markus, 1997).

In order to overcome perceived incompatibility of values, behaviours and performance attributes, IS/IT specialists need to build positive relationships with their clients. This requires sustained interaction between them and their clients, as trustworthiness takes time to develop and is only incrementally cumulative. In the trust building process, it is also desired that appropriate behaviour be consistently applied, which helps make people appear predictable and which, in turn, promotes trusting relationships (Bashein and Markus, 1997).

No schooling adequately prepares one for all of the demands of modern IS/IT professional practice. The schooling available from corporate IS/IT departments, software enterprises and hardware manufacturers generally recognises the professional deficiencies of their new and existing personnel and they have introduced programmes offering a mixture of continuing professional education and work experiences designed to overcome those deficiencies. Although the new professional receives encouragement and support with regard to continuing professional education, only the slightest encouragement is offered to continue general intellectual development beyond the stage of professional skills acquisition. A by-product of employers' emphasis on professional development is the virtual exclusion of overall intellectual and vocational development, which is inevitably an outcome of the barbarism of specialisation (Drucker, 1951).

As Gantz (1997) argues that IS/IT is rapidly becoming a business and not just a support function, the IS/IT professional will be increasingly included in major operating decisions and will work more directly with key clients (Gantz, 1997). In order to meet the challenge, gaining new skills and capabilities is a must! However, the new IS/IT breed will require more attractive pay than traditional IS/IT compensation, although pay alone will not ensure IS/IT staff retention (Foote, 1996). Changes of compensation for IS/IT professionals requires comprehensive changes of corporate culture and overcoming the resistance to cultural change that exists in most companies, and IS/IT departments (Foote, 1996). Changes are taking place in the private and public sector worlds, which will force a reconsideration of current attitudes to performance requirements, compensation and career path. Downsizing and re-engineering provides for exciting times for those who do not mind change and have developed the new IS/IT managerial skills and leadership capabilities.

The demand to attract IS/IT professionals with solid business backgrounds is increasingly being met through the appointment of business professionals, who may then be taught the technical prerequisites to help plan and implement IS/IT for business (Israel, 1990). In the UK this has initiated a debate on the role of the 'hybrid manager', as the more effective CIO of the future (Earl and Feeny, 1994). The renewed interest surrounding the effective management and development of IS/IT human resources, is likely to require of the IS/IT professional the capability for mobility across the three contexts of job, organisation and strategy (Figure 7.3). The alternative is to appoint managers already well versed in the skills and capabilities of management and leadership and who just need enhancing in the areas of IS/IT. The question remaining is, will the IS/IT profession allow itself to be so outflanked when both the alternatives and pathway forward are eminently clear and achievable?

Note

1   This chapter was originally presented at BITWorld'98 Conference, Delhi, India, February 1998.

8 'Profession' and Professional Ethics: An IT Perspective

ANDREW K. KAKABADSE AND NADA K. KAKABADSE

Abstract

In the last 15 years, there has been a growing interest in the subject of professional and business ethics. Organisations are becoming increasingly aware of the effects of (un)ethical practices on stakeholders (Adams et al.. 1991). Public awareness of unethical business behaviour has sharpened, as the climate of deregulation and competition has shifted, impacting on the boundaries of accepted practice, with the media and investigative reporting surfacing many incidents. Public awareness has been facilitated by multimedia that rests on the advancements in information technologies (IT).

Furthermore, economies that are shifting from material growth towards added value in all its varied forms through information, ideas and intelligence, the 'three I's economy', in healthcare, the arts and environment, leisure, travel, sport and service sectors, are increasingly becoming information intensive and at the same time IS/IT driven (Handy, 1995). Consequently these economies are increasingly dependent on the knowledge and services of IS/IT specialists. Although these IS/IT specialists are increasingly referred to in the literature as professionals, they operate as an occupation and at best can be seen as para-specialists, without professional certification and codes of conduct.

This chapter[1] examines what constitutes profession, through an analysis of the pros and cons of a profession. The chapter also explores the emerging need for IS/IT 'professionals' and/or para-professionals to adopt codes of conduct. It is argued that sustained research output in this area is important in order to establish IS/IT ethics on an equal footing with other topics in applied ethics and the establishment of an ethical code of conduct for IS/IT 'professionals'.

Introduction

For some years now, the topic of professionalism and ethics has been gaining increased exposure across the ranks of the management community, its advisors and regulators. While the 'excesses of the 80s' gave impetus to the current wave of interest in professional and business ethics, there are many other forces driving the process. Of these, the most important is the rate and process of change. As the rate of change accelerates, so novel problems arise with increasing frequency. Some of the most obvious challenges come about because of developments in technology. Particular technology issues arise which are to do with equity and the allocation of community resources. Although 'biotechnology' questions capture the popular imagination, technology development in other areas give rise to equally pressing issues. The use and potential abuse of information is one issue. An additional issue is the degree to which communication technology has the power to affect radically the nature of society (Longstaff, 1995). Undoubtedly, telecommunications are essential to public order and to national and global security, but the ever-creeping infringement on the lives of citizens gives rise to considerable concern. New forms of surveillance may limit our effective zones of privacy. Overall, IT/IS underpins the economic development of whole societies as well as business activities in every sector of the economy (MacLean, 1997).

IT is no longer restricted to the automation of organisational processes. Once valued primarily for its capacity to raise productivity by automating routine transactions, today IT means new business ventures, electronic commerce and partnership, management of change, new opportunities for the development of innovative products and services, enhancing customer services, integration and group solutions, information superhighway, facilities enhancement, virtual office and teleworking, and better co-ordination with superior and dramatic improvements in internal processes (Pacheco, 1995). For example, office inter-organisational systems, such as electronic data interchange (EDI), provides new ways of handling business documents and person-to-person communication (Pacheco, 1995). For most people, IS/IT, in terms of telecommunications, offers an important social convenience. For others, such as the elderly, the isolated, the disabled, it has become a lifeline (MacLean, 1997). Although all these IS/IT facilities are supported by the IS/IT specialists and 'professionals', the very same professionals have not, to date, adopted a professional code of ethics, such as the right to privacy (ITU, 1993). Through providing service to the rest of the organisation in particular, and society in general, IS/IT specialists will inevitably be confronted by the implications of the nature of their contribution to the accomplishment of organisational goals and results.

With such challenges at hand, IS/IT professionals, like other employees, need guidance and direction concerning appropriate and inappropriate ways of behaving and when their activities are infringing on the unacceptable. It is postulated that a code of ethics is required to keep IT professionals motivated to adhere to the highest standards of their profession. As it is, professionals, in general, use their professional organisations as communities within which to articulate ethics that can inform other employees, especially ones in related professions (Glazer and Glazer, 1989).

This chapter provides analysis of what constitutes a profession and professional ethics. In so doing, a sociological analysis of professions is undertaken. The changing nature of social responsibility and its impact on IS/IT professionals is also considered. What constitutes professional ethics and the 'real' need for the IS/IT profession to adopt a professional code is further examined, concluding with a view as to what constitutes critical mass for the effective adoption of a code of ethics. The view emerging is that adopting a code of ethics for IS/IT professionals is no longer a 'nice to have' opinion, but a necessity.

The Sociology of Profession

Professionalism refers to the thinking, values, methods and behaviour dominant in a profession or discipline (Chambers, 1993, p.4). It is a phenomenon that has built in

> 'stability from its link with knowledge and power, reverence for established method, capacity to reproduce itself, and defence against threat. It is sustained by the core-periphery structure of knowledge and knowledge-generation, by education and training, by organisational hierarchy and by rewards and career patterns' (Chambers, 1993, p.4).

'Profession' seeks security through specialisation, simplification, rejection and assimilation.

A sociological interpretation of profession has tended to adopt one of two approaches. The conventional approach is to treat the characterisation of a profession primarily as question of definition. By this interpretation, the central concern is with the traits or characteristics which define the profession and justify their high levels of status and remuneration, and which separate them from occupational groups lacking such attributes. Typical characteristics would include, the possession of a body of theoretical knowledge linked to high educational achievement; education and training in skills based on that knowledge; competence standards, and methodological and procedural criteria: a code of conduct providing a licence to practice controlled by an occupational association; commitment to an altruistic public service; and considerable occupational autonomy (Laffin, 1986, p.5).

However, if one explores what constitutes a profession, it is considered that IS/IT emerges only as an occupation which, it is argued in this chapter, needs to be recognised as a profession. In its simplest definition, a profession is an occupation where taking advantage of the client is against the rules (Burke, 1994). For an occupation, *caveat emptor* applies, in that the buyer of goods or services must look out for his or her own interests. Thus, for example, a merchant is permitted to negotiate the best deal he or she can obtain and need not consider what is in the best interest of the customer. However, within a profession, such self-interest is not permitted.

The concept that certain occupations have a duty to act on behalf of the interests of those they serve, is an ancient one. The provision of professional service arose from the days when the wealthy could not read and required lawyers to prepare their deeds, wills and contracts. Such relationships conducted to the advantage of the client are based entirely on trust. The need for trust eliminated the rule of *caveat emptor* and substituted it by a moral and professional obligation to act in the client's best interest. This ancient beginning led to the following generally recognised requirement of a profession (Burke, 1994):

- The subject matter must be sufficiently esoteric that the common person does not generally understand it and must rely upon the expertise of another for proper completion of the task;

- The subject matter must require a period of academic study in order to master the complexities of the topic;
- There must be a barrier to entry into the field which excludes those who are not competent;
- There must be a code of ethics which requires the members of the profession to conduct their affairs at a level which exceeds the mere requirements of the law. The core concept of a code of ethics must be the requirement that the professional will not take advantage of the public's inability to understand the profession's work;
- There should be a professional society to monitor the actions of its members and to enforce the code of ethics.

The alternative view of profession, focuses on the process of negotiation to attain professional status, highlighting profession as a political phenomenon, and emphasises the ways in which occupations are accepted as 'professions', relative to other power centres in society. Adopting this view, the identification of particular attributes which support the case of transition to a profession are, in reality, the means by which a profession can seek support for its own elevation of status, and actively maintain its social boundary (Laffin, 1986, p.196). On the one hand, a political interpretation of profession avoids the functionalist trap, namely the view that privilege exists because society is in need of valued services. Through the exercise of power, the political intervention promotes dynamism and change. On the other, such change is accommodated in the evolution of the relationship of professions to the society in which they are embodied. It is evident, for example, that occupations can both lose and gain 'professional identity' and, also, that occupations which share with professions many of their defining characteristics, may not gain public recognition as 'professions', precisely because they lack the power to establish the independence of action integral to the gaining of their new identity.

However, a political view of profession suggests a definition of professionalism as a 'peculiar type of occupational control, rather than an expression of the inherent nature of particular occupations' (Johnson T, 1974, p.57), and emphasises the crucial element of self determination - 'the right to control its own work' (Friedson, 1970, p.71) which a profession claims for itself. Laffin (1986, p.21) argues that the 'central and defining aim of a profession is the maximisation of ties, autonomy or freedom from control by others, both within the immediate work setting and in the institutionalised regulation of the relations between the professionals and the consumers of their services'.

Change and Social Responsibility

It is, however, possible to overplay the issue of self-determination, for absolute autonomy is not necessarily the sole influence determining the public's perception of a 'profession'. For example, recent changes in western societies in the IS/IT arena can be seen as the transition from professionalism to managerialism, in the sense of a move from IT autonomy in the centralised IT departments to decentralisation throughout the organisation. One consequence of this development is that 'increase in external control implies a reduction of professionalism' (Flynn, 1990, p.56). However, this notion imposes a rather simplistic view of the independence of the profession from the organisation. Professions are always subject to some degree of external influence. Therefore, the issue at stake is less the case of the establishment of new mechanisms of control, but rather one of more involving politically-induced changes in the locus and extent of external influence. What is likely to happen is thus, 'less a matter of managerialism versus professionals, than of competing interests trying to establish control' (Laffin, 1986, p.56). One way in which individual interest groups may seek to increase their influence over a profession is by appealing to the consensus of the society and, at the same time, attempt to undermine its existing claims to legitimacy. Changes in professional status may be more the result of a change in the areas of influence over occupational decision-making, than the imposition of a hierarchical relationship. Thus, the defining characteristic is not absolute independence, but maximisation of autonomy and, as such, there is an important element of subjectivity in the propensity of society to recognise an occupational grouping as meriting 'professional' identity, according to the nature of the external influence upon it.

The Downside of Professions

The debate in support of profession and professionals has its critics. Ortega y Gasset (1961, p.110), for example, argue that the narrow specialisation of a profession produces 'dilettantism' that is ignorant of social issues and professionals' impact on the profession and society. Quinn et al. (1996) are critical of professions on three accounts.

First, in group situations, when professionals are required to collaborate as equals with other organisational members in problem solving situations, a slow response is a commonplace experience, as specialists try to refine their particular solutions to fine technical details (Quinn et al. 1996). Because a professional's knowledge is their power base, the motivation to share needs to be induced. The tendency of each profession is to regard itself as en elite, with special values, often getting in the way of cross-disciplinary sharing required by contemporary organisations (Quinn et al. 1996).

Second, often the loyalty of professionals would be more aligned with their profession than with the organisation which employs them (Quinn et al. 1996). Many professionals are considered to display little respect for those outside their field, even when all parties are supposedly seeking the same goals (Quinn et al. 1996). Doctors, for example, have been known to resist the attempts by the National Health Service's (NHS) management to tell them how to practice medicine. Such a position as the source of tension lies in the professional/organisational relationship.

Third, professionals tend to surround themselves with people who have similar backgrounds and values (Quinn et al. 1996). Unless deliberately fractured, these discipline-based cocoons quickly become inward-looking bureaucracies that are resistant to change and detached from their customers (Quinn et al. 1996). For example, many software or basic research units become isolated inside large organisations, generating poor relationships with other professional groups such as marketing, manufacturing or sales departments (Quinn et al. 1996).

Development of Professional Ethics

A particular distinguishing feature between professional and other groupings, is that professionals have drafted their own code of ethics.

Although individual provision may differ, all codes generally require that its members maintain a higher standard of conduct than that required by law (Backof and Martin, 1991). The codes of ethics embraced by the legal, medical and accounting professions are examples, as ones which have developed over time and are sensitive to changing events. Sometimes a profession is affected by certain events, such as the new privacy code adopted by Britain's Press Commission, driven by the death of Diana, Princes of Wales *(Times,* 1997). The self-regulated press body adopted a code that prohibits the publication of photographs obtained illegally or by 'persistent pursuit' *(Times,* 1997). However, codes are not static, for the codes of a profession may be changed in response to changes in the social, economic and political environment, as well as changes in the growth and development of professional practice (Backof and Martin, 1991). For example, the legal profession's code of ethics in the USA underwent considerable change through the federal government's *War and Poverty* policy during the 1960s (Backof and Martin, 1991).

Yet, despite a profession's capacity to respond to change, looking through history it can been seen that it took a number of occupations many years before they become recognised as professions. The medical profession, for example, was the first to develop a modern code of ethics, based on the work in 1803 of a British physician, Thomas Percival. In an attempt to abate the decline of the status of the medical profession, at the first meeting of the American Medical Association (AMA) in 1846, a committee was appointed to report on a code of ethics for the organisation (Fishbein, 1947). Some 60 years later the legal profession, through the American Bar Association (ABA), adopted its first code of professional ethics, *Canons of Ethics,* in 1908 based on the work of Judge George Sharswood, written some 50 years prior in 1854. The accountant's desire for professional prestige led to the development of a code of professional ethics in 1907 (Backof and Martin, 1991).

More recently, the development of a market forces ideology was the major force underpinning the development of a business code of ethics. Prior to 1960 business ethics were primarily considered from a theological and religious perspective (De George, 1982). The emerging interest in social issues in business during the 1960's corresponded to the anti-business and anti-military movement amongst the youth of the US, a movement partly responsible in the 1970s for the rise of business ethics (De George, 1982). Whilst the 1980s could be viewed as the period of initial consolidation of business ethics (De George, 1982), the 1990s can be seen as the era of ethics codification.

However, a fundamental difference exists between professional ethics, centred on particular professions, such as law, medicine, communications, counselling, journalism, engineering, accountancy, as opposed to business ethics, namely that most professions work to a code of ethics *(un code de deontologie)* that often provides the focus of that profession's ethical behaviour. Unlike corporate codes of ethics, professional codes in western societies are often legally enforceable. Moreover, entry into professional life is usually much more uniform and regulated than is entry into a career in business (McDonald, 1992).

IT and the Need for a Professional Code of Ethics

Having examined the nature of social responsibility, its influence on the development of professions and the varying nature of professional and business ethics, attention is now given to examining the needs and requirements of IS/IT as a movement requiring the involvement of professionals.

Perhaps one of the current and more significant social developments is that of the new employment trend, the 'externalised' work force, with its emphasis on fixed-term contracts rather than lifelong careers. Increasingly, externalised employees are professionals, such as accountants, healthcare workers and IT specialists (Davis-Blake and Uzzi, 1993), of whom has been demanded a requirement for certification, whether on the basis of continuous professional development or vocational qualifications (Kavanagh, 1996). The new employment patterns mean demand for IT qualifications is growing and raising new issues concerning training quality and accreditation (Kavanagh, 1996). At a time of skill shortages, changing employment patterns and the growing emphasis on qualifications, accreditation is one development which can help to unify the training industry, employers, individuals, professional societies and academic institutions (Kavanagh, 1996).

Further, the proliferation of IT and the associated ease of information sharing, the flattening of organisational hierarchies and the increase of formal and informal networks, pose difficulties for privacy and confidentiality. As never before IT-based systems provide organisations with the opportunity to have an almost instantaneous access to vast amounts of critical information concerning customers, competitors, employees, suppliers and products/services. An error or deliberate action can have considerable impact on privacy. For example, an error in a computer program carried out by a Department of Social Security employee in Australia caused the distribution of thousands of social benefit payments to be sent to the wrong addressees (Korac-Boisvert and Kouzmin, 1994).

Additionally, (un)intentional commercial actions may place IS/IT specialists in a compromising ethical situation. For example, during the launch of the new software product, *Natural New Dimension* for personal computers, the software corporation SPL Worldgroup (Australia) presented each attendant with a free software package. Of the 210 IS specialists attending, 180 were public sector employees who attended the two hour presentation, during working hours, as part of a government initiative to keep abreast of IT developments (SPL Worldgroup Australia, 1995). Considering that software licences were issued under individual names, not the organisation's, and that individuals were IT professionals, each individual took home a package worth AUS$2100 (SPL Worldgroup Australia, 1995).

Furthermore, unethical acts are not only performed by businesses, but also by IS/IT specialists. For example, in the Australian Commonwealth Department of Customs, an information technology consultant dealing with diesel excise rebates, managed to channel funds into numerous bank accounts over a period of time, amounting to AUS$1.3 million *(The Daily Telegraph Mirror,* 1994, p.9; Korac-Boisvert and Kouzmin, 1994). Similarly, the two largest Australian social benefits departments, the Department of Social Security (DSS) and the Department of Employment, Education and Training (DEET) have encountered similar financial embellishments, not only by clients but by employees dealing with IS/IT systems (Ives, 1993; Korac-Boisvert and Kouzmin, 1994), which, after media leaks, led to the adoption of the Fraud Control Action Plan (Ives, 1993; Korac-Boisvert and Kouzmin, 1994). These examples do not suggest that IT professionals in other societies are more ethical than in Australia, but rather that Australian's have more open access to information. Unfortunately, recent incidents involving software piracy, computer viruses, data thefts, system espionage and employee monitoring in the USA and elsewhere, have emphasised the potential for unethical behaviour associated with the use of IS/IT and the IS/IT occupation (Kidwell et al., 1987; Straub and Collins, 1990; Shim and Taylor, 1991).

The growing literature on IS/IT project failures suggests that one in two IS/IT development projects will not come to fruition as successful systems (Butler Cox Foundation, 1986; Lyytinen, 1988; Galloway and Whyte, 1989). Although there exists a variety of reasons for such a poor track record, a certain degree of responsibility lies with IS/IT developers. For example, Whyte and Bytheway (1996) argue that systems that score low on the 'necessity' scale (the degree to which systems are really contributory to the business), suggest that the IT department is spending the company's money pursuing their own pet IT projects. This indulgence in technical objectives at the expense of the business can be viewed as an ethical issue.

However, some have argued that the standards IS/IT professionals accept would hardly be acceptable for a doctor, dentist or architect. The reasons are quite understandable given the nature of problems and solutions (Sims, 1996). Shifting requirements, unstable technology, a mobile work force, unrealistic schedules, over-sold software assistance and lack of comprehension of limitations, all make the IS/IT professional's work difficult (Sims, 1996).

Optimistic futurists predicted a society transformed radically for the better by IS/IT, with IS/IT being the tool of liberation (Turkle, 1984). Critics viewed IS/IT as a tool for increasingly inhumane and despotic capitalism (Webster, 1990). However, the reality of the IS/IT revolution has been, that like all technical innovations, its impact has varied across different categories of social sectors and classes. However, there exist several reasons for special concern about IS/IT. First and foremost, it is ubiquitous. Whereas most labour-saving technologies in the past affected a small part of the economy, IS/IT affects everybody including the service sector. It is the service sector where all the employment growth in the western world has occurred over two or three decades, giving opportunity for female employment and part-time jobs, which are now being replaced by automation (Brame, 1996), exemplified by the ATMs and bank tellers. Second and apart from being ubiquitous, IS/IT is also evolving rapidly and creating new market forces than new technologies have done in the past (Rifkin, 1994). IS/IT makes work more portable; more people can work at home, by 'telecommuting', an already significant trend. However, it also means that telecommuters may live in other countries, where wages are lower.   Telecommuting is also a way of exporting jobs.   For example, Swissair has moved its entire reservation service to Bangalore, India, and Lufthansa has announced that it intends to follow suit.   Providing better, more valuable services to consumers, without necessarily consuming more physical resources, is current economic strategy.   Third, the delinking of economic activity from energy and materials ('de-materialisation') (Ayres, 1991) could be dysfunctional in the long term.   For example, adopting more costly 'flexible' manufacturing systems, capable of being reprogrammed to deal with new design and customisation, incurs productivity penalties. Technological change also accelerates capital depreciation which, in turn, requires more investment to replace each generation of depreciated capital goods, which means that less net growth is delivered.   Current technological progress, especially in the field of IS/IT, can negatively impact on economic growth, as the price of manufacturing goods will lower economic growth and lead, ultimately, to higher unemployment.   Overall, technology and the responsibilities computer professionals have as custodians of IS/IT, spans almost all aspects of human life.   Society at large is becoming more aware of the fact that IS/IT can empower or enslave and the choice made, quite often, is reliant upon the 'professional attitudes' of the technologists (Rogerson, 1996).

With the arguments in mind, some have argued that special attention should be paid to ethical issues and problems unique to the field of IS/IT. These are those issues that are characterised by the primary and essential involvement of IS/IT; exploit some unique property of IS/IT; and would not have arisen without the essential involvement of IT (Rogerson, 1996). Uniqueness includes storage, complexity, adaptability and versatility, reproduction and coding.   This IT uniqueness has resulted in a failure to find satisfactory non-computer analogies that might resolve IT-related ethical dilemmas, and therefore no guidelines exist as to how to resolve these new moral dilemmas.   Although the IS/IT occupation has an immense impact on all spheres of organisational life, there is still no code of ethics to highlight pathways through, at times, overwhelming paradox.

Adopting a Code of Ethics: Critical Mass for IS/IT

IS/IT specialists are considered an influential force in contemporary organisations for a number of reasons.   First, as IS/IT attains greater strategic importance, the IS/IT professional's actions will have, a significant impact on the success or failure of their organisation (Pearson et al.. 1997, p.276). Second, decisions, whether ethical or unethical, can be influenced by, the availability and/or quality of the information provided by an organisation's information system (Pearson et al.. 1997, p.276). Since IS/IT professionals typically have responsibility for the development, distribution and maintenance of these systems, the decisions and/or actions for this group of professionals can impact the quality of the information received by decision-makers within the organisation (Pearson et al.. 1997, p.276). Third, unlike other professional groups, IS/IT personnel are still struggling to become a profession and develop a single, agreed-upon code of ethics that is appropriate for their profession (Johnson, 1985; Oz, 1992, 1993; Pearson et al.. 1997), despite the fact that some IT specialists have started forming professional associations (Association of Computing Machinery, ACM; British Computer Society, BCS; Data Processing Management Association, DPMA).

However, the more IS/IT professionals join professional associations according to critical mass theory, the higher the likelihood of the IS/IT occupation attaining the status of a certificated profession, with a professional code of ethics. Currently three major professional IS associations have proposed ethical standards for the IS profession: The Data Processing Management Association (DPMA), the Institute for Certification of Computer Professionals (ICCP), and the Association for Computing Machinery (ACM) (Oz, 1993). Oz (1993) reviewed the codes of ethics proposed by those professional associations and concluded that while these codes have many differing and conflicting principles, they also have several principles in common.

The framework Oz (1993) used to compare those different ethical codes was based on work done by Johnson (1985). Johnson (1985) identified four criteria that should be present within a comprehensive professional code of ethics: obligation to society; obligation to employers; obligation to clients; and obligation to colleagues and to professional organisations. Oz (1993) divided the last obligation into three different obligations and modified the framework to include obligation to colleagues; obligation to professional organisation and obligation to profession. Both Johnson (1985) and Oz (1993) argue that these obligations represent a comprehensive set of criteria for evaluating the ethical behaviour of professional individuals. Both conclude that IS/IT professionals must strive for one, coherent code of professional conduct which can be used as a guide (Johnson, 1985; Oz, 1992, 1993).

Conclusion

Notwithstanding that expunging unethical behaviour is an impossible task, minimising the more unsavoury, negative practices is necessary for any organisation and society at large. Certain values, such as honesty, respect for the person (which suggests *inter alia* that professionals should avoid patronage and favouritism and exercise powers fairly and equitably); integrity and justice appear equally respected by professionals and non-professionals alike. Socratic virtues (Plato, 1961): namely a willingness to talk, to listen to other people, to weigh the consequences of our actions upon other people, are moral virtues that are widely acclaimed in the current leadership and management literature (Kakabadse, 1991; Fairholm, 1991, 1993; Korac-Boisvert and Kouzmin, 1995).

It is strongly argued in this chapter that a concern about ethics needs to become a vital component of the process of IS/IT strategy development. Policies and procedures need to reflect a genuine commitment to building a culture in which ethical values are explicitly acknowledged. This means going beyond a commitment to commercial values of profit maximisation and instead allowing a full appreciation of what underlines such commitments (Longstaff, 1995). Organisations need to know why profits are important and how professionals add value to organisations. Furthermore, an essential element of self-regulation is to be allowed, otherwise organisations will find that individuals and corporations surrender their judgement about the rights and wrongs of a situation to a group of people who will favour a limited and strict interruption of the law (Longstaff, 1995). The advantages of membership of a professional body can also give security and assurance to 'whistle blowers', without the ethical principles being reduced to an administrative code (Vincent, 1995). Although codes of ethics are probably the most visible signs of an organisational ethical philosophy, codes are not an absolute guarantee of ethical behaviour within an organisation, they are merely a set of guidelines available to be followed (Alderson and Kakabadse, 1994). Organisational codes have been viewed as the major organisational mechanism for implementing ethical policies. These codes commonly address issues such as conflict of interests, privacy, and the receiving and giving of gifts (Wiley, 1995). However, in order to make a powerful impact, the code must be tailored to focus on its major line of business. Furthermore, codes should be specific (interpreting individual actions); public (available to the whole constituency to determine the organisation's commitment to fair and ethical practice); clear and practical (realistic and to the point about what happens to violators); revisable (leaving documents open to revision); enforceable (must be enforced); and audible (regular social or moral audit).

Cicero (1981, p.161) observed that, 'to everyone who proposes to have a good career, moral philosophy is indispensable'. Professionalism, like pragmatism, is a synthesis of the, 'theory and practice of enlarging human freedom in a precarious and tragic world by the arts of intelligent social control' (Hook, 1974). Perhaps this synthesis may present a lost cause, however, there may not be a better one. This cause is contingent on the formulation of moral principles and moral education, which in turn requires choosing and defending a cause. Each person's own level of cognitive moral development strongly influences their decision, 'regarding what is right or wrong; the rights, duties, and obligations involved in a particular ethical dilemma' (Kohlberg, 1981; Trevino, 1986). Ethical decision-making is contingent on the interaction of individual variables, and 'formative context' situation moderators and is made vulnerable in circumstances of continuous and dramatic change. For IS/IT professionals, straddling between acceptable professional practice and the pragmatic nature of business enhancement, being respectful to the rights of all concerned whilst exercising professional duty, is not easy. Thus IS/IT professionals require a code of ethics that defines a discernible philosophical direction, be substantial enough in detail to be used as a framework to guide ethical conduct and contain specific topics of concern.

Note

1   This chapter was originally presented as a paper at the ETHICOMP'98 Conference, Rotterdam, The Netherlands, March 1998.

9 Leadership Determinants for Effective IS/IT Adoption

ANDREW K. KAKABADSE AND NADA K. KAKABADSE

Abstract

The importance of information technology (IT) and quality of leadership to business are widely acknowledged in both academic and praxis literature alike. The need for top management involvement in the strategic management of IS/IT for competitive advantage has been a recurring theme, with increasing vigour since the en masse creation of Chief Information Officer (CIO) positions in private and public sector organisations. Previous research has suggested that IS/IT adoption implies organisational innovation and as such there is a need for senior executive involvement. This chapter[1] presents an exploratory framework that links the quality of the leadership to the effective adoption of new IS/IT in organisations. The chapter also explores the demographic influence on leadership philosophy. Data from senior managers and executives in the Australian Public Service (APS) shows how different aspects of leadership philosophies influence (positively and negatively) four integral facets of IS/IT adoption - IS/IT Training, IS/IT Deployment, IS/IT Skills, and IS/IT Impact on the Organisation.

Introduction

Some scholars argue that IS/IT is a sufficiently strategic issue requiring the appointment of a senior executive to represent IS/IT at board level (Earl, 1989; Rowe and Herbert, 1990). Along the same lines, Farbey et al. (1993, p.7) give four key reasons why senior general managers today need to be more involved with IS/IT. Firstly, IS/IT affects strategic issues; secondly, IS/IT is at the core of business processes; thirdly, IS/IT accounts for large expenditure; and fourthly, IS/IT is complex. Others assert that the success of IS/IT adoption depends on the notions held at corporate levels concerning decision processes where IS/IT strategies are formed (Alder et al. 1992; Boynton et al. 1992; Schein, 1994). Equally, successful IS/IT adoption depends on the nature of the strategic planning process (Ciborra and Jelassi, 1994); on the key 'stakeholders', or personnel responsible for implementing IS/IT strategies (Rowe and Herbert, 1990; Earl, 1993); on the role of the technical champion and external agents (management consultants) in the strategy process; and on any other current developments in the IS/IT industry which are likely to influence the IS/IT adoption strategy formulation and implementation, such as outsourcing (Currie, 1994).

One idea that has been strongly linked to the success of technological innovation is the presence of a champion. The champion is an individual who formally or informally emerges in the organisation (Schön, 1963; Tushman and Nadler, 1986) and makes a 'decisive contribution to innovation by actively and enthusiastically promoting its progress through the critical organisational stages' (Achilladelis et al. 1971, p.14). Although personality characteristics, leadership behaviour, and influence tactics are frequently discussed in the championing literature (Schön, 1963; Burgelman, 1983; Van de Ven, 1986; Dean, 1987), for the most part, the results of different studies are increasingly emphasising the powerful influence of leadership. Technological innovation literature argues for the importance of the leadership factor on innovation success, namely that those who allocate organisational resources influence innovation adoption (Wilson, 1966; Sapolsky, 1967; Hage and Dewar, 1973; Dewar and Dutton, 1986; Thong and Yap, 1995). Similarly, the information technology literature suggests that leadership is influential in the effective adoption of IS/IT (McFarlan and McKenney, 1983; Dewar and Dutton, 1986; Gibson and Jackson, 1987; Gerstein, 1987; Long, 1987; Keen, 1988; Zuboff, 1988; Earl, 1989; Walton, 1989; Rowe and Herbert, 1990; Grindley, 1991; Farbey et al. 1993; Davenport, 1993, 1994; Currie, 1995).

The study reported in this chapter examines the influence of aspects of leadership on IS/IT adoption in the Australian Public Service (APS). The chapter equally enters into an examination of the current thoughts surrounding the impact of leadership on the effective adoption of information technology in the organisation. An overview of the demographic characteristics that influence leadership philosophy is also provided. This is followed by an outline of the study, research methodology and hypothesis to be explored. The findings from the research are then presented and the chapter concludes with an outline of the policy design implication for IS/IT adoption. The main findings are threefold. Firstly, organisational demographics are identified as a potent influence in shaping leadership philosophies. Secondly, leadership philosophies are a prime determinant of effective IS/IT adoption in the organisation. Thirdly, that effective IS/IT adoption requires consideration of a comprehensive approach to IS/IT consisting of IS/IT training, tailored to meet the organisation's needs, the deployment of IS/IT systems to meet organisational requirements, the adoption of IS/IT skills needed to meet the above identified needs, and consideration as to how the IS/IT systems are to impact on the organisation. The findings of this survey contradict the results of certain previous studies on the adoption of IS/IT innovation in organisations, in that previous research has focused on organisational characteristics, without giving due emphasis to leadership philosophy characteristics, and/or addressing only one aspect of IS/IT policy such as IS/IT deployment or IS/IT training.

Leadership Influence on Effective IS/IT Adoption

The emerging empirical data shows that leaders and top management teams have considerable impact on organisational outcomes (Romanelli and Tushman, 1986; Finklestein and Hambrick, 1990; Kakabadse, 1991, 1993; Kakabadse et al. 1996; Kakabadse and Myers, 1996a, 1996b; Korac-Kakabadse and Korac-Kakabadse, 1996). Finkelstein and Hambrick's (1990) study found that in high-discretion industries, such as the computer industry, managers seem to 'matter greatly'. Kakabadse's (1991, 1993) extensive study of 'top teams' (5,500 executives in the UK, Australia, Ireland, France, Germany, Sweden, Austria, Spain, Finland and Japan) across private and public sector organisations, found that leadership has the strongest impact on organisational effectiveness.

Equally, several writers conceptually link transformational leadership to the effectiveness of the innovation processes (Bass, 1985; Conger and Kanungo, 1987, 1988; Conger, 1989; Kakabadse, 1991; Korac-Kakabadse et al. 1996), of which IS/IT is one example. A large number of studies link IS/IT with radical changes in the workplace, economy and society (Forester, 1985, 1987). Kakabadse (1991) and others (Korac-Kakabadse and Korac-Kakabadse, 1996; Korac-Kakabadse et al. 1996) show empirically that leadership philosophy influences all aspects of organisational life, while some (Walton, 1989; Grindley, 1991; Thong and Yap, 1995; Chittister and Haimes, 1996) show empirically that leadership is critical for successful adoption and utilisation of IS/IT as, through their skills and competencies, leaders influence the organisational level of innovation. Thus, it is implied that organisational adoption of new IS/IT is determined by leadership choice, or at least strongly influenced by the organisation's executives, whilst leadership philosophy, in turn, is considered as determined by the demographic characteristics (Kakabadse et al. 1996).

Organisational Demography

Research regarding the consequences of organisational demography spans a wide breadth of organisational outcomes, from Kanter's (1977) study on how the proportions of men and women in corporations affect group process and individual outcomes, to Michel and Hambrick's (1992) study of how the diversity of top management teams affects organisational performance, and Ely's (1994) study of how the positions of women at the top levels of law firms influence women lawyers' professional relationships. The basic assumption underpinning demography theory is that demographic characteristics influence social dynamics, which in turn influence organisational outputs and outcomes (Pfeffer, 1983; Stinchcombe et al. 1986). Pfeffer (1983, p.348) argues that 'demography is an important, causal variable that affects a number of intervening variables and processes and through them, a number of organisation outcomes'. Demography theory focuses on compositional characteristics that influence interpersonal and group dynamics, and is particularly relevant to understanding outcomes involving 'top teams' (Pfeffer, 1983; Kakabadse, 1991; Kakabadse and Myers, 1996a, 1996b; Kakabadse et al. 1996; Korac-Kakabadse and Korac-Kakabadse, 1998).

Group demography attributes (age, tenure, occupation, gender and ethnicity) may be used as surrogate measures for the common experiences and background that shape human development and influence, amongst others, language, quality and frequency of communication (March and Simon, 1958; Pelz and Andrews, 1966; Allen and Cohen, 1969; Rogers and Shoemaker, 1971). Group demography reflects similarity and dissimilarity among individuals, making it a meaningful perspective for understanding processes affected by group dynamics, such as the level and extent of within-group communication, as well as outcomes of group dynamics, including such phenomena as the level of consensus within a group, innovation, and turnover. Group demography influences organisational groups' actions and behaviour, for example, communication and psychological dimensions such as social integration (Smith et al. 1994, p.412; Kakabadse, 1991). In the study reported in this chapter, five demographic dimensions - organisational tenure, tenure in the Australian Public Service (APS), job tenure, number of senior appointments, and size of organisation - were used for data pooling for cluster formulation and analysis of leadership philosophies (Kakabadse, 1991; Kakabadse et al. 1996; Kakabadse and Myers, 1996a, 1996b; Korac-Kakabadse and Korac-Kakabadse, 1996; Korac-Kakabadse et al. 1996).

According to Cyert and March's (1963) concept of the 'dominant coalition', Hambrick and Mason's (1984) 'upper-echelons' theory, and Kakabadse's (1991) discretionary leadership theory of the 'top team', upper-level management has an important impact on organisational outcomes because of the discretionary decisions they are empowered to make on behalf of the organisation. Since these managers pursue discretionary choices consistent with their cognitive base, which is, in part, a function of their personal values and experiences, their past experiences and values can be linked to organisational outcomes (Kakabadse, 1991). Based on discretionary leadership logic, scholars link top teams to organisational innovation (Bantel and Jackson, 1989; O'Reilly and Flatt, 1989) and performance (Waldman and Avolio, 1986; Murray, 1989; O'Reilly and Flatt, 1989; Eisenhardt and Schoonhoven, 1990; Michel and Hambrick, 1992; Hambrick and D'Aveni, 1992; Kakabadse, 1991, 1993; Smith et al. 1994; Kakabadse et al. 1996; Kakabadse and Myers, 1996a, 1996b; Korac-Kakabadse and Korac-Kakabadse, 1996).

Three main conceptual perspectives that emerge from 'top team' research focus on the top team's demography, process and organisation performance. Top team demography refers to the aggregated external characteristics of the top team (heterogeneity, tenure, size), while process concerns the team's actions and behaviours (communication, and psychological dimensions, social integration). Broader, qualitative organisational goals, beyond traditional profit-maximisation measures, are developed for performance, such as clear vision, unity of strategic direction, and quality of dialogue. Although some earlier researchers argue that leaders and top management teams have little impact on organisational outcomes (Lieberson and O'Connor, 1972; Aldrich, 1979; Astley and Van de Ven, 1983), the emerging view from recent research suggests otherwise (Romanelli and Tushman, 1986; Finkelstein and Hambrick, 1990; Kakabadse, 1991; Korac-Kakabadse and Korac-Kakabadse, 1996). Finkelstein and Hambrick (1990, p.500) found that in high-decision industries, such as the information industry for example, managers seem to 'matter greatly'. This recent stream of thinking and study findings have been facilitated by the Hambrick and Mason's (1984) upper-echelons theory that was inspired by Cyert and March's (1963) concept of 'dominant coalitions', and Kakabadse's (1991) 'top team' and 'wealth creators' concepts. According to these findings, 'top team' managers have an important impact on organisational outcomes because of the decisions they are empowered to make for the organisation. They are the ones who influence the wealth creation process (Kakabadse, 1991), thereby determining strategy (Finkelstein and Hambrick, 1990; Michel and Hambrick, 1992), strategic change (Grimm and Smith, 1991; Wiersema and Bantel, 1992) and strategic performance (O'Reilly and Flatt, 1989; Michel and Hambrick, 1992; Hambrick and D'Aveni, 1992). In this study, Information Technology (IS/IT) is conceptualised as a function of leadership philosophies, context and IS/IT strategic choice. Thus, organisational IS/IT can be viewed as opportunities for action as well as avenues for uncertainty avoidance, influenced by strategic choice (Child, 1972a, 1972b).

Study Design

The primary purpose of this study is to identify the important factors that lead to effective adoption of IS/IT. This study explores the influence of leadership philosophies on the effective adoption of IS/IT in the Australian Public Service (APS). The participants are senior public sector managers, henceforth referred to as the 'Top Team' (Kakabadse, 1991, 1993), and their constituencies. The study focuses on an examination of two specific issues:

1. Kakabadse's (1991) typology of the analysis of leadership philosophy in the organisation, comprising three facets:

    - The leadership philosophy of intent (what leaders intend to endeavour);
    - The leadership philosophy of approach (how leaders treat others and how others like to be treated); and
    - The leader's behaviour (what leaders do as a result of their philosophy).

2. Korac-Boisvert's (1990) and others' (Anderson and Tushman, 1990; Grindley, 1991) typology of IS/IT dimensions, concentrating on four areas:

- IS/IT Training;
- IS/IT Deployment;
- IS/IT Skills; and
- IS/IT Impact on the Organisation.

Leadership philosophy is taken as discretionary leadership (Kakabadse, 1991, p.20) and classifies executives' roles into two categories: the 'discretionary' or leadership role, and the 'prescribed' or management role. The discretionary, or leadership, role is defined as the role in which an executive exercises choice in identifying and pursuing policies, strategies and determining organisational or sub-unit direction, as 51 per cent or more of their role provides for such freedom and flexibility. In prescribed, or management roles an executive's choice is limited, as 51 per cent or more of that role is predetermined, leaving the role incumbent little option other than to pursue the tasks and duties they are required to perform (Kakabadse, 1991).

The interdependent technological variable, effective adoption of IS/IT, consists of four dimensions: IS/IT training (Davenport, 1993, 1994; Currie, 1995), IS/IT deployment (IS/IT infrastructure and IS/IT utilisation) (Keen and Scott-Morton, 1978; Grindley, 1991; DeMarco and Lister, 1987; Tushman and Anderson, 1986; Currie, 1995); IS/IT skills (Tushman and Anderson, 1986; Grindley, 1991; Currie, 1995; Thong and Yap, 1995); and IS/IT impact on the organisation (DeMarco and Lister, 1987; Tushman and Anderson, 1986; Grindley, 1991). IS/IT innovation research has argued that it may not be possible to develop a unifying theory of innovation due to the fundamental differences between innovation methodologies and IS/IT spread of diversity (Downs and Mohr, 1976; Kirton, 1976). Hence, the selected factors are those that are considered more applicable to the adoption of IS/IT in a public sector organisation context, namely IS/IT training, IS/IT deployment, IS/IT skills, and IS/IT impact on the organisation.

This exploratory study was conducted in two stages. Stage 1 of the study primarily ascertained face validity responses towards Kakabadse's (1991) questionnaire and whether the IS/IT issues identified in the instrument were considered pertinent by the respondents. The Kakabadse (1991) instrument explores leadership philosophies, organisational context and strategy, and has been tested on over 5,500 executives in private and public sector organisations in the UK, Ireland, France, Germany, Sweden, Austria, Spain, Finland, Hong Kong, USA, China and Japan. The pilot survey for face validity was undertaken within the Department of

Employment, Education and Training Secretary (DEET), and 86 questionnaires were distributed to senior civil servants, who were members of the Senior Executive Service (SES), 27 of whom responded. On receipt of these responses and having duly made the necessary adjustment, the Australian Public Service Commission (PSC) staff reviewed the questionnaire for face validity. The PSC is a public sector organisation responsible for the training and development of senior executive service (SES) officers and senior officers (SO).[2] Based on feedback from the 27 respondents and on the PSC staff's recommendations, questionnaire modification was subjected to eight iterations for face validity, with most changes made to item terminology. The 27 responses from the pilot study were not included in the final sample.

For the second stage, the main study, all departments across the Australian Public Service (APS) across the board were chosen rather than a specific number of departments, as the APS represents the necessary strategic level to examine IS/IT implementation, from a policy perspective. Owing to the Australian Commonwealth Privacy Act (1988), mailing addresses of senior executive services (SESs) and senior officers (SOs) were unobtainable. Thus, in order to get access to the APS sample, it was necessary to enter into negotiation with the Public Service Commission (PSC) and obtain their support for the research.

Etzioni (1970) argues that the only way to enter any client system is with the permission of the executive strata. The sample size, instrument distribution and data collection were carried out by the PSC. A total of 1,500 questionnaires were randomly distributed to 750 (46 per cent of the total population) executive officers (SESs) and 750 (5 per cent of the total population) senior officers (SOs) across all federal departments and variety of functions. The PSC ensured that everyone in the sample held a leadership or management position (irrespective of whether they were managers, professional lawyers, medical officers, accountants), and that smaller departments were equitably represented.[3] The response rate was 50 per cent, a rate considered by the researchers as positive, given the sensitivity of the questionnaire and the seniority of the respondents (Norburn and Birley, 1986; Finkelstein, 1992). A response rate of 40 per cent or more is deemed reasonably high (Finkelstein, 1992, p.522). Measures of demographic attributes were collected for all 750 participating APS managers.

Research Hypotheses

The hypotheses outlined below are derived from a literature search, in particular the work of Kakabadse (1991, 1993), Korac-Kakabadse and Korac-Kakabadse (1996), Korac-Kakabadse et al. (1996) and others (McFarlan and McKenney, 1983; Dewar and Dutton, 1986; Gibson and Jackson, 1987; Gerstein, 1987; Long, 1987; Keen, 1988; Zuboff, 1988; Earl, 1989; Walton, 1989; Korac-Boisvert, 1990; Rowe and Herbert, 1990; Grindley, 1991; Farbey et al. 1993; Davenport, 1993, 1994; Currie, 1995; Thong and Yap, 1995), as well as the researchers' personal experience of managing adaptation of new IS/IT in organisations.

Hypothesis 1:   Effective adoption of IS/IT is dependent on the appropriate mix of transformational and transactional leadership approaches adopted by the Top Team.

Several writers conceptually link transformational leadership to innovation processes (Bass, 1985; Conger and Kanungo, 1987, 1988; Conger, 1989; Kakabadse, 1991; Korac-Kakabadse et al. 1996) of which IT is one example. A large number of studies link IT with revolutionary changes in the workplace, economy and society (Forester, 1985, 1987). Kakabadse (1991) and others (Korac-Kakabadse and Korac-Kakabadse, 1996; Korac-Kakabadse et al. 1996) show empirically that leadership philosophy influences all aspects of organisational life, while others (Walton, 1989; Grindley, 1991; Thong and Yap, 1995; Chittister and Haimes, 1996) show empirically that leadership is critical for the successful adoption and utilisation of IT, as by using their skills and competencies, leaders influence the pursuit and application of skills at the organisational level and the pursuit of innovation. Thus, it is implied that organisational adoption of new IT is determined by leadership choice, or at least strongly influenced by the organisation's executives.

Hypothesis 2:   Effective adoption of new IS/IT is dependent on implementing a relevant and complete IS/IT package, consisting of four aspects: IS/IT training, IS/IT deployment (infrastructure and utilisation), IS/IT skills, and assessment of IS/IT impact.

Both vertical technology transfer (the transformation of ideas into products) and horizontal technology transfer (the application of an idea into different domains) are long, expensive and difficult processes which require technological, physical and intellectual infrastructures (Korac-Kakabadse and Kouzmin, 1996). Others argue that IS/IT adoption is dependent on the level of existing IS/IT skills and, as a consequence, reinforce the provision of training, as well as the mode of utilisation, and infrastructure (Keen and Scott-Morton, 1978; Perrow, 1984; DeMarco and Lister, 1987; Tushman and Anderson, 1986; Walton, 1989; Korac-Boisvert, 1990; Grindley, 1991; Davenport, 1993, 1994; Margetts and Willcocks, 1993; Currie, 1995; Korac-Boisvert and Kouzmin, 1995; Chittister and Haimes, 1996). In examining hypothesis 2, both vertical and horizontal technology transfer and IS/IT skills levels are explored.

Methodology

Building on the theoretical work of organisational demography (Pfeffer, 1983; Mittman, 1992), and related studies of leadership (Tushman and Romanelli, 1985), and top teams (Kakabadse, 1991; Kakabadse et al. 1996; Kakabadse and Myers, 1996a, 1996b; Korac-Kakabadse and Korac-Kakabadse, 1996), this study has adopted organisational demography theory as the basis for the clustering criterion. Data collected was analysed with respect to the level in the public service organisations; age; gender; background; professional qualifications; tenure in APS; organisational tenure; job tenure; number of senior appointments held; number of appointments held outside the APS; and size of organisation.

Factor analyses were then carried out within each cluster. As Pfeffer (1983) has suggested, demography needs to be assessed in a way that enables the researcher to capture the distribution and compositional effects of variations in group demography. In this study, both variable interdependency (factor analysis) and inter-object similarity (cluster analysis) techniques are used for data analysis, as well as multiple regression analysis for model predictability.

Leadership Philosophy Cluster Analysis

This study used a quick clustering (hierarchical top-down) approach for leadership philosophy data analysis, because of its clarity, ease of use, and previous distinguishable research results in the private and public sectors (Kakabadse, 1991; Kakabadse et al. 1996; Kakabadse and Myers, 1996a, 1996b; Korac-Kakabadse and Korac-Kakabadse, 1996). Quick clustering has been carried out with a pattern of five, four and three clusters. Only five demographic dimensions displayed significant differences in determining significant response clusters: namely, organisational tenure; job tenure; number of senior appointments; size of organisation; and tenure in APS. Three clusters emerged with significant differences determined by the aforementioned five demographic dimensions. This was compatible with earlier research in the private sector organisations, whereby three separate leadership clusters emerged (Kakabadse, 1991; Kakabadse et al. 1996).

The analysis of the statistical data presented in Table 9.1 defines the three clusters determined by the organisational demographics adopted.

Table 9.1 Three Cluster Analysis

Cluster	No of Cases	Organisation Size	Years in APS	Years in Orgn	Years in Job	Number of Senior Appointments
Cluster 1	244.0	2500-5000	10 >	16-25	5-10	2.8
Cluster 2	218.0	500-2000	10 >	1-4	1.2	2.6
Cluster 3	175.0	5000-10000	10 >	10-15	2.3	3.4

Factor Analysis

The input variables were then factor analysed until construct groupings emerged as factors. Variables that load on to a common factor were grouped into indices. To ensure that a given item represents the construct underlying each factor, a minimum item loading at .40 after varimax rotation was deemed acceptable (Nunnally, 1967; Finkelstein, 1992). When cross loading occurred, the following criterion of inclusion was adopted; the highest loading contribution was accepted while the lesser contribution was ignored (Nunnally, 1967). Similarly, if a difference between weights for any given cross-loading item was less then .1 across factors, the item was deleted from the final scale (Snell and Dean, 1992). In this study, the majority of items loaded on only one factor. However, some split-loading occurred predominately in factors with low internal constancy (low Cronbach *Alphas)*, which were duly deleted from the study.

IS/IT factors analysis Valid responses to 26 IS/IT questions, along a five-point interval scale, were factor analysed. From a principal components factor analysis of 26 items, eight factors with eigenvalues greater than one were extracted (Bagozzi, 1980; Finkelstein, 1992), and only those with loadings greater than .40 were reported (Finkelstein, 1992). The factors that survived demonstrated Cronbach's internal constancy of .65 and above (Table 9.2).

Additionally, 22 IS/IT questions with a bipolar (Yes/No) nominal scale were factor analysed. In factor analysis,[4] a loading for 0 - 1 scaled variables can be interpreted as the probability of the object's presence (if the loading is positive), or absence (if negative), given that the factor exists (Guildford, 1963). From the resulting principal components factor analysis of 22 items, factors with eigenvalues greater than one (Bagozzi, 1980; Aaker et al. 1995; Finkelstein, 1992) and after Cronbach's significance testing, factors displaying an internal consistency of .65 and greater, survived (Table 9.2).

Table 9.2 Summary of IS/IT Factors

Factor Type	Factor Title	Factor Loadings Range	No of Items	Cronbach's Alpha
IS/IT 1	IS/IT-Training	.82986 - .56508	6	.82986
IS/IT 2	IS/IT-Deployment	.80449 - .63898	4	.7952
IS/IT 3	IS/IT-Skills	.87259 - .74883	3	.8388
IS/IT 4	IS/IT-Impact	.72495 - .59655	7	.8165

Leadership philosophy factor analysis   Two constructs of concepts emerged from factor analysis: leadership attitudes and leadership values, with each construct dealing with a distinctive aspect of leadership. Eighty-eight and sixty-six Likert (five-point) interval scale items were entered into factor analysis examining leadership attitudes and leadership values respectively. The summary of the factor analysis for each cluster is provided below (Tables 9.3, 9.4 and 9.5):

Table 9.3 Cluster 1 (Team Players) - Factor Summary

Factor Type	Factor Title	Factor Loadings Range	No of Items	*Alpha* Score
Attitude 1	Promoting Performance	.68037 - .41528	19	.8788
Attitude 2	Disciplined	.71012 - .46653	7	.7071
Attitude 3	Independence	.67652 - .54018	7	.7424
Attitude 4	Specialist Orientation	.68486 - .55036	5	.7036
Value 1	Service Values	.85714 - .43291	18	.8489
Value 2	Responsibilities (Sense of Organisational Responsibilities)	.85609 - .45168	14	.8492
Value 3	Leading through Example	.81384 - .50463	10	.8327
Value 4	Response to Challenge	.78129 - .49355	8	.7461
Value 5	Professionalism and Conduct	.77564 - .47984	6	.7874
Value 6	Development for Others	.68931 - .47528	9	.8875

Table 9.4 Cluster 2 (Radicals) - Factor Summary

Factor Type	Factor Title	Factor Loadings Range	No of Items	*Alpha* Score
Attitude 1	Critical	.74616 - .40043	12	.8241
Attitude 2	Job Satisfaction	.73942 - .45929	8	.8320
Attitude 3	Discipline	.60442 - .43098	9	.6570
Attitude 4	Specialist Orientation	.66506 - .41997	7	.6508
Attitude 5	Independence	.58265 - .40195	8	.6701
Value 1	Outward Focused	.89042 - .47310	12	.8550
Value 2	Respect for People	.77145 - .41224	13	.9000
Value 3	Service Values	.75060 - .40354	16	.8445
Value 4	Open Accountability for Performance	.80367 - .52378	10	.8754
Value 5	Freedom to Perform	-.76310 - .46572	11	.7163

Table 9.5 Cluster 3 (Bureaucrats) - Factor Summary

Factor Type	Factor Title	Factor Loadings Range	No of Items	*Alpha* Score
Attitude 1	Cynical	.76311 - .46451	19	.8855
Attitude 2	Job Satisfaction	.64572 - .43982	6	.7109
Attitude 3	Specialist Orientation	.75911 - .48631	8	.7460
Attitude 4	Discipline	.59917 - .41851	10	.7032
Attitude 5	Independence	.54100 - .42456	8	.6668
Value 1	Professional Impartiality	.79082 - .51590	18	.8823
Value 2	Personal Conduct	.82795 - .42770	15	.8736
Value 3	Service Orientation	.87890 - .50859	9	.8440
Value 4	Accountability	.81459 - .64724	7	.7607

Internal constancy was assessed by calculating Cronbach *Alphas*[5] to obtain reliability estimates for each factor. Although a literature search suggests that there are no standard guidelines available on appropriate magnitudes for the *Alpha* coefficient (Van de Ven and Feraiy, 1980; Finkelstein, 1992, p.519), 'in practice, an *Alpha* greater than .60 is considered reasonable in organisational research' (Finkelstein, 1992, p.519; Eisenhardt, 1988; Van de Ven and Feraiy, 1980). Van de Ven and Feraiy (1980), for example, use .63 as a cut-off point for *Alpha,* and Finkelstein (1992) uses .65. Nunnally (1967) suggests that for large samples ($N \geq 450$) mediocre to good reliability ranges from .5 to .8. In this study, the higher standard of the *Alpha* coefficient magnitude is taken, with the cut-off point of .65.

Leadership Philosophy Profiles

From the analysis of SESs' and SOs' styles, values, attitudes and approaches to leadership practice at senior levels in the APS, three fundamentally different philosophies, approaches and ways of thinking of leadership emerged, significantly driven by the five demographic variables mentioned above.

The three different leader groups identified are: Team Players (Table 9.6), Radicals (Table 9.7) and Bureaucrats[6] (Table 9.8).

Team Players   Team Players are typically employed in large sized government organisations, have spent longest in any one organisation, have spent longest in any one job, and have held, on average, 2.8 senior managerial appointments (Table 9.6).

Table 9.6 Team Players - Demographic Characteristics

• Size	2,500 - 5,000 persons
• Years in Organisation	16 - 25 years
• Years in APS	more than 10 years
• Years in Job	5 - 10 years
• Number of Senior Appointments	2.8

The long stay nature of Team Players is strongly influential in the forming of their views concerning what it means to lead and promote a performance oriented culture in the organisation (Table 9.3). Part of generating a positive performance ethos in the organisation is due to the fact that Team Players display a positive attitude towards most challenges. Team Players lead through example. The positive orientation displayed towards colleagues, subordinates, superiors and towards work activities is extended to include the organisation. Team Players indicate that change initiatives undertaken in the past have attained positive results. They equally display positive views concerning present and likely future changes. One reason for their positive attitude towards change in the organisation, is that they actively encourage their peers and subordinates to undertake a broader corporate view over issues, a perspective they adopt themselves. In effect, working as a team and adopting an organisation-wide perspective, are for them, inter-related. Team Players highlight respect of tradition as well as of people.

Engendering high levels of morale in their staff and management is their key lever for attaining a positive orientation towards the provision of service. Team Players have recognised that in order to provide service externally, they, and through example to others, have to provide service to staff and lower level management, internally. Towards this end, professionalism and conduct in the workplace and quality of relationships and personal development are highly valued.

Radicals Radicals tend to have a background of having worked in smaller government departments/agencies, have spent few years in any one organisation and have the fewest number of senior management appointments (Table 9.7).

Table 9.7 Radicals - Demographic Characteristics

- Size of Organisation   500 - 2,000 persons
- Years in Organisation   1 - 4 years
- Years in APS   more than 10 years
- Years in Job   1 - 2 years
- Number of Senior Appointments   2.6

For Radicals, teamwork and discipline are considered as the important levers for effective policy and strategy implementation (Table 9.7). Radicals are also identified as self disciplined in terms of their approach to their daily work activities. They are equally conscious of the need to promote discipline in others. They are insistent that regular briefings on developments on projects and other initiatives are vital for effective communication.

Effective teamwork is also viewed as resulting from being disciplined in the pursuit and implementation of tasks and activities. Radicals recognise that being disciplined leads to cohesive teamwork, which is considered as necessary for effective policy implementation. They also recognise that positive teamwork helps people to better identify with, and own, the challenges and activities they have undertaken. For Radicals, teamwork and discipline are considered as the important levers for effective policy and strategy implementation.

However, being disciplined is accompanied by strong feelings of independence and needing the freedom to pursue their own courses of action. Radicals highlight that they dislike interference in their daily work activities. They are resentful of being directed on operational matters or broader policy matters. However, they highlight that they do find positions of command stimulating, as they can then pursue and apply their views and ideas in the organisation. Leadership is not just seen as command or taking charge, but the leadership necessary for the provision of service to communities and clients.

They equally attempt to inculcate the same high standards in others by working towards promoting trusting relationships. Their perspective is that if people trust each other, then they can accept feedback, then they can improve. The frustration of the Radicals is that they expect the same high standards from others as they do of themselves, and when disappointed, they display their frustration through being critical about the organisation and its management, which can induce a defensive response from others.

Bureaucrats   Bureaucrats typically have worked in larger government departments, have changed jobs considerably and have held the greatest number of senior management positions in comparison with the other two leader profiles (Table 9.8).

Table 9.8 Bureaucrats - Demographic Characteristics

• Size of Organisation	5,000 - 10,000 persons
• Years in Organisation	10 - 15 years
• Years in APS	more than 10 years
• Years in Job	2 - 3 years
• Number of Senior Appointments	3.4

Bureaucrats are identified as displaying a cynical style of leadership, in that they view their organisation as being constraining and themselves as hard done by (Table 9.8). Yet, these are the very same people who have more experience of senior management than others, but seem to be unwilling to do anything about their circumstances. The Bureaucrats' more cynical view of the organisation does not undermine their drive for effective job related performance.   Bureaucrats see themselves as disciplined in terms of attention to detail. Equally, the same degree of discipline is applied to following established procedures.   They see themselves as setting realistic targets within realistic time frames for their subordinates. Respect is shown for those who are disciplined and for those who respect the rules and procedures laid down in the organisation. They feel that, generally, greater discipline needs to be applied by senior management, as they strongly believe that greater discipline leads to greater success for the organisation.

Bureaucrats equally hold strong values determining what they consider to be professionalism, standards of personal conduct, performance, service and the development of the organisation through effective accountability. Professionalism for Bureaucrats is displayed by a concern with high standards of application of skills and competencies, whilst maintaining their impartiality, and a sense of fairness. Hence, displaying commitment, being timely, diligent and responsible, whilst at the same time remaining neutral, are important balances to achieve in order to provide for, what they consider as, value to the community and equally to protect and enhance the reputation of the organisation.

Regression Analysis

Each of the accepted IS/IT factors: IS/IT-training, IS/IT-deployment, IS/IT-skills, IS/IT-impact on the organisation are defined as dependent variables and are regressed against the leadership factors. Results with R-square values of less than .4 were discarded. Independent variables included only the factors that survived .65 *Alpha* reliability analysis. The acceptable level of significance was .05 and above.[7]

Leadership Influence on IS/IT

In line with the original hypothesis that leadership philosophies influence IS/IT adoption, regression analysis was undertaken for each IS/IT construct obtained from factor analysis, namely, IS/IT-training, IS/IT-deployment, IS/IT-skills, and IS/IT-impact. In each regression, one IS/IT factor was defined as the dependent variable while the other three IS/IT factors and 29 Leadership Philosophy indices were defined as independent variables. The lowest accepted level of significance in all regression is .05.

Regression Analysis Results

Particular elements of each of the three leadership philosophies emerge as positively influencing IS/IT adaptation. As for IS/IT training, two aspects of the Team Players' leadership philosophies negatively impact on how effectively IS/IT training is applied in the organisation (Table 9.9). The Team Players' approach to discipline and responding to challenge induces the adoption of basic IS/IT training in the enterprise. However, effective IS/IT deployment produces a positive influence on the application of higher order IS/IT training in the organisation (Table 9.10). Similarly, if the impact of IS/IT on the organisation is positive, managers in the organisation are likely to be more positively inclined to desire to pursue higher order IS/IT skills through training. Further, having staff and managers in the organisation who are already well skilled in IS/IT, applying their skills in an innovative manner, is likely to motivate others to improve their levels of capability and who, in turn, will push for improvements in IS/IT training standards in the organisation.

Table 9.9 Leadership Influence on IS/IT-Training (IS/IT1)

Significant T	Variable
.0098xx	IS/IT-Impact on the Organisation
-.0140x	Discipline (Team Players)
-.0329x	Responding to Challenge (Team Players)

Levels of Significance: XX - .01;   X - .05;   R-square = .81282

In terms of IS/IT deployment, namely the degree to which the IS/IT infrastructure is effectively utilised in the organisation, elements of both Team Leaders' and Bureaucrats' philosophy impacts on how effectively IS/IT is utilised (Table 9.10).   The independence orientation of Team Players has a positive impact on effective IS/IT deployment in the organisation. In contrast, the independence orientation of the Bureaucrats' leadership philosophy emerges as having a negative impact on effective IS/IT deployment in the organisation. A more consistent picture emerges concerning the influence of the other IS/IT factors on IS/IT deployment. The shared view that IS/IT is having a positive impact on the organisation supports the further deployment of IS/IT in the enterprise.

Table 9.10 Leadership Influence on IS/IT-Deployment (IS/IT2)

Significant T	Variable
.0059xx	IS/IT-Impact on the Organisation
.0285xx	IS/IT-Skills
.0179x	Independence (Team Players)
-.0453x	Independence (Bureaucrats)

Levels of Significance: XX - .01;   X - .05;   R-square = .77853

Further, the existence of an advanced level of IS/IT skills amongst the staff and managers in the organisation has a positive impact on the effectiveness of IS/IT deployment within the organisation. Due to their understanding of IS/IT, people are motivated to further utilise IS/IT in their daily practice. For similar reasons, well applied IS/IT training has a positive impact on IS/IT deployment in the organisation.

The development and effective utilisation of IS/IT skills in the organisation emerges as being influenced by two elements of leadership philosophy (Table 9.11). The independence orientation of Team Players is identified as having a negative impact on the development of IS/IT skills in the organisation. In contrast, the independence orientation of Radicals is supportive towards the development and utilisation of advanced and innovative IS/IT skills in the organisation. In addition, two elements of IS/IT applications are identified as influencing the manner in which IS/IT skills are developed in the organisation. Perceived effective IS/IT deployment influences the development and utilisation of advanced/innovative IS/IT skills in the organisation. On this basis, the more IS/IT is seen to have a positive impact on the organisation, the more senior management are likely to wish to sponsor, on behalf of their staff and management, advanced, more specialised/innovative IS/IT skills.

Table 9.11 Leadership Influence on IS/IT-Skills (IS/IT3)

Significant T	Variable
.0269x	Independence (Radicals)
.0285x	IS/IT-Deployment
-.0450x	Independence (Team Players)
.0465x	IS/IT-Impact on the Organisation

Levels of Significance: X - .05;   R-square = .70647

Concerning the perceived impact of IS/IT on the organisation, the two aspects of leadership philosophy and the nature of the IS/IT package being utilised in the organisation, influence, positively and negatively, perceptions of impact (Table 9.12). The discipline perspective of Team Players is recognised as having a positive impact on IS/IT being accepted in the organisation.

Table 9.12 Leadership Influence on IS/IT-Impact (IS/IT4)

Significant T	Variable
.0059xx	IS/IT-Deployment
.0098xx	IS/IT-Training
.0094xx	Discipline (Team Players)
-.0121x	Independence (Team Players)
-.0464x	Discipline (Bureaucrats)
-.0465x	IS/IT-Skills
.0215x	Independence (Radicals)

Levels of Significance: XX - .01;   X - .05;   R-square = .80768

However, the independence orientation of Team Players is identified as having a negative impact on IS/IT application and usage in the organisation, generating resistance to the usage of IS/IT. The discipline orientation of Bureaucrats induces a similar negative effect, whereas the independence orientation of Radicals is identified as having a more positive effect on the utilisation and acceptance of IS/IT in the organisation. In terms of the impact of other elements of the IS/IT package, it is identified that effective adoption of IS/IT training induces a positive view of IS/IT in the organisation, reducing resistance to the usage of IS/IT. Equally, effective deployment of IS/IT promotes a positive image of IS/IT in the organisation. In contrast, the adoption of innovative and specialist IS/IT skills has the opposite effect of generating resistance to the application of IS/IT.

Discussion of Findings

Hypothesis 1 asserts that the effective adoption of IS/IT is dependent on a mix of transformational and transactional leadership approaches adopted by the Top Team. Empirical testing of this hypothesis highlights how aspects of three distinct leadership philosophies, namely, Team Players, Radicals and Bureaucrats (Tables 9.3, 9.4, and 9.5) impact on the effective IS/IT adoption. Regression analysis (Tables 9.9, 9.10, 9.11 and 9.12) shows that certain aspects (attitudes, values) of each of the three leadership philosophies have a different impact on IS/IT factors, namely IS/IT skills, deployment, training and impact on organisation (Table 9.2). Some of these leadership aspects have an enhancing effect, whilst others have a detracting effect. For example, responsiveness to challenge and disciplined Team Players induce a more negative impact on IT training, in that they motivate people to only adopt basic training. Similarly independent Bureaucrats have a negative influence on effective IS/IT deployment, whilst the orientation of independent Team Players has a positive impact. Independent Radicals have positive impact on the IT skills adoption, whilst independent Team Players have negative impact on IS/IT skills adoption. Equally, the orientation of disciplined Team Players and independent Radicals has a positive impact on the organisation, reducing the number of sensitivities inhibiting dialogue, whilst disciplined Bureaucrats and independent Team Players have a negative impact promoting greater sensitivities which act as inhibitors to discussion and relationship building.

Hypothesis 2 argued that the adoption of new IS/IT is dependent on the complete IS/IT package consisting of four aspects: IS/IT training, IS/IT deployment (infrastructure and utilisation), IS/IT skills, and assessment of IS/IT impact. Empirical testing supports this hypothesis, as the study results highlight that identified IS/IT factors are influenced by each other (see Figure 9.1).

Figure 9.1 captures the relationship between leadership philosophy and effective IS/IT adoption. Equally, Figure 9.1 emphasises the need for a complete IS/IT package being implemented in the organisation, consisting of consideration of appropriate IS/IT skills, well thought through IS/IT deployment and a comprehensive training programme, so that IS/IT can have a positive impact on the organisation. Further, in order for IS/IT to have a positive impact on the organisation, the transformational combination of disciplined Team Players and independent Radicals is identified as having an enhancing influence. In contrast, a more detracting influence is provided by the transactional combination of independent Team Players and disciplined Bureaucrats.

For staff and management to adopt more innovative IS/IT skills requires the leadership philosophy of independent Radicals. The influence of Team Players is likely to induce basic IS/IT skills adoption amongst personnel in the organisation.

Consideration of appropriate IS/IT deployment in the organisation requires a more people sensitive, transactional leadership application. An enhancing influence to positive IS/IT deployment is that of the independent Team Players. A more detractional influence is that of the independent Bureaucrats. Both leadership approaches highlight a transactional philosophy, but the more people sensitive approach is identified as positive and contributory.

Effectiveness of IS/IT training is identified as more driven by the manner in which the whole IS/IT package is structured and implemented in the organisation than by leadership approach. The results indicate that leaders who adopt the philosophy of being challenging and disciplined Team Players, only induce the need to adopt more basic IS/IT training.

The results emphasise that appropriate leadership in combination with a well conceived and structured package of IS/IT services, allows for effectiveness of IS/IT adoption in the organisation. Appropriateness of leadership philosophy involves applying a combination of transformational and transactional approaches, emphasising independence of approach (Radicals), in combination with a people centred style, but which in itself highlights consistency, discipline and an ability to stand back and reflect on circumstances (disciplined/independent Team players). A detracting leadership influence is one of being people centred, disciplined and reflective but in combination with a more systems/'politically correct' approach (disciplined/independent Bureaucrats). The study reveals that there exists the need for a leader to champion IS/IT in the organisation, through utilising an apt combination of transformational and transactional behaviours, as opposed to a subtle combination of transactional behaviours which emphasise the maintenance of the status quo. In effect, when IS/IT is utilised as an organisational change tool, transformational philosophies and processes, reflective and supportive of that change, need to be adopted by leaders.

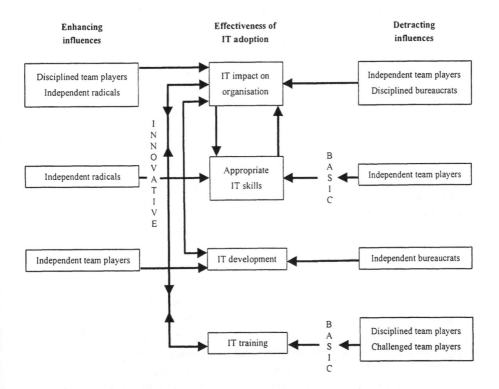

Figure 9.1 Leadership Philosophy Impact on Effective IS/IT Adoption

Conclusions: Leadership Philosophy Influence on IS/IT

The findings of this study, that leadership is influential in IS/IT adoption, is in agreement with the technological innovation literature (Wilson, 1966; Sapolsky, 1967; Hage and Dewar, 1973; Dewar and Dutton, 1986; Thong and Yap, 1995). The impact of leadership on the organisation influences a number of transactional and transformational decisions. Transformational decisions may relate to what to do to achieve budget savings, improve client services or gain and maintain competitive edge. The adoption of IS/IT would be one possible avenue towards gaining competitive advantage, exemplified by the increasing trend towards business process re-engineering (BPR) applications, where IS/IT plays a major role (Davenport, 1993, 1994; Currie, 1995). For most organisations, the adoption of new IS/IT represents a radical innovation that not only requires large outlays of financial resources, but also utilises innovative complex technology (Yap et al. 1994). Similarly, other studies have suggested that perseverance and discipline to see things through, amongst other attributes, are, in fact, characteristics of successful champions of technological innovation (Howell and Higgins, 1990).

Overall, leadership influence on effective IS/IT adoption has been supported by a number of studies, in particular McFarlan and McKenney (1983); Dewar and Dutton (1986); Gibson and Jackson (1987); Gerstein (1987); Long (1987); Keen (1988); Zuboff (1988); Earl (1989); Walton (1989); Rowe and Herbert, (1990); Grindley, (1991); Farbey et al. (1993); Davenport, (1993, 1994); Currie (1995); and Thong and Yap (1995), whose hypotheses and findings support those of this study, especially regarding the role of leadership and/or skills for effective IS/IT adoption.

In addition, a complete IS/IT package consisting of IS/IT training, IS/IT deployment, IS/IT skills, and positive IS/IT impact on the organisation is identified as necessary for effective IS/IT adoption in organisations. This finding is in line with the findings of other studies, which portray the ways in which the lack of knowledge and skill in the IS/IT adoption process, and insufficient awareness of the potential benefits may be inhibiting a business from adopting IS/IT (Senn and Gibson, 1981; Attewell, 1992; Yap et al. 1994). To the extent that a leadership philosophy can develop a knowledge capacity through job related development, is supported by the results of this study. This finding is also supported by evidence from the technological innovation literature. For example, Dewar and Dutton (1986) found that extensive knowledge is important for the adoption of technical process innovations. Similarly, other researchers have found that IS/IT skills, knowledge and training are important for effective IS/IT adoption (Walton, 1989; Grindley, 1991; Davenport, 1993, 1994; Currie, 1995).

This study contributes to the IS/IT and leadership literature by providing empirical evidence that highlights the significant role played by leaders in the adoption of IS/IT innovation, especially in public sector organisations and, in particular, the need for leaders to adopt transformational and transactional behaviours interchangeably; that is, the need for a transformational approach in conceptualising IS/IT and reformulating processes in the organisations, and transactional behaviours in order to adopt IS/IT as a tool for achieving these transformations.

Furthermore, to increase their chances of success, IS/IT consultants and vendors need to examine the whole IS/IT package which, besides new IS/IT products (software or hardware) or services, needs also to have included IS/IT training towards innovative IS/IT skills, which can encompass both horizontal and vertical technology transfer, and also to have incorporated an impact study that shows positive and negative correlations between the new IS/IT product or service, and the needs of the organisation.

However, this study has one limitation. Due to the time constraints and nature of this study (it represents a snap-shot in time), it was not possible to measure the dynamics of leadership philosophies and their effects on IS/IT, over time. Different technologies and executive experiences may have different effects on leadership philosophy which, in turn, may produce a different impact on IS/IT adoption. Longitudinal studies would have to be conducted to explicitly determine links of causality. In this way, the management and use of IS/IT across government can be examined especially during periods of change, when the scope of the IS/IT service is contributing to changing the role of individual agencies. Further, a longitudinal study can also examine the dramatic changes in the speed and scope of IS/IT, and its impact on the balance between the co-ordination of a whole-of-government approach to key issues, and the operational freedom needed for line agencies to deliver services to clients.

Notes

1   This chapter was originally presented as a paper at the UKAIS'98 Conference, Lincoln, UK, April 1998.

2   Each individual department also provides training for senior officers (SOs).

3   Within the last ten years the PSC has undertaken the distribution of three surveys amongst SESs.

4   The loading plays the role in factor analysis of the regression coefficient in multiple regression (Rummel, 1970).

5   The model, termed alpha factor analysis, attempts to maximise the fit of the common factors for the sample of variables to the factors for the universe of variables in the domain. Employing the alpha coefficient of generalisability, derived from the Kudar-Richardson (1937) reliability coefficient or Cronbach coefficient (Cronbach, 1951; Cronbach et al. 1963), Kaiser and Caffrey (1965) derive a scaling and matrix transformation of the data that yields common factors with maximum generalisability to the universe.

6   Terminology: Team Players, Radicals and Bureaucrats are used as labels for the leadership characteristics driven by demographics in the Korac-Kakabadse and Korac-Kakabadse (1998) studies and are not related to the literature usage (Presthus, 1958, 1962; Hampden-Turner, 1972).

7   Level of significance and their labels used are: XXX - .001; XX - .01 and X - .05.

10 Technostress: Over Identification with Information Technology and Its Impact on Employees and Managerial Effectiveness

NADA K. KAKABADSE, ALEXANDER KOUZMIN AND
ANDREW K. KAKABADSE

Abstract

The proliferation of information technology (IT) at the workplace constitutes an extraordinary opportunity for access to information and new ways of working. At the same time, IT presents work-related and social challenges which are, as yet, not adequately addressed. This chapter outlines major work-related challenges that management has to contend with and the published literature has to acknowledge. In particular, the focus is on issues related to information overload, responding to demands in real time, working in 'lean' organisations and these impacts on individual effectiveness.

A review is carried out to see whether these issues are over-stated. In order to work 'smarter', not harder, using IT effectively and lowering the individual and social cost of technostress and burnout, there is a need to identify critical value-adding in organisations and in individual roles. Re-examining current ways of working is proposed as a way forward in overcoming many of these unexamined IT-related issues.[1]

Introduction

IT's discursive presence is most prominent in a cultural setting concerned with the future of work and organisations (Forester, 1985; 1989; Roszak,

1986; Webster and Robins, 1986). Within a sociological context, IT influences social system continuity, control, identity and the integration of members. For example, the micro-electronic advancements of the last decade have been particularly influential on labour organisations. The use of job clustering (combining several jobs into one) is often facilitated by the use of IT, as opposed to job simplification (a reduced task set), emphasised by the Taylorist influence (Hammer and Champy, 1993: pp.51-52). Furthermore, when assisted by direct access to centrally-formed databanks, by means of computer networks and other forms of interactive IT, employees at the lower levels of organisational structure have the potential to become multi-skilled; equipped with the kind of planning and logistical information hitherto held only at the disposal of middle managers. The distribution of power within the work force, however, is not pre-determined (Child, 1987).

During the 1980s, the cost of IT's material components (hardware) continued to decline (Kauffman and Weill, 1990), resulting in IT permeating every facet of organisation and, concurrently, becoming available for individual use. In the 1990s and beyond, IT further intensified its dominant role by the ever-increasing *societal* dependence on IT systems (Rochlin, 1997). Parallel with the introduction of modern information technology in the workplace, is an ever-increasing management move to create 'leaner' and more 'efficient' organisations. Corporations expect productivity and efficiency increases as they introduce new and more sophisticated forms of IT systems, equipment and aids in 'de-layering' their structures and reducing the number of employees. The transition to an economy where value adding is through information, ideas and intelligence, the 'Three-I- Economy', is based on IT. To some, IT is forging a productivity revolution as it enables flexibility in working arrangements previously unavailable (Fritz et al. 1994). The most often quoted benefits from IT are timeliness and connectivity, as IT breaks down barriers of geography and time (Toffler, 1980). Furthermore, IT has also flattened organisational structure and eliminated a vast number of jobs, whilst making others more demanding and effective (Rockart and Short, 1989; Powell and Dente-Micallef, 1997).

Notwithstanding the fact that the fundamental factor of globalisation rests first and foremost in reducing the costs of information and its transmission, not everyone subscribes to the view that IT is responsible for a new paradigm of inflation-free economic growth (Houlder, 1998). Moreover, the positive results from radical re-engineering and downsizing are increasingly questioned as it is becoming apparent that the more important determinants of enhanced efficiency are the manner in which professional work is performed and the effective design of work processes (Kelly and Caplan, 1993). Even Porter (1985: p.165) observed that not all technological change is strategically beneficial and suggested that it may, even, worsen a firm's competitive position and industry attractiveness; that high technology does not guarantee profitability. Some argue that 'the productivity gains of the Information Age are just a myth' and that 'organisational changes that have accompanied the introduction of new IT may have increased the pressure on employees in a way that damages the organisation as a whole' (Roach, quoted in Houlder, 1998: p.14). Research carried out by a KPMG consultancy found that apparent productivity gains from computers in the US are explained by the longer hours Americans are spending at work (Houlder, 1998). By the year 2001, three-quarters of the households in the US, along with over a half a billion people globally, are expected to subscribe to a wireless communication service (Korac-Kakabadse et al. 1998).

Research in the area of changing models of work shows that, in the last ten to 15 years, IT has improved existing processes, increased efficiency and has enabled innovation but, at the same time, warns that 40 per cent of UK professionals will be facing high levels of stress at work as IT changes thinking about how society works (Millard, 1999). A complete re-assessment of what work is, how people value work and how people spend their time is taking place as lines between work and other aspects of life are increasingly blurring (Hardill et al. 1997; Millard, 1999). For example, over the last five to ten years, the UK has adopted the 'flexible work force' concept more than any other European country but its work force still has the longest working hours in Europe, with one in eight UK managers working more than 60 hours a week (DEMOS, 1995).

Similarly, an inquiry in the quality of working life of 5000 UK managers (executives and middle managers), over a five-year period at UMIST, reveals that 77 per cent work over their contact hours each week, 54 per cent work every evening and 34 per cent work every weekend (Worall and Cooper, 1997). A study of work practices amongst merchant bankers reveals that bankers (men and women) work 10 to 12 hours a day (McDowell and Court, 1994). Research at Macquarie University, sponsored by the Australian Government, on the prevention of child abuse, found that Australian fathers suffer from high stress, work long hours (47 hours a week) and blame their jobs for preventing them from being more effective parents (Walsh, 1999).

The literature reveals that there are two majority streams dealing with IT in organisations; the IT-enabling and the IT-consequences streams. The IT-enabling stream of thought encompasses the majority of the literature and addresses Gutek's (1983: p.163) question: 'What can technology do *for* you?'. IT benefits are exemplified by IT facilitation of individual capacity to telecommute (Toffler, 1980); perform 'mobile' work (Di Martina and Wirth, 1990; Fritz et al. 1994); perform computer-supported supplemental work-at-home (Venkatesh and Vitalari, 1992); and provide organisations and individuals with efficiencies, competitive advantages and the ability to carry out work processes that would be impossible, or less effective, without IT use (Smith, 1997). Some of the ramifications of the rapid influx of technology into society are blatant, while others quite subtle. A smaller, but steadily increasing, literature is trying to answer Gutek's (1983: p.163) second question: 'What can technology do *to* you?'. The negative consequences of the ubiquity of technology (Johnson, M., 1997; Johnson, S., 1997; Rochlin, 1997) are exemplified by information overload (Houlder, 1998); responding to the demands of IT in near-real time; encroachment of work on discretionary time; and IT surveillance and political control (Kirby, 1995; Carey, 1996; EUDGR, 1998; Terrorism and Security Monitor, 1998) - often leading to 'technostress' (Arnetz and Wihlom, 1997) and burnout (McGee, 1996). This chapter examines the *negative* impacts of IT on ways of working which result in technostress and burnout, with a particular focus on the work of specialists and managers.

Technostress

In the last decade, face-to-face communication has increasingly been replaced by V-mail, E-mail and video conferencing. Many have fallen victim to 'virtuosity', as increasing numbers of people work at home or are, otherwise, off-site with little physical interaction with focal organisations (Hallowell, 1999). Many people cannot imagine life without such technology and the freedom it grants. Hallowell (1999) argues that, with increased dependency on IT, there is a danger of losing the 'human moment', an authentic psychological encounter that can happen only when two people share the same physical space. The destructive power of the absence of the human moment can be felt and can damage a person's emotional health (Hallowell, 1999). An in-depth forecast of the technological impact on human lives, *The Next Step*, carried out by the British IT systems and service company, ICL, concludes that beside enormous benefits, IT will also create new *diseases* and medical conditions such as 'information overload' and 'information shock'. The concept of the 'weekend' will disappear, as people mix work and discretionary time to fit their chosen lifestyle (ICL, 1998). Similarly, a study carried out by the World Health Organisation (WHO) predicts that of all diseases in the next decades, depression will rank second among leading illnesses (World Economic Forum, 1997).

The excitement created around new IT was not only the promise of enhanced performance and productivity but, also, the promise of a better quality of life - such as a 30-hour working week; elimination of routine, dull operations; monetary savings; happy and satisfied patrons; and new flexibility to enjoy leisure and thoughtful pursuits (Clark and Kalin, 1996). Although IT facilitates many labour-saving tools, many people find IT a source of mounting stress (Ganzel, 1998), because computerised jobs are more sedentary, require less physical energy expenditure and also require more cognitive processing and mental attention (Smith, 1997). Proliferation of high-technology tools requires coping with multiple software interfaces, varying equipment configurations, escalating performance demands and perpetual change (Moreland, 1993).

Technostress research has been conducted from a variety of perspectives and models, each offering a unique and complementary framework of which epidemology, ergonomics and organisational behaviour lead to a field of understanding how work influences individual well-being (Amicil and Celentano, 1984; Smith and Salvendy, 1993; Anzai et al. 1995). Although technology is usually considered to be a process for transforming physical and informational inputs into outputs and, as such, technological decisions, directly or indirectly, structure the work process (Rousseau, 1983), the use of various models, exemplified by the stress-reaction model (Kasl and Cooper, 1987; Frese and Zapf, 1988), the accumulation model (Frese and Okonek, 1984), the dynamic-accumulation model (Bamberg, 1992), the adjustment model (Lazarus and Folkman, 1984; Schonfeld, 1992) and the sleeper effect model (Theorell et al. 1994), research perspectives and methodologies have contributed to a plethora of findings, of which some are consistent and some contradictory. For example, job demand, job control, social support and job satisfaction have been consistently identified as predictors of employee well-being (Karasek et al. 1981; Schnall et al. 1990).

Although the term 'technostress' (Brod, 1984a; 1984b) has been variously defined, it generally refers to the state of mental and physiological arousal, and consequent pressure, observed in some employees who are heavily dependent on technology in their work (Arntez and Wihlom, 1997). Some consider technostress to be a modern disease of adaptation caused by an inability to cope with new technologies in a 'healthy' manner (Brod, 1984a; 1984b; Clark and Kalin, 1996). This can also occur in circumstances where employees perceive their job as stimulating at the same time that they feel that they do not quite master the necessary skills (Brod, 1984a; 1984b; Arnetz et al. 1997). New equipment, increased amount of equipment, software updates and inadequate or non-existent user support can cause strain on the individual left to deal with technology. Strain is considered to be the state of being stressed, as evidenced by physiological, psychological or medical indices (Fletcher and Payne, 1980). In addition to technology, poor response to performance, sub-optimal organisational efficiency and a partial mis-match between the skills and competence available in the work force, and those required for new product development, add to the mental strain (Arnetz, 1997). Some have suggested that different aspects of technology produce greater stress for different kinds of 'psychological types' of people (Moreland, 1993). Organisational behaviour research has shown that the characteristics of the organisation which structure jobs, by placing limits on what one can do, such as technology, affect attitudes and behaviour (Rousseau, 1977; Abdel-Halim, 1981; Brass, 1985).

Psychologists Weil and Rosen (1998) define 'technostress' as any negative impact on attitudes, thoughts, behaviour or body physiology caused either directly or indirectly by technology. They also define 'technosis' as the dissolution of human-technology boundaries and increased dependency on technological aids, wherein humans begin thinking they should act and perform as quickly as their machines (Weil and Rosen, 1998) - for example, when humans start to believe that technology, such as the telephone, should always be available and is the only means to getting something done or, more extremely, cases of technosis occur when actors actually begin defining their persona based on what brand, or power, of computer they own. These actors are overly positive technology users who often have the attitude that 'technology solves all problems' and are often referred to as 'technofreaks' (Bichteler, 1987). There are two general areas of technostress manifestation - the struggle of individuals to accept, or adjust to, present or emerging technologies and an individual's over-identification with, and/or dependency on, new technology.

Technostress Due to Conflict Over Accepting, or Adjusting, to New Technology

The individual struggle or resistance to new technologies has been explained by individual-level perspective theories such as Rational Choice Theory and by collective-level perspective theories exemplified by Social Construction Theory (Markus, 1994). Actor's conservatism, fear of change, lack of involvement and motivation and incompatible cognitive styles have been major issues identified by individual-level theories trying to explain resistance to innovation (Markus, 1994). The individual struggles to accept technology, as a stream of thought, is based on the premise that technostress is a modern disease of adaptation caused by individual inability to cope with new technologies in a 'healthy manner' (Brod, 1982; 1984a; 1984b; Clark and Kalin, 1996). In the 1980s, Brod (1982; 1984a; 1984b) coined the term 'technostress' to depict stress due to individual inability to adjust to technology, while others used terms 'technophobia' (Bichteler, 1987) and 'terminal paralysis' (Fine, 1986).

The effects of new technology at the workplace have reportedly increased strain (Brod, 1982; 1984a; 1984b; Stellman et al. 1989; Steffy and Jones, 1989). Brod (1984a; 1984b) argues that whether people love technology - 'technocentered' or hate it - 'technoanxious', they lose. Brod (1984a; 1984b) suggests that 'technoanxious' people feel threatened and alienated by machines that do instantly and perfectly a job that has taken the worker years to learn. 'Technocentered' people, on the other hand, identify so closely with the computer that it supplies nourishment even for his/her emotions. The inability of people to adjust to technology may be exemplified by a range of attitudes, such as indifference and hostility due to irrational fear of technology, fear of replacement by technology, fear of loss of status or a strong preference for the *status quo* (Bichteler, 1987). However, technostress can occur in circumstances where employees perceive their job as stimulating and, at the same time, feel that they have not quite mastered the necessary skills. People can be open-minded, enthusiastic about the automation, show genuine interest in learning more and being included in training and development and still suffer from technostress (Bichteler, 1987).

The individual struggle to accept technology can result from a number of sources:

- Having continuously to learn about newer technology (for example, software updates);

- Increased amount of equipment and technological aids;
- Inadequate training and, thus, a fear of making irrecoverable mistakes or breaking equipment;
- Inadequate or non-existent technical support;
- Frustration with incompatibility between software/hardware and their equipment;
- Outdated equipment;
- Over exposure to technology;
- Inconsistent/infrequent use of technology;
- Management decisions that do not adequately consider the operator/user of the new technology;
- Poor communication with others who are at various technology skill levels;
- Fear of being replaced by technology or loss of status;
- Fear of change introduced by technology; and
- Tyranny of errors (errors are often visible to multiple constituencies).

The consequences can be linked to behavioural changes (Bichteler, 1987) exemplified by:

- Absenteeism, tardiness or unusual number of personal 'emergencies';
- Aggressiveness;
- Negativism;
- Withdrawal;
- Argumentativeness;
- Denigration of colleagues; and
- Various health issues.

Health issues identified, so far, include psycho-physiological (Berg at al, 1992; Arnetz, 1997), exemplified by reduced job satisfaction (Korunka et al. 1995) and stress (Agervold, 1987; Cooper and Payne, 1988); psycho-social aspects (Kasl and Cooper, 1987; Amicil and Celentano, 1991, Hackett et al. 1991), exemplified by depression (WHO, 1989; 1990); the musculo-skeletal system (Zeier et al. 1987; Nibel and Ghem, 1990), exemplified by repetitive strain injuries (RSI) (Miller and Topliss, 1988; Ong, 1993; Sauter et al. 1993); eye discomfort (Berqvist et al. 1992); headaches (Berg et al. 1992); threats to the foetus (Ericson and Kallen, 1986; Schnorr et al. 1991); skin diseases (Carmichael and Roberts, 1992; Berg et al. 1992); hypersensitivity to electricity and video display units

(VDU); Chronic Fatigue Syndrome (CFS) caused by emission of Electro Magnetic Forces (EMF) or electro-magnetic pollution from IT equipment (Herrmann, 1999); and Alzheimer's disease, memory loss and lack concentration (*Hotline*, 1999). This initial concern has increasingly received empirical evidence. For example, research into electro-magnetic fields (EMFs) emitted by electronic equipment suggests that the current generation is apparently exposed to 100 million times more man-made electromagnetic radiation than their grandparents (*Hotline*, 1999). VDUs, for example, are charged with up to 100 volts, alone. Electronic clock radios, microwaves, TV sets, videos and electrical cables have similar emissions (*Hotline*, 1999).

Recommended maximum exposure to electric fields (EF) at home should not exceed one volt/meter and to magnetic fields (MF) exposure should not exceed 20 Nanotesla (nT). Long term exposure to EF levels up to 50 volts/meter and MF above 70 nT are not considered safe by Swedish norms (Herrmann, 1999). A 25 year study, including 436,000 people, conducted by the Swedish government in cooperation with a utility, found that childhood leukaemia was four times greater where children lived in a 300-nT field or greater, three times greater when living in a 200-nT field and two times greater in a 100-nT field (Herrmann, 1999). Furthermore, mobile phones owned by 16 per cent of the UK population have been linked to asthma, Alzheimer's disease, memory loss and lack concentration (*Hotline*, 1999).

Technostress Due to Over-Identification with, and/or Dependency on, New Technology

Although, more recently, the term 'technostress' has been used to describe the psycho-physiological consequences of a poor interface between individuals and IT systems (Arnetz, 1997; Weil and Rosen, 1998), with rapidly blurring boundaries between work and the private sphere, technostress is increasingly used to describe irritation people feel as these boundaries are constantly invaded by beepers, pagers, computers and cell phone conversations in trains, restaurants, theatres or anywhere where, previously, individuals enjoyed peace and quiet (Weil and Rosen, 1998: viii).

Technostress due to an individual's over-identification with, or over dependency on, technology is based on the premise that people adopt technology and then become over dependent on their use - such as E-mail and cellular phones. This technostress can be attributed to number of factors such as:

- Information overload (quantitative and qualitative) (for example, Information Fatigue Syndrome);
- Responding to the demands in near-real time (for example, E-mail, V-mail, video conferencing);
- Encroachment of work on discretionary time (for example, E-mails, laptops, cellular phones);
- Multi-tasking (for example, juggling six applications simultaneously);
- Loss of privacy (for example, cellular phones, E-mails, smart cards); and
- Addiction to technology or technosis (for example, internet addiction disorder).

The consequences can be linked to lower productivity (McGee, 1996) due to:

- Lower motivation at work;
- Extreme dissatisfaction with the job;
- Lagging effectiveness;
- Feeling of lost control, helplessness, dread, resentment, stress;
- Burnout; and
- Various health issues due to stress (Weil and Rosen, 1998), burn-out and emotional breakdown (McGee, 1996).

Although stress is considered to be a physiological state preparing people for action, an under-stimulation and over-stimulation can both produce negative consequences for individuals (Hamilton and Warburton, 1981). Experience during certain stress reactions can lead to pleasure, enjoyment or the sense of fulfilment - 'eustress', whilst an excess of demand causes hyper-stress and pathogenic occurrence of unpleasant, unhealthy or damaging distress (Hamilton and Warburton 1981). Thus, in response to conditions produced by transactions between individuals and IT systems/aids, individuals can experience stress, strain, load, distress or fulfilment. Longitudinal studies amongst information system professionals developing software found that work-related stress among IS professionals is affected more by task-specific work stressors, such as communication problems and ambiguity in specifications, than by reward, human resource development or role ambiguity (Fujigaki and Mori, 1997). This study shows a link between increases in bio-chemical stress and job events. The results show that increased adrenalin hormones in the blood reflects acute job events, such as the beginning of new project, deadlines, sudden increases in amount of work and budget negotiation (Fujigaki and Mori, 1997).

Whilst increased levels of the hormone Cortisol represent a chronic state of work stress, Cortisol increases after the continuation of a busy state, such as just after having finished a big project or after getting used to the job (Fujigaki and Mori, 1997). Prolonged stress leads the cascade of neuro-hormonal changes as well as immunological changes that follow (Arnetz, 1997). This state is reflected both in higher circulating levels of stress-sensitive hormones (Adrenaline and Cortisol), Serum Frucosamine and Haemoglobin A1c (Arnetz, 1984; Arnetz et al. 1988) as well as cognitive symptoms fundamental to physiological consequences, such as poor concentration, irritability and memory disorder (Arnetz and Wihlom, 1997: p.41). Increased Serum Cortisol levels in humans have been linked to situations characterised by hopelessness and depressed moods (Irwin et al. 1988; Nowak, 1991).

A study of employees using VDUs reveals that they had significantly higher levels of circulating Prolactin, a stress-sensitive hormone (Arnetz, 1996). Prolactin levels have been reported to increase in situations of high mental demand, with feelings of not being in complete control, and during negative events (Berg et al. 1992; Theorell and Emlund, 1993). Elevated Prolactin levels are known to influence established or putative auto-immune disease and may also partly contribute to symptoms such as neuro-behavioural changes, dermatological symptoms and repetitive strain disorder in workers suing VDUs (Ong, 1993; Reichlin, 1993; Sauter et al. 1993). Characteristically, those who work with VDUs and other IT aids complain about symptoms such as headache; fatigue; nausea; and mucousal erruption (Arnetz and Wihlom, 1997). Because technostress has a real physiological component, the wear and tear of humans might very well increase a person's susceptibility to the effects of the physio-chemical environment (Arnetz and Wihlom, 1997). The cost of stress-related ailments, including those stemming from burnout, in the US, is estimated by some to be as much as US$300 billion a year (McGee, 1996) and, lately, between five and ten per cent of Gross National Product (Vernon, 1998).

A survey carried by the PSI health and safety specialists, among more than 150 leading private and public companies in the UK, revealed that the cost of stress is estimated at £4 billion (*Management Services*, 1996). Similarly, a survey carried by Mind, UK's biggest mental-health charity organisation, revealed that over 20 per cent of companies believe illnesses related to stress now account for between quarter and half of all days off sick (*Computer Weekly*, 1992). The World Health Organisation's (WHO) Working Group Five (WHO, 1989: p.957; 1990) also declared that 'psycho-social are at least as important as the physical ergonomics of the work situation and the working environment'.

'Technocentredness' (Brod, 1984a; 1984b), 'technofreaks' (Bichteler, 1987), 'addiction to technology' (Weil and Rosen, 1998) or 'technosis' (Weil and Rosen, 1998) are considered to be a problem among children. Brod (1984a) argues that technocentred children are developing their sense of objective reality and their perception of cause and effect in an electronic space that has no counterpart in daily work. As a result, children, many of whom become fanatic programmers, lose hand-eye co-ordination, develop a distorted sense of time and gradually withdraw from friendships (Brod, 1984a; 1984b).

Depression

Stress is amongst the leading factors contributing to depression and growing alienation in the informatised world. According to the US National Institute for Public Health Service (PHS), 11 million Americans, or one in every 20, will have a depressive episode in any given year (Hancock, 1998). The psychological disorders are most common among US adults, in their productive working years, between the age of 25 to 44 years (Freedman, 1984; Smith and Carayon, 1995). Depression is considered to be a mental illness with psychiatric and emotional symptoms (Hancock, 1998). It covers a range of moods, from low-grade chronic malaise to deep and wrenching anguish, and affects both men and woman. It has been estimated that in the US, alone, the cost of mental disorders in terms of work-time lost, medication and insurance is over US$700 billion per year (Karuppan, 1997; Vernon, 1998).

Depressed employees face a double burden of overwhelming symptoms of apathy, anxiety and irritability, as well as stigma of the illness itself. They worry that if they do not seek treatment they will be fired, and if they do, they will be branded unemployable. Research in a large high-tech company, in the US, found that 20 per cent of the Information Systems Department employees showed signs of clinical depression. At Xerox Corp, for example, numerous IT employees have taken disability leave because of depression (Hancock, 1998). Portable PCs, pagers, cellular phones and wireless E-mail ensure that one can stay out of the office for a long time (McGee, 1996). Demand from increasingly 'tech-savvy' users and executives who want more results from IT; unrealistic demands; expectation of IS employees to keep other departments wired around the clock; hype surrounding the Internet; less time to support increasing IT users; being on call 24-hours a day, seven-days a week and insufficient time to distance oneself from the job, are attributing factors in higher burnout among IS/IT professionals (McGee, 1996).

The electronic media, such as Intranets, GroupWare and intelligent agents, CAD-CAM, project management software tools as well as video-conferencing and 'distributed' white boards used in international project design, allowing teams in London, New Delhi and Oregon to work together, sharing - in real time - voice, computer data and graphics, have consequences. 'Live' and 'synchronous' multimedia communication often play havoc with the sleeping habits of team members (Price Waterhouse Coopers, 1998). Research amongst professionals who work on designing and developing high-tech telecommunication systems reveals that although the work environment is highly intellectually stimulating, and provides a high degree of control over the work process, at the same time, stress stems from the constant development of new software tools, rapidly changing technical and business environments and an increased focus on shortening the time-to-customer period (Arnetz, 1997).

In a study of the bodily, mental and psycho-physiological reactions of employees involved in the design of advanced telecommunications systems and office employees using regular video display technology, several stress-related psychosomatic disorders have been identified, such as sleep disturbance, psycho-physiological stress and somatic complaints (Arnetz, 1997). Although depression is no more common in information technology than in other fields, some argue that it is hardest to recognise within IT professionals as much of IT involves working with computers, not people (Hancock, 1998; Fawn, 1998). IT work also tends to attract a large percentage of introverts who prefer to work alone and are attracted to jobs that allow them do so.

Burnout

Burnout is the ultimate in job dissatisfaction and loss of control (McGee, 1996). Some of the symptoms of burnout are lower motivation at work, extreme dissatisfaction, sharply lower productivity and effectiveness and persistent feelings of depression and panic attacks (McGee, 1996). Individuals suffering from burnout, use different expressions to describe their experiences - can't cope; have lost energy; just could not face what could previously be handled; just too much for me; emotionally choked up (Korac-Kakabadse and Korac-Kakabadse, 1999, p.349). The constant repetition of tasks, activities and demands that may previously have been experienced as positive, are perceived as routine, dull and de-motivational; to the point of the individual becoming pathological and leading to burnout (Korac-Kakabadse and Korac-Kakabadse, 1999).

Owing to advances in IT, to globalisation and the need to cut costs, many organisations have chosen downsizing and re-engineering to achieve productivity gains, using IT as a lever for change. IT can contribute to heighten burnout through greater individual accessibility through portable laptops, home-PCs equipped with modems, E-mail, cellular phones and other IT-aids, forcing employees to be linked with the office anytime and anywhere (McGee, 1996). Similarly, unrealistic demands placed on technical and non-technical users of IT systems and the speed of expected responses can contribute to burnout (McGee, 1996). Although burnout involves an experience of stress, it is different from stress as it is not only person related but, also, consistently situational driven. Often, it is time critical and can be an outcome of boredom (Korac-Kakabadse and Korac-Kakabadse, 1999).

Burnout is defined as 'an emotional deterioration arising from prolonged exposure to perceived debilitating circumstances, resulting in not being able to continue doing that in which the person was previously accomplished' (Korac-Kakabadse and Korac-Kakabadse, 1999, p.350). The most obvious consequences of burnout are an individual's inability to manage interpersonal relationships. These include social isolation; long hours at work; little or no recreation time - which often creates alcohol and drug abuse by partners and/or children; poor school performance of children; increased fighting among family partners and sexual problems (Greenfield and Raskin, 1984; McGee, 1996). Burnout can trigger panic instincts, hindering effective communication and personal growth, and can destroy confidence. The negative physiological and psychological toll that burnout exacts from individuals can be devastating, with the final costs being the disability of mind and spirit. Burnout robs individuals of resilience to adapt, being able to effectively communicate with others and having a will to continue. Some symptoms of burnout are:

- Lower motivation at work;

- Extreme dissatisfaction and loss of control;
- Sharp drop in productivity and effectiveness;
- Persistent feeling of depression and panic attacks;
- Emotionally choked up, helplessness, dread, resentment;
- Increased irritability, nervousness, worry;
- Relationship problems, including family and marital;
- Persistent headaches, fatigue and eating and sleeping disorders; and
- Substance abuse.

Emergent from the Cranfield School of Management research project, namely 'IT Roles and Work Practices', 'diversity' and 'learning', based on interviews with 160 professionals, managers and executives in Motorola, GlaxoWelcome, NCR and Thames Valley Police (Korac-Kakabadse and Korac-Kakabadse, 1998), it becomes apparent that a majority of interviewees identified information overload (E-mail, corporate web sites), responding in near-real time, extended working hours through technology, encroachment of work into discretionary time and multi-tasking as the main sources of pressure and major challenge. Guided by the results of these interview outcomes, the remaining focus of this chapter is on technostress due to individual over-identification with, or dependency on, technology, as exemplified by information overload; the need to respond to the demands in near-real time; multi-tasking; encroachment of work on discretionary time; loss of privacy and addiction to technology (technosis).

Information Overload

Many organisations are rapidly shifting from a work force that produces products and services to one that primarily manages information (Barner, 1996). This shift also creates movement from information 'pull' to information 'push', or information 'overload', as there is more information and less time for processing and less time for thinking about the implications of action taken (Bowman, 1997). IT proliferation which facilitates digital transfer of multimedia (video, audio and text) information, the rapid spread of IT-networks that enable faster response to customers independently of their spatial position and the privilege of working anywhere, at any time, increasingly leads to a growth of 'virtual' organisations. IT also facilitates information 'push', such as list-servers, in one big disorganised batch, creating a glut of information (Ganzel, 1998). Many organisations have not found effective ways of handling information 'push' as they emotionally still operate in the old paradigm of information 'pull' or information 'search'.

Information overload usually describes a situation when an employee finds 20 V-mail and 60 E-mail messages waiting and a stack of paper in the facsimile machine (Ganzel, 1998). E-mail makes it technically feasible for employees to skip levels in the chain of command, providing senior managers with direct feedback on performance problems and rising organisational issues (Barner, 1996). Although some find ways to counter the flood of E-mails by using 'bozo filters', software programmes that automatically screen-out the messages of certain E-mail senders, individuals cannot filter all work-related messages. E-mail can be time-saving but it can just as easy take over one's life, rendering employees less productive (Carey, 1996). Interviews conducted by the Cranfield School of Management (Korac-Kakabadse and Korac-Kakabadse, 1998) reveal that 80 per cent of interviewees considered information overload as an issue that adds to a work pressure. Asked to identify current issues and work pressures, interviewees identified information overload as the second factor. The first was the time pressure (having to meet many tight deadlines) and quantitative overload (having too many things to do). Other identified work pressures were role ambiguities (lack of defined objectives, expectations and scope of responsibility); prolonged working hours; ineffective communication; psychological role demands (increased amount of concentration and vigilance and cost of errors associated with the role); continuous restructuring and/or mergers; and poorly defined merit system criteria.

Research carried out by the Institute For the Future and Gallup Studies suggests that the average employee sends and receives 178 V-mail, E-mail and fax messages each day (Heine, 1997). The onslaught of correspondence has 71 per cent of respondents feeling overwhelmed (Carey, 1996), whilst 84 per cent reported being interrupted three or more times per hour as a result of 'layering' - such as receiving the initial letter, followed by an E-mail and, then, even, a fax (Heine, 1997). Research carried out by School of Business Study at the University of Connecticut, reveals that almost 60 per cent of respondents declared that E-mail, V-mail and other new communication mediums have not made their lives better, only busier, whilst 54 per cent concluded that IT wastes as much times as it saves (Heine, 1997). The University of Connecticut study found that IT has eroded work relationships between people, with 44 per cent of the respondents feeling that the work environment has become too cold and impersonal - people are not forming true relationships through IT (Heine,

1997). 42.1 per cent felt that IT is the most abused managerial tool and that the use of E-mail is a 'cop-out' for addressing personal issues (Heine, 1997). Increased reliance on IT has produced an increased torrent of data and information or information 'push'. Some argue that instead of an information age we have entered an age of information glut (Ganzel, 1998). In changing environments, the endless problem is not that 'we have less information than we need, but more information than we can use' (Clark and Kalin, 1996, p.33).

Pushing professionals into overload conditions are video- and teleconferencing sessions; focus group transcripts; clipping services; government studies; trading magazines; electronic monitors of market surveys and a mountain of archived research reports (externally commissioned and generated in-house) on the corporate, electronic knowledge base. Executives, for example, are called on to assimilate ever-growing amounts of information, from an ever-mounting number of sources. Those who are unable to create strategies to cope with information intake are vulnerable to Information Fatigue Syndrome (IFS), a malady that senior executives often recognise privately, but one that is still officially 'invisible' in most organisations (Young, 1998).

In Australia, for example, a society with the highest executive redundancy rate in the OECD countries, anxious executives work harder, adopting an attitude that 'more information is better', thus perpetuating an information overload (Hind, 1998). Research carried out by the news agency Reuters, found that two thirds of respondents consider that stress induced by information overload is an important force in loss of job satisfaction, whilst 42 per cent blame it for ill health (Young, 1998). Six out of ten declared that they need high levels of information to perform effectively, whilst half admitted that they were unable to properly process the amount of information they had collected and to extract value-added information buried in encyclopaedic volumes of electronic data (Young, 1998).

Increasingly, knowledge workers are suffering from IFS, with more information than can be read and digested in a lifetime, seemingly coming at them, via technology, every day (Weil and Rosen, 1998). Filtering information, as well as keeping the lines of communication open, is critical for coping with change and high performance. Employees are also feeling frustrated by the pace at which they are asked to adapt to new technologies. Even when they master one computer programme, they often are asked to change to another one that can 'do more', but takes time to learn (Weil and Rosen, 1998). However, they are rarely given adequate time to learn.

More often than not they are offered an 'eight-hour intensive seminar' to prepare for the transition.

A key issue identified from this focus on the human aspects of information and knowledge management is the fact that whilst there are no fundamental technical barriers to information availability (Evans, 1999), the human capacity for attention has remained constant, as has the ability to allocate it (Davenport, 1999). As the amount of information with which people are bombarded continues to accelerate, it is now associated as being a negative stimulus to organisational performance. Shenk (1997) shows that this information overload is making employees more anxious, less effective and, sometimes, even 'sick'. In addition, the endless analysis and morass of expert information has begun to undermine logical approaches to deliberation and problem solving. Unfortunately, some scholars continually assert that with regard to information, addiction must be the goal without any address to any negative implications of addiction (Shenk, 1997; 1999).

The Reuters Agency (1996; 1997; 1998a; 1998b) research shows the burden of keeping up with an information explosion, exemplified by stress generated in a number of ways. The fear of failure to understand critical information leads to making expensive mistakes; there is the threat of being overwhelmed by the sheer quantity of information that must be mastered to perform efficiently. Stress is also caused by not knowing whether crucial information exists, or, if it exists, of not being sure where and how to locate it (Reuters Agency, 1996; 1997; 1998a; 1998b). Furthermore, there is the frustration associated with the location of the information being known but not the method of being able to access it (Reuters Agency, 1996; 1997; 1998a; 1998b). Underlying and intensifying information stress are time pressures. The research also shows that when compelled to choose among a series of options, in the face of vast amounts of potentially important information and against the clock, individuals move into a state of excessive stress, often resulting in foolish decisions and flawed conclusions (Lewis, 1998).

Consequently, the focus on the relationship between a firm's competitive advantage and its use of its information systems has shifted so that, increasingly, smart organisations are beginning to draw the distinction between accessibility and value (Buchanan, 1999) and are, consequently, investigating how they can filter this volume of information so that individuals within the organisation receive the information they require and the support to be able to manage, effectively, both the inputs and outputs expected for optimum performance (Shenk, 1999). Indeed, Drucker

(1999), whilst not working from the perspective of information overload, is still concerned that for data and information to be meaningful it has to be organised; the same information may have to be organised in different ways for different purposes - in other words, customised.

Increasingly, this information filtration and customisation is becoming an important issue (Buchanan, 1999) and, thus, the emergence of the role of information intermediaries. Considering that unsolicited electronic junk mail, known as 'spam', now makes up about 10 per cent of all E-mail around the world (Hagell and Singer, 1999), the need of information filtering and customising is on the increase. However, in addition to data and information customising, there is a need for understanding how data and information customisation can be utilised to contribute to the achievement of competitive advantage.

Furthermore, there is a need for increased understanding of :

- What is information overload?
- How does information overload affect the performance of individuals within the organisation?
- What impact, if any, does information overload have on the competitive advantage of an organisation?, and
- What actions have been identified as providing a solution to the effects of information overload?

Responding to Demands in Near-Real Time

Some argue that new organisations capture value in shifting from the traditional 'make and sell' to the new, IT-enabled, paradigm of 'sense and respond' (Bradley and Nolan, 1998). The new, interactive communication networks enable organisations to sense, in real time, customers' needs and enable them to respond swiftly and effectively but, at the same time, create an expectation that the recipient of the message will respond immediately (Bowman, 1997). IT networks, or virtual organisations, require responses and decision-making in real time. IT has eliminated a safety buffer, or a 'float', in finances and decision-making (Barner, 1996). For example, the gap between the time an individual writes a cheque and the bank actually cashing it has disappeared. Equally, E-mail and V-mail, around the clock, have replaced responding to written requests during designated working hours, eliminating decision 'float'. Paradoxically, saving time can cost a company more by making every situation an 'emergency' (Bowman, 1997).

For example, IT enabled communication can facilitate working on reports right to the last minute of the deadline, eliminating traditional three days of transport/postage time and, thus, giving more time to get things right. However, the down side is that it leaves less time before the next deadline is set (Ganzel, 1998). The ever-increasing speed of IT increases the speed of workflow and heightens people's expectations for productivity (Clark and Kalin, 1996).

Many organisations, such as in insurance and banking, use IT - supported workflow systems which set the speed of response time. The anytime/anyplace worker is more likely to work a longer day, but not in the usual segments - rather, in spurts of activity throughout the day and night (Devoito, 1996). Many employees tote their laptops on vacation whilst their bosses expect them to carry sky pagers (Weil and Rosen, 1998). Some feel invaded by technology on all fronts; by the beeps of their pagers, cell phones, incoming faxes and by those of others around them. Embedded controllers, the silicon chips that run everything from coffee makers to carburettors, also invade the home. By year 2001, it is estimated that there will be more than 200 embedded chips in every US home (Licking, 1999). As personal and work boundaries are blurred, many never experience true 'down time' (Weil and Rosen, 1998). Some studies suggest that within the past 20 years, working hours have increased in the US by the equivalent of one extra month a year (Handy, 1995). A poll conducted by the *Wall Street Journal*, found that 80 per cent of US respondents describe their lives as busy to the point of discomfort, as the info-age produces a society in 'real time' response, composed of people that are 'economically pressed, politically depressed and socially stressed' (Beeman, 1996: p.3).

Technology has produced perpetual urgency (Mankin et al. 1982; Marshall, 1995). Because it is easier to generate data, the expectation is that people need the data faster (Hind, 1998). Very few people pause to assess what they need to respond to as, often, no one qualifies for their 'time' investment. Technology seems to generate a 'Pavlov's dog' response among knowledge workers (Hind, 1998). Owing to IT advances, downsized business survivors can follow their executive itineraries that place them on a global, round-the-clock time schedule, subject to laptops, modems, faxes and E-mail at any time of the day (Tonn and Petrich, 1998: p.270). E-mail, V-mail and mobile phones, and the constant demand for attention by the electronic environment, can wear down the strongest of executives committed to ensuring some residue of discretionary time (Hind, 1998). Technology has even transformed one of the world's oldest communal rituals, a meal together, as cell-phones are common place in restaurants as well as at home (Ganzel, 1998). Availability of IT systems and appliances add an increased demand on employees to process information, and act on it, in, or near-, real-time. Such pressures pose increased stress on employees (Vernon, 1998).

Multi-Tasking

Clark and Kalin (1996) argue that people have set themselves work rhythms to correspond to the steady, quick pace of the computer. The faster the machines, the faster the work flows and the higher the expectation of productivity. They argue that although IT provides the capacity to multi-task, or performing several things at one time, humans are capable of focusing on only one thing and that humans become quantitatively and qualitatively overloaded. Individuals become unable to think clearly and can become forgetful and incapable of having a restful sleep as the stimulation from the overload keeps their brain working overtime (Weil and Rosen, 1998). A variety of studies have suggested that machine-paced work processes are at an elevated risk of being a stress-related disease (Caplan et al. 1975; Jenner et al. 1980; Lacroix, 1984). Most machine-pacing studies were not designed to address illness and disease outcomes *per se;* rather, the focus was on documenting indicators of stress - such as Catecholamine levels (Johansson, 1979) or job dissatisfaction (Wilkes et al. 1981). These studies suggest that ethnological systems affect employee's health through changes in the nature of work. Machine-paced technological systems create conditions of heavy job demands and work pressure, little control over the work processes and both physical and psychological job conditions which lead to socially-isolating work environments (Johansson, 1979; Wilkes et al. 1981).

Juggling six open applications on a computer screen, subscribing to too many list-servers and sending and receiving an increased number of E-mails - more than one can handle - all add to increased stress levels (Clark and Kalin, 1996). Even those who choose to work at home, find themselves multi-tasking, cooking dinner in the microwave oven, talking on a cellular phone, sending an E-mail and printing a document, all at the same time. Given the time pressure and deluge of data, the only way an executive can get though a day is by multi-tasking (Young, 1998). But the knack of doing several things at once, using electronic gadgets, can be taken to outrageous extremes, exemplified by use of laptops for clearing E-mails during meetings.

Encroachment of Work on Discretionary Time

Every IT innovation, from cell phone to E-mail, from facsimiles to Web-sites, demands new skills, speedier reaction times and creativity on call 24-hours a day (Weil and Rosen, 1998). In addition to career pressures to work past 5:00 pm, the very speed with which technology develops means people have to put in the extra hours in order to cope with innovation and work (Vernon, 1998). For example, the US work force is moving steadily towards a 24-hour-a-day, 7-days-a-week economy with only 55 per cent of workers employed full-time during the day (Presser, quoted in Kleiman, 1996, p.7).

In the UK, like in the US, a high proportion of interviewed executives stated that there was no point in the day when they are not reachable or accessible (Vernon, 1998). For many executives, this is ultimate irony - as the E-mail, faxes and V-mail, created to make working lives easier, have, instead, made things more difficult (Vernon, 1998). With new technology, there are more avenues to be reached and with that comes higher expectations and, consequently, the pressure for higher performance. The question of how one escapes from the tentacles of IT-facilitated accessibility and reclaims one's own life again is unanswered. Furthermore, as many corporations are moving towards the virtual organisation, it will become even more difficult to delineate the dividing line between work and home; to determine when an employee's rights of privacy have been violated (Barner, 1996, p.15). Traditionally, organisations with a genuine 24-hour, seven-day work ethic, such as the military, the medical profession and the police, were also very rigid in exercising work and leisure discipline (Boyd, 1997) which new entrants to the 24-hour, seven-day work ethic do not have. This need for instant response, with no buffer or cover to hide behind, is acknowledged, even by one of the inventors of the personal computer, Steven Jobs, who admits that technology has invaded his personal life as it is follows him everywhere (McKenna R, 1997).

Although there has always been tension in capitalist society between work, family and leisure, it is more so in an information-economy where work places major constraints on the amount and quality of people's discretionary time and attention (Lobel, 1992). Living in electronic 'real time' causes 'time poverty' in both spheres. Information technology facilitates work encroachment into personal life. Although the work of the owner/manager, especially in small- and medium-sized enterprises (SMEs), has traditionally encroached into personal and family life, this was not true for employees. For example, owners of restaurants and small factories always mixed work and discretionary times. However, information technology facilitates work encroachment into the personal life of employees without individuals having any financial stake in the business. In a sense, information technology, such as laptops, modems and cellular phones, blur the boundary between home and work for ordinary employees.

An alternative viewpoint is that although work life encroached into the personal life of the owner/manager, she/he developed a greater sense of responsibility, maturity and robustness to cope with such encroachment (Vernon, 1998). Furthermore, owner/managers often create family structures intricately involved with a business, thus giving him/her time together with family members. Information technology does not necessarily integrate the family into the work situation in the way owners/managers integrate their families into SMEs. Information technology facilitates work encroachment on an individual's private life but without the flexibility of an owner/manager who has a choice to allow work to encroach on his/her private life or to allow work to encroach into family life in a way that facilitates family integration and provides work for family members. The average employee does not have an opportunity to turn individual work encroachment into family integration; thus creating increased work and private life conflict. This increasing conflict between work and discretionary time is partly attributed to information technology's facility to extend the working place into the most intimate times and places and to build the pressure to succeed at both spheres, thus adversely affecting the well-being of men and women in both domains (Cooper, quoted in Vernon, 1998). Increasingly, more people are working longer hours, seemingly by choice, but, in actuality, with little recourse (Vernon, 1998:p.30). Lives are harried and, increasingly, self-focused.

The HomeNet study, undertaken at Carnegie Mellon University in the US, examines the social and psychological impact of the Internet on 169 people in 73 households during their first one to two years on-line (Kraut et al. 1998). The study suggests that, within their sample, greater use of the Internet was associated with declines in participants' communication with family members in the household, declines in the size of their social circle and increases in their depression and loneliness (Kraut et al. 1998).

Although electronic communication is a valuable tool for keeping in touch with 'offline' friends and pre-existing social networks, thus using cyberspace for interaction for reasons of convenience and practicality, it is still held that relationships conducted offline through face-to-face interaction are qualitatively better than relationships conducted on-line through computer-mediated communication or interaction with on-line virtual friends. Turkle (1984; 1997: p.34) questions whether it is sensible 'to sit alone in our rooms, typing at our networked computers and filling our lives with 'virtual' friends'?

Loss of Privacy

A 1998 survey of 1085 corporations, conducted by the American Management Association, shows that more than 40 per cent engaged in some kind of intrusive employee monitoring. Such monitoring includes checking of E-mail, V-mail and telephone conversations; recording of computer keystrokes; video recording of job performance; video monitoring in the locker rooms and bathrooms; and secret monitoring of employees (Doyle, 1999). Random drug testing was carried out by 61 per cent of those surveyed. Psychological testing, which often attempts to probe intimate thoughts and attitudes, is carried out by 15 per cent of surveyed corporations (Doyle, 1999). Furthermore, genetic testing, which creates the potential for discrimination, is practised by one per cent of surveyed corporations (Doyle, 1999). A survey, carried out by the University of Illinois, reveals that one quarter of 84 surveyed corporations, from *Fortune 500*, released confidential employee information to government agencies without a *subpoena* and that 70 per cent gave information to credit guarantors (Doyle, 1999).

Addiction to Technology

The rapid change facilitated by IT produces the feeling of 'technophobia' in some individuals - the feeling that the new technology is 'leaving them behind' and that this anxiety is extending to a pathology. Others are positively addicted to E-mail, the Web and on-line chatting, to the point that they suffer from an 'Internet Addiction Disorder' (IAD) (Ganzel, 1998). IAD is a condition characterised by spending up to 10 hours a day surfing the Net and with physical symptoms such as shaking hands

(Cantelmi, quoted in Elliot, 1998: p.6). Victims can become so fixated on the computer that they lose all social contact and, in some cases, their jobs (Elliot, 1998; Sinha, 1999). The majority of surfers are educated men in the 27 to 31 age group. The Internet can be mesmerising for some (Fawn, 1998). A study at the Carnegie Mellon University examined how people were affected by spending time on-line. Contrary to their expectation, they found higher levels of depression and loneliness in people who spend even a few hours per week connected to the Internet (Hallowell, 1999; Sinha, 1999).

Working Hours in the 'Lean' Organisation

The concept of 'lean' production was developed in the car manufacturing industry in the 1980s (Krafcik, 1988) but it has been extended to all other sectors. In response to changing market demands, such as shorter and more reliable delivery times; a higher and constant product quality; a higher flexibility of both production quantities and variants; shortening product innovation time; and greater customer orientations, organisations have adopted lean production concepts (van Amelsvoort et al. 1991). The basic goal of the lean production concept is to maximise a company's economic performance, accomplished by focusing on four sub-goals (Monden, 1983):

- Cost reduction by eliminating waste;
- Quality assurance so that each process supplies only goods and services to units to the next processes;
- Quantity control, or just-in-time techniques, facilitating daily and monthly fluctuations; and
- Respectful utilisation of human resources in a way that the system can attain its cost objectives.

These new organisational demands and the 'lean' concept could not be met by traditional organisational structures. Information technology is increasingly used as a lever for achieving improvement in competitive status through the achievement of economic benefits, such as lower production cost through the use of more efficient machines; reduced work force; a cheaper, less-skilled work force; improved product or service quality and conformity; increased up-time or production time; enhanced flexibility of the production system to meet customer needs; and lowered insurance costs by a reduction in worker risks (Smith and Carayon, 1995).

However, the extensive downsizing through informatisation and management restructuring throughout the global economy have led to longer hours for those who have jobs (Sharp, 1996). For example, in Canada, the major banks received a $350M R & D tax credit from federal tax for installing ATMs, whilst 60,000 tellers lost their jobs. For some businesses in mature economies, exemplified by software design, work can be performed though 'telework' or 'remote-work'. For example, using Web sites on the Internet and GroupWare software, such as Lotus Notes, employees from different departments, countries and time-zones are able to work together on electronically-stored documents and can contribute to on-line bulletins. However, telework facilitates overseas outsourcing at a fraction of the cost - the worker can be located on the other side of the world, such as India or Eastern Europe, increasing local employees vulnerability to redundancies (Houlder, 1998). In its extreme form, the use of IT and communication technologies has fostered the emergence of the 'virtual office', where instead of the office, there exists a web site. Instead of salaried employees, work is outsourced either to other companies or to a team of freelancers (Houlder, 1998).

Those employees who survive reorganisations suffer from survival syndrome and are working longer hours (Korac-Kakabadse et al. 1998). In US, for example, employees believe that working harder and longer is necessary to keep a job (Sharp, 1996). In self-imposed, downsized, 'lean' and, in some cases, 'anorexic' organisations, top management assumes that remaining employee will devote 50, 60 or 70 hour a week to get the job done (Clark, 1997). Even the White House administration, under President Clinton's leadership, has become leaner as it has cut down 25 per cent of its staff since the Bush years (Milbank, 1998). This has produced a relentless work ethic which encourages late-night work and regular 12-hour workdays for President Clinton's aides (Milbank, 1998). As a result, staff last an average 18 months before being burnt out (Milbank, 1998).

Research shows that IT users face heavier workloads as the initial higher speed of output provided by IT-aids is quickly matched by management's higher expectations in terms of productivity, creating qualitative and quantitative overload (Karuppan, 1997). Quantitative overload is experienced in situations where the quality of work to be performed within a certain time frame exceeds an individual's capability. Qualitative overload arises when the nature of the work to be performed exceeds an individual's knowledge and capabilities (French and Wall, 1972; Karuppan, 1997). Studies of employees in high-technology industries suggest that psychosomatic symptoms are related, in part, to high perceived mental demands in combination with the lack of sufficient skills (Arnetz and Wihlom, 1997) which can be interpreted as qualitative overload. Often, IT systems affect individual roles in ways that have decreased control over jobs, further compounded with lack of job security and psychological demands of increased vigilance and the cost of errors associated with the job (Martin and Wall, 1989). Making skilled and important decisions under pressure of time contributes to higher levels of strain on the individual. In stress research, there has been an increased focus on the factors mediating between workplace and the experience of stress, especially in relation to control and influence (Turner, 1984; Smith, 1987a; 1987b). Control is understood to be a 'power', 'mastery' or 'influence' over the environment (Fisher, 1985; 1986) and job control is exercised over various facets of the job, such as work place, task order, work methods, schedule and organisational policies (Smith, 1987a; 1987b). However, research shows that the pressure and complexity of work are higher among those working with new technologies (Agervold, 1987). Thus, the increased workload is often seen as a consequence of these changes in organisational work (Agervold, 1987). Whilst an increase in the pressure of work is now associated with feelings of stress (Buchanan and Boddy, 1982; Agervold and Kristensen, 1986; Agervold, 1987), research shows that, where new technology affects working conditions in such a way that the quality of work deteriorates and pressure of work increases, there is a higher incidence of stress (Agervold, 1987).

The time pressure associated with prolonged working hours has a negative impact on the quality of life, often leading to higher levels of stress and burnout (El-Shinnawy and Markus, 1997). This finding is explicitly addressed in the stress reaction model that suggests that the impact of stressors increase psychological dysfunctioning with exposure to time (Zapf et al. 1996). Furthermore, IT networks require faster decisions from both individuals and groups whilst, paradoxically, research suggests that decisions in IT facilitated groups takes a longer time (El-Shinnawy and Markus, 1997), creating additional stress on individuals. This is further compounded by the fear of redundancy as electronic networking facilitates redistribution of power in organisations. It is technically feasible for employees to communicate directly with executives (Barner, 1996). Other factors, such as coping skills (Parkers, 1990), commitment (Begley and Czaika, 1993) and behavioural types (Orpen, 1982), all mediate the individual experience of stress.

IT-Extended Working Hours and Consequences

In the US, employees are working an hour longer than in 1982, before computers first moved into office *en masse* and laptops, cellular phones and other electronic business gadgets become the norm (Carey, 1996). In the past 20 years, vacation time in the US has decreased for the average employee by three-and-a-half days whilst commuting time has increased by 23 hours per year (Tonn and Petrich, 1998). The UK also has a culture of long working hours which may pose a threat to the stability of family life and the erosion of the quality of life. A study of 6000 couples, aged 33, found that more than one in four fathers work more than 50 hours a week and that their absence had a detrimental effect on joint family activities (Ferri and Smith, 1996). A survey on the quality of working life found that 82 per cent of managers in the UK regularly work more than 40 hours a week, of which nearly four in ten reported working more than 50 hours a week (Vernon, 1998). For many, the working week extends beyond Friday with 41 per cent stating that they regularly take work home at the weekend (Vernon, 1998). Related Cranfield studies (Korac-Kakabadse and Korac-Kakabadse, 1998) reveal that of 160 interviewed managers and professionals, 60 per cent have a working week somewhere near 60 hours. UK national statistics show that the highest divorce rate in Europe - 45 per cent, second only to US.

Like their counterparts in US, UK men who work longer hours admit to having poor relationships with their children, causing family distress and negatively impacting on relationships with a partner (Delong and Delong, 1992). Longer working hours among men also places a disproportional burden on women who often combine the double shift of care and work with paid work (Lewis, 1998). The sense that families increasingly live in a situation of 'compressed time', as work pervades both the public and private sphere, is equally shared in the UK (Daly, 1996: p.117). Technology is becoming increasingly invasive in employee's personal lives (Boyd, 1997). Research shows that people who work long hours are often unable to communicate on an emotional level in a private sphere, further producing stress (Delong and Dellong, 1992). Career individuals with high family expectations (greater responsibility for child care and home chores) are increasingly augmenting time spent at the office with work done at home by utilisation of IT aids (Venkatesh and Vitalari, 1992). This trend has been linked to an increase in family conflict (Bird et al. 1980).

Although the demographics of work have changed drastically in last 30 years, work remains a place built on 'face time' or long hours in the office for any recognition, reward and advancement (McKenna, 1997). In today's organisations, 80 per cent of managers work in an office and only 4 per cent work from home (Vernon, 1998). Thus, although companies do make provisions for flexible working hours and working from home, they often marginalise those who use those provisions, such as women and disabled (McKenna, 1997).

A study, commissioned by *Computer Weekly*, of 500 IT directors in the UK, across all industry sectors, reveals that 62 per cent of respondents spend up to 48 hours in the office (Vernon, 1998). However, experience of IT industry employees in the UK is shared by others according to an Institute of Management report that concludes that continuous change and restructuring in organisations has led to long working hours, job insecurity and lower morale (Vernon, 1998). The increased and continuous changes to work practices posed by IT proliferation, outsourcing and downsizing create an era of casual professionals, in which short-term contracts run alongside an information overload culture (Cooper, quoted in Vernon, 1988). Current business practices are often destructive and costly in the long term.

In the UK, the pressure to perform at work is considered to be the biggest cause of stress, followed by fear of redundancy; lack of trust in other people to make correct decisions; information overload; excessive working hours; and deadlines and project deliveries (*Computer Weekly*, 1992; Taylor, 1998). Research findings suggest that children of successful US executives are more likely to suffer a range of emotional and health problems than children of 'less successful' parents (Tonn and Petrich, 1998). For example, 36 per cent of the children of executives undergo psychiatric treatment or drug abuse attention each year versus 15 per cent of non-executive children in the same company (Arbor, quoted in Tonn and Petrich, 1998). Furthermore, parents are spending 40 per cent less time with their children than they did thirty years ago (Tonn and Petrich, 1998).

Teleworking and the Web 'Chat Room': The New 'Water Cooler' of the Virtual Office

To date, much of the relevant research has been in the area of telecommuting or teleworking. Research from the University of California shows that telecommuting boosts productivity and reduces costs, helping to break down office politics as it focuses employees on results (Hind, 1998). Other studies suggest that one-too-many capabilities of E-mail, that makes it an invaluable tool for workplace collaboration, also makes it an equally potent weapon for political manipulation (Young, 1998). E-mail has a democratising effect as it opens lines of communications which make issues suppressed into common property. While its decentralising power enhances organisational efficiencies for some organisations, it can lead to disruption and erosion of productivity at others (Young, 1998). The pattern usually consists of employees short-circuiting established managerial channels by using E-mail campaigns to air anti-managerial sentiments (Young, 1998). However, the changes to people's lives that may be a result of the movement to 'virtual societies' encompass far more than alterations to the way one performs work in the future (Agres, Edberg and Igbaria, 1998).

For some, the Internet has magical and/or frightening opportunities - it frees the imagination from the everyday world and facilitates remote-working and timeliness (Sinha, 1999). For others, it creates information overload, imposes working around the clock and poses employment threats. The concept of 'telework', 'remote-work' or 'telecommuting' refers to the use of computers and telecommunication aids to do office work away from a central, conventional office during regular office hours (Kraut, 1987). Most people need a sense of being connected to others and belonging to a social group. Although the trend towards a work force linked by technology and not by common place provides a sense of connectiveness, it falls short of belonging. On-line contact can remove people from a proper understanding of reality and of the proper test for trust, as it is difficult to verify people's identity and to connect, on-line, with 'real' life. It is persuasive, far reaching and clandestine (Lacayo, 1993). Building a common work culture without a common workplace and face-to-face interaction is a challenge to information age. The isolation created in a telecommuting environment can lead to stress (Devoito, 1996). Savings in eliminating lost time at the water cooler may not be real as the need to be connected can take a 15-minute phone which often stretches to 45 minutes (Devoito, 1996). Furthermore, frustration awaits the worker who attempts to telephone a colleague, only to reach V-mail time after time.

Despite the advances in the virtual office, there remains no substitute for bringing people together. Often those who work remotely and lack the informal bonds necessary to connect them to their co-worker have no common sense of value and purpose. Increasingly, teleworkers find themselves aligned along shared technical skills or interests (Devoito, 1996). Working from home, for example, which is equipped with two phone lines (one for voice, one for data); facsimiles; E-mail; file transfer capabilities; and delivery services can be a lonely experience, as well as overwhelming, as there is no place to go to after work. Furthermore, it poses difficulties for personal and others' development and mentoring (Graham, 1998). According to a fax poll of 247 members of the American Management Association, the most frequently felt emotions in the office are enthusiasm (62.8 per cent), frustration (51.0 per cent) and stress (49.4 per cent) (Romano, 1995). Considering that frustration in the workplace is also often dealt with in the workplace, it is difficult to ascertain whether company Web pages, with electronic bulletin boards or 'chat rooms', can provide opportunities for frequent exchange of knowledge and venting of frustration.

Information technologies ratchet change upward faster than humans can cope (Pascarella, 1997). The speed with which advances are currently being made in the business applications of information and communication technologies triggers unprecedented change in organisations which industries, agencies and society, and those who study them, are only beginning to understand (Bradley and Nolan, 1998).

Where is the Added Value?

Many organisations have been through re-engineering and de-layering to the point that they cannot provide their employees the time necessary to develop further and share existing knowledge (Houlder, 1998). These changes have a price. A survey carried out by a KPMG consultancy reveals that nearly half of the companies that survived had damaged a relationship with an important client or supplier because they had failed to turn human intellectual capital into organisational intellectual capital (Houlder, 1998). Knowledge sharing requires forming true relationships (Houlder, 1998). Employees carry information and experience within themselves and, when they leave, they take this 'wealth' with them. With large-scale redundancies and a more mobile work force, companies risk losing the intellectual capital that constitutes their 'corporate memory' (Houlder, 1998; Korac-Kakabadse et al. 1998; Scarnati, 1998).

The problem often lies with tacit, rather than explicit, knowledge that governs the way people do their jobs. Explicit knowledge is easier captured and shared through IT. Companies find it relatively easy to store, retrieve and share reports and documents, but far harder to deal with the less formal knowledge that governs the way people do their jobs and make decisions. Explicit knowledge can be shared through organisations by a variety of means; electronic bulletin boards, Internet, Intranet and electronic mail. However, attempts to develop expert systems, that involve creating rules that reflect an expert's know-how, have found only limited application; such as systems diagnostics and computer simulations. Some organisations, such as Arthur Anderson, the consultancy firm, for example, use an on-line system that allows consultants worldwide to initiate and participate in discussions as part of a much larger knowledge network. Others, such as BP Oil company, use a desktop video-conferencing system, document scanning, electronic mail and the Internet to encourage knowledge sharing amongst employees and to create 'virtual teams'. However, these initiatives also create additional pressure as they create information overload. Furthermore, many employees feel threatened by being asked to share their personal expertise in a knowledge management system.

Although some organisations appear to be more successful than others in knowledge sharing, there is no panacea for knowledge sharing, as it is contextually dependent. First, organisations need to define where the value-added in their business activity is and, then, where the value-added may reside in each role. Creative organisations, such as advertising agencies, where pressure to be original makes employees reluctant to consider second-hand ideas, may need different technologies than those that need to introduce consistency in the service or the product. Similarly, organisations with intellectually curious and confident employees may be enthusiastic in sharing knowledge, such as in R & D organisations, than organisations with excessive layoffs.

Finding where the value-added is in a role requires role analysis as well as organisation design and understanding of organisational culture. Effective role design can then take place. Furthermore, communication systems need to be designed that facilitate sharing but do not produce information overload. Having a Web page or Intranet does not mean that organisation has effective communication systems; rather, the organisation has an electronic system for merely accessing information. Furthermore, the access to Internet al.so requires skill for *finding* required information. Creating information librarian position(s) within large teams, for example, may reduce information overload and increase effectiveness of team members. Information librarians can add value by being involved in selecting and implementing the company-wide crawler and search engines, indexing and cataloguing major content sites and overseeing the process for authenticating Web sites. The value of library expertise in information retrieval, in cataloguing and indexing, is increasingly more important in the Web context.

Similarly, carrying an audit of current work practices and making them congruent with current demands can eliminate many historical tasks being carried out, devoid of any value adding to the role of the organisation. Certain working methods do not match existing technologies and require different prioritising and ways of working. Weil and Rosen (1998) argue that people allow themselves to be sucked into this technological abyss and, in doing so, they become more machine-oriented and less sensitive to their own needs and the needs of others. Some people become so immersed in technology that they risk losing their own identity (Weil and Rosen, 1998; Sinha, 1999). Others challenge the notion that being on-line, all the time, is equal to being 'on the ball'; rather, it can be counter-productive (Hind, 1998).

Current Ways of Working and Organisational Policies

Weil and Rosen (1998) argue that 85 per cent of the population feel uncomfortable with technology and that even people who are comfortable and confident with technology can feel frustrated, intimidated and/or distressed in many ways. Weil and Rosen (1998) devised three categories, or 'technotypes', of people's attitudes towards technology: 'eager adopters', which comprise about 10-15 per cent of the industrialised population; 'hesitant' or 'prove its', which make up about 50-60 per cent of population; and the 'resisters', the remaining 25-40 per cent. Depending on the technology and the context, an individual can be one, or all three, technotypes (Weil and Rosen, 1998). Weil and Rosen (1998) found that of people currently using the Web, cell phones or the Net, 52 per cent feel technophobic about it, resulting in higher stress, lower productivity, less efficiency and higher worker-compensation claims.

Similarly, the UK report, *IT For All*, showed that although the UK has, in many respects, embraced the applications of the information society, patterns of usage are mixed and there exists considerable confusion about its meaning and doubt about potential benefits. Around half of the population claimed never to use computers and only 13 per cent claimed ever to have used the Internet (BMRB International, 1997). In segmenting attitudes, the BMRB study identifies five categories, or technotypes, into which the UK adult population might be divided (BMRB International, 1997):

- *Enthusiasts* - 25 per cent of the population (men, aged between 16 and 34);
- *Acceptors* - 21 per cent of population (men, but slightly older, aged 25-44);
- *Unconvinced* - 20 per cent of the population (principally, more upmarket women, aged 25-54);
- *Concerned* - 18 per cent of the population - typical many older people (women and men, aged 45 plus); and
- *Alienated* - 16 per cent of the population (women, aged 55 plus).

A research study, conducted by Dixons Stores Group, found that household penetration of PCs (the more advanced versions with multimedia potential) was 18 per cent in the UK, compared to 35 per cent in the US (Dixons Stores Group, 1996). However, the problem of technostress goes beyond computers and the Internet, as IT is pervasive, whether one purchases it or not. People are experiencing a reaction to the omnipresence of technology and that reaction often manifests itself as technostress (Weil and Rosen, 1998).

These statistics suggest that similar attitudes can be found in the work place, as they are representative of the researched population. Furthermore, many employment policies are less than friendly towards family life. The lower extent of reconciliation of family-friendly employment provisions in UK, in comparison with other European countries, is sometimes blamed on the lack of clear government initiatives. The voluntary nature of the reconciliation polices in the UK means that the 'trickle down' effect can be slow and is subject to local labour market conditions (Scheibl and Dex, 1998a; 1998b). French public policy, for example, offers employees wider scope for a reconciliation of home and work due to extensive public child-care provision. In Germany, and to some extent in UK, where women have lengthy informal and formal leave periods from the labour market, and public child-care is scant, the policy environment does not seek to reconcile the two spheres. Rather, in many respects it reinforces them (Schiersmann, 1996). In the US, where government has not led in reconciliation policies, some employees have taken responsibility for reconciliation in forms of flexibility of the work force. Some organisations have a wide range of policies that have been considered family-friendly. These are policies concerned with employees' hours of work (job sharing, part-time work, flexi-time), leave entitlements (parental leave, career breaks), financial assistance (child care, maternity pay) and specific responsibilities (elder care or children).

At Achieve Global, a consultancy company, in Tampa, reconciliation policy also includes premises for nursery care for six week to 18 month olds. To ease the personal burdens of stressed-out, dual-career couples and single parents, and to reduce time of work, KPMG, also a consultancy house, allows employees to tap, via an 800 number, the services of Work Family Directions, a counselling and referral agency. About 500 KPMG employees call the 800 number each year for assistance and referrals to adoption agencies, nursing homes, day care, legal and other services (Gordon, 1998). Similarly, Partemps, recruitment consultants, are paying staff to join dating agencies in a similar manner to health-care and pension schemes. The emergence of family-friendly policies is more prominent in consultancy organisations, where intellectual capital is now the scarce resource rather than financial capital (Ghoshal, 1997: p.630). The '24-hour laboratory', a concept that actively makes use of global time differences, and particularly suitable to software development in organisations with round-the clock development ethics, has been tried by Canon in its new 'product development initiative', at Headquarters in Tokyo, drawing on a distributed technical community located in Europe, North America and Japan (Price Waterhouse Coopers, 1998).

Woodall's (1997) study of corporate commitment to *Opportunity 2000,* in a large UK-based corporation, shows that re-structuring, de-layering and the competitive nature of the business environment can force the reconciliation issue down the list of corporate priorities. Gordon (1998) suggests that a similar trend can be found in the US, when the economy heads south. He suggests that, unlike the family, corporate support is not unconditional (Gordon, 1998: p.70). During the *Year of Family*, in 1994, the United Nations set an agenda for action within organisations to expand reconciliation polices. The Agenda's major recommendation was that managers should lead by example and cut their own working hours as well as offering flexibility to staff (UN, 1994) - highlighting the fact that behaviour and expectations are set by the top layers of the organisation and these should be targeted for reform. Organisations need to recognise that employees need time away from the office, when they can be deemed *inaccessible* to all but their most important contacts, not only to preserve the employees' mental-heath but also their value to the organisation (Carey, 1996). A formal and informal set of terms and conditions designed to enable an employee to combine family responsibility with employment, are necessary. Whilst focused provision is directed towards helping a particular group of employees, such as parents with young children, an unfocused provision could benefit a wider range of employees with different needs; including the fulfilment of care for elderly relatives (Forth et al. 1996). IT can be used effectively to facilitate flexibility and value-creation and, at the same time, provide scope to cut costs for employers through staff retention, reduced absenteeism and reduced turnover.

The value-creating role, in turn, gives corporations enormous influence in defining social norms and expectations, making them one of society's primary agents of change (Bartlett and Ghoshal, 1994). This requires changing a traditional culture of long working hours and using 'face time' hours in the office as a means for recognition, reward and advancement (McKenna, 1997), as well as for the adoption of new ways of working. Similarly, the way IT is used needs to be re-examined. For example, instead of using E-mail for self promotion and, at the same time, creating unnecessary information overload for others, as in the case of one large chemical company in UK, employees need to use E-mail only when necessary - as they would have used the office memo in the past. This requires employee education and awareness of their own responsibility and accountability in using technology dysfunctionally and impacting on others.

Although some employers have taken a paternalistic approach to helping employees reduce general levels of stress, there is no evidence that similar initiatives have been undertaken to *reduce* technostress. However, individuals can take initiatives themselves in fighting technostress. Awareness is the first step. Individuals need to see that technology does create stress in their personal, family and work lives. Some of the following may help to reduce technostress:

- Interact with others to establish whether others have an effective solution to a particular problem. Seek IT-related information from many sources;
- Evaluate IT-technology in terms of one's own culture. What value is it going to add?
- Learn to be the driver of IT-technology and not to be driven. Put the IT-technology, such as computers and cellular phones, into perspective. They are only tools;
- Try to participate in decision-making processes on the issue of adapting new technologies;
- Decide on reasonable boundaries for what can be handled, in what time frame. Try to negotiate these boundaries with one's work environment, if possible;
- Apply for appropriate training to learn how to use new IT technology;

- Be assertive, set boundaries around private or discretionary time, even if only for a few hours;
- Request safer technology (modern monitors with emissions of less than 10 volts per metre);
- Observe ergonomic guidelines (for example, do not sit less than one metre from a VDU). When using mobile phones, use an ear piece;
- Choose minimal contact with IT technology during holidays and discretionary time;
- Raditech multi-wave oscillators have been found effective in neutralising electro-magnetic stress in the home.

Conclusion

As social, rather than merely economic, entities, corporations provide important forums for interpersonal inter-action and personal fulfilment for many people. Workplace interactions should, above all, do no harm. However, there is a danger that increased dependence on IT technology will obfuscate the value of personhood. Both managers and employees are 'concerned with life values, fulfilment and a sense of wholeness' (Ferri and Smith, 1996: p.44). People desire what some call 'quality work', which is more than a source of financial support. People who have quality work are able to use their own unique skills and abilities and be in respectful relationships with one another. Human resource managers are increasingly challenged to provide quality work in workplaces where IT technology is replacing human contact. Creating a quality workplace requires, at a minimum, addressing the following questions:

- Where is the value-added in the organisation?
- Where is the value-added in each role?
- What do employees feel about the benefits and problems of using IT which blurs boundaries between work and discretionary time?
- What contributes to productivity of employees who telecommute?
- What is the role of the human resource manager in fostering new ways of working?

Most issues are not technological but human and organisational. Thus, those who are in management roles need to look for ways to mitigate the effects of IT change by effectively responding to IT and adopting new ways of working. They are also being required to attend to the needs of staff members and user communities while responding to pressures to continually adopt and develop new technologies (Clark and Kalin, 1996). Critical skills for the future will be to maintain team performance in turbulent, highly-pressured, IT-supported organisations. Managers will need to strategically use the 'human moment', through face-to-face communication, in order to add colour to employees' lives, help build confidence and develop trust at work (Hallowell, 1999). This skill is currently ignored - at the peril of organisational fragmentation (Hallowell, 1999). While managers will not be expected to be therapists, they will be expected to identify warning signs of impending employee burnout and to help employees deal with high-stress situations (Barner, 1996).

Research has shown that stress reduction programmes based on improving personal stress-management skill have a palliative effect on mental strain, or stress load, and a beneficial and lasting effect on social interactions and support, as well as on a psycho-physiological markers such as lower circulating levels of Prolactin (Arnetz, 1997: p.101). Research suggest that there is a learning curve - that it takes some time to reset the neurocortical-hypothalamic-pituitary axis (Arnetz, 1997, p.101). However, structural changes need to be considered as well (Arnetz, 1997). When correctly designed and implemented, with proper organisational adaptation and change management programmes, IT technology *may* significantly enhance business effectiveness (Arnetz at al, 1992; Arnetz, 1997).

Note

1   This chapter was a paper presented at the Curtin Business School and the ACER National Business Education and Research Conference on 'Directions for Business Education and Research: The Industry and University Interface', Perth, October 1999.

Bibliography

Aaker, D.A., Kumar, V. and Day, G.S. (1995), *Marketing Research,* Fifth Edition, John Wiley and Sons, New York.

Abdel-Halim, A.A. (1981), 'Effects of Role Stress-Job Design-Technology on Employee Work Satisfaction', *Academy of Management Journal,* Vol 24, No 2, June, pp. 260-273.

Abegglen, J.C. (1958). *The Japanese Factory: Aspects Of Its Social Organisation,* Free Press, Glencoe.

Abramis, F.J. (1994), Relationship of Job Stressors to Job Performance: Linear or an Inverted-U?, *Psychological Reports,* Vol 75, No 4, pp. 547-555.

Achilladelis, B., Jervis, P. and Robertson, A. (1971), *A Study of Success and Failure in Industrial Innovation,* University of Sussex Press, Sussex.

Adams, D.A., Todd, P.A. and Nelson, R.R. (1993), 'A Comparative Evaluation of the Impact of Electronic and Voice Mail on Organisational Communication', *Information and Management,* Vol 24, No 1, pp. 9-21.

Adams, R., Carruthers, J. and Hamil, S. (1991), *Changing Corporate Values*, Kogan Page, London.

Adonis, A. and Mulgan, G. (1994), 'Back to Greece: The Scope for Direct Democracy', *Demos,* issue 3, pp. 3-9.

Agervold, M. (1987), 'New Technology in the Office: Attitudes and Consequences', *Work and Stress,* Vol 1, No 2, pp. 143-153.

Agervold, M. and Kristensen, O.S. (1986), *Experienced Workers and New Technology,* The European Foundation for the Improvement of Living and Working Conditions, Dublin.

Agi, M. (1987), Communication and Third-World Development. *Transnational Data and Communications Report* 12(6), pp.10-14.

Agres, C., Edberg, D, and Igbaria, M. (1998), 'Transformation to Virtual Societies: Forces and Issues', *Information Society,* Vol 14, No 2, pp. 71-82.

Ahuja, A. (1997), 'A Price We Must Pay for Progress', *The Times,* Interface Supplement, June 18, p. 14.

Alder, P.S., MacDonald, D.W. and MacDonald, F. (1992), 'Strategic Management of Technical Functions', *Sloan Management Review*, Winter, pp. 19-37.

Alderson, A. and Kakabadse, A. (1994), 'Business Ethics and Irish Management: A Cross-Cultural Study', *European Management Journal*, Vol 12, No 4, pp. 432-441.

Aldrich, H. (1979), *Organisations and Environments,* Prentice-Hall, Englewood Cliffs.

Allen, T.J. and Cohen, S. (1969), 'Information Flow in Research and Development Laboratories', *Administrative Science Quarterly*, Vol 14, No 1, pp. 12-19.

Allison, G. (1971), *Essence of Decision-Making*, Little Brown, Boston.

Amicil, B.C. and Celentano, D.D. (1984), 'Human Factors Epidiemology: An Integrated Approach to the Study of Health Issues in Office Work', in Cohen, B.G.F. (ed.), *Human Aspects of Office Automation*, Elsevier Press, Amsterdam, pp. 78-82.

Amicil, B.C. and Celentano, D.D. (1991), 'Structural Determinates of the Psycho-Social Work Environment: Introducing Technology in the Work Stress Framework', *Ergonomics,* Vol 34, No 5, pp. 625-646.

Anderson, J.R. (1983), *The Architecture of Cognition*, Harvard University Press, Cambridge.

Anderson, J.R. (1987), 'Methodologies of Studying Human Knowledge', *Behavioural and Brain Science*, Vol 10, No 3, pp. 467-505.

Anderson, P. and Tushman, M.L. (1990), 'Technological Discontinuities and Dominant Designs: A Cyclical Model of Technological Change', *Administrative Science Quarterly*, Vol 35, No 4, December, pp. 604-633.

Andrews, C. and Kouzmin, A. (1999), '"Naming the Rose": New Public Management Discourse in the Brazilian Context', *International Review of Public Administration*, Vol 4, No 1, pp. 11-20.

Annis S. (1987), The Shifting Grounds of Poverty Lending at the World Bank. In *Between Two Worlds: The World Bank's Next Decade*. Feinberg, R. (ed.). Overseas Development Council and Transaction Books, Washington, pp. 27-36.

Anzai, Y., Katsuhiko, O. and Mori, H. (eds.), (1995), *Symbiosis of Human and Artifact,* Elsevier, Amsterdam.

Applegate, L.M. and Elam, J.J. (1992), 'New Information Systems Leaders: A Changing Role in a Changing World', *MIS Quarterly,* Vol 16, No 4. pp. 469-490.

Applegate, P.D. and Zawacki, R.A. (1997), 'A Balanced Approach to IT Transformation', *Information Systems Management,* Summer, pp. 6-22.

Argenti, P.A. (1996), 'Corporate Communication as a Discipline: Toward a Definition', *Management Communication Quarterly,* Vol 10, No 1, pp. 73-97.

Argyris, C. (1964), *Integrating the Individual and the Organisation,* Wiley, New York.

Argyris, C. and Schon, D.A. (1978), *Organisational Learning,* Addison-Wesley, Reading.

Aristotle (1928), 'Analytical Posterior', in *The Oxford Translation of Aristotle, Vol 1* (translated by Mure, G.R.G and Ross, W.D.), Oxford University Press, Oxford, pp. 83-94.

Aristotle (1984), *The Complete Work of Aristotle, Vol 2* (edited by Burns, J.), Princeton University Press, Princeton.

Aristotle (1987), *Politics,* Penguin Classics, London.

Arnetz, B.B. (1984), 'The Potential Role of Psycho-Social Stress on Levels of Haemoglobin A1c (Hba1c) and Fasting Plasma Glucose in Elderly People', *Journal of Gerontology,* Vol 39, No 3, pp. 424-429.

Arnetz, B.B. (1996), 'Technostress: A Prospective Psycho-Physiological Study of the Impact of a Controlled Stress-Reduction Programme in Advanced Telecommunication Systems Design Work', *Journal of Occupational Environmental Medicine,* Vol 38, No 1, pp. 53-65.

Arnetz, B.B. (1997), 'Technological Stress: Psycho-Physiological Aspects of Working With Modern Information Technology', *Scandinavian Journal of Work Environment and Health,* Vol 23, No S3, pp. 97-103.

Arnetz, B.B., Anderson, B.B., Strandberg, S., Eneroth, M. and Kallner, P.A. (1988), 'Comparison Between Surgeons and General Practitioners With Respect to Cardiovascular and Psycho-Social Risk Factors Among Physicians', *Scandinavian Journal of Social Medicine,* Vol 21, No 1, pp. 122-125.

Arnetz, B.B., Berg, M. and Arnetz, J.E. (1997), 'Mental Strain and Psychological Symptoms Among Employees in Modern Environment's, *Architecture, Environment, Health,* Vol 51, No 1, pp. 63-67.

Arnetz, B.B., Franberg, M. and Axling, C. (1992), 'Occupational Stress in a Swedish High-Tech Telecommunicaton Corporation: An Integrated Approach to an Occupational Health Challenge. Case Study No 14', in

International Labour Office (ILO) (Ed.), *Conditions of Work Digest: Preventing Stress At Work, Vol II,* ILO, Geneva, pp. 233-238.

Arnetz, B.B. and Wihlom, C. (1997), 'Technological Stress: Psycho-Physiological Symptoms in Modern Offices', *Journal of Psychosmomatic Research,* Vol 43, No 1, pp.35-42.

Asiaweek (1999a), 'Dream Career Track', Vol 25, No 5, February, p. 59.

Asiaweek (1999b), 'Net Tales', Vol 35, No 3, December, p. 28.

Asiaweek (1999c), 'Trouble in E-Timor', Vol 25, No 5, February, p. 59.

Aspect Computing Pty. Ltd. (ACPL), Thompsett R. 1988. Information Systems Project Management. *Course Notes.* Aspect Computing Pty. Ltd. and Thompsett, Canberra. Appendix 7, pp. 1-15.

Astley, W.G. and Van de Ven, A.H. (1983), 'Central Perspectives and Debates in Organisation Theory', *Administrative Science Quarterly,* Vol 29, No 2, pp. 245-273.

Attewell, P. (1992), 'Technology Diffusion and Organisational Learning: The Case of Business Computing', *Organisational Science,* Vol 3, No 1, pp. 1-19.

Auchincloss, K. (1998), 'Real Men Don't Click', *Newsweek,* Vol CXXXII, No 23, 7 December, pp. 4-5.

Austin, J.E. (1990), *Managing in Developing Countries: Strategic Analysis and Operating Technologies,* Free Press, New York.

Australia, Parliament (1988), *Privacy Act Commonwealth 1988,* AGPS, Canberra.

Ayres, R.U. (1991), *Computer Integrated Manufacturing: Revolution in Progress, IIASA CIM Project,* Chapman and Hall, London.

Backof, J.F. and Martin, C.L., Jr. (1991), 'Historical Perspective: Development of the Code of Ethics in the Legal, Medical and Accounting Professions', *Journal of Business Ethics,* Vol 10, No 1, pp. 99-110.

Bagozzi, R. (1980), *Casual Models,* Wiley, New York.

Bahalla A.S. and James D.D. (1991), Integrating new technologies with traditional economic activities in developing countries: an evaluative look at "technology blending". *The Journal of Developing Areas.* 25. October, pp. 477-496.

Balagopal, K. (1989), 'Ruling Class Politics and People's Rights', in S. Kothari and H. Sethi (eds), *Rethinking Human Rights,* New Horizon Press, New York, pp. 83-92.

Bamberg, E. (1992), 'Stressoren in der Erwerbsarbeit und in der Freizeit: ZUSmmenhangemit Psychischen Befindensbeeintrachitigungen'

(Stressors at Work and in Leisure Time: Their Relationship With Psychological Dysfunctioning), *Zeitschrift Fur Arbeits- Und Organisationspsychologie,* Vol 36, No 1, pp. 84-91.

Bankers Magazine (1997), 'Alternative Delivery Systems: Supermarkets, ATMs, Telephone Banking, PCs and On-line Banking', May, pp. 5-12.

Bantel, K. and Jackson, S. (1989), 'Top Management and Innovations in Banking: Does the Composition of the Top Team Make a Difference?' *Strategic Management Journal,* Vol 10, No 1, pp. 107-124.

Barley S.R. (1990), The alignment of technology and structure through roles and networks. *Administrative Science Quarterly* 24(2), pp. 286-308.

Barley, S.R. (1996), 'Technicians in the Workplace: Ethnographic Evidence For Bringing Work Into Organisation Studies', *Administrative Science Quarterly,* Vol 41, No 3, September, pp. 404-441.

Barnard, C. (1938), *The Functions of the Executive,* Harvard University Press, Cambridge.

Barner, R. (1996), 'The New Millennium Workplace: Seven Changes That Will Challenge Managers and Workers', *The Futurist,* Vol 30, No 2, pp. 14-21.

Barnouw, E. (1982), 'Historical Survey of Communication Breakthrough', in G. Benjamin (ed), *Communications Revolution in Politics,* Academy of Political Science, New York, pp. 13-23.

Barthes, R. (1967), *Writing Degree Zero* (translated by Lavers, A. and Smith, C.), Cape, London.

Bartlett, C.A. and Ghoshal, S. (1994), 'Beyond Strategy, Structure, Systems To Purpose, Process, People: Reflections on a Voyage of Discovery', in Duffy, P.B. (Ed.), *The Relevance of A Decade,* Harvard Business School Press, Boston, pp. 72-85.

Bashein, B. and Markus, L.M. (1997), 'Credibility Equation for IT Specialists', *Sloan Management Review,* Vol 38, No 4, pp. 35-44.

Bass, B.M. (1985), *Leadership and Perfomance Beyond Expectations,* Free Press, New York.

Bateson, G. (1973), *Steps to an Ecology of Mind,* Paladin, London.

Beckman, T. (1997), *A Methodology For Knowledge Management,* International Association of Science and Technology For Development (IASTFD) AI and Soft Computing Conference, July, Banff, Canada.

Beckman, T. (1998), *Knowledge Management: A Technical Review*, GWU Working Paper, Washington.

Beeman, L. (1996), 'Too Many Things to Do and Too Little Time to Do Them', *The Oak Ridger,* 3 May, p. 3.

Begley, T.M. and Czaika, J.M. (1993), 'Panel Analysis of the Moderating Effects of Commitment on Job Satisfaction, Intent to Quit and Health Following Organisational Change', *Journal of Applied Psychology,* Vol 78, No 4, pp. 552-556.

Belkin N.J. and Robertson S.E. (1975), Information Science and the Phenomenon of Information. *Journal of the American Society for Information Science* 27(4), pp. 197-204.

Bell, D. (1976), *The Cultural Contradiction of Capitalism,* Heinmann, London.

Bell, D. (1980), The Social Framework of the Information Society. In *The Computer Age: Twenty-Year View.* Dertouzos M.L, Moses J. (eds), MIT Press, Cambridge, pp. 159-167.

Benjamin, R., Dickinson, C. and Rockart, J. (1985), 'Changing Role of the Corporate Information Systems Officer', *MIS Quarterly,* Vol 9, No 3, pp. 177-188.

Bennett, M. (1998), 'The Worldwide Sell', *CIO,* September, pp. 44-45.

Bennis, W. and Nanus, B. (1985), *Leaders: The Strategies for Taking Charge,* Harper and Row, New York.

Benston, G.J. (1982), 'Accounting and Corporate Accountability', *Accounting, Organisation and Society,* Vol 7, No 2, pp. 87-105.

Berg, M., Ametz, B.B., Liden, S., Eneroth, P. and Kallner, A. (1992), 'Technostress: A Psycho-Physiological Study of Employees With VDU-Associated Skin Complaints', *Journal of Occupational Medicine,* No 34, pp. 698-701.

Berners-Lee, T. (1990), *Information Management: A Proposal* [On-line], available at WWW URL,
    http://www.w3.org/pub/www/History/1989/Proposal.html.

Berners-Lee, T. and Cailliau, R. (1990), *WorldWideWeb: Proposal For a HyperText Project* (On-line), available at WWW URL,
    http://www.w3.org/pub/www/Proposal.html.

Berqvist, U., Knave, B., Voss, M. and Wibom, R. (1992), 'A Longitudinal Study of VDT Work and Health', *International Journal of Human-Computer Interaction,* Vol 4, No 2, pp. 197-219.

Berry, J.N., III (1992), 'If Words Will Never Hurt Me, Then ...?', *Library Journal,* January, pp. 6-7.

Bichteler, J. (1987), 'Technostress in Libraries: Causes, Effects and Solutions', *The Electronic Library,* Vol 5, No 5, pp. 282-287.

Bickel, A.M. (1986), *The Least Dangerous Branch: The Supreme Court at the Bar of Politics,* Second Edition, Yale University Press, Yale.

Bird, G., Gross, R. and Bird, G. (1980), 'Effects of Home Computer Use on Fathers' Lives', *Family Relations,* Vol 39, No 3, pp. 438-442.

Birdwhistell, R. (1952), *Introduction to Kinestics,* University of Louisville, Louisville.

Bishop, J.D. (1991), 'The Moral Responsibility of Corporate Executives for Disasters', *Journal of Business Ethics,* Vol 10, No 5, pp. 377-383.

Blythe, J. (1997), *The Essence of Consumer Behaviour,* Prentice Hall, London.

BMRB International (1997), *IT For All 2: Report* (unpublished report), BMRB International, London, September.

Bock, G., Carpenter, K. and Ellen, J. (1986), 'Management's Newest Star: Meet the Chief Information Officer', *Business Week,* October, pp. 84-92.

Bollard, A. and Harper, D. (1987), *Research and Development in New Zealand,* Allen and Unwin, Wellington.

Borda, O.F. (1986), *Retorno a La Tierra,* Carlos Valencia Editores, Bogota.

Bork, R.H. (1990), *The Tempting of America: The Political Seduction of the Law,* Free Press, New York.

Botelho, A.J.J. (1989), Brazil's Independent Computer Strategy. In *Computers in the Human Context: Information Technology, Productivity and People,* Forester T. (ed.), Basil Blackwell, Oxford, pp. 509-517.

Boucher, E.L. (1981), L'impact de l'informatique sur l'emploi en france. *Problems Economique* 8(3), pp. 112-124.

Bourdieu, P. (1971), 'Intellectual Field and Creative Project', in Young, M. (ed.) *Knowledge and Control,* Collier-Macmillan, London, pp. 64-83.

Bourdieu, P. (1979), 'The Production of Belief: Contribution to an Economy of Symbolic Goods', *Media, Culture and Society,* Vol 2, No 1, pp. 48-53.

Bowman, R.J. (1997), 'High Technology: Dream or Nightmare?', *Distribution,* Vol 96, No 13, December, pp. 30-34.

Boyd, F. (1997), 'The Puppet on the String', *Management Services,* Vol 41, No 1, January, pp.38-39.

Boyer, R. and Drache, D. (1996), *States Against Markets: The Limits of Globalisation,* Routledge, New York.

Boynton, A.C., Jacobs, G.C. and Zmud, R.W. (1992), 'Whose Responsibility is IT Management?', *Sloan Management Review,* Summer, pp. 32-38.

Bozeman, D.P. (1993), 'Toward a Limited Rationality Perspective of Managerial Media Selection in Organisations', *Academy of Management Best Paper Proceeding,* The Academy of Management, Columbia SC, pp. 278-282.

Bradley, S.B. and Nolan, R.L. (1998), 'Capturing Value in the Network Era', in Bradley, S.B. and Nolan, R.L. (Eds.) *Sense and Response,* Harvard Business School Press, Boston, pp. 3-29.

Braman, S. (1994), 'The Autopoietic State: Communication and Democratic Potential in the Net', *Journal of the American Society for Information Science,* Vol 45, No 6, pp. 358-368.

Brame, G.G. (1996), 'Seismic Shift', *Working Women,* Vol 21, No 6, pp. 30-33.

Branscum, D. (1998), 'Web Sites For All Eyes', *Newsweek* (Special Issue), Winter, pp. 20-25.

Bransford, J.D. and Johnson, M.K. (1972), 'Contextual Prerequisites for Understanding: Some Investigations of Comprehension and Recall', *Journal of Verbal Learning and Verbal Behaviour,* Vol 11, No 4, pp. 717-726.

Brass, D.J. (1985), 'Technology and the Structuring of Jobs: Employee Satisfaction, Performance and Influence', *Organisational Behaviour and Human Decision Processes,* Vol 35, No 2, pp.215-240.

Braverman, H. (1974), *Labour and Monopoly Capital: The Degradation of Work in the Twentieth Century,* Monthly Review Press, New York.

Bray, P. (1997), 'Yield to Electronic Impulse: The Internet', *The Sunday Times,* 20 April, p. 18 and p. 22.

Brewer, G.D. (1986), 'Methods for Synthesis: Policy Exercises', in W.C. Clark and R.E. Munn (eds), *Sustainable Development of the Biosphere,* Cambridge University Press, Cambridge, pp. 455-475.

Brod, C. (1982), 'Managing Technostress: Optimising the Use of Computer Technology', *Personal Journal,* Vol 61, No 10, pp. 753-757.

Brod, C. (1984a),Technostress: *The Human Cost of the Computer Revolution,* Addison-Wesley, Reading.

Brod, C. (1984b), 'How to Deal with Technostress?' *Office Automation and Administration,* Vol 45, No 7, August, pp. 28-34.

Brooking, A. (1996), *Introduction to Intellectual Capital,* Knowledge Broker Ltd., Cambridge.

Brookings, J.B. (1985), 'Self-Reported Job Burnout among Female Human Service Professionals', *Journal of Occupational Behaviour,* Vol 6, No 2, pp. 143-150.

Brown, A.L.(1982), 'Learning and Development: The Problem of Compatibility, Access and Induction', *Human Development,* Vol 25, No 1, pp. 89-115.

Bruce, W. (1990), *Managing the Problem Employee,* Quorum, New York.

Bruce, W. (1997), 'Communication in Human Resource Management', in Garnett, J.L. and Koumzin, A. (eds.),

Brunsson, N. (1985), *The Irational Organisation,* John Wiley, New York.

Buchanan, D. and Boddy, D. (1982), 'Advanced Technology and the Quality of Working Life', *Journal of Occupational Psychology,* Vol 55, No 1, pp. 1-55.

Buchanan L. (1999), *The Smartest Little Company in America,* Reuters Inc.

Burgelman, R.A. (1983), 'A Process Model of Internal Corporate Venturing in the Diversified Major Firm', *Administrative Science Quarterly,* Vol 28, No 2, pp. 223-244.

Burke, C.A. (1994), 'What is Profession?' *Journal of the American Society of CLU and ChFC,* Vol 48, No 1, pp. 28-30.

Burns, J.M. (1978), *Leadership,* Harper and Row, New York

Burns, T. and Stalker, G.M. (1961), *The Management of Innovation,* Tavistock. London

Business Week (1985), A cotton plantation in a test tube? 11 November, pp. 17-18.

Butler Cox Foundation (1986), *Information Technology: Value for Money,* CSC Index, Bloomsbury Square, London.

Cadbury, A. (1995), *The Company Chairman: New Edition,* Fitzwilliam Publishing, Hemel Hempstead.

Caldwell, B.S. and Taha, L.H. (1993), 'Starving at the Banquet: Social Isolation in Electronic Communication Media', *Interpersonal Computing and Technology: An Electronic Journal For 21st Century,* Vol 1, No 1, January, pp. 11-28.

Campbell, D. (1979), 'Interior Office Design and Visitor Response', *Journal of Applied Psychology,* Vol 64, No 6, pp. 648-653.

Caplin, R.D., Cobb, S., French, J.R.P., Harrison, R.V. and Pinneau, S.R. (1975), *Job Demands and Work Health: Main Effects and*

Occupational Differences, US Government Printing Office, Washington.

Carey, R. (1996),'A Balancing Act', *Sale and Marketing Management,* June, pp. 14-18.

Carmichael, A.J. and Roberts, D.L. (1992), 'Visual Display Units and Facial Rashes', *Contact Dermatitis,* Vol 26, No 1, pp. 63-64.

Carmody, M.J. (1989), Modernisation: The Australian Taxation Office Approach to Introducing New Technologies, *Proceedings of the International Working Conference on Shaping Organisations - Shaping Technology,* Terrigal. May.

Castelles, M. (1986), High technology, world development and structural transformation: the trends and the debate. *Alternatives: Social Transformation And Human Governance.* 11(3) pp. 297-343.

Castelles, M. (1988), High Technology and the New International Division of Labour. Paper presented to the International Institute for Labour Studies. Indiana Council of Social Science Research Seminar on the Diffusion of High Technology and the Labour Market, Asian Experience. New Delhi, March.

Castelles, M. (1989), 'High Technology and the New International Division of Labour', *Labour and Society,* Vol 14, No 1, pp. 7-42.

Cauldfield, C. (1998), *Masters of Illusion: The World Bank and the Poverty of Nations,* Pan Books, London.

Cavanaugh, K. (1998), 'Bandwidth's New Bargains', *Magazine of Innovation Technology Review,* Vol 101, No 4, November-December, pp. 63-65.

Cetron, M. (1994), 'The Future Face of Terrorism', *The Futurist,* November-December, pp. 74-83.

Chambers, R. (1993), *Challenging the Professions: Frontiers for Rural Development,* IT Publication, London.

Chandler, A.D. (1962), *Strategy and Structure: Chapters in the History of American Enterprise,* MIT Press, Cambridge.

Chartland, R.L. and Morentz, J.W. (eds.) (1979), *Information Technology Serving Society,* Pergamon, New York.

Chau, P.Y.K. and Tye Ng, E.M.W. (1993), 'IS/IT Skills Required for the 1990s': The Hong Kong Scenario', *Proceedings of the International Academy of Information Management Conference,* Florida, December, pp. 99-109.

Cheney, P.H., Hale, D.P. and Kasper, G.M. (1990), 'Knowledge, Skills and Abilities of Information Systems Professionals: Past Present and Future', *Information and Management,* Vol 19, No 4, pp. 237-247.

Chesebro, J.W. and Bertelsen, D.A. (1996), *Analysing Media: Communication Technologies as Symbolic and Cognitive Systems,* Guilford Press, New York.

Chia, S.Y. (1985), The Role of Foreign Trade in Investment in the Development of Singapore. In *Foreign Trade and Investment: Economic Growth in the Newly Industrialising Asian Countries,* Galenson, W. (ed.), University of Wisconsin Press, Madison, pp. 84-96.

Chidambaram, L. and Jones, B. (1993), 'Impact of Communication Medium and Computer Support on Group Perceptions and Performance: A Comparison of Face-to-Face and Dispersed Meetings', *MIS Quarterly,* Vol 17, No 4, pp. 465-491.

Child, J. (1972a), 'Organisation, Structure and Strategies of Control: A Replication of the Aston Study', *Administrative Science Quarterly,* Vol 17, pp. 163-177.

Child, J. (1972b), 'Organisational Structure, Environment, and Performance: The Role of Strategic Choice', *Sociology,* Vol 6, No 1, January, pp. 1-22.

Child, J. (1987), 'Information Technology, Organisation and the Response to Strategic Challenges', *California Management Review,* Vol 30, No 1, pp.33-50.

Chittister, C.G. and Haimes, Y.Y. (1996), 'System Integration via Software Risk Management', *Systems and Humans,* Vol 26, No 5, September, pp. 521-532.

Choo, W.C. (1998), *The Knowing Organisation: How Organisations Use Information to Construct Meaning, Create Knowledge and Make Decisions,* Oxford University Press, Oxford.

Choo, W.C. (1999), 'Closing the Cognitive Gaps: Mastering Information Management', *The Financial Times,* 22 March, p. 17.

Christensen, H.K. and Montgomery, C.A. (1981), 'Corporate Economic Performance: Diversification Strategy Versus Market Structure', *Strategic Management Journal,* Vol 2, No 4, pp. 327-343.

Ciborra, C. and Jelassi, T. (1994), *Strategic Information Systems,* Wiley, New York.

Cicero (1981), *Cicero Selected Works,* Trans. M. Grabt, Penguin Classics, New York.

Clark, K. (1997), 'How to Make Traffic Jams a Thing of the Past', *Fortune,* 31 March, p. 34.

Clark, K. and Kalin, S. (1996), 'Technostressed Out?: How to Cope in the Digital Age', *Library Journal,* Vol 121, No 13, pp. 30-35.

Clark, P. (1985), A Review of the Theories of Time and Structure for Organisational Sociology. *Working Paper Series No 6,* University of Birmingham Working Organisations Research Centre, pp. 1-43.

Clarke, M. and Stewart, J. (1997), *Partnership and the Management of Co-operation,* Institute of Local Government Studies, London.

Clegg, S. and Dunkerley, D. (1980), *Organisation, Class and Control,* Routledge and Kegan Paul, London.

Cleland, K. (1995), 'On-Line Offers Truly Receptive Promotion Target's, *Advertising Age,* 20 March, p. 18.

Clift, S.E. (1997), 'Putting Pen to Paper: Electronic Democracy, Write Oo!', *International E-Democracy,* http://freenet.mps.mn.us/govt/e-democracy.

Cohen, B. (1999), 'The Job Network Puzzle', *HQ Magazine,* No 62, January-February, pp. 34-36.

Cohen, S. (1980), 'After Effects of Stress on Human Performance and Social Behaviour: A Review or Research and Theory', *Psychological Bulletin,* Vol 88, No 1, pp. 82-108.

Cohen, S. and Brand, R. (1993), *Total Quality Management in Government: A Practical Guide For the Real World,* Jossey-Bass, San Francisco.

Collins, J.C. and Porras, J.I. (1994), *Built to Last: Successful Habits of Visionary Companies,* Harper Business, New York.

Comer, J.P. (1988), 'Educating Poor Minority Children', *Scientific American,* issue 259, pp. 42-48.

Comfort, L.K. (1993), 'Integrating Information Technology Into International Crisis Management and Policy', *Journal of Contingencies and Crisis Management,* Vol 1, No 1, March, pp. 15-26.

Comfort, L.K. (1994), 'Risk and Resilience: Inter-Organisational Learning Following the Northridge Earthquake of 17 January 1994', *The Journal of Contingencies and Crisis Management,* Vol 2, No 3, September, pp. 157-170.

Computer Weekly (1992), 'Stress Costs UK Firms £7000m Every Year', 12 March, p. 82.

Conger, J.A. (1989), *The Charismatic Leader: Behind the Mystique of Exceptional Leadership,* Jossey-Bass, San Francisco.

Conger, J.A. and Kanungo, R.N. (1987), 'Toward a Behavioural Theory of Charismatic Leadership in Organisational Settings', *Academy of Management Review,* Vol 12, No 4, pp. 637-647.

Conger, J.A. and Kanungo, R.N. (1988), 'The Empowerment Process: Integrating Theory and Practice', *Academy of Management Review,* Vol 13, No 3, pp. 471-482.

Contractor, N.S. and Eisenberg, E.M. (1990), 'Communication Networks and New Media in Organisations', in Fulk, J. and Steinfield, C. (Eds), *Organisations and Communication Technology,* Sage Publications, Newbury Park, pp. 143-172.

Cool, K. and Dierickx, I. (1993), 'Rivalry, Strategic Groups and Firm Profitability', *Strategic Management Journal,* Vol 14, No 1, pp. 47-59.

Cooper, C.L. and Payne, R. (Eds.) (1988), *Causes, Coping and Consequences of Stress at Work,* John Wiley, Chichester.

Crane, D. (1987), *The Transformation of the Avant-Garde,* Chicago University Press, Chicago.

Crawford, R. (1991), *In the Era of Human Capital,* Harper Collins, New York.

Creedy, S. (1997), 'Computer Crimes: Police Get Serious', *The Australian,* February 25, pp. 52-53.

Croft, S. (1989), Military technological innovation and stability *Futures* 21(5), pp. 444-479.

Croley, S.P. (1995), 'The Majoritarian Difficulty: Elective Judiciaries and the Rule of Law', *The University of Chicago Law Review,* Vol 62, No 2, Spring, pp. 689-794.

Cronbach, L.J. (1951), 'Coefficient Alpha and the Internal Structure Test', *Psychometrika,* Vol 16, No 2, pp. 297-334.

Cronbach, L.J., Rajaratnam, N. and Glesar, G.C. (1963), 'Theory of Generalisability: A Liberalisation of Reliability Theory', *British Journal of Statistical Psychology,* Vol 16, No 2, pp. 137-163.

Crowther, C. (1987), Information Systems Analysis for Development Countries: What is Wrong and How Action Research Can Help. *Data for Development Newsletter 22,* pp. 19-31.

Crozier, M., Friedberg, E. (1977), *L'Actuer et le System,* Le Seuil, Paris.

Culnan, M.J. and Markus, M.L. (1987), 'Information Technologies: Electronic Media and Inter-Organisational Communication', in Jablin, F.M., Putnam, L.L., Roberts, K.H. and Porter, L.W. (eds.), *Handbook of Organisational Communication: An Interdisciplinary Perspective,* Sage, Newbury Park, pp. 420-443.

Currie, W. (1994), *Outsourcing: Friend or Foe?*, Research Workshop - Management and New Technology, University Pierre Mendes-France, Grenoble, October.

Currie, W. (1995), *Management Strategy For IT: An International Perspective*, Pitman Publishing, London.

Cyert, R.M. and March, J.G. (1963), *A Behavioural Theory of the Firm,* Prentice-Hall, Englewood Cliffs.

Dadzie, K.K.S. (1988), Services in the World Economy. *Transnational Data and Communications Report* 12(1), pp. 17-20.

Daft, R.L. and Lengel, R.H. (1984), 'Information Richness: A New Approach to Managerial Behaviour and Organisational Design', *Research in Organisational Behaviour, Vol 6*, JAI Press, Greenwhich, pp. 191-233.

Daft, R.L. and Lengel, R.H. (1986), 'Organisational Information Requirements, Media Richness and Structural Design', *Management Science*, Vol 32, No 5, pp. 554-571,

Daft, R.L., Lengel, R.H. and Trevino, L.K. (1987), 'Message Equivocality, Media Selection, No and Manager Performance: Implications For Information Systems', *MIS Quarterly,* Vol 1, No 1, pp. 355-366.

Dahl, R.A. (1985), *After the Revolution?: Authority in a Good Society,* Yale University Press, New Haven.

Dahl, R.A. (1989), *Democracy and Its Critics*, Yale University Press, Yale.

Daly, K.J. (1996), *Family and Time: Keeping Pace in a Hurried Culture,* Sage Publications, London.

Damon, N. (1997), 'Old IT Methods Die Hard', *IBM Today*, September, p. 26.

Daniel, D. (1996), 'The IS Profession Comes of Age', *Computer Canada,* Special Issue: Twenty Years of Computing, pp. 14-24.

Davenport, T.H. (1993), *Process Innovation: Re-Engineering Work Through Information Technology,* Harvard Business School Press, Boston.

Davenport, T.H. (1994), 'Saving IT's Soul: Human-Centred Information Management', *Harvard Business Review,* Vol 72, No 2, March-April, pp. 119-131.

Davenport, T.H. (1999), 'Attention: The Next Information Frontier: Mastering Information Management', *The Financial Times*, 8 February, p. 17.

Davenport, T.H. and Marchand D.A. (1999), 'Is KM Just Good Information Management: Mastering Information Management', *The Financial Times*, 8 March, pp. 11-12.

Davenport,T.H. and Prusak, L. (1997), *Information Ecology: Mastering the Information and Knowledge Environment*, Oxford University Press, New York.

Davenport, T.H. and Prusak, L. (1998), *Working Knowledge: How Organisations Manage What They Know*, Harvard Business School Press, Boston.

Davies, M.W. (1988), *Knowing One Another: Shaping an Islamic Anthropology*, Mansell, London.

Davies, S. (1999), 'Europeans Angered by US Espionage', *The Sydney Morning Herald*, 9 August, p.8.

Davis, S. and Davidson, B. (1991), *2020 Vision*, Simon and Schuster, New York.

Davis-Blake, A. and Uzzi, B. (1993), 'Determinants of Employee Externalization: A Study of Temporary Workers and Independent Contractors', *Administrative Science Quarterly*, Vol 38, No 2, pp. 201-221.

De Courcey, A. (1998), 'From Clinic to Classroom: Power of Experimental Learning, *Collage Teaching*, Vol 46, No 4, Fall, pp. 40-45.

De George, R.R. (1982), *Business Ethics*, 2nd Edition, MacMillan Publishing, New York.

De Soto, H. (1989), *The Other Path: The Invisible Revolution in the Third World*. Harper and Row, New York.

de Spinoza, B. (1951), *Works of Spinoza*, translated by R.H.M. Elwes, vols. 1 and 2, Dover, New York.

de Tocqueville, A. (1994), *Democracy in America*,, edited by J.P. Nater, translated by G. Lawrence, Fontane, London.

De Vito, J. (1989), 'Silence and Para-language as Communication', *Ethics*, Vol 46, No 2, pp. 150-153.

Dean, J.W. (1987), 'Building the Future: The Justification Process for New Technology', in P.M. Johannes and A. Buitendam (eds), *New Technology as Organisational Innovation*, Ballinger, Cambridge, pp. 35-58.

Dejean, D. and Dejean, S.B. (1991), *Lotus Notes at Work*, Lotus Books, New York.

Deleone, P. (1994), 'Reinventing the Policy Sciences: Three Steps Back to the Future', *Policy Science*, Vol 27, No 1, pp. 77-95.

Delong, T.J. and Delong, C.C. (1992), 'Managers as Fathers: Hope on the Home Front', *Human Resource Management,* Vol 31, No 2, December, pp. 171-181.

DeMarco, T. and Lister, T. (1987), *Peopleware: Productive Projects and Teams,* Dorset House, New York.

DEMOS (1995), *Time Squeeze,* Demos, London.

Dempsey, M. (1999), 'The Role of the Chief Knowledge Officer: Buzzword Has Already Made a Lot of Enemies', *The Financial Times,* 28 April, p. 11.

Derlega, V.J. and Margulis, S.T. (1982), 'Why Loneliness Occurs: The Inter-Relationship of Social-Psychological and Privacy Concepts', in Peplau, L.A. and Perlman, D. (eds.), *Loneliness: A Sourcebook of Current Theory, Research and Therapy,* John Wiley and Sons, New York, pp. 152 -165.

Dertouzos, M.L. (1998), *What Will Be: How the New World of Information Will Change Our Lives*, Harper Edge, New York.

Descartes, R. (1911), 'Discourses on the Methods' in *The Philosophical Works of Descarte, Vol 1* (translated by Haled, E.I. and Ross, GR. T.), Cambridge University Press, Cambridge, pp. 217-224.

Devoito, M.D. (1996), 'Blueprint For Office 2000: The Adventure Continues...', *Managing Office Technology,* Vol 41, No 12, pp. 16-21.

Dewar, R.D. and Dutton, J.E. (1986), 'The Adoption of Radical and Incremental Innovations: An Empirical Analysis', *Management Science,* Vol 32, No 11, November, pp. 1422-1433.

Dewey, J. (1927), *The Public and Its Problems,* Free Press, New York.

Dewey, J. (1929), *The Quest For Certainty*, Putnam, New York.

Di Giovanni, J. (1998), 'The Big Cover-up', *Vogue Australia,* No 12, December, pp. 144-147.

Di Martina, V. and Wirth, L. (1990), 'Teleworking: A New Way of Working and Living', *International Labour Organisation,* Vol 9, No 4, pp. 529-554.

Dixons Stores Group Plc. (1996), 'UK Home Market For PC's' - Presentation by John Clare, Chief Executive, to Multimedia Industry Advisory Group, Department of Trade and Industry (unpublished), London, October.

Dodgson, M. (1989), 'National Policies - Research and Technology Policy in Australia: Legitimacy in Intervention', *Science and Public Policy*, Vol 16, No 3, pp. 159-166.

Dodgson, M. (1991), The Future for Technological Collaboration. *Emerging*

New International Technology Order: Opportunities and Challenges for Korea, STPI International Conference, Seoul. September.

Donaton, S. (1995), 'Pathfinder Blazes a Trail to Ads', *Advertising Age,* 10 April, p. 19.

Douglas, M. and Wildavsky, A. (1982), *Risk and Culture,* University of California Press, Berkeley.

Dowling, J. and Pfeffer, J. (1975), 'Organisational Legitimacy: Social Values and Organisational Behaviour', *Pacific Sociological Review,* Vol 18, No 1, pp. 122-136.

Downs, A. (1957), *An Economic Theory of Democracy,* Free Press, New York.

Downs, G.W., Jr. and Mohr, L.B. (1976), 'Conceptual Issues in the Study of Innovation', *Administration Science Quarterly,* Vol 21, No 4, pp. 700-714.

Doyle, R. (1999), 'Privacy in the Workplace', *Scientifc American,* Vol 280, No 1, p.19.

Driscoll, M. (1999), 'You've Got Mail: "Scream"', *The Australian,* 8 March, p.15.

Dror, Y. (1987), 'Retrofitting Central Mind of Government', *Research in Public Policy Analysis and Management,* Vol 69, No 4, pp. 79-107.

Drucker, P. (1951), *The New Society,* Heinemann, London.

Drucker, P. (1959), 'Challenge to Management Science', *Long Range Planning,* Vol 5, No 2, pp. 238-242.

Drucker, P. (1993), *Post-Capitalist Society,* Harper Business, New York.

Drucker, P. (1994), 'The Age of Social Transformation', *Atlantic Monthly,* November, pp. 42-43.

Drucker, P. (1999), 'What Information Do Executives Need: Mastering Information Management', *The Financial Times,* 19 April, p. 18.

Dryzek, J.S. (1990), *Discursive Democracy,* Cambridge University Press, New York.

Dunham, R.S. (1999), 'Across America: A Troubling "Digital Divide"', *Business Week,* (European Edition), 2 August, p. 39.

Dworkin, R. (1977), *Taking Rights Seriously,* Harvard University Press, Harvard.

Earl, M. (1989), *Management Strategies for Information Technology,* Prentice Hall, New York.

Earl, M. (1993), 'Experiences in Strategic Information System Planning', *MIS Quarterly,* Vol 17, March, pp. 1-21.

Earl, M.J. and Feeny, D.F. (1994), 'Is Your CIO Adding Value?', *Sloan Management Review,* Vol 35, No 3, pp. 11-17.

Ebin, V. (1979), *The Body Decorated,* Thames and Hudson, New York.

Eisenhardt, K. (1988), 'Agency - and Institutional-Theory Explanations: The Case of Retail Sales Compensation', *Academy of Management Journal,* Vol 31, No 3, pp. 488-511.

Eisenhardt, K. and Schoonhoven, C. (1990), 'Organisational Growth: Linking Founding Team, Strategy and Growth Among US Semi-Conductors Ventures 1978-1988', *Administrative Science Quarterly,* Vol 35, No 4, pp. 504-529.

Elias, N. (1987), 'The Retreat of Sociologists Into the Present', *Theory, Culture and Society,* Vol 4, Nos 2 and 3, pp. 112-120.

Elias, N. and Scotson, J. (1965), *The Established and the Outsiders,* Cass, London.

Elliot, J. (1998), 'Bill Gates Calling or Maybe Not ', *The Daily Telegraph,* 2 June, p. 6.

El-Shinnawy, M. and Markus, M.L. (1997), 'The Poverty of Media Richness Theory: Explaining People's Choice of Electronic Mail versus V-mail', *International Journal of Human-Computer Studies,* Vol 46, No 3, pp. 443-467.

Ely, R.J. (1994), 'The Effects of Organisational Demographics and Social Identity on Relationships Among Professional Women', *Administrative Science Quarterly,* Vol 39, No 2, pp. 203-238.

Emery, F.E. and Thorsrud, E. (1976), *Democracy at Work,* Nijoff, Leiden.

Employment Service (1992), *Corporate IT Strategy: April 92 - March 96.* ES/IT Branch. London. April, pp. 2-42.

Ericson, A. and Kallen, B. (1986), 'An Ediemological Study of Work With Video Screens and Pregnancy Outcome: A Case-Referent Study', *American Journal of Industrial Medicine,* Issue 9, pp. 459-475.

Ericsson, K.A. and Simon, H.A. (1984), *Protocol Analysis: Verbal Reports as Data,* MIT Press, Cambridge.

Erikson, J. (1999), 'Middlemen Beware', *Asiaweek,* Vol 25, No 3, 19 March, p. 46.

Escobar, A. (1992), Reflection on "Development": Grassroots Approaches and Alternative Politics in the Third World. *Futures* 24(6), pp. 411-436.

Esteva, G. (1987), Regenerating People's Space. *Alternatives* 12(1), pp. 129-136.

Etzioni, A. (1970), *Intervention Theory and Method: A Behavioural View,* Addison-Wesley, Mass.

European Commission (1987), *FAST II Programme 1984-87: European Futures. Prospects and Issues in Science and Technology - Summaries of Research Reports,* European Commission, Brussels.

European Union Directorate General For Research (EUDGR) (1998), *An Appraisal of the Technologies of Political Control, Report,* European Union Directorate General For Research, Brussels.

Evans, P. (1999), 'Strategy and the New Economics of Information: Mastering Information Management'. *The Financial Times,* 8 February, p. 12 and p. 14.

Evans, P.B. and Wurster, T.S. (1997), 'Strategy and the New Economics of Information', *Harvard Business Review,* Vol 75, No 5, September-October, pp. 71-82.

External Affairs and International Trade Canada (EAITC) (1991), *Information Technology Strategic Plan: 1991-1996,* Information System Bureau (MSD, December, Ottawa.

Fairholm, G.W. (1991), *Values Leadership: Towards a New Philosophy of Leadership,* Praeger, London.

Fairholm, G.W. (1993), *Organisational Power Politics: Tactics in Organisational Leadership,* Praeger, London.

Falcione, R.L., Daley, J.A. and McCroskey, J.C. (1977), 'Job Satisfaction as a Function of Employees' Communication Apprehension, Self-Esteem and Perceptions of Their Immediate Supervisors', in Rubin, B.D. (ed.) *Communication Yearbook, Vol 1,* Transaction Books, New Brunswick, pp. 363-376.

Fallows, J. (1996), 'Why Americans Hate the Media', *Atlantic Monthly,* February, p. 62.

Farbey, B., Land, F. and Targett, D. (1993), *IT Investment: A Study of Methods and Practice,* Butterworth-Heinemann, London.

Farjoun, M. and Lai, L. (1997), 'Similarity Judgements in Strategy Formulation: Role, Process and Implications', *Strategic Management Journal,* Vol 18, No 4, pp. 255-273.

Farrell, R. (1998), 'Electronic Commerce: Basics For Beginners', *Briefings,* Issue 59, December, p. 11.

Farwell, D.W., Kuramoto, L., Lee, D., Trauth, E.M. and Winslow, C. (1992), 'A New Paradigm for IS - The Education Implications', *Information System Management,* Spring, pp. 7-14.

Fawn, F. (1998), 'Singing the IT Blues', *Computerworld,* Vol 29, Issue, 59, 20 July, pp. 59-60.

Fayol, H. (1949), *General and Industrial Administration,* Piman and Sons, London.

Fedanzo, A. (1995), 'Breaking the Glass Ceiling', *Informationweek,* Issue 528, May 22, p. 127.

Feeny, D.F., Edwards, B.R. and Simpson, K.M. (1992), 'Understanding the CEO/CIO Relationship', *MIS Quarterly,* December, pp. 435-448.

Feinberg R. (ed.) (1987), *Between Two Worlds: The World Bank's Next Decade,* Overseas Development Council and Transaction Books, Washington.

Fels, X. (1988), Technological Co-operation. *Science and Public Policy* 15(6), pp. 373-375.

Ferrer, A. (1985), Argentina's Foreign Debt Crisis. *Third World Affairs.* Third World Foundation, London, pp. 1-14.

Ferri, E. and Smith, K. (1996), *Parenting in the 1990s,* Family Policies Study Centre, London.

Fine, S.F. (1986), 'Terminal Paralysis or Showdown at the Interface', in Urbana, I.L., (Ed.), *Human Aspects of Libarry Automatissation: Helping Staff and Patrons,* Graduate School of Library Information Science, University of Illinois, pp. 214-223.

Finer, H. (1932), *The Theory and Practice of Modern Government,* Metheuen, London.

Finholt, T. and Sproull, L.S. (1990), 'Electronic Groups at Work', *Organisation Science,* Vol 1, No 1, pp. 41-64.

Finkelstein, S. (1992), 'Power in Top Management Teams: Dimensions, Measurement and Validation', *Academy of Management Journal,* Vol 35, No 3, pp. 505-538.

Finkelstein, S. and Hambrick, D. (1990), 'Top Management Team Tenure and Organisational Outcomes: The Moderating Role of Managerial Discretion', *Administrative Science Quarterly,* Vol 35, No 4, pp. 484-503.

Fischer, C.S. and Phillips, S.L. (1982), 'Who is Alone? Social Characteristics of People with Small Networks', in Peplau, L.A. and Perlman, D. (eds.), *Loneliness: A Sourcebook of Current Theory, Research and Therapy,* John Wiley and Sons, New York pp .21-39.

Fischer, F. and Forester, J. (eds.) (1993), *The Argumentative Turn in Policy Analysis and Planning,* Duke University Press, Durham.

Fishbein, M. (1947), *A History of the American Medical Association 1842 to 1847*, W.B. Saunders Co., Philadelphia.

Fisher, G.B. (1950), Alternative Techniques for Promoting Equality in a Capitalist Society. *American Economic Review*. 15 May, pp. 356-368.

Fisher, S. (1985), 'Control and Blue-Collar Work', in Cooper, C.L. and Smith, M.J. (eds.), *Job Stress and Blue Collar Work*, Wiley, New York, pp. 112-121.

Fisher, S. (1986), *Stress and Strategy*, Psychology Publisher, New York.

Fletcher, B. C. and Payne, R.L. (1980), 'Stress at the Workplace: A Review and Theoretical Framework - Part II', *Personnel Review*, Vol 9, No 2, pp. 4-8.

Flynn, L. (1999), 'Testing the Links', *The Sunday Morning Herald*, 23 February, p. 4c.

Flynn, N. (1990), *Public Sector Management*, Harvester Wheatsheaf, London.

Fogelman, M. (1994), 'Freedom and Censorship in the Emerging Electronic Environment', *The Information Society*, Vol 10, No 4, pp. 295-303.

Follett, M.P. (1940), *Dynamic Administration: The Collected Papers of Mary Parker Follett* (edited by Metcalf, H. and Urwick, L.), Haper and Brothers, New York.

Foote, D. (1996), 'The New Breed', *CIO*, Vol 10, No 3, pp. 38-42.

Foreign and Commonwealth Office (1997), *Britain's System of Government*, Foreign and Commonwealth Office, October, London

Forester T. (ed.) (1985), *The Information Technology Revolution*, Basil Blackwell, Oxford.

Forester, T. (1987), *High-Tech Society*, Basil Blackwell, Oxford.

Forester, T. (ed.) (1989), *Computers in the Human Context: Information Technology, Productivity and People*, Basil Blackwell, Oxford.

Forth, J., Lissenburgh, S., Callender, C. and Millward, N. (1996), *Family-Friendly Working Arrangements in Britain*, Research Report No 16, Department For Education and Employment, London.

Fosu, A.K. (1991), Capital instability and economic growth in sub-saharan Africa. *The Journal of Development Studies* 28(1), pp. 74-85.

Foucault, M. (1980), *Power/Knowledge; Selected Essays and Other Writings: 1972-1977* (translated and edited by Gordon, C.), Harvester Press, Brighton.

France, M. (1999), 'The Net: How to Head off Big-Time Regulation', *Business Week*, 10 May, pp. 33-34.

Freedman, D.X. (1984), 'Psychiatric Epidemiology Counts,' *Archives of General Psychiatry,* Vol 41, pp. 931-933.

Freeman, L. (1995), 'From Salesman's Web to On-line Web', *Advertising Age,* 3 April, p.7. and On-line: http://www.helsinki.fi/science/optek/1993/n1/caldwell.txt.

French, J.R.P. and Wall, T.D. (1972), 'Organisational Stress and Individual Strain', in Marrow, A.J. (Ed.), *The Failure of Success,* AMACOM, New York, pp. 89-96.

Frese, M. and Okonek, K. (1984), 'Reasons to Leave Shift-Work and Psychological and Psychosomatic Reactions of Former Shift-Workers', *Journal of Applied Psychology,* Vol 69, No 4, pp. 509-414.

Frese, M. and Zapf, D. (1988), 'Methodological Issues in the Study of Work Stress; Objective versus Subjective Measurement of Work Stress and the Question of Longitudinal Studies', in Cooper, C.L. and Payne, R. (Eds.), *Causes, Coping and Consequences of Stress at Work,* John Wiley, Chichester, pp. 375-411.

Friedman, T.L. (1999), 'Judgment Not Included', *The New York Times,* 27 April, p. 18.

Friedson, E. (1970), 'Professions and the Occupational Principle', in E. Friedson (ed), *Professions and their Prospects*, Sage, New York.

Fritz, W., Higa, K. and Narasimhan, S. (1994), 'Telework: Exploring the Broderless Office', in Nunamker, J.F. and Sprague, R.H., (eds.), *Proceedings of the 27th Annual Hawaii International Conference on Systems Science, Vol 4,* IEEE Computer Society, Los Alamitos, pp. 149-158.

Fujigaki, Y. and Mori, K. (1997), 'Longitudinal Study of Work Stress Among Information System Professionals', *International Journal of Human-Centred Interaction,* Vol 9, No 4, pp. 369-381.

Fukuyama, F. (1992), *The End of History and the Last Man,* Hamish Hamilton, London.

Fulk, J. and Boyd, B. (1991), 'Emerging Theories of Communication in Organisations', *Journal of Management,* Vol 17, No 2, pp. 407-446.

Fulk, J., Schmitz, J. and Rye, D. (1995), 'Cognitive Elements in the Social Construction of Communication Technology', *Management Communication Quarterly,* No 18, No 3, pp. 259-288.

Fulk, J., Schmitz, J. and Steinfield, C.W. (1990), 'A Social Influence Model of Technology Use', in Fulk, J. and Steinfield, C. (Eds.), *Organisations and Communication Technology,* Sage Publications, Newbury Park, pp. 117-139.

Gaffin, A. (1994), 'Mall-Hopping on the Internet', *Network World*, No 4, 10 October, pp. 11-41.

Galbraith, J.K. (1992), *The Culture of Contentment*, Sinclair-Stevenson, London.

Galbraith, J.K. (1995), The *World Economy Since the Wars: A Personal View*, Mandarin Paperbacks, London.

Galloway, R.L. and Whyte, G.A. (1989), The Information Systems Function as a Service Operation', *International Journal of Operations and Production Management*, Vol 9, No 4, pp. 14-23.

Gantz, J. (1997), 'E-Commerce puts IS in the Fast Lane', *Computerworld*, Vol 31, No 5, p. 33.

Ganzel, R. (1998), 'Feeling Squeezed by Technology?', *Training*, Vol 35, No 4, pp. 62-70.

Gardner, J.W. (1990), *On Leadership*, Free Press, New York.

Garfinkel, S.L. (1998), 'The Web's Un-Elected Government', *Technology Review*, Vol 101, No 6, pp. 38-46.

Garnett, J.L. (1997), 'Administrative Communication: Domain, Threats and Legitimacy', in Garnett, J.L. and Kouzmin, A. (eds.), *Handbook of Administrative Communication*, Marcel Dekker, New York, pp. 1-35.

Garnett, J. and Kouzmin, A. (1999), 'Communication During Crises: From Bullhorn to Mass Media to High Technology to Organisational Networking', in Kouzmin, A. and Hayne, A. (Eds.), *Essays in Economic Globalisation, Transnational Policies and Vulnerability*, IOP Press, Brussels (in press).

Garton, L. and Wellman, B. (1995), 'Social Impacts of Electronic Mail in Organisations: A Review of the Research Literature', *Communication Yearbook, Vol 18*, Transaction Books, New Brunswick, pp. 434-453.

Geertz, C. (1973), *The Interpretations of Cultures*, Basic Books, New York.

Gelwick, R. (1977), *The Way of Discovery: An Introduction to the Thoughts of Michael Polanyi*, Oxford University Press, Oxford.

Gerstein, M.C. (1987), *The Technology Connection: Strategy and Change in the Information Age*, Addison-Wesley, Reading.

Ghiselli, E.E. (1971), *Explorations in Managerial Talent*, Goodyear, Glenview.

Ghiselli, E.E. (1973), 'The Validity of Aptitude Tests in Personnel Selection', *Personnel Psychology*, Vol 26, pp. 461-477.

Ghoshal, S. (1997), 'The Individualised Corporation', *European Management Journal*, Vol 15, No 5, December, pp. 625-632.

Gibson, C.F. and Jackson, B.B. (1987), *The Information Imperative,* Lexington Books, Lexington.

Gibson, H. (1999), 'Web of Spies', *Time,* Vol 153, No 20, p. 35.

Giddens, A. (1984), *The Constitution of Society,* University of California Press, Berkeley.

Giddens, A. (1984), *The Constitution of Society: Outline of the Theory of Structure,* University of California Press, Berkeley.

Gillwald, K., Sandi, A.M. and van Steenbergen, B. (eds) (1992), 'Central and East European Futures', *Futures,* Special Issue, Vol 24, No 2, March.

Ginsberg, A. (1990), 'Connecting Diversification to Performance: A Socio-Cognitive Approach', *Academy of Management Review,* Vol 15, No 3, pp. 514-535.

Girdner, E.J. (1987), Economic Liberalisation in India: The New Electronic Policy. *Asian Survey* 27(11), pp. 1188-1204.

Glazer, M. and Glazer, P. (1989), *The Whistleblowers: Exposing Corruption in Government and Industry,* Basic Books, New York.

Goffman, E. (1963), *Frame Analysis: An Essay on the Organisational Experience,* North Eastern University Press, New York.

Goldhaber, G. (1993), *Organisational Communication* (Sixth Edition), Brown and Benchmark, Madison.

Goleman, D. (1995), *Emotional Intelligence: What can Matter more than IQ?,* Bloomsbury, London.

Gordon, J. (1998), 'The New Paternalism', *Forbes,* Vol 162, No 10, November, pp. 68-70.

Gore, A. (1994), 'The Deadly Age of Cynicism', *The Aspen Institute Quarterly,* Vol 6, No 4, pp. 7-21.

Graham, A. (1998), 'Rethinking The Workplace', *The Magazine For Magazine Management,* Vol 27, No 7, pp. 65-66.

Granovetter, M. (1985), 'Economic Action and Social Structure: The Problem of Embededness', *American Journal of Sociology,* Vol 91, No 3, November, pp. 481-510.

Gray, R. (1983), 'Accounting, Financial Reporting and Not-for-Profit Organisations', *AUTA Review,* Vol 15, No 1, pp. 3-23.

Gray, R., Owen, D. and Maunders, K. (1987), *Corporate Social Reporting: Accounting and Accountability,* Prentice-Hall International, Hemel Hempstead, Herts.

Gray, R., Owen, D. and Maunders, K. (1988), 'Corporate Social Reporting: Emerging Trends in Accountability and Social Contract', *Accounting, Auditing and Accountability Journal,* Vol 1, No 1, pp. 6-20.

Gray, R., Owen, D. and Maunders, K. (1991), 'Accountability, Corporate Social Reporting and the External Social Audits', *Advances in Public Interest Accounting,* Vol 4, No 1, pp. 1-21.

Green, G.I. (1989), 'Perceived Importance of System Analysts' Job Skills, Roles and Non-Salary Incentives', *MIS Quarterly,* Vol 13, No 2, pp. 115-133.

Greenfield, P.E. and Raskin, L. (1984), 'Watch For Signs of Stress That Threaten Your DP Site – Part 2', *Computerworld,* June 18, Vol 18, Issue 25, p. 20.

Grieco, J.M. (1984), *Between Dependency and Autonomy; India's Experience with the International Computer Industry,* University of California Press, Berkeley.

Grimm, C. and Smith, K. (1991), 'Management and Organisational Change: A Note on the Railroad Industry', *Strategic Management Journal,* Vol 12, No 4, pp. 557-562.

Grindley, K. (1991), *Changing IT at Board Level: The Hidden Agenda Exposed,* Price Waterhouse, London.

Gross, E. (1978), 'Organisations as Criminal Actors', in P.R. Wilson and J. Braithwaite (eds), *The Two Faces of Deviance: Crimes of the Powerful and Powerless,* University of Queensland Press, St Lucia, Brisbane, pp. 119-213.

Guildford, J.P. (1963), 'Preparation of Item Scores for the Correlations Between Persons in a Q Factor Analysis', *Educational and Psychological Measurement,* Vol 23, pp. 13-22.

Gulick, L.H. (1937), 'Notes on Theory of Organisation', in Gulick, L.H. and Urwick, L., (eds.), *Papers on the Science and Administration,* Institute of Public Administration, New York, pp. 1-32.

Gunasinghe, N. (1984), The Open Economy and Its Impact on Ethnic Relations in Sri Lanka. In *Sri Lanka: The Ethnic Conflict.* Committee for Rational Development (ed.), Navranga Publishers, New Delhi, pp. 45-61.

Gupte, P. (1999), 'Water: Not a Drop to Drink', *Newsweek,* Vol CXXXIII, No 13, 29 March, p. 4.

Gutek, B.A. (1983), 'Changing Boundaries', in Zimmerman, J. (ed.), *The Technological Woman: Interfacing With Tomorrow,* Preager, New York, pp. 157-172.

Guthrie, J. and Parker, L.D. (1989), 'Corporate Social Disclosures: A Rebuttal of Legitimacy Theory', *Accounting and Business Research,* Vol 19, No 76, pp. 343-352.

Habermas, J. (1971), *Towards a Rational Society: Student Protest, Science and Politics,* Heinemann, London.

Habermas, J. (1972), *Knowledge and Human Interests*, Beacon Press, Boston.

Habermas, J. (1972), 'Towards a Theory of Communication Competence', in Dreizl, H. (Ed.), *Recent Sociology, Vol 2,* Macmillan, New York, pp. 114-150.

Habermas, J. (1990), *Moral Consciousness and Communicative Action,* MIT Press, Cambridge.

Hackett, E.J., Mirvis, P.H. and Sales, A.L. (1991), 'Women's and Men's Expectations About the Effects of New Technology at Work', *Group and Organisational Studies,* Vol 16, No 1, pp. 60-85.

Hage, J. and Dewar, R. (1973), 'Elite Values Versus Organisational Structure in Predicting Innovation', *Administrative Science Quarterly,* Vol 18, No 2, pp. 279-290.

Hage, J, and Finsterbusch, K. (1987), *Organisational Change as a Development Strategy: Models and Tactics for Improving Third World Organisations,* Lynne Rienner, Boulder.

Hagell, III, J. and Singer, M. (1999), 'Private Lives', *The McKinsey Quarterly*, No 1, pp. 6-15.

Hall, M. (1991), *Detecting Deception in the Voice: An Analysis of the Fundamental Frequency, Syllabic Duration and Amplitude of the Human Voice,* University Microfilm, Ann Arbor, Michigan.

Hallowell, E.M. (1999), 'The Human Moment at Work', *Harvard Business Review,* Vol 77, No 1, January-February, pp. 58-152.

Hambrick, D.C. and D'Aveni, R.A. (1992), 'Top Team Detonation as Part of the Downward Spiral of Large Corporate Bankruptcies', *Management Science,* Vol 38, No 6, pp. 1445-1466.

Hambrick, D.C. and Mason, P.A. (1984), 'Upper Echelons: The Organisation as a Reflection of Its Top Managers', *Academy of Management Review,* Vol 9, No 2, pp. 193-207.

Hamilton, A. (1999), 'Super-Charging Snail Mail', *Asiaweek,* Vol 25, No 5, February, p. 59.

Hamilton, V. and Warburton, D.M. (1981), *Human Stress and Cognition,* John Wiley and Sons, New York.

Hammer, M. and Champy, J. (1993), *Re-Engineering the Corporation: A Manifesto For Business Revolution,* Harper Business, New York.

Hampden-Turner, C. (1972), *Radical Man,* Free Press, New York.

Hancock, B. (1998), 'Security Views', *Computers and Security,* Vol 17, No 2, pp. 99-109.

Handbook of Administrative Communication, Marcel Dekker, New York, pp. 413-432.

Handy, C. (1995), 'How do you Manage People whom you do not see? - Trust and the Virtual Organisation', *Harvard Business Review,* Vol 73, No 2, pp. 40-50.

Handy, C. (1995), *Beyond Certainty: The Changing Worlds of Organisations,* Harvard Business School Press, Boston.

Hanna, N. (1990), The Information Technology Revolution and Economic Development. *World Bank Working Paper,* Task Force on Information Technology for Development. World Bank. January.

Hardill, I., Green, A.E. and Dudleson, A.C. (1997), 'The "Blurring of Boundaries" Between "Work" and "Home": Perspectives From Case Studies in the East Midlands', *Area,* Vol 29, No 4, pp. 335-343.

Harmon, M.M. and Meyer, R.R. (1986), *Organisation Theory For Public Administration,* Little Brown and Company, Chicago.

Harshman, C.L. and Phillip, S.L. (1994), *Teaming up: Achieving Organisational Transformation,* Pfeiffer and Co, San Diego.

Harvey, B., Smith, S. and Wilkinson, B. (1984), *Managers and Corporate Social Policy,* The Macmillan Press, London.

Hegel, G.W.F. (1977), *Hegel's Phenomenology of Spirit* (translated by Miller, A.V.), Oxford University Press, Oxford.

Heidegger, M. (1962), *Being and Time* (translated by Macquarie, J. and Robinson, E.), Harper and Row, Boston.

Heine, K. (1997), 'Communication Breakdown', *Incentive,* Vol 171, No 7, pp. 24-27.

Henderson, J. (1991), *The Globalisation of High Technology Production: Society, Space and Semiconductors in the Restructuring of the Modern World,* Routledge, London.

Henley, N. (1977), *Body Politics,* Prentice-Hall, Englewood Cliffs.

Herrmann, P. (1999), 'Electro-Magnetic Radiation', *International Well Being Magazine: Annual,* No 74, pp.45-46.

Hill, S. (1988), *Competition and Control at Work: The New Industrial Sociology,* Gower, London.

Hill, S. (1990), Changing the Technological Trajectory: Addressing the

"Trailing Edge" of Australia's Historical Culture. *Future* 22(6), pp. 272-297.

Hills, J. (1990), The telecommunications: rich and poor. *Third World Quarterly* 12(2), pp. 12-15.

Hiltz, R.S. and Turoff, M. (1993), *The Network Nation: Human Communication via Computer*, MIT Press, Cambridge.

Hind, P. (1998), 'Captured by Technology', *CIO Magazine,* September, pp. 22-23.

Hirsch, E.D. and Mulcahy, P. (eds) (1987), *Cultural Literacy: What Every American Needs to Know,* Houghton Mifflin, Boston.

Hirschheim, R. and Klein, H.K. (1994), 'Realizing Emancipatory Principles in Information Systems Development; The Case For Ethics', *MIS Quarterly,* Vol 18, No 1, pp. 83-109.

Hirschman, A.O. (1970), *Exit, Voice and Loyalty: Responses to Decline in Firms, Organisations and States,* Harvard University Press, Cambridge.

Hirschman, A.O. (1991), *The Rhetoric of Reaction: Perversity, Futility, Jeopardy,* Harvard University Press, Cambridge.

Hirschman, A.O. (1995), 'Convergences with Michel Crozier', in Hirschman, A. O. (ed.), *A Propensity of Subversion,* Harvard University Press, Cambridge, pp. 139-153.

Hobday, M. (1985), The Impact of Microelectronics on Developing Countries; The Case of Brazilian Telecommunications. *Development and Changes* 16(2), pp. 13-34.

Hoffman, D.L. and Novak, T.P. (1995), 'Marketing in Hypermedia, Computer-Mediated Environments: Conceptual Foundations', Working Paper No 1, Project 2000 Research Programme, available at http://www.2000.ogsm.vanderbilt.edu.

Hollands, M. (1999), 'Softcore Solution to Clean up the E-mail,' *The Australian*, 25 May, p. 7.

Holliday, S.G. and Chandler, M.J. (1986), *Wisdom: Explorations in Adult Competence*, Karger, Basel.

Holmes, S. (1988), 'Precommitment and the Paradox of Democracy', in J. Elster and R. Slagstad (eds), *Constitutionalism and Democracy,* Cambridge University Press, Cambridge.

Hong Kong Business (1998), 'For the Record: Internet Users - Asia Pacific', Vol 17, No 198, December, p.2.

Hook, S. (1974), *Pragmatism and the Tragic Sense of Life*, Basic Books, New York.

Horkheimer, M. (1974), *Critique of Instrumental Reason,* Seabury Press, New York.

Hosenball, M. and Thomas, E. (1997), 'A China Connection? How Charges of Clinton Campaign Sleaze Could Turn into A Spy Scandal', *Newsweek,* February 24, pp. 38-40.

Hotline (1999), 'I am Alright, It is Just the Building That is Ill', Issue 5, Winter, p. 22.

Houlder, V. (1998), 'Spreading the Message Inside the Organisation', *The Financial Times - Digital Business Supplement,* 10 November, p.14.

Howell, J.M. and Higgins, C.A. (1990), 'Champions of Technological Innovation', *Administrative Science Quarterly,* Vol 35, pp. 317-343, http://www.euronet.nl/~rembert/echelon/16119801.htm.

Hubber, S. (1989), *The Impact of Stereotypes on Person Judgement,* Lang, New York.

Hughes, R. (1993), *The Culture of Complaint,* Oxford University Press, Oxford.

Husserl, E.(1931), *Ideas General Introduction to Pure Phenomenology* (translated by Royce Gibson, W.R.), Allen and Unwin, London.

Husserl, E. (1964), *The Idea of Phenomenology* (translated by Alston, W.P. and Nakhnikian, G.), Nijhoff, The Hague.

ICL (1996), 'The Hedsor Memorandum: A Call for Europe to Embrace the Full Potential of the Global Information Society', Hedsor Park, Berkshire, September, pp. 1-54.

ICL (1997), 'The Information Society Symposium', Civil Service College, Sunningdale Park, 13-14 January, pp. 1-9.

ICL Systems (1998), *The Next Step,* ICL, London.

Ijiri, Y. (1983), 'On the Accountability-Based Conceptual Framework of Accounting', *Journal of Accounting and Public Policy,* Vol 2, No 2, pp. 75-81.

Inayatullah, C. (1992), 'Democracy, Ethnic Nationalism and Emerging World Order', in S. Kumur (ed), *Gorbachev's Reforms and International Change,* Lancer Books, Delhi, pp. 72-84.

International Data Corporation (1998), 'Internet Users - Asia Pacific', *Hong Kong Business,* Vol 17, No 198, December, p .2.

International Development Research Centre (IDRC) (1989), *Sharing Knowledge for Development: IDRC's Information Strategy for Africa,* International Development Research Centre, Ottawa.

International Monetary Fund (IMF) (1986),*World Economic Outlook,* IMF. October.

International Telecommunication Union (ITU) (1993), *Constitution of the International Telecommunication*, ITU, Geneva.

Irwin, M., Daniels, M., Risch, S.C., Bloom, E. and Weiner, H. (1988), 'Plasma Cortisol and Natural Killer Cell Activity During Bereavement', *Biological Psychiatry*, Vol 24, No 1, pp. 173-178.

Israel, B. (1990), 'Hiring System Analysts for the 1990s', *Information Executive*, Vol 3, No 1, pp. 35-36.

IT Directors' Forum (1997), *IT Directors' Forum - Focus Group Meeting*, Cranfield, October 14.

Ives, B. and Learmonth, G.P. (1984), 'The Information Systems as a Competitive Weapon', *Communications of the ACM*, Vol 27, No 12, pp. 17-34.

Ives, D. (1993), Millions Lost by Government Software, The Canberra Times, 11 October, pp. 1-2.

Jackson, M.H. (1997), 'Assessing the Structure of Communication on the World Wide Web, *Journal of Computer Mediated Communication*, Vol 3, No 1, pp. 17-23.

Jackson, S.E. and Schulrer, R.S. (1985), A Meta-Analysis and Conceptual Critique of Research on Role Ambiguity and Role Conflict in Work Settings', *Organisational Behaviour and Human Decision Processes*, Vol 37, No 1, pp. 16-78.

Jackson, S.E., Turner, J.A. and Brief, A.P. (1987), 'Correlates of Burnout among Public Service Lawyers', *Journal of Occupational Behaviour*, Vol 8, No 3, pp. 339-349.

James, G. (1998) 'Stock Scams and Spams on the Internet', *Upside* (9th Anniversary Issue), Vol 9, No 1, November, pp. 77-86.

James, J. (1985), *The Employment and Income Distribution Impact of Microelectronics: A Prospective Analysis for the Third World*. World Employment Programme Research Working Paper No 153. International Labour Office, Geneva.

James, W. (1966), *Psychology: The Brief Course* (edited by Allport, G.), Harper and Row, New York.

Janis, I.L. and Mann, L. (1977), *Decision Making*, Free Press, New York.

Jarman, A.M.G. and Kouzmin, A. (1994), 'Creeping Crises, Environmental Agendas and Expert Systems: A Research Note', *International Review of Administrative Sciences*, Vol 60, No 3, September, pp. 399-422.

Jeannot, T.M. (1989), 'Moral Leadership and Practical Wisdom', *International Journal of Social Economics*, Vol 16, No 6, pp. 14-48.

Jenner, D.A., Reynolds, V. and Harrison, G.A. (1980), 'Catecholamine Excretion Rates and Occupation', *Ergonomics,* Vol 23, No 2, pp. 237-246.

Johansson, G. (1979), 'Psycho-Neuroendocrine Reactions to Mechanised and Computerised Work Routines', in Mackay, C. and Cox, T. (Eds.), *Response to Stress: Occupational Aspects,* IPC Science and Technology Press, Guildford, pp. 214-221.

Johnson, D. (1985), *Computer Ethics*, Prentice Hall, Englewood.

Johnson, M. (1997), 'Extracting Value From Data', *Management Consultancy*, February, p. 23.

Johnson, O.E.G. (1991), The Integration in Africa: Enhancing Prospects for Success. *The Journal of Modern African Studies* 29(1), pp. 1-26.

Johnson, S. (1997), *Interface Culture,* Delacrote, New York.

Johnson, T. (1974), *Professions and Power*, MacMillan, London.

Johnson-Laird, P.N. (1983), *Mental Models*, Cambridge University Press, Cambridge.

Johnston, J. and Kouzmin, A. (1998), 'Who are the Rent-Seekers?: From the Ideological Attack on Public Officials to the "Pork Barrell" *Par Excellence* - Privatisation and Outsourcing as Oligarchic Corruption', *Administrative Theory and Praxis*, Vol 20, No 4, pp. 491-507.

Jones, C.B. (1991), 'Eco-Democracy: Synthesising Feminism, Ecology and Participatory Organisations' in B. von Steenbergen, R. Nakarada, F. Marti and J. Dator (eds), *Advancing Democracy and Participation: Challenges for the Future,* Centre Catala de Prospectova, Barcelona, pp. 96-112.

Jonish, J. (1988), Laser Technology For Land Levelling in Egypt. In *New Technologies and Development: Experiments in Technology Blending,* Bahalla, A.S, James, D.D. (eds.), Lynne Rienner, Boulder, pp. 105-119.

Journal of Advertising Research (1997), 'Advertising: Brand Communications Styles in Established Media and the Internet', March, pp. 17-23.

Kahneman, D., Slovic, P. and Tversky, A. (Eds.) (1984), *Judgement Under Uncertainty: Heuristics and Biases*, Cambridge University Press, Cambridge.

Kaiser, H.F. and Caffrey, J. (1965), 'Alpha Factor Analysis', *Psychometrika*, Vol 30, No 1, pp. 1-14.

Kakabadse, A. (1991), *The Wealth Creators: Top People, Top Teams and Executive Best Practice*, Kogan Page, London.

Kakabadse, A. (1993), 'Success Levers For Europe: The Cranfield Executive Competencies Survey', *Journal of Management Development*, Vol 13, No 1, pp. 75-96.

Kakabadse, A. and Kakabadse, N. (1998), *Essence of Leadership*, International Thomson, London.

Kakabadse, A.P., Korac-Kakabadse, N. and Myers, A. (1996), *Leadership and the Public Sector: An Internationally Comparative Benchmarking Analysis*, Paper presented at the Commonwealth Association for Public Administration and Management (CAPAM), Second Biennial Conference on the New Public Administration: Global Challenges - Local Solutions, 21-24 April, Malta.

Kakabadse, A. and Myers, A. (1995a), 'Qualities of Top Management: Comparisons of European Manufacturers', *Journal of Management Development*, Vol 14, No 1, pp. 5-15.

Kakabadse, A. and Myers, A. (1995b), *Boardroom Skills For Europe*, International Management Development Centre, Cranfield School of Management, Cranfield.

Kakabadse, A.P. and Myers, A. (1996a), *NHS Trust Survey*, Cranfield University, School of Management, Cranfield.

Kakabadse, A.P. and Myers, A. (1996b), 'Boardroom Skills for Europe', *European Management Journal*, Vol 4, No 2, pp. 189-200.

Kant, I. (1960), *Religion Within The Limits of Reason Alone*, Harper and Row, New York.

Kant, I. (1965), *Critique of Pure Reason* (translated by Smith, N.K.), St. Martin's Press, New York.

Kanter, R.M. (1977), *Men and Women of the Corporation*, Basic Books, New York.

Kanter, R.M. (1985), *The Change Masters: Innovation and Entrepreneurship in the American Corporations*, Simon and Schuster, New York.

Kanter, R.M. (1986), 'Innovation: The Only Hope for Times Ahead?', *Sloan Management Review*, Vol 27, Special Issue, pp. 51-55.

Kapor, M. (1992), 'Where is the Digital Highway Really Heading? The Case for a Jefersonian Information Policy', *WiReD*, Vol 1, No 3, pp. 47-52.

Karasek, R.A., Baker, D., Marxer, F., Ahlbom, A. and Theorell, T. (1981), 'Job Decision Latitude, Job Demands and Cardiovascular Disease: A Prospective Study of Swedish Men', *American Journal of Public Health*, Vol 71, No 4, pp. 694-705.

Karuppan, C.M. (1997), 'Advanced Manufacturing Technology and Stress: Technology and Management Support Polices', *International Journal of Technology Management,* Vol 14, Nos 2-4, pp. 254-264.

Kasl, S.V. and Cooper, C.L. (1987), *Research Methods in Health Psychology,* John Wiley, Chichester.

Katz, D. and Khan, R.L. (1996), *The Social Psychology of Organisations,* John Wiley, New York.

Katzenbach, J.R. and Smith, D.K. (1993), *The Wisdom of Team,* Harvard Business School Press, Boston.

Kauffman, R. J. and Weill, P. (1990), 'An Evaluative Framework For Research on the Performance Effects on Information Technology Investment', *Information System Research,* Vol 1, No 4, pp. 377-388.

Kaufman, H. and Couzens, M. (1973), *Administrative Feedback: Monitoring Subordinates' Behaviour,* Brookings Institute, Washington.

Kaufmann, F.X. (ed.) (1991), *The Public Sector: Challenge for Co-ordination and Learning,* Walter de Gruyter (de Gruyter Studies in Organisation: Organisation Theory and Research), Berlin.

Kavanagh, J. (1996), 'Quality Safeguards in the Training Market', *IDPM Journal,* Vol 6, No 4, pp. 10-11.

Kavanagh, J. (1997), 'Why IT Staff are Losers with an Attitude Problem', *Interface,* August 27, p. 10.

Keely, S. (1992), 'Psychometric Testing', *IDPM Journal,* Vol 3, No 1, pp. 22-23.

Keen, P.G.W. (1988), *Computing in Time: Using Telecommunications for Competitive Advantage,* Ballinger, Cambridge.

Keen, P.G.W. and Scott-Morton, M.S. (1978), *Decision Support Systems: An Organisational Perspective,* Addison-Wesley.

Kelly, R. and Caplin, I. (1993), 'How Bell Labs Create Star Performers', *Harvard Business Review,* Vol 71, No 1, January-February, pp. 128-139.

Keynes, J.M. (1981), *The Collected Writings of John Maynard Keynes, Vol 19: Activities 1922-1929 - Return to Gold and Industrial Policy,* Cambridge University Press, Cambridge.

Khan, M.N. (1984), Public libraries in Bangladesh. *International Library Review* 16(2), pp. 125-241.

Khan, S. (1978), 'Job Burnout: Prevention and Remedies', *Public Welfare,* Vol 26, No 1, pp. 53-61.

Kidwell, J.M., Stevens, R.E. and Bethke, A. (1987), 'Differences in Ethical Perceptions between Male and Female Managers: Myth or Reality?', *Journal of Business Ethics*, Vol 6, No 2, pp. 95-103.

Kiesler, S. (1986), 'The Hidden Messages in Computer Networks', *Harvard Business Review,* Vol 64, No 1, January-February, pp. 46-60.

King, J. (1995), 'Stress Rattles "Help" Desks', *Computerworld,* Vol 29, No 11, pp. 1-16.

King, R.C. and Sethi, V. (1997), 'The Moderating Effect of Organisational Commitment on Burnout in Information Systems Professionals', *European Journal of Information Systems,* Vol 6, No 2, pp. 86-96.

Kirby, J. (1995), 'Artificial Intelligence and Knowledge-Based Systems: A New Challenge For the Human-Centred Perspective?', in Benders, J., De Haan, J. and Bennett, D. (Eds.), *The Symbiosis of Work and Technology,* Taylor and Francis, London, pp. 142-153.

Kirton, M.J. (1976), 'Adopters and Innovators: A Description and Measure', *Journal of Applied Psychology,* Vol 61, No 4, pp. 622-629.

Kleiman, C. (1996), 'More Workdays Are Work-Nights', *Chicago Tribune,* 30 March, p. 7.

Klenke, K. (1993), 'Changing Roles of Information Systems Professionals: From Technical Managers to Strategic Leaders', *Proceeding of SIGCPR Conference,* St Louis, March, pp. 214-225.

Kohlberg, L. (1981), *The Meaning and Measurement of Moral Development*, Clark University Press, Worcester.

Korac-Boisvert, N. (1990), *Management of Information Technology: A Contingency Pathway,* Unpublished Master Thesis, University of Canberra, Canberra.

Korac-Boisvert, N. (1992), 'Developing Economies and Information Technology: A Meta-Policy Review', paper presented at the Australian and New Zealand Academy of Management's (ANZAM) Annual Conference on 'Re-discovering Australasian Management Competence in a Global Context', Sydney, December, pp. 1-34.

Korac-Boisvert, N. (1994), 'The Need For Cultural Change', *Case Analysis, Vol 2*, November, DEET, Canberra, pp. 1-3.

Korac-Boisvert, N. and Kouzmin, A. (1994), 'The Dark Side of Info-Age Social Networks in Public Organisations and Creeping Crises', *Administrative Theory and Praxis: A Journal of Dialogue in Public Administrative Theory,* Vol 16, No 1, April, pp. 57-82.

Korac-Boisvert, N. and Kouzmin, A. (1995), 'IT Development:
Methodology Overload or Crisis?', *Science Communication: An
Interdisciplinary Science Journal*, Vol 17, No 1, September, pp. 57-89.

Korac-Boisvert, N. and Kouzmin, A. (1995), 'Re-Engineering and the Role
of IT in Australia's Largest "Firm", The Australian Public Service
(APS)', paper presented at the Annual Conference on the European
Group of Public Administration (EGPA), Erasmus University,
Rotterdam, September, pp. 1-22.

Korac-Boisvert, N. and Kouzmin, A. (1995a), 'IT Development:
Methodology Overload or Crisis?', *Science Communication: An
Interdisciplinary Social Science Journal,* Vol 17, No 1, September, pp.
57-89.

Korac-Boisvert, N. and Kouzmin, A. (1995b), 'Transcending Softcore IT
Disasters in Public Sector Organisations', *Information Infrastructure
and Policy,* Vol 4, No 2, pp. 131-161.

Korac-Boisvert, N. and Kouzmin, A. (1995c), 'After the Re-Engineering
and the Role of IT in Australia's Largest "Firm": The Australian
Public Service (APS)', paper presented at the Annual Conference on
the European Group of Public Administration (EGPA), Erasmus
University, Rotterdam, September, pp. 1-22.

Korac-Kakabadse, A. and Korac-Kakabadse, N. (1996), *The Kakabadse
Report/Leadership in Government: Study of the Australian Public
Service*, Report to the Commonwealth Government of Australia,
Cranfield School of Management, Cranfield.

Korac-Kakabadse, A. and Korac-Kakabadse, N. (1998), *Leadership in
Government: Study of the Australian Public Service*, Ashgate,
Aldershot.

Korac-Kakabadse, A. and Korac-Kakabadse, N. (1999), *Essence of
Leadership,* International Thomson Business Press, London.

Korac-Kakabadse, A., Korac-Kakabadse, N. and Kouzmin, A. (1998),
'Negotiating Consultant Links With the Top Team: Transacting
Meaning and Obligations or Executive Failure Through Excessive
Outsourcing?', *Journal of Contemporary Issues in Business and
Government*, Vol 4, No 2, November, pp. 4-17.

Korac-Kakabadse, A.P., Korac-Kakabadse, N. and Myers, A. (1996), 'Leadership and the Public Sector: An Internationally Comparative Benchmarking Analysis', *Journal of Public Administration,* Vol 16, No 4, October, pp. 377-396.

Korac-Kakabadse, N. and Knyght, P.R. (1996), 'The Impact of Technological Advancement on the Ethics and the Morality of the Public Sector Management in the Third Millennium', paper presented at the International Research Symposium on the Public Services Management, Aston Business School, Aston University, Birmingham, 25-26 March.

Korac-Kakabadse, N. and Kouzmin, A. (1996), 'Innovation Strategies for the Adoption of New IT in Government: An Australian Experience', *Journal of Public Administration,* Vol 16, No 4, October, pp. 317-330.

Korac-Kakabadse, N. and Kouzmin, A. (1996), 'Molecular Innovation and Molar Scanning Strategies for the Adoption of New Information Technology (IT) in Learning Organisations', *Public Productivity and Management Review,* Vol 19, No 4, June, pp. 434-454.

Korac-Kakabadse, N. and Kouzmin, A. (1997), 'Maintaining the Rage: From "Glass and Concrete Ceilings" and Metaphorical Sex Changes to Psychological Audits and Re-negotiating Organisational Scripts', *Women in Management Review,* Vol 12, Nos 5 and 6, pp. 182-195 and pp. 207-221.

Korac-Kakabadse, N. and Kouzmin, A. (1999), 'Designing For Cultural Diversity in an IT and Globalised Milieu: Some Real Leadership Dilemmas For the New Millenium', *Journal of Management Development,* Vol 18, No 3, October, pp. 291-319.

Korac-Kakabadse, N., Korac-Kakabadse, A. (1998), *The Future Role of IS/IT Professions: A Survey,* ISRC, Cranfield School of Management, Bedford.

Korac-Kakabadse, N., Korac-Kakabadse, A. and Kouzmin, A. (1998), 'The Role of IT in Changing Psycho-Social Contracts: A Multi-Stakeholder's perspective', *Knowledge and Process Management,* Special Issue on Business Process Phenomenon: Consequences and New Horizons, Vol 5, No 2, June, pp. 132-140.

Korac-Kakabadse, N., Kouzmin, A. and Korac-Kakabadse, A. (1996), 'Information Technology and Development: Designing Relevant Infrastructure Capability or New Colonialism?', paper presented at the 5th International Speyer Workshop on Assessing and Evaluating Public Service Reforms, Speyer, 20-22 November.

Korale, S.R. (1984), National Library Development and Legislation in Sri Lanka: A Review. *Journal of Library and Information Science.* 9(2), pp. 118-145.

Korunaka, C., Weiss, A., Huemoer, K-H. and Karatta, B. (1995), 'The Effect of New Technologies on Job Satisfaction and Psychosomatic Complaints', *Applied Psychology: An International Review,* Vol 44, No 2, pp. 123-142.

Kotler, P. (1992), Megamarketing. In *Managing the External Environment: A Strategic Perspective.* Mercer, D. (ed.), Sage, London, pp. 38-51.

Kotter, J.P. (1982), *The General Managers,* Free Press, New York.

Kouzmin, A. (1983), Centrifugal Organisations: Technology and "Voice" in Organisational Analysis. In *Public Sector Administration: New Perspectives.* Kouzmin, A. (ed.), Longman Cheshire, Melbourne, pp. 232-267.

Kouzmin, A., Dixon, J. and Wilson, J. (1995), 'Commercializing "Washminster" in Australia: What Lessons?', *Public Money and Management,* Vol 15, No 2, April-June, pp. 55-62.

Kouzmin, A. and Jarman, A. (1989), 'Crisis Decision-Making: Towards a Contingent Decision Path Perspective', in Rosenthal, U., Charles, M.T. and Hart 't, P., (Eds.), *Coping with Crises: The Management of Disasters, Riots and Terrorism,* Charles C Thomas, Springfield, pp. 397-435.

Kouzmin, A. and Jarman A. (1990), Decision Pathways from Crisis: A Contingency-Theory Simulation Heuristic for the Challenger Shuttle Disaster (1983-1988). *Contemporary Crises: Law, Crime and Social Policy* 14(4), December, pp. 399-433.

Kouzmin, A. and Korac-Boisvert, N. (1995), 'Soft-Core Disasters: A Multiple Realities Crisis Perspective on IT Development Failures', in Hill, H. and Klages, H. (Eds.), *Trends in Public Sector Renewal: Recent Developments and Concepts of Awarding Excellence,* Peter Lang, Berlin, pp. 89-132.

Kouzmin, A. and Korac-Kakabadse, N. (1997), 'From Phobias and Ideological Prescription: Towards Multiple Models in Transformation Management For Socialist Economies in Transition, *Administration and Society,* Vol 29, No 2, May, pp. 139-188.

Kouzmin, A. and Korac-Kakabadse, N. (1999), 'Mapping the Institutional Impact of "Lean" Communication in "Lean" Agencies: IT Literacy and Leadership Failure', *Administration and Society,* Vol 31, No 4, September (in press).

Kouzmin, A., Korac-Kakabadse, N. and Jarman, A. (1996), 'Economic Rationalism, Risk and Institutional Vulnerability', *Risk, Decision and Policy,* Vol 1, No 2, December, pp. 229-256.

Kouzmin, A., Korac-Kakabadse, N. and Korac-Kakabadse, A. (1999a), 'Information Technology and Development: Creating "IT-Harems", Fostering New Colonialism or Solving "Wicked" Policy Problems?', paper presented at the Public Administration and Development Jubilee Conference on the Last 50 years and the Next 50 years: A Century of Public Administration and Development, St Anne's College, Oxford University, 12-14 April.

Kouzmin, A., Korac-Kakabadse, N. and Korac-Kakabadse, A. (1999b), 'Globalization and Information Technology: Vanishing Social Contracts, the "Pink Collar" Work force and Public Policy Challenges', *Women in Management Review,* Vol 14, No 6, pp. 230-251.

Kouzmin, A., Leivesley, R. and Carr, A. (1997), 'From Managerial Dysfunction, Towards Communicative Competence: Re-discovering "Dramaturgy" and "Voice" in Communicating Risk', in Garnett, J.L and Kouzmin, A., (eds.), *Handbook of Administrative Communication,* Marcel Dekker, New York, pp. 661-679.

Kouzmin, A., Leivesley, R. and Korac-Kakabadse, N. (1997), 'From Managerialism and Economic Rationalism: Towards "Re-inventing" Economic Ideology and Administrative Diversity,' *Administrative Theory and Praxis,* Vol 19, No 1, pp. 19-42.

Krafcik, J.F. (1988), 'Triumph of the Lean Production System', *Sloan Management Review,* Vol 30, No 1, pp. 41-52.

Kraft, P. (1979), The Industrialisation of Computer Programming: From Programming to Software Production. In *Case Studies in the Labour Process,* Zimbalist A. (ed.), Monthly Review Press, New York, pp. 1-17.

Krause, L., Ai Tee Koh, Yuan Lee (1987), *The Singapore Economy Reconsidered,* Institute of Southeast Asian Studies, Singapore.

Kraut, R.E. (1987), 'Telework as a Workstyle Innovation', in Kraut, R.E. (ed.), *Technology and the Transformation of White Collar Work,* Lawrence Erlbaum, Hillsdale, pp. 49-64.

Kraut, R.E., Patterson, M., Lundmark, V., Keisler, S., Mukophadhyay, T. and Scherlis, W. (1998), 'Internet Paradox: A Social Technology that Reduces Social Involvement and Psychological Well-Being', *American Psychologist,* Vol 53, No 9, pp. 89-79.

Kreamer, K. and Pinsonneault, A.L. (1993), 'The Impact of Information Technology on Middle Managers', *MIS Quarterly,* Vol 17, September, pp. 271-292.

Krol, E. and Hoffman, E. (1993), *FYI on What is the Internet? Network Working Group Request For Comments*: 1462, FYI: 20. URL:gopher://dsl.internic.net/00/fyi/fyi20.txt

Krugaman, P. (1999), *The Return of Depression Economics*, Norton and Company, New York.

Kudar, G.F. and Richardson, M.W. (1937), 'The Theory of the Estimation of Test Reliability', *Psychometrika*, Vol 29, pp. 115-129.

Kwan, T. (1992), *Briefing Reports and Notes from Overseas Study Tour,* Working Papers. June. DEET. Canberra, pp. 1-20.

Labouvie-Vief, G. (1989), 'Modes of Knowledge and the Organisation of Development', in Commons, M.L., Sinnott, J.D., Richards, F.A. and Armon, C. (Eds.), *Beyond Formal Operations II: Comparisons and Applications of Adolescent and Adult Development Models*, Preager, New York, pp. 109-119.

Lacayo, R. (1993), 'The Lure of the Cult', *Times,* Vol 149, No 14, pp. 39-40.

Lacity, M.C., Willcocks, L.P. and Feeny, D.J. (1995), 'IT Outsourcing: Maximise Flexibility and Control', *Harvard Business Review,* Vol 73, No 3, pp. 84-93.

Lacroix, A.Z. (1984), 'Occupational Exposure to High Demand/Local Control Work and Coronary Heart Disease Incidence in the Framingham Cohort', *Dissertation Abstracts International*, Vol 45, No 2521B, pp. 575-579.

Laffin, M. (1986), *Professionalism and Policy: The Role of the Professions in the Central-Local Government Relationship*, Gower, London.

LaPorte, T.R. (ed) (1975), *Organised Social Complexity: Challenge to Politics and Policy,* Princeton University Press, Princeton.

Latham, M. (1998), *Civilising Global Capital: New Thinking For Australian Labor*, Allen and Unwin, Sydney.

Laughlin, R.C. (1996), 'Rethinking Models of Accountability: The Influence of Professionalism and "Higher" Principals on Actions and Reactions of "Agents" in the Caring Professions', in R. Munro and J. Mouritsen (eds), *Accountability, Power and Ethos,* Chapman and Hall, London.

Lavakare, P.J. (1985), Scientific and Technological Information Experiences and Activities in India: Problems and Future Prospects. In *Scientific and Technological Information for Development: Proceedings of the Ad Hoc Panel of Experts on Information Systems for Science and Technology for Development,* United Nations, New York, pp. 72-79.

Lawrence, P. and Lorsch, J. (1967), *Organisation and Environment,* Harvard University Press, Cambridge.

Lazarus, R.S. and Folkman, S. (1984), *Stress, Appraisal and Coping,* Springer, New York.

Lazonick, W. (1992), Business Organisation and Competitive Advantage: Capitalist Transformation in the Twentieth Century. In *Technology and Enterprise in a Historical Perspective.* Dosi, G., Giannettti, R. and Toninelli, P.A. (eds.), Clarendon Press, Oxford, pp. 32-47.

Le Monde (1990), 11 May, Section B.

Lea, M. (1991), 'Rationalist Assumptions in Cross-Media Comparisons of Computer-Mediated Communication', *Behaviour and Information Technology,* Vol 10, No 2, pp. 153-172.

Leiter, M.P. (1991), 'Coping Patterns as Predictors of Burnout: The Action of Control and Escapist Coping Patterns', *Journal of Organisational Behaviour,* Vol 12, No 1, pp. 123-144.

Leitheiser, R.L. (1992), 'MIS Skills for the 1990s: A Survey of MIS Managers' Perceptions', *Journal of Management Information Systems,* Vol 9, No 1, pp. 68-91.

Leonard, P. (1998), *Wellsprings of Knowledge: Building and Sustaining the Sources of Innovation,* Harvard Business School Press, Boston.

Levy, S. (1998), 'Christms.com', *Newsweek,* Vol CXXXII, No 23, 7 December, pp. 46-50.

Lewis, D. (1998), *Forward to Reuters 1998 Information Overload Survey,* Reuters Inc. Lewis, S. (1997), 'Family-Friendly Employment Polices; A Route to Change Organisational Culture or Playing About at the Margins?', *Gender, Work and Organisation,* Vol 4, No 3, pp. 13-23.

Licking, E. (Ed.) (1999), 'A Smarter Path to Smart Appliances', *Business Week (*European Edition), 1 February, p. 62.

Lieberson, S. and O'Connor, J. (1972), 'Leadership and Organisational Performance', *American Sociological Review,* Vol 37, pp. 117-130.

Likert, R. (1961), *New Patterns of Management,* McGraw-Hill, New York.

Lintner, B. (1998), ' Fantasy Island', *Far Eastern Economic Review,* Vol 161, No 50, 10 December, pp. 32-35.

Lipton, M. (1977), *Why Poor People Stay Poor: A Study of Urban Bias in World Development.,* Temple Smith, London.

Lobel, S.A. (1992), 'A Value Laden Approach to Integrating Work and Family Life', *Human Resource Management'*, Vol 31, No 2, pp. 244-265.

Locke, J. (1987), *An Essay Concerning Human Understanding: Book II*, Oxford University Press, Oxford.

London, S. (1994), 'Electronic Democracy: A Literature Survey', paper prepared for the Kattering Foundation, March, Santa Barbara.

Long, G. (1999), 'World Body Shakes Up Net Rules', *The Australian*, 9 March , p.33.

Long, R.J. (1987), *New Office Information Technology: Human and Managerial Implications*, Croom Helm, New York.

Longstaff, S. (1995), 'Why all the Fuss about Ethics?', *Management*, June, pp. 5-7.

Ludlum, D.A. (1989), 'I Am OK: Top Management's So-So', *Computerworld*, Vol 23, No 37, pp. 73-74.

Lyons, J. (1987), *Ecology of the Body: Styles of Behaviour in Human Life*, Duke University Press, Durham.

Lyytinen, K. (1988), 'Expectation, Concept and Systems Analysts' View of Information System Failures: Results of an Exploratory Study', *Information and Management* (North-Holland), Vol 14, No 1, pp. 45-56.

Machlup, F. (1962), *The Production and Distribution of Knowledge in the United States*, Princeton University Press, Princeton.

MacLean, D.J. (1997), 'Ethical Dilemmas in the Global Telecommunications Revolution', *Business Ethics*, Vol 6, No 3, pp. 175-183.

Madu, C.N. (1990), 'Prescriptive Framework For the Transfer of Appropriate Technology', *Futures*, Vol 22, No 9, pp. 523-550.

Management Services (1996), 'Information Technology: The Key to Corporate Stress Management', Vol 40, No 9, pp. 3-4.

Mankin, D., Bikson, T.K. and Gutek, B.A. (1982), 'The Office of the Future: Prison or Paradise?', *Futurist*, Vol16, No 3, June, pp. 333-337.

Manktelow, N. (1999), 'Users Open to Abuse', *The Australian*, 8 March, p. 15.

Mantovani, G. (1996), *New Communication Environments: From Everyday to Virtual*, Taylor and Francis, London.

March, J.G. (1962), 'The Business Firm as a Political Coalition', *Journal of Politics*, Vol 24, No 4, pp. 662-678.

March, J.G. and Simon, H.A. (1958), *Organisations*, John Wiley, New York.

Marcuse, H. (1967), *The Critical Spirit: Essays in Honour of Herbert Marcuse,* Beacon Press, Boston.

Margetts, H. and Willcocks, L. (1993), 'Information Technology in Public Sectors: Disaster Faster?', *Public Money and Management,* Vol 13, No 2, April-June, pp. 49-56.

Marglin, S.A. (1971), *What Do Bosses Do?: The Origins and Functions of Hierarchy in Capitalist Production,* Discussion Paper No 222, Harvard Institute of Economic Research, Harvard University Press, Cambridge.

Marien, M. (1989), IT: You Ain't Seen Nothing Yet. In *Computers in the Human Context: Information Technology. Productivity and People.* Forester, T. (ed.), Basil Blackwell, Oxford, pp. 41-47.

Markus, M.L. (1990), 'Toward a "Critical Mass" Theory of Interactive Media', in Fulk, J. and Steinfield, C. (Eds.), *Organisations and Communication Technology,* Sage Publications, Newbury Park, pp. 194-218.

Markus, M.L. (1994), 'Electronic Mail: A Medium of Managerial Choice', *Organisational Science,* Vol 5, No 4, pp. 502-527.

Markus, M.L. and Benjamin, R.I. (1997), 'The Magic Bullit Theory in IT-Enabled Transformation', *Sloan Management Review,* Vol 38, No 2, pp. 55-68.

Markus, M.L. and Robey, D. (1983), 'The Organisational Validity of Management Information Systems', *Human Relations,* Vol 36, No 3, pp. 203-226.

Marlow, E. and Wilson, P. O. (1997), *The Breakdown of Hierarchy: Communicating in the Evolving Workplace*, Butterworth-Heinemann, Boston.

Marphy, R. (1989), *Social Closure: The Theory of Monopolisation and Exposure,* Clarendon Press, New York.

Marshall, A. (1965), *Principles of Economics*, Macmillan, London.

Marshall, E.M. (1995), *Transforming the Way We Work: The Power of the Collaborative Workplace*, Amacom, New York.

Martin, R. (1965), *The Cities and the Federal System,* Atherton Press, New York.

Martin, R. and Wall, T.D. (1989), 'Attentional Demand and Cost Responsibility as Stressors in Shop-Floor Jobs', *Academy of Management Journal,* Vol 32, No 1, March, pp. 69-86.

Martinez, M.E. (1994), 'Access to Information Technologies Among School-Age Children: Implications for a Democratic Society', *Journal of the American Society for Information Science,* Vol 45, No 6, pp. 395-400.

Marx, K. (1964), *Economic and Philosophic Manuscripts of 1844,* International Publishers, New York.

Marx, K. (1976), *Capital,* Penguin, Hammondsworth.

Maslach, C. (1976), 'Burnout', *Human Behaviour,* Vol 5, No 9, pp. 16-22.

Maslach, C. (1978a), 'Job Burnout: How People Cope', *Public Welfare,* Vol 36, No 1, pp. 56-58.

Maslach, C. (1978b), 'The Client Role in Staff Burnout', *Journal of Social Issues,* Vol 34, No 4, pp. 111-124.

Maslach, C. (1979), 'The Burnout Syndrome and Patient Care', in Garfield, C. (Ed.), *Stress and Survival: The Emotional Realties of Life-Threatening Illness,* Mosby, St. Louse.

Maslach, C. and Jackson, S.E. (1981), 'The Measurement of Experienced Burnout', *Journal of Occupational Behaviour,* Vol 2, No 1, pp. 99-113.

Mathews, M.R. (1993), *Socially Responsible Accounting,* Chapman and Hall, London.

Mathieu, J.E. and Zajac, D. (1990), 'A Review and Meta-Analysis of the Antecedents, Correlates and Consequences of Organisational Commitment', *Psychological Bulletin,* Vol 108, No 2, pp. 171-194.

Maurer, J.G. (1971), *Readings in Organisation Theory: Open-System Approaches,* Random House, New York.

Maynard, H. and Mehrtens, S. (1993), *The Forth Wave: Business in the 21st Century,* Berrett, San Francisco.

Mayo, E. (1933), *The Human Problems of Industrial Civilization,* Macmillan, New York.

Mazuri, A. (1990), *Cultural Forces in World Politics,* James Currey, London.

McAteer, P.F. (1994), 'Harnessing the Power of Technology', *Training and Development,* Vol 4, No 8, pp. 64-68.

McCarteny, L. (1996), 'IS Gears up for the New Millennium', *Informationweek,* Issue 599, September, pp. 65-72.

McClelland, D.C. and Boyatzis, R.E. (1982), 'Leadership Motive Pattern and Long-term Sucess in Management', *Journal of Applied Psychology,* Vol 67, No 4, pp. 737-743.

McDonald, M. (1992), 'The Canadian Research Strategy for Applied Ethics: A New Opportunity for Research in Business and Professional Ethics', *Journal of Business Ethics*, Vol 11, No 8, pp. 569-583.

McDowell, L. and Court, G. (1994), 'Gender Divisions of Labour in the Post-Fordist Economy: The Maintenance of Occupational Sex Segregation in the Financial Service Sector', *Environment and Planning*, Vol 26, No 7, pp. 1397-1418.

McFarlan, W.F. and McKenney, J.L. (1983), *Corporate Information Systems Management: The Issues Facing Senior Executives,* Richard D. Irwin, Homewood.

McGee, M.K. (1996), 'Burnout', *Information Week,* Issue 569, 4 March, pp. 34-40.

McGrath, J.E. and Hollingshead, A.B. (1994), *Groups Interacting With Technology: Ideas, Evidence, Issues and an Agenda*, Sage, Thousand Oaks.

McGregor, D. (1960), *The Human Side of Enterprize,* McGraw-Hill, New York.

McKenna, E.P. (1997), *When Work Doesn't Work Anymore: Women, Work and Identity*, Delacrote, New York.

McKenna, R. (1997), *Real Time,* Free Press, New York.

McKenney, J.L., Zack, M.H. and Doherty, V.S. (1992), 'Complementary Communication Media: A Comparison of Electronic Mail and Face-to-Face Communication in a Programming Team', in Nohria, N. and Eccles, R.G., (eds.), *Networks and Organisations: Structure, Form and Action,* Harvard Business School Press, Boston, pp. 262-287.

McLagan, P. and Christo, N. (1995), 'The Dawning of a New Age in the Workplace', *Journal for Quality and Participation,* Vol 18, iss. 2, March, pp. 10-15.

McLean, I. (1989), *Democracy and New Technology,* Polity Press, Cambridge.

McLeod, R., Jr. and Jones, J.W. (1986), 'Making Executive Information Systems More Effective', *Business Horizons*, September-October, pp. 24-32.

McLuhan, M. (1964), *Understanding Media: The Extension of Man,* MIT Press, Cambridge.

Meacham, J.A. (1983), 'Wisdom and the Context of Knowledge: Knowing What One Don't Know', in Kuhn, D. And Meacham, J.A. (eds.), *On the Development of Developmental Psychology*, Karger, Basel, pp. 111-134.

Mereau-Ponty, M. (1962), *The Phenomenology of Perception* (translated by Smith, C.), Routledge and Kegan Paul, London.

Merritt, D. (1995), *Public Journalism and Public Life: Why Telling the News is not Enough,* Erlbaum, Hillsdale.

Meyer, J.P. and Allen, N.J. (1984), 'Testing the "Side-Bet Theory" of Organisational Commitment: Some Methodological Considerations', *Journal of Applied Psychology,* Vol 69, No 3, pp. 372-378.

Meyer, R. and Rowen, B. (1977), 'Institutionalised Organisation: Formal Structure as Myth and Ceremony', *American Journal of Sociology,* Vol 83, No 3, pp. 340-363.

Michalski, A. (1994), 'Swedish Local Democracy: A Viable Model for Europe?', *European Business Review,* Vol 94, No 5, pp. X-XII.

Michel, J. and Hambrick, D. (1992), 'Diversification Posture and Top Team Characteristics', *Academy of Management Journal,* Vol 35, No 1, pp. 9-37.

Micklethwait, J. and Wooldridge, A. (1997), *The Witch Doctors: What the Management Gurus are Saying, Why it Matters and How to Make Sense of it?,* Mandarin Paperbacks, London.

Middle East Executive Report (1990), November.

Milbank, D. (1998), 'The White House is Anti-Family', *The Week,* 28 November, Issues 181, p. 11.

Miles, R.H. (1980), *Macro Organisatonal Behaviour,* Scotto Foresman, Glenview.

Miles, R.H. and Perreault, W.D., Jr. (1976), 'Organisational Role Conflict: Its Antecedents and Consequences', *Organisational Behaviour and Human Performance,* Vol 71, No 1, pp. 19-44.

Mill, J.S. (1991), *Consideration on Representative Government,* Prometheus Book, Essex.

Millard, J.(1999), 'Insights From the ACTS and TAP Research Programmes', *The New Methods of Work Workshop,* The Fifth Framework Stream, 23 February, Paris.

Miller, J. (ed.)(1996),IT in South Africa. *Information Technology in Developing Countries* 6(1), p. 6.

Miller, M.H. and Topliss, D.J. (1988), 'Chronic Upper Limb Pain Syndrome (Repetitive Strain Injury) in the Australian Work force: A Systematic Cross-Sectional Rheumatological Study of 229 Patients', *Journal of Rheumatology,* Issue 15, pp. 1705-1712.

Miller, R. (1996), *Marketing Technology: IT and Miss-Marketing,* Haymarket Publishing, London.

Miller, R. (1997), *Point-of-Purchase: Banks Branch Into POP Marketing*, Marketing Publications, London.

Miller, S. (1996), *Civilising Cyberspace: Policy, Power and the Information Superhighway*, ACM Press, New York.

MINTEL (1996), 'Banks and Building Societies', *Financial Data Report*, MINTEL, London.

Mintzberg, H. (1973), *The Nature of Managerial Work*, Harper and Row, New York.

Mittman, B.S. (1992), 'Theoretical and Methodological Issues in the Study of Organisation Demography and Demographic Change', in P.S. Tolbert and S.B. Bacharach (eds), *Research in the Sociology of Organisation,* JAI Press, Greenwich, pp. 3-53.

Moberg, D.J. and Koch J.L. (1975), E.W. 1981. *Understanding Cost Growth and Performance Shortfalls in Pioneer Process Plans,* RAND Corporation Report, Santa Monica. November, pp. 27-42.

Moberg D.J, Koch, J.L. (1975), A Critical Appraisal of Integrated Treatments of Contingency Findings. *Academy of Management Journal* 18(1), pp. 109-124.

Moerman, M. (1988), *Talking Culture: Ethnography and Conversation Analysis,* University of Pennsylvania Press, Philadelphia.

Mollay, J. (1987), *The Women's Dress for Success Book,* Warner Books, New York.

Mollay, J. (1988), *New Dress for Success,* Warren Books, New York.

Monden, Y. (1983), *Toyota Production System,* Industrial Engineering and Management Press, Norcross.

Moor, J.H. (1985), 'What Is Computer Ethics', in Terrell Ward Bynum, (ed.), *Computers and Ethics* (Meta-philosophy Journal) (Special Issue), October, pp. 266-275.

Moore, R.A. (1998), 'The Police State Conspiracy', *New Darwin,* No 51, November-December, pp. 57-62.

Moreland, V. (1993), 'Technostress and Personality Type', *On-line,* Vol 17, No 4, pp. 59-62.

Morgan, G. (1986), *Images of Organisations,* Sage, Beverly Hills.

Morrow, P. and McElroy, J. (1981), 'Interior Office Design and Visitor Response', *Journal of Applied Psychology,* Vol 66, No 5, pp. 645-650.

Mouffe, C. (ed) (1992), *Dimensions of Radical Democracy: Pluralism, Citizenship, Community,* Verso, London.

Mowlana, H. (1985), *International Flow of Information: A Global Report and Analysis,* Reports and Papers on Mass Communications. Vol 99.

UNESCO, Paris.

Muetzelfeldt, M. (1988), *'The Ideology of Consumption Within the Mode of Production'*, paper presented to the Sociological Association of Australia and New Zealand Annual Conference, Canberra, May.

Muller, D. (1998), 'Behind the World Financial Crisis', *New Darwin,* No 51, November-December, pp. 17-20.

Murray, A. (1989), 'Top Management Group Heterogeneity and Firm Performance', *Strategic Management Journal*, Vol 10, No 1, pp. 125-141.

Murray, P. (1999), 'How Smarter Companies Get Results from KM: Mastering Information Management', *The Financial Times,* 9 March, p. 10, http://www.globalarchive.ft.com.

Murray, P. and Myers, A. (1997), 'The Facts About Knowledge', *Information Strategy*, Vol 2, No 7, September, pp. 29-33.

Muzaffar, C. (1993), *Human Rights and the New World Order,* Just World Trust, Penang.

Myers, A., Kakabadse, A. and Gordon, C. (1995), 'Effectiveness of French Management: Analysis of the Behaviour, Attitudes and Business Impact of Top Managers', *Journal of Management Development*, Vol 14, No 6, pp. 56-72.

Myers, P. (ed.) (1996), *Knowledge Management and Organisational Design*, Butterworth-Heinemann, London.

Naisbitt, J. (1994), *Global Paradox*, William Morrow and Company, New York.

Nass, C. and Mason, L. (1990), 'On The Study of Technology and Task: A Variable-Based Approach', in Fulk, J. and Steinfield, C. (eds.), *Organisations and Communication Technology*, Sage Publications, Dewberry Park, pp. 91-102.

Nayyar, P.R. (1992), 'On the Measurement of Corporate Diversification Strategy: Evidence from Large US Service Firms', *Strategic Management Journal,* Vol 13, No 3, pp. 219-235.

Nelson, R.R. (1991), 'Educational Needs as Perceived by IS and End-User Personnel: A Survey of Knowledge and Skills Requirements', *MIS Quarterly,* Vol 15, No 4, pp. 503-525.

Neuman, P.G. (1995), *Computer-Related Risks*, Addison-Wesley/CM Press, New York.

Ngwenyama, O. (1991), 'The Critical Social Theory Approach to Information Systems: Problems and Challenges', in Nissen, E., Klein,

H. and Hirschheim, R. (eds.), *Information Systems Research and Emergent Traditions,* North Holland, Amsterdam, pp. 267-280.

Ngwenyama, O. and Lee, A. S. (1997), 'Communication Richness in Electronic Mail: Critical Social Theory and Contextuality of Meaning', *MIS Quarterly,* Vol 21, No 2, June, pp. 145-167.

Ngwenyama, O. and Lyytinen, K. (1997), 'GroupWare Environments as Action Constitutive Resources: A Social Action Framework for Analyzing GroupWare Technologies', *Computer Supported Co-operative Work, The Journal of Collaborative Computing,* Vol 6, No 1, pp. 1-23.

Nibel, H. and Ghem, Th. (1990), 'Macht Der Computer Doch Nicht Krank? (Do Computers Make Us Ill or Not?)', *Zeitschrift Fur Arbeits- Und Organisationspsychologie,* Vol 34, No 4, pp. 192-198.

Nijsmans, M. (1992), 'A Dionysian Way To Organisational Effectiveness', in Stein, M. and Hollwitz, J. (Eds.), *Psyche at Work: Workplace Application of Jungian Analytical Psychology,* Chiron Publications, Illinois, pp. 136-155.

Noble, D.F. (1984), *Forces of Production: A Social History of Industrial Automation,* Knopf, New York.

Nohria, N. and Eccles, R.G. (1992), 'Face-to-Face: Making Network Organisations Work', in Nohria, N. and Eccles, R.G. (eds.), *Networks and Organisations: Structure, Form and Action,* Harvard Business School Press, Boston, pp. 288-308.

Noi, C. (1999), 'Capital Offensive', *The Guardian,* 16 June, pp. 4-5.

Nolan, R. (1979), 'Managing the Crises in Data Processing', *Harvard Business Review,* Vol 73, No 2, March-April, pp. 115-126.

Nonaka, I. (1990), 'Redundant, Overlapping Organisations: A Japanese Approach to Managing the Innovation Processes', *Californian Management Review,* Vol 32, No 3, pp. 27-38.

Nonaka, I. and Takeuchi, H. (1995), *The Knowledge-Creating Company,* Oxford University Press, Oxford

Norburn, D. and Birley, S. (1996), *An Empirical Test of Upper-Echelons Theory,* Paper presented at the Annual Meeting of the Academy of Management, Chicago.

Nowak, R. (1991), 'Windows on the Brain: Cortisol Secretion and Depression', *Journal of NIH Research,* Vol 3, No 1, pp. 62-67.

NTIA Office of Assistant Secretary (1995), *Electronic Commerce* [On-line], available at http://www.ntia.doc.gov:80/opadhome/ecom3.html, December.

Nunnally, J.C. (1967), *Psychometric Theory,* McGraw-Hill, New York.

O'Connor, D.C. (1985), The Computer Industry in the Third World: Policy Options and Constraints. *World Development* 13(3), pp. 311-332.

O'Meara, K. (1998), 'That Fast Count can be Crooked', *Insight,* Vol 14, No 41, pp. 18-20.

O'Reilly, III, C.A. and Flatt, S. (1989), *Executive Team Demography, Organisational Innovation and Firm Performance,* Working Paper, Haas School of Business, University of California, Berkeley.

Ogden, M.R. (1994), 'Politics in Parallel Universe: Is There a Future for Cyberdemocracy?', *Futures,* Vol 26, No 7, September, pp. 713-29.

Ohmae, K. (1995), *The End of the National State: The Rise of Regional Economics,* Free Press, New York.

Olsen, J.P. (1997), 'Institutional Design in Democratic Context', *Journal of Political Philosophy,* Vol 5, No 3, September, pp. 203-229.

Olson, D.R. (1977), 'From Utterance to Text: The Bias of Language in Speech and Writing', *Harvard Educational Review,* Vol 47, No 2, pp. 257-281.

Olson, R. (1996), 'Information Technology in Home Health Care', in C. Bezold and E. Mayer (eds.), *Future Care: Responding to the Demand for Change,* Faulkner, New York, pp. 87-103.

Ong, C.O. (1993), 'Musculo-Skeletal Disorder, Visual Fatigue and Psychological Stess of Working With Display Units: Current Issues and Research Needs', in Luczak, H., Cakir, A., and Cakir, G. (Eds.), *Work With Display Units - 92,* North Holland, New York, pp.221-228.

Organisation for Economic Co-operation and Development (1987), *Structural Adjustment and Economic Performance,* OECD, Paris.

Organisation for Economic Co-operation and Development (OECD) (1996), *Ministerial Symposium on the Future of Public Service,* Organisation for Economic Co-operation and Development Public Management Service, OECD, March, Paris.

Organisation for Economic Co-operation and Development (OECD) (1997), *Citycard - Opening Channels Between the Citizen and Local Government,* Information Society European Style, http://www.oecd.org/puma/governance/it.

Orlikowski, W. J. (1992), 'The Duality of Technology: Rethinking the Concept of Technology in Organisations', *Organisation Science,* Vol 3, No 3, pp.398-427.

Orlikowski, W.J. (1999), 'Managing Use, Not Technology - A View From the Trenches: Mastering Information Management', *The Financial Times*, 22 March, pp. 7-8.

Orlikowski, W.J. and Hofman, D.J. (1997), 'An Improvisation Mode for Change Management: The Case of Groupware Technologies', *Sloan Management Review*, Vol 38, No 2, pp. 11-21.

Ormerod, P. (1994), *The Death of Economics*, Faber and Faber, London.

Orpen, C. (1982), 'Type A Personality as a Moderator For the Effects of Role Conflict, Role Ambiguity and Role Overload on Individual Strain', *Journal of Human Stress*, Vol 8, No 1, pp. 8-14.

Ortega y Gasset, J. (1961), *Meditations on Quixote*, Norton, New York.

Osborne, D. and Gaebler, T. (1992), *Reinventing Government: How the Entrepreneurial Spirit is Transforming the Public Sector*, Addison-Wesley, Reading.

Ostrom, V. (1973), *The Intellectual Crises in American Public Administration*, University of Alabama Press, Alabama.

OXIRM (Oxford Institute of Retail Management) and KPMG (1996), *The Internet: Its Potential and Use by European Retailers*, Templeton College, Oxford.

Oz, E. (1992), 'Ethical Standards for Information System Professionals: A Case for a Unified Code', *MIS Quarterly*, Vol 16, No 4, pp. 423-433.

Oz, E. (1993), 'Ethical Standards for Computer Professionals: A Combative Analysis of Four Major Codes', *Journal of Business Ethics*, Vol 12, No 7, pp. 709-726.

Pacheco, A. (1995), 'Use Information Technology to Improve Efficiency and Accountability', *Management*, June, pp. 7-8.

Paisley, W. (1987), 'Many Literacies, Many Challenges', paper presented at the American Library Association Conference, June, San Francisco.

Pallot, J. (1991), 'The Legitimate Concern with Fairness: A Comment', *Accounting, Organisations and Society*, Vol 16, No 2, pp. 201-208.

Palvia, P.C. and Palvia, S. (1992), 'MIS Issues in India and a Comparison with the United States', *International Information Systems*, HBJ Professional Publishing, Special Issue, pp. 101-110.

Parekh, B. (1993), 'The Cultural Particularity of Liberal Democracy', in D. Held (ed), *Prospects for Democracy*, Polity Press, Cambridge, pp. 127-136.

Parkers, K.R. (1990), 'Coping, Negative Affectivity and The Work Environment: Additive and Interactive Predictors of Mental Health', *Journal of Applied Psychology*, Vol 75, No 3, pp. 399-409.

Parsons, T. (1956), 'Suggestions for a Sociological Approach to the Theory of Organisations', *Administrative Science Quarterly,* Vol 6, No 1, June, pp. 63-85.

Parsons, T. (1960), *Structure and Process in Modern Societies,* Free Press, New York.

Pascarella, P. (1997), 'Spinning a Web of Technophobia', *Management Review,* Vol 86, No 3, March, pp. 43-43.

Pattel, P. (1988), Measuring the economic effects of technology. *STI Review* 4 (December), pp. 121-166.

Patterson, B.A.S. (1992), 'Training the Hybrid Manager', *IDPM Journal,* Vol 3, No 2, pp. 8-9

Pearson, M.J., Crosby, L. and Shim, J.P. (1997), 'Modelling the Relative Importance of Ethical Behaviour Criteria: A Simulation for Information Systems Professionals' Ethical Decisions', *Journal of Strategic Information Systems,* Vol 5, No 4, pp. 275-291.

Pelz, D. and Andrews, F. (1966), *Scientists in Organisations,* Wiley, New York.

Peres, L. (1968), 'The Resurrection of Autonomy: Organisational Theory and the Statutory Corporation', *Public Administration* (Sydney), Vol 27, No 4, December, pp. 361-370.

Perez, C., Soete, L. (1988), 'Catch Up in Technology: Entry Barriers and Windows of Opportunity', in Dosi, G., Freeman, C., Nelson, R., Silverberg, G. and Soete, L. (eds.) *Technical Changes and Economic Theory,* Pinter, London, pp. 458-479.

Perri 6 (1997), 'Information Society Symposium Quality of Democracy Working Group', E-Mail to A. Kakabadse, Demos, London.

Perrow, C.C. (1967), A Framework for the Comparative Analysis of Organisations. *American Sociological Review* 32, pp. 194-208.

Perrow, C.C. (1968), The Effect of Technological Change on the Structure of Business Firms. In *Industrial Relations: Contemporary Issues,* Roberts, N.C. (ed.), MacMillan, London, pp. 205-219.

Perrow, C.C. (1970), *Organisational Analysis: A Sociological View,* Wadsworth, Belmont.

Perrow, C.C. (1972), *Complex Organisations: A Critical Essay,* Scott Foresman and Co., Glenview.

Perrow, C.C. (1984), *Normal Accidents: Living with High Risk Technologies,* Basic Books, New York.

Peters, T.J. and Waterman, R.H. (1982), *In Search of Excellence,* Harper and Row, New York.

Peterson, J.L. (1994), *The Road to 2015: Profile of the Future,* Waite Group Press, San Francisco.

Peterson, R.A. (ed.) (1997), *Electronic Marketing and the Consumer*, Sage, London.

Pfeffer, J. (1983), 'Organisational Demography', in L.L. Cummings and B.M. Staw (eds), *Research in Organisational Behaviour*, JAI Press, Greenwich, pp. 299-357.

Phillips, A.W. (1958), 'The Relationship Between Unemployment and Rate of Change of Money Wages in the United Kingdom, 1861-1957', *Economics,* November, pp. 283-299.

Pike, J. (1998), 'ECHELON: The Global Spy Network', *Coalition For Constitutional Liberties,* Vol 1, No 12, 5 May, on-line citation at http://www.freecongress.org

Plato (1953), 'Phaedo', in *Plato I* (translated by Gowler, H. N.), Harvard University Press/The Loeb Classical Library, Cambridge, pp. 117-124.

Plato (1961), 'Collected Dialogues', in E. Hamilton and H. Cairns (eds.), *The Collected Dialogues of Plato, Including the Letters*, Princeton University Press, Princeton.

Plato (1987), *The Republic,* Penguin Classics, London.

Plato (1997), 'The Phaedara', in *Plato: The Complete Works* (edited by Cooper, J.M. and Hutchinson, D.S.), Hacket Publishing Company, New York, pp. 230-238.

Pliskin, N., Romm, T., Lee, A.S. and Weber, Y. (1993), 'Presumed Versus Actual Organisational Culture: Managerial Implications For Implementation of Information Systems', *Computer Journal,* Vol 36, No 2, pp. 1-10.

Polanyi, M. (1958), *Personal Knowledge*, University of Chicago Press, Chicago.

Polanyi, M. (1966), *The Tacit Dimension*, Routledge and Kegan Paul, London.

Poole, M.S. and DeSanctis, G. (1990), 'Understanding the Use of Group Decision Support Systems: The Theory of Adaptive Structuration', in Fulk, J. and Steinfield, C. (eds.), *Organisations and Communication Technology*, Sage Publications, Newbury Park, pp. 173-193.

Poole, M.S. and DeSanctis, G. (1992), 'Micro-Level Structuration in Computer-Supported Group Decision-making', *Human Communication Research,* Vol 19, No 1, pp. 5-49.

Poole, M.S., Holmes, M. and DeSanctis, G. (1991), 'Conflict Management in Computer-Supported Meeting Environments', *Management Science,* Vol 42, No 2, pp. 143-161.

Poole, P.S. (1998), 'ECHELON: America's Secret Global Surveillance Network, http://www.euronet.nl/~rembert/echelon/16119801 and http://www.euronet.nl/~rembert/echelon/1998.html

Porac, J.F. and Thomas, H. (1990), 'Taxonomic Mental Models in Competitor Definition', *Academy of Management Review,* Vol 15, No 2, pp. 224-240.

Porac, J.F., Thomas, H. and Badon-Fuller, C. (1989), 'Competitive Groups and Cognitive Communities: The Case of Scottish Knitwear Manufacturers', *Journal of Management Studies,* Vol 26, No 3, pp. 397-416.

Port, O. and Resch, I. (1999), 'They're Listening to Your Calls', *Business Week,* 31 May, pp. 58-60.

Porter, M. (1980), *Competitive Strategy,* Basic Books, New York.

Porter, M. (1985), *Competitive Advantage,* Free Press, New York.

Powell, T.C. and Dente-Micallef, A. (1997), 'Information Technology as Competitive Advantage, The Role of Human, Business and Technology Resources', *Strategic Management Journal,* Vol 18, No 5, pp. 375-405.

Power, M. (1991), 'Auditing and Environmental Expertise: Between Protest and Professionalisation', *Accounting, Auditing and Accountability Journal,* Vol 4, No 3, pp. 30-42.

Prahalad, C.K. and Hamel, G. (1990), 'The Core Competencies of the Organisation', *Harvard Business Review,* Vol 68, No 3, pp. 79-91.

Premeaux, S.R. and Mondy, R.W. (1993), 'Linking Management Behaviour to Ethical Philosophy', *Journal of Business Ethics,* Vol 12, No 5, pp. 349-357.

Presthus, R.V. (1958), 'Towards a Theory of Organisational Behaviour', *Administrative Science Quarterly,* Vol 3, pp. 48-72.

Presthus, R.V. (1962), *The Organisational Society,* Vintage Books, New York.

Price Waterhouse (1993), *Information Technology Review 1993/94,* Price Waterhouse, London.

Price Waterhouse Coopers (1998), *Mastering Global Business,* Financial Times, London.

Prodromou, A. (1998), 'Walk "This Way",' *Information Age,* August September, pp. 10-14.

Proudhon, P.J. (1923), *General Idea of the Revolution in the Nineteenth Century*, (translated by Robinson, J.B.), Freedom Press, London.

Pugh, D., Hickson, D., Hinings, C., MacDonald, D., Turner, C. and Lipton, T. (1963), 'A Conceptual Scheme For Organisational Analysis', *Administration Science Quarterly*, Vol 8, No 2, June, pp. 289-315.

Quinn, J.B., Anderson, P. and Finkelstein, S. (1996), 'Managing Professional Intellect: Making the Most of the Best', *Harvard Business Review*, Vol 74, No 2, pp. 71-80.

Rafaeli, S. and Sudweeks, F. (1994), 'Interactively on the Nets', paper presented at The Information Systems and Human Communication Technology Division, ICA Annual Conference, Sydney.

Rafaeli, S. and Sudweeks, F. (1997), 'Networked Interactively', *Journal of Computer-Mediated Communication*, Vol 2, No 4, pp. 118-124.

Raghunathan, B. and Raghunathan, T.S. (1989), 'Relationship of the Rank of Information Systems Executive to the Organisational Role and Planning Dimension of Information Systems', *Journal of Management Information Systems*, Vol 6, No 1, pp. 111-126.

Rahnema, M. (1988), On a New Variety of Aids and its Pathogens: Homo Economicus, Development and Aid. *Alternatives* 3(1), pp. 117-136.

Rahnema, M. (1990), Participatory Action Research: the Last Temptation of Saint Development. *Alternatives* 15(2), pp. 199-226.

Rajan, A. (1985), *New Technology and Employment in Insurance, Banking and Building Societies: Recent Experience and Future Impact*, Aldershot, Gower.

Ramos, A.G. (1981), *The New Science of Organisations: A Reconceptualisation of the Wealth of Nations*, University of Toronto Press, Toronto.

Ravenhill (ed.) (1986), *Africa in Economic Crisis*, Basingstoke, London.

Redfield, C.E. (1958), *Communication in Management: The Theory and Practice of Administrative Communication*, University of Chicago Press, Chicago.

Reed, D. (1997), 'Marketing Technology: Up Close and Personal: One-to-One Targeting is Definitely on the Marketing Agenda But is That Personal Touch Always Welcome', *Marketing Week*, Centaur Communications, 5 June, pp. 6-7.

Reger, R.K. and Huff, A.S. (1993), 'Strategic Groups: A Cognitive Perspective', *Strategic Management Journal*, Vol 14, No 2, pp. 103-124.

Reich, R. B. (1993), *The Work of Nations Preparing Ourselves For 21st Century Capitalism*, Simon and Schuster, London.

Reichlin, S. (1993), 'Neuroendocrine-Immune Interactions', *New England Journal of Medicine,* Issue 329, pp. 1246-1253.

Reilly, N.P. and Orsak, C.L. (1991), 'A Career Stage Analysis of Career and Organisational Commitment in Nursing', *Journal of Vocational Behaviour,* Vol 39, No 2, pp. 311-330.

Rein, M. (1978), *Social Science and Public Policy,* Penguin, New York.

Rein, M. (1983), *From Policy to Practice,* M.E. Share, New York.

Reuters (1996), *Dying for Information: An Investigation Into the Effects of Information Overload Worldwide*, Reuters Inc.

Reuters (1997), *Glued to the Screen: An Investigation Into the Effects of Information Addiction Worldwide*, Reuters Inc.

Reuters (1998a), *Out of the Abyss: Surviving the Information Age*, Reuters Inc.

Reuters (1998b), *The Reuters Guide to Good Information Strategy*, Reuters Inc.

Reynolds, J. (1994), 'Is There a Market For Teleshopping': The Home Network Case', in McGoldrick, P. (ed.), *Cases in Retail Management*, Pitman, London, pp. 112-123.

Reynolds, J. and Davies, R.L. (1988), *The Development of Teleshopping and Teleservices*, Longman, London.

Rheingold, H. (1993), *The Virtual Community: Homesteading on the Electronic Frontier,* Addision-Wesley, New York.

Rice, A.K. (1958), *Productivity and Social Organisation: The Ahmedabad Experiment.*, Tavistock, London.

Rice, R.E. (1984a), 'Mediated Group Communication', in Rice, R. and Associates (eds.), *The New Media,* Academic Press, New York, pp. 129-153.

Rice, R.E. (1984b), *The New Media: Communication, Research and Technology*, Sage Publications, Beverly Hills.

Rice, R.E. and Aydin, C. (1991), 'Attitudes Toward New Organisational Technology: Network Proximity as a Mechanism For Social Information Processing', *Administrative Science Quarterly*, Vol 36, No 2, June, pp. 219-244.

Rice, R.E., Grant, A.E., Schmitz, J. and Torobin, J. (1990), 'Individual and Network Influences on the Adoption and Perceived Outcomes of Electronic Messaging', *Social Networks* , Vol 12, No 1, pp. 27-55.

Rice, R.E., Kraut, R.E., Cool, C. and Fish, R.S. (1994), 'Individual,

Structural and Social Influences on Use of a New Communication Medium', *Academy of Management Best Papers Proceedings,* The Academy of Management, Columbia SC, pp. 285-289.

Rice, R.E. and Shook, D.E. (1990), 'Relationships of Job Categories and Organisational Levels to Use of Communication Channels, Including Electronic Mail: A Meta-Analysis and Extension', *Journal of Management Studies,* Vol 27, No 2, pp. 195-229.

Rifkin, J. (1994), *The End of Work,* Putnam and Sons, New York.

Rittal, H.W.J. and Webber, M. (1973), 'Dilemmas in a General Theory of Planning', *Policy Sciences,* Vol 6, No 1, pp. 76-84.

Rizzo, J.R., House, R.J. and Lirtezman, S.I. (1970), 'Role Conflict and Ambiguity in Complex Organisations', *Administrative Science Quarterly,* Vol 15, No 2, pp. 150-163.

Robbins, S.P. (1994), *Organisational Behaviour,* Prentice Hall, New York.

Roberts, J. and Scapens, R. (1985), 'Accounting Systems and Systems of Accountability: Understanding Accounting Practices in the Organisational Context', *Accounting, Organisations and Society,* Vol 10, No 4, pp. 443-456.

Robertson, R. (1990), 'Mapping the Global Conditions', *Theory, Culture and Society,* Vol 7, Nos 2 and 3, pp. 63-99.

Rochester, J.B. and Douglas, D.P. (1990), 'Change Management and Information Systems', *I/S Analyzer,* Vol 28, No 8, pp. 14-22.

Rochlin, G. (1997), *Trapped in the Net: The Unanticipated Consequences of Computerisation,* Free Press, New York.

Rockart, J., Earl, M. and Ross, R. (1996), 'Eight Imperatives for the New IT Organisation' *Sloan Management Review,* Vol 37, No 1, pp. 37-42.

Rockart, J. and Short, J. (1989), 'IT in the 1990s: Managing Organisational Interdependence', *Sloan Management Review,* Vol 30, No 2, Winter, pp. 7-17.

Rogers, E.M. and Shoemaker, F. (1971), *Communication of Innovations,* Free Press, New York.

Rogerson, S. (1996), 'Social Responsibility', *IDPM Journal,* July, p. 17.

Rokkan, S. (1966), 'Numerical Democracy and Corporate Pluralism', in Dahl, R. (ed.) *Political Oppositions in Western Democracies,* Yale University Press, New Haven, pp. 94-105.

Romanelli, E. and Tushman, M. (1986), 'Executive Leadership and Organisational Outcomes: An Evolutionary Perspective', in D. Hambrick (ed), *The Executive Effect: Concept and Methods for Studying Top Managers,* JAI Press, Greenwich, pp. 129-140.

Romano, C. (1995), 'Managing Change, Diversity and Emotions', *Management Review,* Vol 84, No 7, July, pp. 6-7.

Rondinell, D. (1987), *Development Administration and US Foreign Aid Policy,* Lynne Rienner, Boulder.

Roobeek, A.J.M. (1990), The Technological Debacle: European Technology Policy from a Future Perspective. *Futures* 22(9), pp. 904-914.

Rose, R. (1985), *Understanding Big Government: The Programme Approach,* Sage, London.

Rose-Ackerman, S. (1978), *Corruption: A Study in Political Economy,* Academic Press, New York.

Rosell, S.A. (1992), *Governing in an Information Society,* IRPP, Montreal.

Rosell, S.A. (1995), *Changing Maps: Governing in a World of Rapid Change,* Carleton University Press, Ottawa.

Roszak, T. (1986), *The Cult of Information,* Butterworth, Cambridge.

Rousseau, D.M. (1977), 'Technological Differences in Job Characteristics, Employment Satisfaction and Motivation: A Synthesis of Job Design Research and Socio-Technical Systems Theory', *Organisational Behaviour and Human Performance,* Vol 19, No 1, pp. 18-42.

Rousseau, D.M. (1983), 'Technology in Organisation: A Constructive Review and Analytic Framework', in Seashore, S. (ed.), *Assessing Organisational Change,* John Wiley and Sons, New York, pp. 173-182.

Rowe, C. and Herbert, B. (1990), 'IT in the Boardroom: The Growth of Computer Awareness Among Chief Executives', *Journal of General Management,* Vol 15, No 4, pp. 32-44.

Ruch, W. (1989), *International Handbook of Corporate Communication,* McFarland and Co, Jefferson.

Rumelhart, D.E. and Nomran, D.A. (1990), 'Representation of Knowledge', in Aitkenhead, A.M. and Slack, J.M. (Eds.), *Issues in Cognitive Modeling,* Macmillan, New York, pp. 43-52.

Rummel, R.J. (1970), *Applied Factor Analysis,* Northwestern University Press, Evantson.

Sabatier, P.A. (1991), 'Towards Better Theories of the Policy Process', *PS: Political Science and Politics,* Vol 24, No 2, pp. 141-58.

Sadler, P. (1994), 'Gold Collar Workers: What Makes Them Play at Their Best?', *Personnel Management,* April, pp. 14-17.

Sandberg, J. (1998), 'The Electronic Mail', *Newsweek* (Special Issue), Winter, pp. 10-19.

Santikarn, M. (1981), *Technology Transfer: A Case Study,* Singapore University Press, Singapore.

Sapolsky, H.M. (1967), 'Organisational Structure and Innovation', *Journal of Business,* Vol 40, No 4, pp. 497-510.

Saracevic, T., Braga, G. and Afolayan, M.A. (1985), Issues in Information Science Education in Developing Countries. *Journal of the American Society for Information Science* 6(3), pp. 192-199.

Sardar, Z. (1985), *The Future of Muslim Civilisation,* Second Edition, Mansell, London.

Sardar, Z. (1994), *Muhammed for Beginners,* Icon Books, London.

Sardar, Z. (1996), 'The Future of Democracy and Human Rights', *Features,* Vol 28, No 9, pp. 839-859.

Sartre, J.P. (1956), *Being and Nothingness* (translated by Barnes, H.E.), Philosophical Libraries, New York.

Sauter, S., Hales, T., Bernard, B., Fine, L., Peterson, M., Pautz-anderson, V. and Associates (1993), 'Summary of Two NIOSH Field Studies of Musculoskeletal Disorder and VDT Work Among Telecommunication and Newspaper Workers', in Luczak, H., Cakir, A., and Cakir, G. (Eds.), *Work With Diplay Units - 92,* North Holland, New York, pp.229-234.

Scarnati, J. (1998), 'Beyond Technical Competence: Fear - Banish the Beast', *Leadership and Organisational Development,* Vol 19, No 7, pp. 362-373.

Schank, E. and Abelson, R. (1977), *Scripts, Plans, Goals and Understanding: An Inquiry Into Human Knowledge Structures,* Erlbaum, Hillsdale.

Scharge, M. (1997), 'The Problem With Computers', *Harvard Business Review,* Vol 75, No 5, September-October, pp. 178-188.

Scheibl, F. and Dex, S. (1998a), 'Is There a Business Case For Firms to Have Family-Friendly Policies?', *Working Paper,* Judge Institute, University of Cambridge.

Scheibl, F. and Dex, S. (1998b), 'Should We Have More Family-Friendly Policies', *European Management Journal,* Vol 16, No 5, pp. 586-599.

Schein, E.H. (1994), 'The Role of the CEO in the Management of Change: The Case of Information Technology', in T.J. Allen and M.S. Scott-Morton (eds.), *Information Technology and the Corporation of the 1990s,* OUP, New York, pp. 325-345.

Schenker, J.L. (1999), 'Who Watches the Web'', *Time,* Vol 153, No 15, 19 April, p. 64.

Schiersmann, C. (1996), 'A Comparison of the Conditions For Reconciling Professional and Family Life in Europe: With Special Consideration of Regulations Governing Parental Leave', *Transfer,* Vol 1, No 1, pp. 1-23.

Schlenker, B. (1980), *Impression Management,* Wadsworth, Belmont.

Schmitz, J. and Fulk, J. (1991), 'Organisational Colleagues, Media Richness and Electronic Mail: A Test of the Social Influence Model of Technology Use', *Communication Research* , Vol 18, No 4, pp. 487-523.

Schmoranz, I. (1980), *Makroôkonomische Analyse des Informationssektors,* Oldenbourg, Wien-Mûnchen.

Schnall, P.L., Pieper, C., Schwats, J.E., Karasek, R.A., Schlussel, Y., Devereux, R., Ganau, A., Alderman, M., Warren, K. and Pickering, T. (1990), 'The Relationship Between "Job Strain" Workplace Diastolic Blood Pressure and Left Ventricular Mass Index: Results of A Cross-Control Study', *Journal of the American Medical Association,* Vol 23, No 6, pp. 1929-1935.

Schneider, M.L. (1997), 'When Overnight Isn't Fast Enough', *Graphic Arts Monthly*, February, Vol 69, No 2, pp. 68-73.

Schnorr, T.M., Grasewski, B.A. and Hornung, R.W. (1991), 'Video Display Terminal and the Risk For Spontaneous Abortion', *New England Journal of Medicine,* Issue 324, pp. 727-733.

Schön, D.A. (1963), 'Champions for Radical New Inventions', *Harvard Business Review,* Vol 41, No 2, March-April, pp. 77-86.

Schonfeld, I.S. (1992), 'A Longitudinal Study of Occupational Stressors and Depressive Symptoms in First-Year Female Teachers', *Teaching and Teacher Education,* Vol 8, No 1, pp. 151-158.

Schutz, A. (1973), *Collected Papers,* Martinus Nijhof, Hague.

Scott, G.E. (1992), Transfer, Economic Structure and Vulnerability of the African Economy. *The Journal of Developing Areas* 26, pp. 213-238.

Scott, S. and Morgan, D. (eds.) (1993), *Body Matters: Essays on the Sociology of the Body,* Falmer Press, Washington.

Scott-Morton, M.S. (ed) (1991), *The Corporation of the 1990s: Information Technology and Organisational Transformation,* Oxford University Press, Oxford.

Seabrook, J. (1993), *Victim of Development: Resistance and Alternatives,* Verso, London.

Selznick, P. (1957), *Leadership in Administrational: A Sociological Perspective,* Harper and Row, New York.

Senge, P.M. (1990), *The Fifth Discipline: The Age and Practice of the Learning Organisation*, Century Business, London.

Senge, P.M. (1993), *The Fifth Discipline: The Art and Practice of Organisational Learning,* Doubleday, New York.

Senker, P. (1992), Technological Changes and the Future of Work: An Approach to an Analysis. *Futures* 24(4), pp. 351-363.

Senn, J.A. and Gibson, V.R. (1981), 'Risk of Investment in Microcomputers for Small Business Management', *Journal of Small Business Management,* Vol 19, No 3, pp. 24-32.

Shannon, C.E. and Weaver, W. (1949), *The Mathematical Theory of Communication,* University of Illinois Press, Illinois.

Sharp, D.E. (1996), 'So Many Lists, So Little Time', *US Weekend,* 15-17 March, pp. 4-6.

Sharp, D.E. (1998), 'Extranets: Borderless Internet/Intranet Networking', *Information Systems Management*, Vol 15, No 2, Summer, pp. 31-33.

Sheldon, A. (1987), The Shifting Grounds of Poverty Lending at the World Bank. In *Between Two Worlds: The World Bank's Next Decade.* Feinberg, R. (ed.), Overseas Development Council and Transaction Books, Washington, pp. 87-103.

Sheldon, A. (1990), Toward a Pro-Poor Information Agenda at the World Bank. *Development* 4(2), pp. 73-76.

Shenk, D. (1997), *Data Smog: Surviving the Information Glut*, Harper-Collins, New York.

Shenk, D. (1999), 'Why You Feel the Way You Do', *Inc.,* January, p. 28.

Shim, J.P. and Taylor, G.S. (1991), 'A Comparative Study of Information Systems Faculty Members' Vs Practising Managers' Perceptions', in R. Dejoie, G. Fowler and D. Paradice (eds), *Ethical Issues in Information Systems*, Boyd and Fraser Publishing, New York, pp. 189-198.

Shocker, A.D. and Sethi, S.P. (1974), 'An Approach to Incorporating Social Preferences in Developing Corporate Action Strategies', in S.P. Sethi (ed), *The Unstable Ground: Corporate Social Policy in a Dynamic Society,* Melvile, California.

Siegel, J., Dubrovsky, V., Kiesler, S. and McGuire, T.W. (1986), 'Group Processes in Computer-Mediated Communication', *Organisational Behaviour and Human Decision Processes*, Vol 37, No 1, pp. 157-187.

Simon, H.A. (1947), *Administrative Behaviour: A Study of Decision-Making Processes in Administrative Organisation,* Macmillan, New York.

Simon, H.A. (1986), 'Rationality in Psychology and Economics', *Journal of Business,* Vol 59, No 4, pp. 209-223.

Sims, R. (1996), 'Professional Education in the Fast Lane', *IDPM Journal,* Vol 6, No 3, pp. 9-11.

Single, M.K. and Anderson, J.R. (1989), *The Transfer of Cognitive Skills,* Harvard University Press, Cambridge.

Sinha, I. (1999), *The Cyber Gypsies: Love, Life and Travels on the Electronic Frontier,* Scribener, London.

Sithole, N. (1959), *African Nationalism,* Oxford University Press, Cape Town.

Sitkin, S.B., Sutcliffe, K. M. and Barrios-Choplin, J.R. (1992), 'A Dual-Capacity Model of Communication Media Choice in Organisations', *Human Communication Research,* Vol 18, No 4, pp. 563-598.

Skyrme, D. (1996), *Creating the Knowledge-Based Business,* Oxford University Press, Oxford.

Slaughter, R. (1999), 'Towards Responsible Dissent and the Rise of Transformational Futures', *Futures,* Vol 31, No 2, pp. 147-154.

Smircich, L. and Stubbart, C. (1985), 'Strategic Management in an Enacted World', *Academy of Management Review,* Vol 10, No 4, pp. 724-736.

Smith, B., Jordan, J. (1990), Technology Transformation and Technology Transfer. In *Technological Challenges in the Asia Pacific Economy.* Soesastro, H. and Pangestu, M. (eds.), Allen and Unwin, Sydney, pp. 3-24.

Smith, K.G., Smith, K.A., Olian, J.D., Sims, H.P., Jr., O'Bannon, D.P. and Scully, J.A. (1994), 'Top Management Team Demography and Process: The Role of Social Integration and Communication', *Administrative Science Quarterly,* Vol 39, No 3, pp. 412-438.

Smith, M.J. (1987a), 'Occupational Stress', in Salvendy, G. (Ed.), *Handbook of Human Factors,* Wiley, New York, pp. 84-93.

Smith, M.J. (1987b), 'Mental and Physical Strain at VDT Workstations', *Behavioural and Information Technology,* Vol 6, No 2, pp. 243-255.

Smith, M.J. (1997), 'Psycho-Social Aspects of Working with Video Display Terminals (VDTs) and Employee Physical and Mental Health', *Ergonomics,* Vol 40, No 10, pp. 1002-1015.

Smith, M.J and Carayon, P. (1995), 'New Technology, Automatisation and Work Organisations: Stress Problems and Improved Technology Implementation Strategies', *The International Journal of Human Factors in Manufacturing,* Vol 5, No 1, pp. 99-116.

Smith, M.J. and Salvendy, G. (1993), *Human-Computer Interaction: Applications and Case Studies,* Elsevier, Amsterdam.

Smith, R.J. (1994), *China's Cultural Heritage,* Westview Press, Boulder.

Snell, S.A. and Dean, J.W., Jr. (1992), 'Integrated Manufacturing and Human Resource Management: A Human Capital Perspective', *Academy of Management Journal,* Vol 35, No 3, pp. 467-504.

Snider, J.H. (1994), 'Democracy On-Line: Tomorrow's Electronic Electorate', *The Futurist,* Vol 28, No 5, September-October, pp. 15-19.

Soesastro, H., Pangestu, M. (eds.) (1990), *Technological Challenges in the Asia Pacific Economy.* Allen and Unwin, Sydney.

Soesastro, H., Pangestu, M., Mckendrick, D. (1990), Summary of Chapters and Discussion. In *Technological Challenges in the Asia Pacific Economy,* Soesastro, H. and Pangestu, M. (eds.), Allen and Unwin, Sydney, pp. 299-323.

Soete, L. (ed.) (1985), *Technology Trends and Employment: Electronics and Communication,* Aldershot, Grower.

Sogolo, G. (1991), 'The Futures of Democracy and Participation in Everyday Life: The African Experience' in B. von Steenbergen, R. Nakarada, F. Marti and J. Dator (eds), *Advancing Democracy and Participation: Challenges for the Future,* Centre Catala de Prospectova, Barcelona, pp. 47-62.

Solomon, J. (1990), 'As Electronic Mail Loosens Inhibitions, Impetuous Senders Feel Anything Goes', *The Wall Street Journal,* 12 October, p. B1.

Sonnentag, S. (1994), 'Stressor-Burnout Relationship in Software Development Teams', *Journal of Occupational and Organisational Behaviour ,* Vol 14, No 1, pp. 37-48.

Soros, G. (1999), *The Crisis of Global Capitalism: Open Society Endangered,* Public Affairs, New York

Sowa, J. (1984), *Conceptual Structures*, Addison-Wesley, London.

Spender, J.C. (1993), 'Competitive Advantage From Tacit Knowledge? Unpacking the Concept and Its Strategic Implication', *Best Paper Proceedings*, Annual Meeting of the Academy of Management, Atlanta, pp. 240-252.

SPL Worldgroup Australia (1995), *Natural New Dimension, Launch at Park Royal,* May 19, Canberra.

Sproull, L. and Kiesler, S. (1986), 'Reducing Social Context Clues: Electronic Mail in Organisational Communication', *Management Science*, Vol 32, No 11, pp. 1492-1512.

Sproull, L. and Kiesler, S. (1991), 'A Two-Level Perspective on Electronic Mail in Organisations', *Journal of Organisational Computing*, Vol 2, No 1, pp. 125-134.

Sproull, L. and Kiesler, S. (1992), *Connections: New Ways of Working in the Networked Organisation*, MIT Press, Cambridge.

State and Local Coalition on Immigration, Immigration Policy Project (SLCI, IPP) (1995), *America's Newcomers: An Immigrant Policy Handbook*, National Conference of State Legislatures, Denver.

Steers, R. and Black, J.S. (1994), *Organisational Behaviour* (Fifth Edition), Harper-Collins, New York.

Steffy, B.D. and Jones, J.W. (1989), 'The Psychological Impact of Video Display Terminals on Employees' Well-Being', *American Journal of Health Promotion*, Vol 4, No 2, pp. 101-107.

Steinfield, C. (1992), 'Computer-Mediated Communications in Organisational Settings: Emerging Conceptual Frameworks and Directions For Research', *Management Communication Quarterly*, Vol 5, No 3, pp. 348-365.

Stellman, J.M., Klitzman, S., Gordon, G.C. and Snow, B.R. (1989), 'Work Environment and the Well-Being of Clerical and VDT Workers', *Journal of Occupational Behaviour*, Vol 8, No 1, pp. 95-114.

Stephenson, N. (1995), 'Global Neighbourhood Watch', *Scenarios: 1.01, Wired Special Edition*, Fall, pp. 96-107.

Stern, P.C. (1986), 'Blind Spots in Policy Analysis: What Economics Doesn't Say About Energy Use', *Journal of Policy Analysis and Management*, Vol 5, No 2, pp. 200-227.

Sternberg, R. (ed) (1990), *Wisdom: Its Nature, Origins, and Development*, Cambridge University Press, Cambridge.

Stewart, J.D. (1984), 'The Role of Information in Public Accountability', in A. Hopwood and C. Tomkins (eds), *Issues in Public Sector Accounting*, Philip Allen, Deddington, Oxford, pp. 13-34.

Stinchcombe, A.L., McDill, M.S. and Walker, D.R. (1986), 'Demography of Organisations', *American Journal of Sociology*, Vol 74, No 2, pp. 221-229.

Stivers, R. (1994), *The Culture of Cynicism*, Blackwell, Oxford.

Stone, L.D. (1991), 'How to Ease the Pain of Difficult Downsizing Choices', *Human Resources Professional,* Vol 3, No 2, Winter, pp. 21-25.

Stone, R.A. (1995), 'Workplace Homicide: A Time for Action', *Business Horizon,* Vol 38, No 2, pp. 3-10.

Strassman, P. (1995), *Information Payoff,* The Information Economics Press, New York.

Straub, D.W. and Collins, R.W. (1990), 'Key Information Liability Issues Facing Managers: Software Piracy, Proprietary Databases and Individual Rights to Privacy', *MIS Quarterly,* Vol 14, No 2, pp. 143-156.

Sussman, G. (1988), Information Technologies for the ASEAN Region: The Political Economy of Privatisation. In *The Political Economy of Information.* Mosco, V. and Wasko, J. (eds.), University of Wisconsin Press, Madison, pp 274-296.

Sutton, R.I. and Kahn, R.L. (1983), *Prediction, Understanding and Control as Antidotes to Organisational Stress,* Institute for Social Research, University of Michigan, Ann Arbor.

Suzuki, H. (1988), General Background and Conceptual Issues. *ILO Labour Relation Series No 68: Technological Change, Work Organisation and Pay, Lessons from Asia,* ILO, Geneva.

Szilagyi, M.N. (1994), *How to Save Our Country: A Non-Partisan Vision for Change,* Pallsas Press, Tucson.

Taylor, D. (1998), 'Stress Management Issues', *Computer Weekly,* 20 August, p. 1.

Taylor, D. (1999), 'Wage Slaves, Throw Off Your Chains!', *The Guardian,* 23 June, p.6.

Taylor, F. (1911), *Principles of Scientific Management,* Harper and Row, New York.

Taylor, F.W. (1911), *Scientific Management,* Harper and Row, New York.

Taylor-Cummins, A. and Feeny, D.F. (1997), 'The Development and Implementation of System Bridging the User-IS Gap', in L. Willcocks and D.F. Feeny (eds), *Managing Information Technology as a Strategic Resource,* McGraw-Hill, London, pp. 171-202.

Team Consulting (1995), *The Developing Skills of the Information Society,* Team Consulting, London.

Teece, D. (1981), 'The Market For "Know-How" and the Efficient International Transfer of Technology', *Annals of the American Academy of Political and Social Science',* Vol 458, pp. 81-95.

Terrorism and Security Monitor (T and SM) (1998), 'Who Will Police the Policemen?', *Special Report*, October, pp. 2-7.

The Cranfield Information Strategy Knowledge Survey (TCISKS) (1998), *Europe's State of the Art in Knowledge Management*, The Economist Group, London.

The Daily Telegraph Mirror (1994), 'Customs Man on $1.3m Charge', March 16, pp. 9.

The Economist (1989), *Algeria: Country Report 1989-1990: Annual Survey of Political and Economic Background,* The Economist Intelligence Unit, London.

The Economist (1995), 'Democracy and Technology', 17-23 June, pp. 21-2.

The Economist (1995), 'The Internet - The Accidental Super Highway, Vol 348, 1 July, pp. 118-119.

The Economist (1998), 'American Democracy: How Far Can You Trust the People?', Vol 348, No 8081, August 15, pp. 41-2.

The Economist (1998), 'Depression: Spirit of the Age', Vol 349, No 8099, pp. 113-121.

The Economist (1998), 'When the Bubble Bursts', Vol 350, No 8104, 30 November, pp. 21-22.

The Economist (1999), 'The End of Privacy: The Surveillance Society', Vol 351, No 8117, pp. 105-107.

The Economist (1999a), 'The Net Imperative: Business and the Internet', Vol 351, No 8125, pp. 5-44.

The Economist (1999b), 'Truth, Lies and Cyberspace', Vol 351, No 8116, 24 April, p. 122.

The European Commission (1994), *Europe and the Global Information Society: Recommendations to the European Council* (Bangemann Report), The European Chancel, Brussels, May.

The Times (1997), 'World Watch: London', October 6, p. 22.

The Weekend Australian (1999), 'The Digital Divide', 27-28 February, pp. 6-7.

Thee, K.W. (1990), Indonesia: Technology Transfer in the Manufacturing Industry. In *Technological Challenges in the Asia Pacific Economy.* Soesastro, H. and Pangestu, M. (eds.), Allen and Unwin, Sydney, pp. 200-232.

Theorell, T. and Emlund, N. (1993), 'On Physiological Effects of Positive and Negative Life-Change: A Longitudional Study', *Journal of Psychosomatic Research,* Vol 37, No 4, pp. 653-659.

Theorell, T., Leymann, H., Jodko, M., Konarski, K. and Norbeck, H.E. (1994), 'Persons Under Train Incidents From the Subway Driver's Point of View: A Prospective one-year Follow-up Study - The Design, Medical and Psychiatric Data', *Social Science and Medicine* (Special Issue on Suicide on Railways), Vol 38, pp. 471-475.

Thompson, J.D. (1957), *Organisations in Action: Social Sciences Bases of Administrative Theory*, McGraw-Hill, New York.

Thong, J. and Yap, C. (1995), 'CEO Characteristics, Organisational Characteristics and Information Technology Adoption in Small Businesses', *Omega International Journal of Management Sciences*, Vol 23, No 4, pp. 429-442.

Thornton, M. (1997), 'Electonic Commerce: 3 Truths for IS', *Computerworld*, Vol 31, No 16, pp. S1-S11.

Tilley, L. (1990), A Revolution in Share Registration. *Banking Technology*. November, pp. 7-17.

Toffler, A. (1980), *The Third Wave*, Morrow, New York.

Tonn, B. (1996), 'A Design for Further-Oriented Government', *Futures*, Vol 28, No 5, pp. 413-431.

Tonn, B.E. and Petrich, C. (1998), 'Everyday Life's Constraints on Citizenship in the United States', *Futures*, Vol 30, No 8, pp. 783-813.

Torgerson, D. (1992), 'Editorial: Priest and Jester in the Policy Sciences: Developing the Focus of Inquiry', *Policy Science*, No 25, No 2, pp. 225-235.

Touraine, A. (1985), 'An Introduction to the Study of Social Movements', *Social Research*, Vol 52, No 4, pp. 45-52.

Townson, P.A. (ed.) (1995), The Internet Society. *TELECOM Digest* 15(345), p. 16.

Trauth, E.M., Farwell, D.W. and Lee, D. (1993), 'The IS Expectation Gap: Industry Expectations versus Academic Perpetration', *MIS Quarterly*, Vol 17, No 3, pp. 213-223.

Treux, D.P. (1993), *Information Systems Development in the Emergent Organisation* (unpublished Phd Dissertation), Watson School of Engineering, State University of New York, Binghamton.

Trevino, L.K. (1986), 'Ethical Decision Making in Organisations: A Person-Situation Interactions Model', *Academy of Management Review*, Vol 11, No 4, pp. 601-617.

Trevino, L.K., Daft, R.L. and Lengel, R.H. (1990), 'Understanding Managers' Media Choices: A Symbolic Interactionist Perspective', in

Fulk, J. and Steinfield, C. (Eds.) *Organisations and Communication Technology*, Sage Publications, Newbury Park, pp. 123-131.

Trevino, L.K., Lengel, R.H. and Daft, R.L. (1987), 'Media Symbolism, Media Richness and Media Choice in Organisations: A Symbolic Interactionist Perspective', *Communication Research*, Vol 14, No 4, pp. 553-574.

Tricker, R.I. (1983), 'Corporate Responsibility, Institutional Governance and the Roles of Accounting Standards', in M. Bromwich and A. Hopwood (eds), *Accounting Standard Setting: An International Perspective,* Pitman, London, pp. 27-41.

Tucker, R.C. (1981), *Politics as Leadership,* University of Missouri Press, Columbia.

Turban, E. (1992), *Expert Systems and Applied Artificial Intelligence*, Macmillan, New York.

Turkle, S. (1984), 'Women and Computer Programming', *Technology Review*, Vol 87, No 8, pp. 48-50.

Turkle, S. (1997), *Life on the Screen: Identity in the Age of the Internet*, Touchstone Books, New York.

Turner, J.A. (1984), 'Computer-Mediated Work: The Interplay Between Technology and Structured Jobs', *Communications of the ACM*, Vol 27, No 6, pp. 1210-1217.

Tushman, M.L. and Anderson, P. (1986), 'Technological Discontinuities and Organisational Environments', *Administrative Science Quarterly,* Vol 31, No 3, pp. 439-465.

Tushman, M.L. and Nadler, D. (1986), 'Organising for Innovation', *California Management Review,* Vol 28, No 3, pp. 74-92.

Tushman, M.L. and Nelson, R.R. (1990), Technology, Organisations and Innovation. *Administrative Science Quarterly* 35(1), pp. 1-8.

Tushman, M.L. and Romanelli, E. (1985), 'Organisation Evaluation: A Metamorphosis Model of Convergence and Reorientation', in L.L. Cummings and B.M. Staw (eds), *Research in Organisational Behaviour*, 7, JAI Press, Greenwich, pp. 171-122.

UK, Department of Trade and Industry, 'IT for All' Project Office (1996), 'Read All about IT: A Survey into Public Awareness of Attitudes Towards, and Access to Information and Communication Technologies', in *The Start of IT,* HM Government, London, December 1996, pp. 1-20.

UK, Department of Trade and Industry (1997), http://www.edma.org., 7 October.

UK, Office of Public Service, Central IT Unit (1997), 'Government Direct', *Information Package,* Office of Public Service, Central IT Unit, London.

Unger, R.M. (1987), *False Necessity,* Cambridge University Press, Cambridge.

United Nations (1985), *The Diffusion of Electronics Technology in the Capital Goods Sector in the Industrialised Countries,* Geneva.

United Nations (1992), Development and the Environment: World Development Indicators *World Development Report 1992,* UN, New York, pp. 47-83.

United Nations (1994), *The Year of The Family,* United Nations Report, New York.

United Nations (1998), *Human Development Report,* United Nations, New York.

United Nations Advisory Committee on Science and Technology for Development (UNACSTD) (1989), Imperatives of Science and Technology in the International Development Strategy for the Fourth United Nations Development Decade. *Draft Report:* United Nations, New York. November.

United Nations Development Programme (UNDP) (1992), *Human Development Report,1992,* Oxford University Press, New York.

United Nations Economic Commission for Africa (UNECA) (1989), Alternative Framework to Structural Adjustment Programme for Socio-economic Recovery and Transformation. *UNECA E/ECA/CM.15/Rev. 3.* UNECA, Paris.

United Nations Economic Commission for Latin America (UNECLA) (1987), National information networks and system development in Latin America and the Caribbean. *Data For Development Newsletter* 22, pp. 42-46.

United Nations Population Fund (1994), *The State of World Population 1994: Choices and Responsibilities,* UNFPA, New York.

Usher, A.P. (1954), *A History of Mechanical Innovation*, Oxford University Press, Cambridge.

Valacich, J. S., Paranka, D., George, J.F. and Nunamaker, J.F. Jr. (1993), 'Communication Concurrency and the New Media', *Communication Research,* Vol 20, No 2, pp. 249-276.

Van Amelsvoort, P., Knol, G., Leyen, D. and De Weerd, H. (1991), 'Integrale Organisatievernieuwing Phillips Stadskanaal',

Bedrijfskunde, Vol 63, No 2, pp. 208-217.

Van de Donk, W.B.H.J. and Tops, W. (1995), 'Orwell or Athens? Information and the Future of Democracy', in W.B.H.J. Van de Donk, I.Th.M Snellen and P.W. Tops (eds.), *Orwell in Athens: A Perspective on Informatiozation and Democracy,* IOS Press, Amsterdam, pp.113-132.

Van de Ven, A.H. (1986), 'Central Problems in the Management of Innovation', *Management Science,* Vol 32, pp. 590-607.

Van de Ven, A.H. and Feraiy, D.L. (1980), *Measuring and Assessing Organisation,* Wiley, New York.

Van der Spek, R. and Spijkervet, A. (1997), 'Knowledge Management: Dealing Intelligently With Knowledge', in Liebowitz and Wilcox (eds.), *Knowledge Management and its Integrative Elements,* CRC Press, London, pp. 114-123.

Venkatesh, A. and Vitalari, N. (1992), 'An Emerging Distributed Work Arrangement: An Investigation of Computer-Based Supplemental Work at Home', *Managing Science,* Vol 12, Not 8, pp. 1887-1906.

Venkatraman, N. (1990), 'Performance Implications of Strategic Coalignment: A Methodological Perspective', *Journal of Management Studies,* Vol 27, No 1, January, pp. 19-41.

Venkatraman, N. and Camillus, J. (1984), 'Exploring the Concept of "Fit" in Strategic Management', *Academy of Management Review,* Vol 9, No 3, July, pp. 513-525.

Vernon, M. (1998), 'Directors Buckle Under Work Pressures', *Computer Weekly,* 4 June, p. 30.

Vickery, G. (1986), Industrial Flows of Technology: Recent Trends and Developments. *STI Review* 1, (Autumn), pp. 9-46.

Vincent, M. (1995), 'Welcome Disclosure: The Decline of Whistleblowing and Ethical Act', *Alternative Law Journal,* Vol 20, No 2, pp. 74-78.

Von Hippel, E.(1994), ' "Sticky Information" and the Locus of Problem Solving: Implications for Innovation', *Management Science,* Vol 40, No 4, pp. 429-439.

Waldman, D.A. and Avolio, B.J. (1986), 'A Meta-Analysis of Age Difference in Job Performance', *Journal of Applied Psychology,* Vol 71, No 1, pp. 33-38.

Waldo, D. (1948), *The Administrative State: A Study of the Political Theory of American Public Administration,* Ronald Press, New York.

Walsh, J. (1995), 'Managerial and Organisational Cognition: Notes From a Trip Down Memory Lane', *Organisation Science*, Vol 6, No 3, May-June, pp. 280-321.

Walsh, P. (1999), 'Dads Want More Time Being Dads', *The Daily Telegraph,* 25 February, p.3.

Walther, J.B. (1992), 'Interpersonal Effects in Computer Mediated Interaction: A Relational Perspective', *Communication Research*, Vol 19, No 1, pp. 52-90.

Walton, E.J. (1986), 'Management Prototypes of Financial Firms', *Journal of Management Studies,* Vol 23, No 5, pp. 679-698.

Walton, R.E. (1989), *Up and Running: Integrating Information Technology and the Organisation,* Harvard Business School Press, Boston.

Wang Ke (1987), Informatisation: A New World Development Strategy and the Choice for China. *Modernisation* 2(1), pp. 8-9.

Ward, J. and Peppard, J. (1996), 'Reconciling the IT/Business Relationship: A Troubled Marriage in Need of Guidance', *Journal of Strategic Information Systems,* Vol 5, No 1, pp. 37-65.

Ward, J., Taylor, P. and Bond, P. (1995), 'Evaluation and Realisation of IS/IT Benefits: An Empirical Study of Current Practice', *European Journal of Information Systems*, Vol 4, pp. 214-225.

Washington Post (1996), 'Postal Voting', 22 January, Section 1, p. 1.

Water, R. (1993a), Tarus the Octopus. *The Financial Times.* 22 January, p. 10.

Water, R. (1993b), The Plan that Fell to Earth. *The Financial Times.* 12 March, p. 19.

Water, R. and Cane, A. (1993), Sudden Death of a Runaway Bull. *The Financial Times.* 19 March, p. 11.

Webster, F. and Robins, K. (1986), *Information Technology: A Luddite Analysis,* Ablex, Norwood.

Webster, J. (1989), 'Gender, Paid Work and Information Technology', paper presented to the PICT Gender and ICT Workshop, Brighton Polytechnic, May.

Webster, J. (1990), *Office Automation: The Secretarial Labour Process and Women's Work in Britain*, Harvester Wheatsheaf, Hemel Hempstead.

Webster, J. and Trevino, L.K. (1995), 'Rational and Social Theories as Complementary Explanations of Communication Media Choices: Two Policy-Capturing Studies', *Academy of Management Journal*, Vol 38, No 6, December, pp. 1544-1572.

Weick, K.E. (1987), 'Theorising About Organisational Communication', In Jablin, F. M., Putnam, L.L., Roberts, K.H. and Porter, L.W. (eds.) *Handbook of Organisational Communication,* Sage Publications, Newbury Park, pp. 97-122.

Weick, K.E. (1995), *Sensemaking in Organisations*, Sage, London.

Weil, M.M. and Rosen, L.D. (1998), Technostress*: Coping With Technology at Work, Home, Play,* John Wiley and Sons Inc., New York.

Weiss, E.B. (1989), *In Fairness to Future Generations: International Law, Common Patrimony and Intergenerational Equity,* Transnational Publications Inc., New York.

Weldon, D. (1996), 'Training for the New Millennium', *Computerworld,* Special Issue: The 100 Best Places to Work Supplement, June, pp. 42-46.

Westley, F. and Mintzberg, H. (1989), 'Visionary Leadership and Strategic Management', *Strategic Management Journal*, Vol 10, Summer, pp. 17-32.

White, R.A. and McDonnell, J. (1983), Priorities for National Communication Policy in the Third World. *The Information Science Journal* 2(1), pp. 5-33.

Whitman, M.E. and Gibson, M.L. (1996), 'Enterprise Modelling for Strategic Support', *Information Systems Management,* Vol 13, No 2, pp. 64-72.

Whyte, G. and Bytheway, A. (1996), 'Factors Affecting Information Systems' Success', *International Journal of Service Industry Management*, Vol 7, No 1, pp. 74-93.

Wick, C.W. and Leon, L.S. (1995), 'From Ideas to Action: Creating a Learning Organisation', *Human Resource Management,* Vol 34, No 2, Summer, pp. 299-311.

Wiersema, M. and Bantel, K. (1992), 'Top Management Team Demography and Corporate Strategic Change', *Academy of Management Journal*, Vol 35, No 1, pp. 91-121.

Wiig, K. (1993), *Knowledge Management Foundation*, Schema Press, New York.

Wildavsky, A. (1987), 'Choosing Preference by Constructing Institutions: A Cultural Theory of Preference Formation', *American Political Science Review,* Vol 81, No 1, pp. 3-22.

Wiley, C. (1995), 'The ABC's of Business Ethics: Definitions, Philosophies and Implementation', *Industrial Management*, Vol 37, No 1, January-February, pp. 22-27.

Wilkes, B., Stammerjohn, L. and Lalish, N. (1981), 'Job Demands and Work Health in Machine-Paced Poultry Inspection', *Scandinavian Journal of Work, Environment and Health,* Vol 7, No 1, pp. 2-19.

Wilkinson, B. (1988), Emergence of an Industrial Economy? The Human Relations Movement in Singapore. In *The Enterprise and Management in Asia.* Clegg, S., Dunphy, D. and Redding, S. (Eds.), Centre of Asian Studies, The University of Hong Kong, Hong Kong, pp. 111-128.

Wilkinson, C. (1983), 'Organisational Control: A Resource Dependence Approach', in T. Lowe and J.L.J. Machin (eds), *New Perspectives in Management Control,* The Macmillan Press, Houndmills, Hants, pp. 188-233.

Williams, E. (1977), 'Experimental Comparisons of Face-to-Face and Mediated Communications: A Review', *Psychological Bulletin,* Vol 84, No 5, September, pp. 963-976.

Williams, M.J. (1987), African Debt and Economic Recovery: Required Adjustments by the IMF and Donor Governments. *Development* 2(3), pp. 6-10.

Williams, T.A. (1987), *Learning to Manage our Future,* John Wiley, New York

Wilson, D.C. (1992), *A Strategy of Change: Concepts and Controversies in the Management of Change,* Routledge, London.

Wilson, J.Q. (1966), 'Risk of Investment in Microcomputers for Small Business Management', *Journal of Small Business Management,* Vol 19, No 3, pp. 24-32.

Wilson, J.Q. (1993), *The Moral Sense,* The Free Press, New York.

Withmore, S. (1999), 'How Not to Get Ripped-off While Shopping', *Asiaweek,* Vol 25, No 11, p. 51.

Wittgenstein, L. (1958), *The Blue and Books*, Basil Blackwell, Oxford.

Wood, S. (1982), *The Degradation of Work: Skill, Deskilling and the Labour Process,* Hutchinson, London.

Woodall, J. (1997), 'Organisational Restructuring and the Achievement on an Equal Opportunity Culture', *Gender, Work and Organisations,* Vol 4, No 1, pp. 1-12.

Woodward, J. (1965), *Industrial Organisation: Theory and Practice,* Oxford University Press, London.

Woolf, H. (1990), *Webster's New World Dictionary of the American Language*, G and C Merriam, New York.

Worall, M. and Cooper, C.L. (1997), *IM-UMIST Quality of Working Life Survey*, Institute of Management, London.

World Bank (1984), *Towards Sustained Development in Sub-Saharan Africa: A Joint Programme of Action*, World Bank, Washington.

World Bank (1988), *World Development Report: 1988*, World Bank, Washington.

World Bank (1989a), *Sub-Saharan Africa: From Crisis to Sustainable Growth*, World Bank, Washington.

World Bank (1989b), *World Tables: 1988-1989*, World Bank, Washington.

World Bank (1989c), *World Debt Tables: 1989-1990*, World Bank, Washington.

World Bank (1990), *World Development Report: 1990*, World Bank, Washington.

World Bank (1990), *World Development Report:1990*, Oxford

World Economic Forum (WEF) (1997), 'Communique', 1997 Annual WEF Meeting, Davos, 20 January - 4 February.

World Health Organisation (1989), 'Work With Visual Display Terminals: Psychosocial Aspects and Health: Report on a World Health Meeting', *Journal of Occupational Medicine*, Vol 31, No 4, pp. 957-968.

World Health Organisation (1990), 'Up-Date on Visual Display Terminals and Workers' Health', *Technical Report No OCH90.3*, Geneva.

Yap, C., Thong, J. and Raman, K. (1994), 'Effect of Government Incentives on Computerisation in Small Business', *European Journal of Information Systems*, Vol 3, No 2, pp. 191-206.

Yates, J. and Orlikowski, W. J. (1992), 'Genres of Organisational Communication: A Structurational Approach to Studying Communication and Media', *Academy of Management Review*, Vol 17, No 2, April, pp. 299-326.

Young, P. (1998), 'Under Fire', *CIO Magazine*, September, pp. 15-20.

Zapf, D., Dormann, C. and Frese, M. (1996), 'Longitudinal Studies in Organisational Stress Research; A Review of the Literature With Reference to Methodological Issues', *Journal of Occupational Health Psychology*, Vol 1, No 2, pp. 145-169.

Zeier, H., Mion, H., Laubli, Th., Thomas, C. and Senn, E. (1987), 'Augen- und Ruckenbeschwerden Bei Bildschirmarbeit in Abhangigkeit Von Ergonomischen und Bioppsychosozialen Faktoren, (Eye and Back Complaint When Working WithVideo Display Units Related to

Ergonomic and Bio-psychosocial Factors)', *Zeitschrit Fur Experimentalle und Angewandte Psychologie,* Vol 34, No 1, pp. 155-179.

Zelany, M. (1982), High technology management. *Human System Management* 11(1), pp. 57-59.

Ziauddin, S. and Davies, M.W. (1992), Lessons from the Third World. *Futures* 24(2), pp. 150-157.

Zuboff, S. (1988), *In the Age of the Smart Machine: The Future of Work and Power,* Basic Books, New York.

Zysman, G. (1995), 'Wireless Networks', *Scientific American,* September, pp. 68-69.

Index

Abelson, R. 161
Achieve Global 293
Adonis, A. 47
Advanced Research Project Agency (ARPA) 66-67, 128
ALTERNEX 92-93
Amazon 135, 146, 147
America On-line (AOL) 130, 135, 136
American Bar Association (ABA) 224
American Management Association 289
Applegate, L.M. 195
Aristotle 32, 37, 160, 177
ARPA Computer Network (ARPANET) 128, 129
Association for Computing Machinery (ACM) 229
Australian Commonwealth Privacy Act (1988) 240
Australian Electronic Democracy 55
Australian Public Service (APS) 204, 233, 234, 238, 240
Australian Taxation Office Re-development Project 84
Axiom Corporation 12

Bangemann Report 55
Bannerstake 146
Barnes and Noble 135, 146
Basic Research in Industrial Technology in Europe (BRITE) 91
Beckman, T. 165
Berkeley Community Memory Project 132
Berners-Lee, T. 133, 152
Bio-technology (BAP) 91
Biotechnology 218
BITNET 128, 129
BMRB study 291-292
Bock, G. 204
Borders 135
Bradley, S.B. 115
Bretton Woods 74, 75-76
Brookings, J.B. 193
Burnout 192-193, 271-273; defined 192, 272; and lower employee commitment 193; and role ambiguity 193; and role conflict 193; stressors 192-193; symptoms 272-273
Business Process Re-engineering (BPR) 190

CERN 133
Chandler, M.J. 164
Chau, P.Y.K. 204
Cheney, P.H. 201
Churchill, W. 32
Cicero 231
Citycard 48-49
Cleveland Free-Net 132
Collective capitalism 98-99
Communaute Economique de l'Afrique de l'ouest (CEAO) 91
communication: audio/visual 110; choosing/managing 123; complexity of 103-104, 122; definitions of 102; determinants of media choice 111-113; diversity of 102-103; diversity of subject domain 102-103; effective 110; face-to-face 119, 123; individual/group choice 124; integrativist approach 105-106; in organisational setting 104, 113, 123-124; process 101-102; rich 110; text-based 110; variables 103
CompuServe 130, 136
Computer bulletin boards (CBB) 104
Computer conferencing 104
Cranfield School of Management IT Directors' Forum 205
crime 58-59
Crozier, M. 81
Csnet 129
Cyberdemocracy 39, 57, 64, 65
Cybershopping 150
CYCLADES 129
Cyert, R.M. 237, 238

Daft, R.L. 111
DARPA 66-67
Data Processing Management Association (DPMA) 229

371

Davenport, T.H. 174
Decision making: cognitive-managerial paradigm 206, 207; rational-economic paradigm 205-206
democracy 31; and access to information 70-71; accessibility, equitability, adaptability 68-69; African 35-36, 43; background 32-33; and citizen choice 47-48; and civic participation 69-70; and constitutional theory 34-35; and context 35-37; and decentralised governance 66-67; and economic prosperity 47; and election procedures 36; and ethnic tensions 46-47; and human rights principles 36-37; and individual rights 33-35; and information infrastructure 69-70; IT and international concern 54-56; liberal 33-34; local (Swedish model) 65-66; models of 37-42; and need to refocus debate 46-48; and new technology 48-51; and people of wisdom 45-46; reinventing 64-70; value component 67-68, 72; and voting procedures 65; *see also* direct democracy; electronic democracy; representative democracy
developing countries: and absence of information infra-structure 75-66; and access to IT 10-12; and cost of information 81; and development problematic 79-81; and dumping of technology 9; and establishment of competitive niches 86, 87-88; investment in 9-10; lessons from developed economies 82-85; limited discourse/paradigm barriers 76-79; loans to 74; market barriers/multinational monopoly problems in 86-87; needs of 74-75; planning introduction of IT 88-91; policy challenges/constraints 86-88; policy recommendations 93-99; poverty of 12-15; and problem of technology transfer 73-75; successful donor programmes 85; and technological imperialism 80; towards policy contingencies/alternatives 88-93
developmental debates: decentralised/ centralised 77-78; dualistic 77; formative context 76; and rhetoric of intransigence 77; single-image formula 77; state control 76-77; and structural adjustment 77; traditional 77
Dewar, R.D. 256
DIAL (Direct Intelligence Access Listening) 16
direct democracy (Aristotelian) 37-38
Direct Record Entry (DRE) 52
Distributed Computing Environments 190
Dixons Stores Group study 292
Drucker, P. 25, 160, 161
Dutton, J.E. 256

Early Wide-Range Scientific and Technology Programme (EUREKA) 91
ECHELON globe-trading system 18-19
Economic exclusion 27-29
Economics: and challenges of public policy 25-28; globalisation of 3-5, 25-27; *laissez-faire* 127; liberalisation of 2-3; models of 3
El-Shinnawy, M. 111, 112
Elam, J.J. 195
Electronic channels (E-channels) 136-137, 142
electronic commerce (E-commerce); business-to-business (B2B) 147, 148: business-to-consumer 147-148; described 136-139, 140-141; developments in 141; issues concerning 139-145; on the Net 146-149
Electronic Cooperation of India Limited (ECIL) 87
electronic democracy: civil society model 41; concept of 39; and crime 53; downside of 51-54; effect on political environment 51-52; effects of 41-42; electronic bureaucracy model 39-40; as emerging global trend 56; information management model 40; and monitoring devices 53-54; populist model 40-41; and possibility of individual alienation 58-59, 60; problems of 57-60; and responsibility/accountability 57-58;

rich/poor division 52-53
electronic mail (E-mail) 103, 110, 111-112, 118-119, 120-121, 141, 262, 295; and stress 271, 274, 277, 278, 279, 280, 287-288
electronic marketing (E-marketing) 136-138
employment: complexity of policy for 24; consequences of extended working hours 286-287; creation of new forms of 27; effect of longer hours on 21-22; impact of IT on 81; working hours in lean organisation 283-286; *see also* unemployment
Enfopol 19
Ethics 217; adapting code of 228-230; background 218-219; development of professional 223-225; importance of 230-231; need for professional code of 225-228
Etzioni, A. 240
'Europe and the Global Information Society' (Bangemann Report) 55
European Commission (EC) 55
European Economic Community (EEC) 88-89, 91
European Research in Advanced Material (EURAM) 91
European Strategic Programme for Research and Development in Information Technology (ESPRIT) 91
European Union Directorate General for Research (EUDGR) 16
Excite 135

Facilitating agents 167-168
Farbey, B. 233
Federal Trade Commission (FTC) 149
Feeny, D.F. 204
FIDOnet 128, 129
Finholt, T. 115
Finsterbusch, K. 85
Flexible labour exchange services (FLEX) 24
Food and Agriculture Organisation (FAO) 85
Forecasting and Development of Advanced Communications Technology for Europe (RACE) 91
Freedom of Information Act 50
Friedberg, E. 81

Fukuyama, F. 47

Galbraith, J.K. 27
Gantz, J. 214
Garnett, J.L. 103
globalisation 2-5; effect on developing nations 12-15; effect on nature of work 29; effect on public policy 25-27; as facilitator of universal prosperity 12-13; as new political structure 21; and outsider groups 168; planning for 20
Gordon, J. 293
'Government Direct' (Green Paper) 40, 56
'Government On-Line' project 55
Grindley, K. 196
group behaviour: attributes of 115-116; identity maintenance 116-117; influence attempts 116; interaction 116; learning 117; member characteristics 115-116; membership criteria 116; organisational consequences of 117-118; participation 117; performance 117; physical setting 115; processes of 116-117; task type 116
group demography 236-237
GroupWare 104, 114-115, 168, 169, 177-178, 188, 192, 271
Gutenberg Project 132

Habermas, J. 164
Hage, J. 85
Hallowell, E.M. 262
Hambrick, D.C. 237, 238
Hamel, G. 199
Hawai FYI 132
Health Management Appraisal Method (Jordan) 85
Hedsor Memorandum 55
Hirschman, A.O. 27
Hogan project 82
Holliday, S.G. 164
HomeNet study 281
Human resource development 98
HUMAN-NETS 129

ICL Systems 20
Information: as definition of pair-wise relationship 167; as knowledge 164-

165, 178-179; rich 105, 107, 113
Information Fatigue Syndrome (IFS) 275
information overload 273-277; studies into
   274-276
'Information Society Project' 55
'Information Society Symposium' (1997)
   55-56
information systems (IS) 103, 160; *see also*
   IS/IT
information technology (IT) 2; access to 10-
   12; and access to public bodies 49-50;
   adoption of 90, 97-98, 164-165;
   benefits 49-50; centrality of computer
   literacy to 60; and citizen/local
   authority dialogue 48-49; cost of 260;
   and democratic potential through 48-
   51; development of 97; effect on
   nature of work 29; expenditure on 79;
   and gap between rich/poor 7; and
   globalisation 260; goals for 89, 90-91,
   95-96; and government/citizen
   communication 54-55; impact on
   citizens/representatives' roles 57-60;
   impact on media/corporations' roles
   61-64; impact of 55-56, 260-261;
   influence on political process 50-51;
   infra-structure for 96-97; international
   concerns 54-56; introduction of 82-
   84; and invisible barriers 6-7;
   liberating power of 11-12; and loss of
   jobs 11; making choices in 88-89; and
   need for professional code of ethics
   225-228; optimist/pessimist views 5-
   6; and political surveillance/control
   15-19; and poverty 12-15; presence of
   259-260; problems with 53; regional
   research programmes 91-93; and
   scenarios for the future 19-22; and
   social isolation 8-9; support for 89-90;
   and SWOT analysis 94; and voting
   procedures 49; as 'wicked' public
   policy problem 22-24; *see also* IS/IT
Information Technology Meta Policy
   (ITMP) 99
innovation 113, 181, 239
Institute for Certification of Computer
   Professionals (ICCP) 229
Institute of Criminology 53
Institute of Social and Economic Analysis
   (IBASE) 92, 93

institutional knowledge:
   alliances/partnerships 172-173;
   codification process 170-171;
   consultant 172; home-grown 172;
   internalisation process 169;
   management/acquisition 171-173;
   socialisation process 170
Integrated Planning and Implementation in
   Rural Development (Colombia) 85
Inter Media Advertising Solution Report
   146
International Benchmarking Study 137
International Development Research Centre
   (IDRC) 10, 80
International Monetary Fund (IMF) 15, 74,
   81
Internet 6, 12, 53, 66, 288, 291; abuse of
   149-152; advertising on 146;
   background 127-128; Chinese whisper
   on 151-152; commercial use of 142;
   community systems on 132; control of
   information on 155-156; and
   cybersquatting 157; as a democracy
   157; and dependence on telephone
   companies 148; development of 128-
   131; Dominion of Melchizedek on
   150, 151; E-commerce on 136-139,
   146-149; and electronic contracts 157;
   free access to 146; information on
   132-133; legal/cultural issues 142-
   145; management of WWW 152-154;
   on-going considerations 139-145;
   ownership of 130; portals on 135-136;
   positive benefits of 154-156; power of
   157; privacy on 153-154, 157;
   slovenly reporting on 151; spam and
   cookies on 151, 152; threats to use of
   147; use of 131-132; what is on the
   Net 132-133; WWW on 131-135
Internet Assigned Numbers Authority
   (IANA) 130
Internet Co-operation For Assigned Names
   and Numbers (ICANN) 130
Internet Service Provider (ISP) 130, 135
IS/IT: academic interest in 187; adopting a
   code of ethics for 228-230; adoption
   of 239; background 186-189; and
   burnout 192-193; challenges of 188-
   189; changes in compensation/
   performance/career path

214-215; characteristics of staff 197-198; competencies 202-203; current trends concerning professionals' skills 200-201; development requirements of professionals 206; effect of globalisation on 189; effect of 185; effectiveness of practice 205-212; failures in 227; glass ceilings/professionals'credibility 189, 194-198; and groupware technologies 188; impact of 218-219, 227-228; influence of leadership adoption of 235-238; and introduction of IT 186-187; and knowledge of programming 186; lack of respect for 195; leadership influence on 250-253, 256-257; nature of third paradigm shift 189-190; need for multi-skills 190; organisational context 209-211; perceived incompatibility of personnel 213-214; recognition of required business skills 198-200; requirements for the future 213-215; research studies in skills 203-205; role ambiguity in 191-192; roles in 207-212; senior management involvement in 233-234; standards in 227; stereotypic images of 196-197; strategic context 211-212; work performance/contribution model 205-212; *see also* information systems (IS); information technology (IT)

IT For All report 291

'IT Roles and Work Practice' 273

IT-harem metaphor 5-6, 7

IT-mediated communication: artefacts 109; basic elements 106-109; channelling 107; characteristics of 106-110; decoding 107; determinants 109-110; distortion 108; effect/implication of 119; and enabling of new structures/designs 114-115; encoding 106; equivocality resolution 109-110; and group behaviour 115-118; and handling of interruptions 114; individual/collective perspectives 113; integrative approach 105; interpretativist approach 104, 105; kinetics 109; lack of social cues 114, 122, 123; leanness 107; level of interactivity 108; linkage 107; mode 108; noise 108; non-verbal cues 108; para-language 109; positivist perspective 104-105; problems with 119; pros/cons of 118-121; proxemics 108-109; reach 108; richness 105, 107; social presence approach 104; task analysability 110; task routine 110; uncertainty reduction 109

J18 movement 14

Job-Seeker/Job-Bank 82

Johnson, D. 229

Jordan, J. 98

Kakabadse, A. 163, 238, 239

Keynes, J.M. 127

King, J. 192

King, R.C. 192

Knowledge 25, 71; acquisition 171-173; application 170-171; behavioural 161; context 161; creation 169; definitions of 165-166; factual 162; general/specific 161-162; information as 164-165; procedural 162; role of symbolic analysts 166-169; scientific 161; sharing 170; tacit/explicit 162-164, 178, 289-290; understanding meaning of 160-164

knowledge leadership 179-182

knowledge management 160, 171-173; barriers that need managing 176-179; Cranfield survey on 173-174, 175, 178; defined 173; different views of 178; effect of IT on 174-175, 177-178; first attempts at 177; further research on 175-176; and knowledge 176-177; and management 176; and people 176; praxis 173-176; process approach to 177; and structure 176

knowledge worker 160, 161, 187

Korac-Boisvert, N. 238

KPMG 293

La Cooperation 74, 85

Laffin, M. 221

Lagos Plan of Action (1980) 91

Latham, M. 25-26

Lazonick, W. 98

Leadership 175; background 233-235; and

dialogue 180-182; discretionary 179-180, 239; influence on effective IS/IT adoption 235-238; influence on IS/IT 250-253, 256-257; and knowledge management 179; philosophy influence on IS/IT 256-257; skills 213
Leadership study: bureaucrats 249; discussion of findings 253-255; factor analysis 243; important factors 238-240; IS/IT factor analysis 243-244; leadership influence on IS/IT 250-253, 256-257; leadership philosophy cluster analysis 242-243; leadership philosophy factor analysis 244-246; leadership philosophy profiles 246; methodology 242-249; radicals 247-248; regression analysis 250-253; research hypothesis 241-242; team players 246-247
Lengel, R.H. 111
Leonard, P. 179
Local Area Network (LAN) 84
Long Term Capital Management (LTCM) 14
Ludlum, D.A. 192
Lycos 135, 146

MacLean, M. Jr 102
Management-Improvement Teams in Agriculture (Guyana) 85
Managerial capitalism 98, 99
Managerial Information Flows 190
MANDATA 82
March, J.G. 237, 238
Marchand, D.A. 174
Market fundamentalism 2
Markus, M.L. 111, 112
Marshall, A. 161
Marx, K. 32
Mason, P.A. 237, 238
Mathieu, J.E. 193
MCI/Worldcom 130
Media, role of 61-63
Media choice: diversity of influence on 112-113; and functionality 112; rational perspective 105, 124; richness of medium vs equivocality of message 111-112, 113; socio-cultural perspective 105, 124; spontaneous vs planned 112; verbal vs written 112

mediated democracy *see* representative (mediated) democracy
Memex surveillance system 15
Meyer, R. 165
micro-computer systems 92
Mill, J.S. 32
Minnesota E-Democracy project 54-55
Morrow, P. 82
MSN 135
Mulgan, G. 47
multi-tasking 279-280
multinational corporations (MNCs) 93

National Capital Free-Net 132
National Information Infrastructure (NII) Task Force 140
National Physical Laboratory 129
National Science Foundation (NSF) 129
National Security Agency (NSA) 18-19
National Unemployment Benefits System 2 (NUBS2) 83, 84
navigators 167
NCP (Network Control Programme) 128
Net *see* Internet
Netcenter 135
Netscape 135, 136
network organisation 114-115
Network Transport Protocol (NNTP) 129
Next Step study 20, 262
Nolan, R.L. 115
Nonaka, I. 163
NSFNet 129
Nua 131
numerically controlled machine tools (NCMT) 86

Opportunity 2000 293
organisation champion 234
Organisation for Economic Cooperation (OECD) 148
Organisational Changes of National Irrigation Administration (Philippines) 85
organisational demography 236-238
Organisational Planning (Jamaica) 85
Organisations: and added value 289-291; communication/dialogue in 180-181; competencies/strategic performance 199-200; competitive forces view 198; context 209-212; cultures in 178;

encouraging/neglecting professionals 196; learning in 180; policies in 291-295; quality of relationships in 181-182; resources based view 198-199; restructuring 191-192, 284; role ambiguity in 191-192; role of 63-64
Ortega y Gasset, J. 223
Oz, E. 229

PEN (Public Electronic Network) 41
Perot, R. 40, 62
Pfeffer, J. 242
Phillips, A.W. 3
Phillips Curve 3
Platform For Internet Content Selection (PICS) 167
Plato 32, 57, 122, 160, 177
Polanyi, M. 163
Prahalad, C.K. 199
profession 217; background 218-219; change/social responsibility 222; downside of 223; importance of 230-231; need for code of ethics 223-225; and negotiation 221; political view of 221-222; requirement of 220-221; and security/assurance for whistle blowers 230; sociology of 219-222
Progressive Policy Institute (PPI) 8
Project Bartleby 132
proprietary capitalism 98
Proudhon, P.J. 5
Public Choice Theory 1, 25

Raghunathan, B. 195
Raghunathan, T.S. 195
Redesigning Network processes 190
Re-engineering Operational Process 190
Re-engineering Support Processes 190
Redfield, C.E. 102
regional systems 91-93
Reich, R.B. 4
Rein, M. 67
representative (mediated) democracy 38-39; adverse effect of technology on 58-59; critiques of current models of 42-46; cynicism concerning 42; individual/collective tension 42-43; interest groups 43-44; lobby groups 44-45; present system of 57-58; re-evaluation/refocus of criticism on 59-

60; redesigning 65-70; and values/morals 45-46; western/non-western tension 43
rich information 105, 107, 113
Rittal, H.W.J. 22
Rizzo, J.R. 193
Rockart, J. 190
Rokkan, S. 2
roles: appropriateness 208; discretionary 207-208, 210; prescribed 207, 208; understanding of 207-212; vale-addition in 290
Roobeek, A.J.M. 89
Rosen, L.D. 264, 291
Rowan, B. 165

Santa Monica Public Electronic Network (PEN) 132
Saville and Holdsworth (SHL) 197
Schank, E. 161
Science and Technology for Regional Innovation and Development in Europe (STRADE) 91
self-managing work groups 98-99
Senge, P. 199
Sethi, V. 192
SF-LOVERS 129
Shannon, C.E. 102
Sithole, N. 35
Smith, B. 98
social isolation 8-9
Society for Information Management 201
Socrates 177
Sonnentag, S. 192
SPRINT 130
Sproull, L.S. 115
state: changing role of 2-5; intervention 1-2, 26-27
Stratplan 82
stress: research into 261-262; *see also* technostress
surveillance 4, 12; political 15-19; range of 16-17; types of 16-19; use of 15-16
symbolic analysts, role of 166-169

Takeuchi, H. 163
TARUS (Transfer and Automated Registration of Uncertificated Stock) 83-84
Taylor, F.W. 161

TCP/IP (Transmission Control Protocol/Internet Protocol) 128, 131
technological capability 79-80
technological dynamics 78-79; diachronic/synchronic analysis of 79
Technology: addiction to 282-283; impact of 278-279; resistance to new 113-114
Technology change 141-142
Technology dumping 9, 76, 79, 87
Technology transfer: cost of 92-93; effective 84-85; and establishment of institutions 94; and financial incentives 96; problematic 9-12; time-lags in 84
Technostress 262-264; and addiction to technology 282-283; behavioural changes 266; and burnout 271-273; consequences of 268; and current ways of working/organisational policies 291-295; defined 263-264; and depression 270-271; due to conflict over accepting/adjusting to new technology 265-267; due to over-identification with and/or dependency on new technology 267-270; effect on children 270; and encroachment of work on discretionary time 280-282; factors causing 268; health issues 266-267; and information overload 273-277; IT-extended working hours/consequences 286-287; and loss of privacy 282; and multi-tasking 279-280; and problem of added value 289-291; reduction programmes for 294-296; research into 263; responding to demands in near-real time 277-279; studies into 268-270; and teleworking/Web Chat Room 287-289; and working hours in lean organisation 283-285
Telecommuting 227-228
Teleconferencing 62
Thee, K.W. 98
Tocqueville, A. de 32
Toffler, A. 61
Top team research 237-238, 238
Training and Visit System (India) 85
Transnational corporations (TNCs) 15, 98
Trauth, E.M. 204
Trevino, L.K. 111

Ts'ai Lun 128
Tye Ng, E.M.W. 204

unemployment 27; as 'wicked' public policy dilemma 22-24; *see also* employment
UNET 130
Union douaniere et Economique de l'Afrique centrale (UDEAC) 91
United Nations 75
United Nations Human Development Report 13
Universal Resource Location (URL) 152
US Agency for International Development (USAID) 74, 85
Usenet 129

virtual office 284, 287-289
virtual organisation 114-115
virtual reality (VR) 51, 59
voice mail (V-mail) 103-104, 111, 118-119, 120-121, 262; and stress 274, 277, 278, 288

W3C (World Wide Web Consortium) 152
Weaver, W. 102
Webber, M. 22
Weil, M.M. 264, 291
Weiss, E.B. 48
Wellington Citynet 132
Westely, B. 102
wicked problems 22-24
Wide Area Network (WAN) 83
Woodall, J. 293
Work performance/contribution model: overview 212-213; in practice 205-212
Work Profiling System (WPS) 197
World Bank 13, 15, 74, 81, 85, 93
World Health Organisation (WHO) 20, 85, 270
World Intellectual Property Organisation (WIPO) 19, 157
World Trade Organisation (WTO) 15
World Wide Web (WWW) 132-133; as collection of destinations 135; content sites 140; described 139; E-commerce on 137, 139; hypertext system 133-134; incentive site 140; and information retrieval 145, 291; main

language on 153; mall 140; managing 152-154; as marketing/advertising medium 131; on-line storefront sites 140; pages on 139-140; pages (URLs) on 135; retail sites 142; search agents 140; sites 133-136, 137, 140, 168, 169; squatters on 135; users of 8; Web rings 134; Web sites 134-135

Yahoo! 135, 136
Year of the Family (1994) 293
Zajac, D. 193